'Based on careful reading of a remarkable coll[illegible] as many fascinating photographs, this meticulously researched and beautifully written biography of the psychiatrist and historian Gregory Zilboorg portrays the life of a remarkable man. The story is nicely embedded into a fascinating social, political, medical, and cultural context, one that includes politics, war, religion, and a psychoanalytic world that has been too-often forgotten. This biography will be of interest to a wide range of readers, including medical historians, psychiatrists, and anyone interested in one fascinating person's journey from pre-revolutionary Russia to the twentieth-century United States.'

— *Joel Howell, MD, PhD, Elizabeth Farrand Professor of the History of Medicine at the University of Michigan*

'There are powerful myths about daughters in search of fathers. This biography equals them. With lucidity, intensity, and vivid words the author Dr. Caroline Zilboorg sets out, 60 years after his passing, to find and better know her father, the psychoanalyst Dr. Gregory Zilboorg. Her search yields a generous gift to readers. Gregory Zilboorg was an extraordinarily brilliant man with a personal history extending from service in the ill-fated Menshevik government of revolutionary Russia to an exceptional American career as a psychiatrist, medical historian, and spellbinding public speaker. To tell his life is also to tell much of the history, not without conflicts, of Freudian analysis in America. Caroline Zilboorg engages us as her companions in a most fruitful search for identity.'

— *Roger Lipsey, author of* Make Peace Before the Sun Goes Down: The Long Encounter of Thomas Merton and His Abbot, James Fox

'How does a poor Russian Jew become a revolutionary socialist, an orthodox Freudian, and a devout Catholic, in that order? Read Caroline Zilboorg's biography of her father Gregory and find out! In addition to providing illuminating commentaries on the evolution of his work in the history of psychiatry, and the social issues that animated Gregory Zilboorg as a public intellectual, Caroline Zilboorg shows a keen and sensitive grasp of the vagaries of Jewish family life in Czarist Russia, the vicissitudes and horrors of the Russian Revolution, the anguish of immigrants adapting to America, and the sheer nastiness of psychoanalytic politics. This is a searching, sympathetic, and richly embroidered biography of a courageous, creative, generous, yet much-misunderstood man. It is "must reading" for anyone interested in the history of psychiatry, psychoanalysis, and the Jewish-American immigrant experience.'

— *Daniel Burston, Founding Scholar, British Psychoanalytic Council; author of* Psychoanalysis, Politics and the Postmodern University *and* The Wing of Madness: The Life and Work of R.D. Laing

The Life of Gregory Zilboorg, 1890–1940

The Life of Gregory Zilboorg, 1890–1940: Psyche, Psychiatry, and Psychoanalysis is the first volume of a meticulously researched two-part biography of the Russian-American psychoanalyst Gregory Zilboorg and chronicles the period from his birth as a Jew in Tsarist Russia to his prominence as a New York psychoanalyst on the eve of the Second World War.

Educated in Kiev and Saint Petersburg, Zilboorg served as a young physician during the First World War and, after the revolution, as secretary to the minister of labour in Kerensky's provisional government. Having escaped following Lenin's takeover, Zilboorg requalified in medicine at Columbia University and underwent analysis with Franz Alexander at the Berlin Psychoanalytic Institute. His American patients ranged from wealthy and artistic figures such as George Gershwin and Lillian Hellman to prison inmates. His writing includes important histories of psychiatry, for which he is still known, as well as examinations of gender, suicide, and the relationship between psychiatry and the law. His socialist politics and late work on Freud's (mis)understanding of religious belief created a wide circle of friends and acquaintances, from members of the Warburg banking family to the Trappist monk Thomas Merton.

Drawing on previously unpublished sources, including family papers and archival material, *The Life of Gregory Zilboorg, 1890–1940: Psyche, Psychiatry, and Psychoanalysis* offers a dramatic narrative that will appeal to general readers as well as scholars interested in the First World War, the Russian revolution, the Jewish diaspora, and the history of psychoanalysis.

Caroline Zilboorg is a life member of Clare Hall, Cambridge University, and a scholar of the British Psychoanalytic Council. Her books include *Richard Aldington and H.D.: Their Lives in Letters*, *The Masks of Mary Renault: A Literary Biography*, and the biographical novel *Transgressions*. She lives in Brittany, France, where she continues to write.

The History of Psychoanalysis Series
Series Editors
Professor Brett Kahr and Professor Peter L. Rudnytsky

This series seeks to present outstanding new books that illuminate any aspect of the history of psychoanalysis from its earliest days to the present, and to reintroduce classic texts to contemporary readers.

Other titles in the series:

The Dreams of Mabel Dodge
Diary of an Analysis with Smith Ely Jelliffe
Patricia R. Everett

Reading Freud's Three Essays on the Theory of Sexuality
From Pleasure to the Object
Philippe Van Haute and Herman Westerink

Reading Freud's Patients
Memoir, Narrative and the Analysand
Anat Tzur Mahalel

Rediscovering Pierre Janet
Trauma, Dissociation, and a New Context for Psychoanalysis
Edited by Giuseppe Craparo, Francesca Ortu, and Onno Van der Hart

Freud/Tiffany
Anna Freud, Dorothy Tiffany Burlingham and the 'Best Possible School'
Edited by Elizabeth Ann Danto and Alexandra Steiner-Strauss

Freud at Work
On the History of Psychoanalytic Theory and Practice, with an Analysis of Freud's Patient Record Books
Ulrike May

For further information about this series please visit www.routledge.com/The-History-of-Psychoanalysis-Series/book-series/KARNHIPSY

The Life of Gregory Zilboorg, 1890–1940

Psyche, Psychiatry, and Psychoanalysis

Caroline Zilboorg

LONDON AND NEW YORK

First published 2022
by Routledge
2 Park Square, Milton Park, Abingdon, Oxon OX14 4RN

and by Routledge
605 Third Avenue, New York, NY 10158

Routledge is an imprint of the Taylor & Francis Group, an informa business

British Library Cataloguing-in-Publication Data
A catalogue record for this book is available from the British Library

Library of Congress Cataloging-in-Publication Data
A catalog record for this book has been requested

ISBN: 978-1-032-04206-0 (hbk)
ISBN: 978-1-032-04207-7 (pbk)
ISBN: 978-1-003-19093-6 (ebk)

DOI: 10.4324/9781003190936

Typeset in Times New Roman
by Apex CoVantage, LLC

To my seven granddaughters:

Adriana Stone Nevin and Alessandra Nevin,
Gita Lovisa Brunn and Elva Roswitha Brunn,
and
Leyla Nevin, Lily Nevin, and Thalia Nevin

Contents

Acknowledgements

Correspondence between Gregory Zilboorg and his brother James Zilboorg and his wife Eugenia Zilboorg is in the James and Eugenia Zilboorg Papers at the Beinecke Rare Book and Manuscript Library at Yale University (JEZB). I am grateful to the late Olga Irvine (daughter of James and Eugenia Zilboorg) and to Peggy Schaeffer (granddaughter of James and Eugenia Zilboorg) for permission to quote from letters by James Zilboorg. These letters are in Russian unless otherwise noted until the end of the summer of 1932, after which this correspondence is in English.

Correspondence between Fera Levitas and James Zilboorg and between Basia Berdychevsky and James Zilboorg is in JEZB. I am grateful to Gloria Levitas for permission to quote from these letters, all of which are in Russian.

Correspondence between Moses and Anna Zilboorg and James and Eugenia Zilboorg is in JEZB. Moses's letters are in Russian and Anna's letters are in Yiddish.

Correspondence between Gregory Zilboorg and George W. Henry is in the Gregory Zilboorg Papers (GZB) at the Beinecke Rare Book and Manuscript Library at Yale University.

Correspondence between Gregory Zilboorg and Noël Mailloux as well as letters and documents related to their relationship and to Mailloux's efforts on his behalf are among Mailloux's papers in Les Archives Provinciales Dominicaines, Montréal, Québec, Canada, and are quoted by permission of the archive.

Correspondence and documents related to the Zilboorg family currently in Schaeffer's possession will in time be deposited in JEZB and GZB.

Correspondence between Gregory Zilboorg and Henry Sigerist and his family are in Marcel H. Bickel's edition of *Correspondence: Henry E. Sigerist-Gregory Zilboorg, 1931–1956*. I am grateful to the late Marcel Bickel for permission to quote from Sigerist's letters.

Correspondence and documents not attributed to an archive are in my possession.

Thomas Irvine's interview with Fera Levitas is quoted with his permission. I am grateful to Etta Fay Orkin for sharing with me copies of her own and Catherine Orkin Oskow's interview with Fera. My interview with Anna (formally Nancy) Zilboorg is quoted with her permission. Tatiana Irvine's interview with

Olga Irvine and Gloria and Mitchel Levitas is quoted with her permission and theirs.

M.L. Cohn's minutes, comprising 752 pages numbered sequentially, of the four special meetings of the New York Psychoanalytic Society's board of directors held at the New York Psychoanalytic Institute, 324 West 86th Street in New York City, between 31 October and 21 December 1941, and related documents are in the Archives and Special Collections of the New York Psychoanalytic Society and Institute and are quoted by permission of the New York Psychoanalytic Society and Institute.

All documents in Russian have been meticulously and sensitively translated by Judith Hehir. I am grateful to Richard Davies, Archivist at the Russian Archive at the University of Leeds, for help in understanding school diplomas and documents relating to Gregory Zilboorg's travel and journalism in Russia. Hanna Nosova provided summaries of Gregory Zilboorg's Russian journalism and letters from Anna and Moses Zilboorg to James and Eugenia Zilboorg. I am grateful to Sima Beeri for translations of letters in Yiddish from Moses and Anna Zilboorg, and for help with Yiddish articles by and about Gregory Zilboorg. I am grateful to Marcel Bickel and Elodie Nevin for translations from German. All translations from French are my own.

As my parents' executor I quote freely from their interviews, correspondence, and writings published and unpublished. I quote from correspondence with me by permission of the individual authors.

All images, unless otherwise noted, are from family files. The photograph of Gregory Zilboorg with George Gershwin in 1935 is reproduced by permission of the Ira and Leonore S. Gershwin Trusts. Gregory Zilboorg's photographs of Diego Rivera and David Siqueiros are owned by the Wach Gallery.

This biography has drawn on both general and specific histories and on archival sources, but the paucity of archival material for Gregory Zilboorg's early life has posed challenges. Indeed, it is remarkable that any records have survived two World Wars, a multi-phased revolution, as well as the Soviet Union and its break-up, and I am grateful to Russian archivists who have searched for information, much of which is now probably unrecoverable. After 1918, archival material has been a rich resource while surviving photographs and letters – testament to social, professional, and intellectual life before the ephemera of the electronic era – have been invaluable. I am grateful to my parents for having preserved so much material still in my possession and to the Beinecke Library for its stewardship of material already donated to them. Many documents I draw upon are, unless otherwise noted, still in my possession at the time of writing, but I intend in due course to deposit all of this material at the Beinecke.

The following institutions and librarians contributed to this volume in significant ways:

A.A. Brill Library, the New York Psychoanalytic Society and Institute, Archives and Special Collections (Nellie L. Thompson, Curator)

Alan Mason Chesney Medical Archives, Johns Hopkins Medical Institutions (Marjorie Winslow Kehoe, Reference Archivist)
American Journal of Psychiatry (Michael D. Roy, Editorial Director)
Archival Sound Labs, Cutting Corporation (Aaron Coe, Sound Engineer)
Archives Provinciales Dominicaines, Montréal, Québec, Canada (Père Rodrigue Guilmette, O.P., Archivist, and Isabel Bigras, Secretary)
The Bancroft Library, Berkeley, California (Dean Smith)
Beinecke Rare Book and Manuscript Library, Yale University (Moira Fitzgerald, Head of Access Services; Elizabeth Frengel, Research Services Librarian; Melissa Barton, Curator of Drama and Prose; Nancy Kuhl, Curator of Poetry, Yale Collection of American Literature)
V.M. Bekhterev Institute, Saint Petersburg, Russia (Marina Akimenko, Archivist)
Berliner Psychoanalytisches Institut and Deutsche Psychoanalytische Vereinigung (Ludger M. Hermanns, Archivist)
Bodleian Library, Oxford University Archives (Alice Millea, Archivist)
Burling Library Archives, Grinnell College (Christopher R. Jones, College Archivist)
Central Archives for the History of the Jewish People, Hebrew University of Jerusalem (Hadassah Assouline and Yochai Ben-Ghedalia, Archivists)
Codrington Library, All Souls College, Oxford University (Gabrielle Matthews, Assistant Librarian)
Columbia University Archives (Jocelyn K. Wilk, Associate University Archivist)
Columbia University Medical Center, A.C. Long Health Sciences Library, Archives and Special Collections (Stephen E. Novak, Head)
Friends Historical Library, Swarthmore College (Christopher Densmore, Archivist)
Historic Synagogue Justo Sierra 71, Mexico City (Monica Unikel)
Howard Gotlieb Archival Research Center, Boston University (Laura Rosso, Archivist)
Lady Margaret Hall Library, Oxford University (Oliver Mahony, Archivist)
Library of Congress, Washington, D.C. (Jennifer Brathovde and Patrick Kerwin, Archivist); George and Ira Gershwin Collection; Manuscript Division; Moving Image Section (Josie Walters-Johnson); Music Division (Cait Miller); Performing Arts Division
Museum of Modern Art, New York City (Danielle King, Manager, Department of Painting and Sculpture)
New York Academy of Medicine (Arlene Shaner, Historical Collections Librarian)
New York-Presbyterian/Weill Cornell, Medical Center Archives (Elizabeth Shepard, Associate Archivist/Photo Archivist)
Nichols House Museum, Boston, Massachusetts (Emma Welty)

Oliver Archives Center, Chautauqua Institution (Amanda Holt)
One Street Museum, Kiev (Dmitry Shlonsky, Director)
Queen's College Library and Archive, Oxford University (Michael Riordan, Archivist)
Rotterdam City Archives (Christa Schepen)
Saint Petersburg State Historical Archives, Saint Petersburg, Russia (Marina Akimenko)
Tate Modern, London (Nathan Ladd, Displays Assistant, Curatorial Department)
Vassar College (Colton Johnson, College Historian, and Dean Rogers, Archivist, Special Collections Library)
Vassar Quarterly, Vassar College (Elizabeth L. Randolph, Director of Alumnae/i)
Wach Gallery (Peter M. Wach, Owner)
Wiley Online Publishers (Romalyn Castellano)

No biography is possible without the interest, help, and encouragement of acquaintances, colleagues, friends, and family. I am indebted to the following in more ways than they know: Tobias Abeloff, Ilonka Venier Alexander, Bert Babcock, Helen Beer, the late Marcel Bickel, Cassandra and Ian Bullock, Daniel Burston, Vitaly Charny, Andrea Marquit Clagget, Michael Copp, Arianne Dar, Richard Davies, Rachel Ertel, Andrew Farah, Cathy Cato Foster, Andrew Frayn, Dorothy Gallagher, the late Gerald Grob, Sharon Hecker, Ludger Hermanns, Joel Howell, the late Olga Zilboorg Irvine, Tatiana Irvine, Thomas Irvine, Brett Kahr, Michail Kalnitsky, Ingrid Kästner, Catriona Kelly, Gloria Levitas, the late Mitchel Levitas, Roger Lipsey, Miranda Machado, Serena Martucci di Scarfizzi, William Maynez, Catherine Zilboorg McMillan, Natan Meir, William Middleton, Mary Miles, Austin Nevin, Elodie Nevin, Thomas Nevin, Tobias Nevin, Abraham Nussbaum, James Oles, Darren Oldridge, Etta Fay Orkin, Michel Peterson, Wendy Pollard, Susan Quinn, Gregory Radick, Natasha Randall, Iona Sachse, Alejandro O. Saitcevsky, Patrick Samway, Max Saunders, Peggy Schaeffer, Emily Schlemowitz, Michael Schröter, Robert Schwartzwald, Margo Stone Shearon, Roger Smith, Jennifer Terry, Daniel Todes, Mary Vance, Leon Wash, Clifton Edward Watkins, Jr., Jared Wickware, Anna Zilboorg, John Zilboorg, and Matthew Zilboorg.

I am finally grateful to my father, the memory of whose hard work and high standards I have carried with me throughout my life.

Series editor's foreword

I shall never forget my utter delight when, at the tender age of 18 years, I stumbled, quite unexpectedly, upon a remarkably special book, while browsing the shelves of my university library.

As a young first-year undergraduate student of psychology, I hoped that I would learn all about the struggles of human beings and, moreover, about the ways in which doctors of the mind might offer assistance. Instead, I received copious instruction in neurobiology, statistical research, and cognitive science – all deeply absorbing and engaging topics of great relevance, but, alas, by no means illuminating of the true plight that each of us must face as we journey through the cycle of life.

Desperate to read something more foundational, I clutched Dr. Gregory Zilboorg's 1941 textbook, *A History of Medical Psychology*, written in collaboration with Dr. George W. Henry, with both curiosity and relish. Within minutes of reading through the introductory chapter, I found myself utterly gripped by the author's superbly written and carefully researched tome on the nature of madness across the centuries, which outlined the dramatic and often shocking ways in which physicians attempted to offer treatments.

After weeks and months of attending lectures, often delivered in a dry style, on the difference between the thalamus and the hypothalamus and, also, on how psychological statisticians distinguish between correlation and causation, I simply could not believe the sheer gripping quality of Dr. Zilboorg's prose and, of course, the breadth and depth of his scholarship.

Indeed, I became extremely impressed that this man could embrace the entire history of medicine from the Paleozoic era to the twentieth century with such thoroughness and clarity. And, as the chapters unfolded, I received a unique education in everything from tuberculosis in the Stone Age, to an examination of Aristotle's 'psychological physiology' (Zilboorg and Henry, 1941, p. 56), to a study of the eighth-century Nestorian physicians who practised 'a rather crude psychotherapy of intimidation and reproach' (Zilboorg and Henry, 1941, p. 120), to the creation of Spanish lunatic asylums in the fifteenth century, and so much more besides.

Zilboorg's broad coverage, underpinned by compelling detail, truly captivated me. And, in due course, I knew that I wished to become both a practitioner of psychoanalysis and, also, an historian of the subject, just like the author.

In the upcoming years, I plunged myself into the works of Zilboorg with unrelenting delight, and he soon became one of my intellectual heroes. I particularly admired his tremendous clinical contributions, especially in relation to the role of parental antagonism in the development of severe mental illness. As a young psychologist working in a backwater psychiatric hospital in the English countryside, I found Zilboorg's (1929, 1931a, 1932, 1941) early papers on the psychoses truly innovative and inspiring.

Zilboorg struck me as an authentic Renaissance man. Not only did he have the capacity to practise medicine, psychiatry, and psychoanalysis, but he boasted many other talents as well, and I soon came to learn about his impressive historical scholarship and his great literary capacities. He also proved himself a most adept translator and, somehow, he even found the time to transform a landmark German-language book, written by the psychoanalysts Dr. Franz Alexander and Dr. Hugo Staub (1929), into a highly readable English edition (Alexander and Staub, 1931; cf. Zilboorg, 1931b), thus illuminating the ways in which psychoanalysts can assist forensic patients who have committed crimes. Zilboorg himself would, in later years, also write about psychoanalytical criminology in a very illuminating manner (e.g., Zilboorg, 1954, 1956).

It saddened me that, some years later, while reading Susan Quinn's (1987) biography of the German-born psychoanalyst Dr. Karen Horney, I encountered a very different Zilboorg. As many readers will appreciate, Gregory Zilboorg, like Karen Horney, immigrated to New York City, and both of these physicians became prominent members of the New York Psychoanalytic Society. In her account, Quinn suggested, much to my chagrin, that Zilboorg, one of Horney's colleagues, had perpetrated many unethical acts, exploiting his psychoanalytical patients for financial gain.

Subsequent to the publication of this exposé by Susan Quinn, other individuals began to allege further transgressions on the part of Gregory Zilboorg. For instance, Katharine Weber, the granddaughter of one of Zilboorg's analysands, Broadway lyricist Kay Swift, claimed that Zilboorg had seduced this woman in the middle of psychoanalytical treatment. According to Katharine Weber, her grandmother confessed, 'He was the only man with whom I ever had a sexual relationship to whom I was not physically attracted' (quoted in Peyser, 1993, p. 263).

Needless to say, these damning portraits of Zilboorg shocked me and challenged my state of admiration, indeed, idealisation, of this great figure in the history of psychoanalysis.

As the years unfolded, I found a way to retain my deep admiration of Zilboorg's scholarship while also appreciating that, back in the olden days, long before the formalisation of more rigorous psychoanalytical training and supervision programmes, many of the early Freudians also engaged in much boundary-breaking behaviour, and that, in consequence, one could forgive Zilboorg for his sins whilst also appreciating his sainthood.

Happily, Dr. Caroline Zilboorg, the daughter of this controversial psychoanalyst and, moreover, a distinguished literary and historical scholar in her own right, has generously devoted herself to a more detailed study of Gregory Zilboorg's life and work than anyone previously. And, after years of painstaking research, Caroline Zilboorg has produced a two-volume masterpiece.

While most children of famous people tend to write personalised, first-hand memoirs of their parents – consider, for instance, Martin Freud's (1957) classic, *Glory Reflected: Sigmund Freud – Man and Father*, based entirely on reminiscences – Caroline Zilboorg has approached this project as a serious academician, conducting oral history interviews, examining unpublished archival materials with microscopic attention, and surveying a wide range of sources of every shape and size. Indeed, Dr. Zilboorg has written her father's biography with such professionalism and with such objectivity, one would presume that an independent scholar, with *no* personal family ties, had actually constructed these impeccable tomes.

This incomparable study of the life and work of Gregory Zilboorg will, in my estimation, never be surpassed. Not only has Caroline Zilboorg studied all of the relevant published and unpublished data but, moreover, she has curated this information in the most thorough manner imaginable, never brushing over the areas of controversy. Instead, she engages with all the Zilboorgian 'scandals' in a truly direct and frank manner. Moreover, she helps us to develop a compassion for her father who, as a refugee to the New World, had to endure innumerable struggles with great fortitude and forbearance.

In spite of the fact that Caroline Zilboorg has written a lengthy, heavily referenced, two-volume biography, this substantial project reads with such fluidity and grace that I simply could not put it down. As a result, I have now come to appreciate that the story of this Russian-born man, regarded by some as a genius and by others as a scoundrel, contains infinitely more nuance and subtlety than we could ever have imagined.

Having now studied the two-volume biography in detail, I have come to acquire a much deeper appreciation of the ways in which Gregory Zilboorg impacted upon his colleagues. Certainly, he evoked a lot of envy from his less talented fellow psychoanalysts, and that factor undoubtedly played a part in the narrative of some of the accusations against him. While maintaining scholarly neutrality, Caroline Zilboorg has, nevertheless, helped us to develop a fuller comprehension of some of the complex dynamics among the members of the New York Psychoanalytic Society in the midst of the Second World War.

Neither idealising nor denigratory, this extraordinary tome – meticulously researched and stunningly crafted – will help us to appreciate the true complexity of the human character. Indeed, as I immersed myself in the book, I became convinced that if Caroline Zilboorg had devoted herself to a career in clinical psychoanalysis, rather than to a more academic lifetime in scholarship, she would absolutely have had all the sensitivity of a great clinician who must recognise the strengths and the vulnerabilities, the brilliance and the madness, and all of the other complexities of being a human.

I thank Caroline Zilboorg warmly for sharing this important story in such an open-hearted and serious manner, helpfully questioning and reconfiguring many of the unsubstantiated myths and rumours. This two-volume biography of Gregory Zilboorg represents, in my estimation, not only a vital contribution to the historiography of psychoanalysis but, also, a wonderful model of how we make sense of the multifaceted, complex, and often contradictory nature of the human mind.

Professor Brett Kahr
August 2021

References

Alexander, Franz, and Staub, Hugo (1929). *Der Verbrecher und seine Richter: Ein psychoanalytischer Einblick in die Welt der Paragraphen*. Vienna: Internationaler Psychoanalytischer Verlag.

Alexander, Franz, and Staub, Hugo (1931). *The Criminal, the Judge, and the Public: A Psychological Analysis*. Gregory Zilboorg (Transl.). New York: Macmillan Company.

Freud, Martin (1957). *Glory Reflected: Sigmund Freud – Man and Father*. London: Angus and Robertson.

Peyser, Joan (1993). *The Memory of All That: The Life of George Gershwin*. New York: Simon & Schuster.

Quinn, Susan (1987). *A Mind of Her Own: The Life of Karen Horney*. New York: Summit Books/Simon & Schuster.

Zilboorg, Gregory (1929). The Dynamics of Schizophrenic Reactions Related to Pregnancy and Childbirth. *American Journal of Psychiatry*, *8*, 733–766.

Zilboorg, Gregory (1931a). Depressive Reactions Related to Parenthood. *American Journal of Psychiatry*, *10*, 927–962.

Zilboorg, Gregory (1931b). Translator's Note. In Franz Alexander and Hugo Staub. *The Criminal, the Judge, and the Public: A Psychological Analysis*. Gregory Zilboorg (Transl.), pp. v–x. New York: Macmillan Company.

Zilboorg, Gregory (1932). Sidelights on Parent-Child Antagonism. *American Journal of Orthopsychiatry*, *2*, 35–42.

Zilboorg, Gregory (1941). Ambulatory Schizophrenias. *Psychiatry*, *4*, 149–155.

Zilboorg, Gregory (1954). *The Psychology of the Criminal Act and Punishment*. New York: Harcourt, Brace & Company.

Zilboorg, Gregory (1956). The Contribution of Psycho-Analysis to Forensic Psychiatry. *International Journal of Psycho-Analysis*, *37*, 318–324.

Zilboorg, Gregory, and George W. Henry (1941). *A History of Medical Psychology*. New York: W.W. Norton & Company.

Preface

When in 1943, five years before I was born, Gregory Zilboorg finished *Mind, Medicine, and Man*, his book on psychiatry for the general reader, he entitled the first chapter 'On Certain Misconceptions'. It is tempting to begin this biography with a similar chapter. My father defended his rationale: In trying to explain psychiatry and his own specialism of psychoanalysis to people who were untrained in either, he needed to address his readers' ignorance. It was not, he insisted, that his readers were uninformed concerning his subjects, in a state of 'not knowing'; rather, quoting Artemus Ward, he pointed out that their ignorance meant 'knowing so many things that ain't so'.[1]

Among those who today know something about Gregory Zilboorg, many are convinced of 'things that ain't so'. The psychiatrist and historian George Mora, once Zilboorg's student, wrote that Zilboorg escaped from Russia after the revolution by simply 'walking out of the country to Finland'. In her introduction to *Psychoanalysis and Religion*, my mother claimed my father knew only three words of English on his arrival in America ('yes', 'no', and 'Bolshevik') but mastered the language in three months. In her biography of Lillian Hellman, Dorothy Gallagher asserted that, as a life-long socialist, Zilboorg felt it was 'legitimate' to 'bilk' wealthy patients. The psychoanalyst Mark Leffert argued that Zilboorg's treatment of George Gershwin in the 1930s offered 'a disturbing narrative of questionable psychoanalytic and medical practices' and that the musician's life could have been saved if his psychoanalyst had made 'an appropriate neurological referral'. Comparing inconsistencies in various biographical accounts, Leffert decided that these narratives could only have originated with Zilboorg, thus he must have lied about his birth, youth, education, experience of war, participation in the revolution, work as a journalist, and escape from Russia. According to Leffert, during a trip to Mexico with Gershwin and Eddie Warburg, to the patients' great discomfort Zilboorg would comment on their analysis over breakfast and intentionally humiliate Gershwin by arranging that they spend time in that Spanish-speaking country 'with people who spoke no English'. If all this were not enough, Leffert stated at the end of his long article that despite his inarguable brilliance, Zilboorg's 'writing was not particularly seminal'. Katharine Weber, the composer

Kay Swift's granddaughter, contended in her family memoir that Swift and her friend the philanthropist Mary Lasker found Zilboorg 'malevolent' and mocked him using 'a private nickname': 'Grischa'. According to Weber, Zilboorg was 'a fraud', 'a duplicitous, immoral Svengali' who even had sexual intercourse with Swift during the analytical hour as part of her therapy. Ron Chernow in *The Warburgs* concluded that Zilboorg 'mesmerized' the Warburg family, extracting his patients' secrets in order to control them.[2]

What follows here will not begin, however, with a countering of all or any of these 'misconceptions'. I am content to let the biography stand on its own, offering a well-documented and careful account of my father's life rather than a polemical refutation or a defence of his reputation. The biography is the result of my efforts to offer a vivid and fair portrait of a complex man who was a fascinating and difficult figure, a person capable of great wisdom, generosity, tenderness, and love, who could also be – or at least appear to be – resentful, manipulative, and unkind. On one hand he could write insightfully,

> when a patient says he has a pain it *is* a pain, whether it is 'purely' psychic, or 'purely' somatic, or a mongrel of the two. There is no 'imaginary' pain except in the imagination of the incredulous physician or the unenlightened sceptic. A pain is a pain – and when a patient has it, he does not like it.

On the other hand, when as a child I complained of a recurrent tummy ache and didn't want to go to school, he was so determined I go that he shouted, 'I don't care if you puke in the street!' The impact of his rage was only slightly mitigated by the fact that I didn't know the word 'puke', but had to get dressed in my school uniform despite my tears, aware that I would need to ask my mother what the word meant and, once I discovered exactly what he intended, be both humiliated in my ignorance and diminished by my father's rage all over again.[3]

I loved my father and feared him; I admired him and identified with him and wanted desperately to please him, but I never thought he was other than a challenging human being. Throughout my childhood and certainly after his death, my mother would speak of him with warmth and humour but also unalloyed adoration. She certainly never acknowledged his complex and contradictory character, apparently forgetting how difficult, egotistic, and domineering he could be. I resolved early on to remember everything – and while I don't remember everything, I have done my best here to find out.

I have thought about biography not only in writing a book about my father but throughout my writing career. This biography's subject has presented special challenges posed not only by the man himself and the available material, but by my relation to the subject, my own place both in the biography and my situation outside the narrative as a responsible writer with a good story to tell about a man who was extremely and protectively private despite having quite a reputation, who was complicated and charismatic, admired and detested, brilliant and misunderstood.

My initial reluctance to write about my father – something that has tempted and been urged upon me since my early twenties – as well as my decision to write about him now, some 60 years after his death, are possibly the subject of another book for another time. My own psychological and authorial efforts to position myself appropriately in relation to the biographical material are also outside the purveyance of this biography. The results of my strategies, however, will be evident throughout. In the early pages I occasionally call Gregory Zilboorg 'my father', but generally I call him 'Gregory'; in the final pages he sometimes becomes 'my father' once again. Still, this biography remains about him and not about me, and if I have done my work well, the reader will understand not only my approach but the man himself.

The matter of evidence and the personal and private nature of much of the material I draw on raise separate questions about the appropriateness of any biography and particularly about an intimate biography like this one. Luckily, my father also thought a great deal about biography. Addressing just these questions, he noted that historians find it 'almost imperative to understand not only the contributions' of their subjects but 'their personalities. Their faces, indeed their innermost lives, while not belonging to their contemporary populace do belong to history.' He thus defended biography:

> the understanding of the intimate structure of a given historical personality tells us a great deal about the specific impact a given historical problem happens to possess, and the reactions of this personality tell us of the force with which this problem was met.[4]

In describing the reasons for biography, one that reveals 'the innermost' element of its subject, a person's 'intimate structure', he also suggested what he felt was good biography. In his review of Ernest Jones's monumental life of Freud, he developed his idea of what good biography ought to entail. Despite his admiration for the work, he finally contended that Jones neither illuminated nor clarified the failings that made Freud human. Jones offered 'masks instead of faces, so many silhouettes instead of statues, so many shadowy outlines instead of presences'; Jones's 'lack of feeling for and about men' resulted in a distortion of Freud's life and achievements. Consequently, his biography contains truth 'but instead of the throbbing *élan vitale*, there is cold fact'. Zilboorg acknowledged the old controversy that it is the poetry of the poet, the art of the artist, the contributions of the scientist that belong to the world and not the poet or artist or scientist as a human being, but he recognised that there is an 'intense need … to catch a glimpse of and into the person'. He mused that 'this need to satisfy one's curiosity about the small things of great men transcends the boundaries of natural or self-imposed objectivity' but cannot be supressed – and it is the effort to satisfy this curiosity that produces a truly worthy biography.[5]

I can only hope that my work satisfies the reader's curiosity about the human being who was Gregory Zilboorg and offers a rounded portrait with the appropriate *élan vitale*.

Notes

1 GZ, MMM, 3.
2 Mora, 'Early American Historians', 59; MSZ, 'Introduction', vii; Gallagher, 93; Leffert, 420, 421, 424, 428, 436; Weber, 196, 197, 212, 147; Chernow, 333.
3 GZ, 'The Struggle', 426.
4 GZ, 'Psychological Sidelights', 562, 563.
5 GZ, review, *The Life and Work*, 254.

Chapter 1

Family and childhood

1890–1909

In 1932, the year that Gregory Zilboorg with three other psychoanalysts founded the *Psychoanalytic Quarterly* in New York, Freud's biographer Ernest Jones discussed with Freud concerns about an American periodical in competition with the journal of the International Psycho-Analytical Association:

> Your inference that the Americans do not feel related to England I should modify by saying this is only true of the foreigners recently arrived in America, who have lost their own civilisation and not acquired any other. Zilboorg, who is a completely wild Russian, is the real centre of this piece of activity. I admire his energy, but wish it could be somewhat directed and controlled.[1]

This 'completely wild Russian' had not entirely lost his own civilisation nor had he failed to adapt to his new environment, but he had certainly come a long way from the world into which he was born. No one could have predicted that the Jewish boy born in Tsarist Russia would make an international name for himself or even that his name would become Gregory Zilboorg.

My father was born in the Podil district of Kiev on 23 December 1890. Eight days later he was circumcised following religious ritual. Because the city had no synagogue, the ceremony probably occurred in his parents' apartment at 32 Kostiantynivska Street. The rabbi recited the traditional Hebrew words as he began to cut: 'Blessed art Thou, O Lord our God, King of the universe, who hast sanctified us with Thy commandments, and hast given us the command concerning circumcision.' My grandfather, cradling his first-born on his lap, then recited, 'Blessed art Thou, O Lord our God, King of the universe, who hast sanctified us with Thy commandments, and hast commanded us to make our sons enter the covenant of Abraham our father.' The male voices in the crowded room responded, 'Even as this child has entered into the covenant, so may he enter into the Torah, into the nuptial canopy, and into good deeds.' Finally the rabbi, dipping his finger into sanctified wine, gently touched the baby's lips and formally named him in Hebrew 'Hirsh' or 'Girsh ben Moses'. The first-born child of Moses and Anna Zil'burg would be known, however, throughout his youth in a curious amalgam of Yiddish and Russian as Girsh Moseevich Zil'burg, but it is unlikely he spoke much

DOI: 10.4324/9781003190936-1

Russian before he started school, for his first language was Yiddish, the language spoken by both of his parents and by Jews throughout the Podil community.[2]

After the ceremony, Anna would have served the many guests an extravagant kosher meal. The menu would likely have included a rich beet and potato borscht, moist rye bread, kasha made with an egg, herring with onions followed by a savoury pirog, and for dessert sweet blinis with jam. The men would have finished the consecrated wine at the end of the bris, but there would have been black tea from the large samovar and kvass for everyone. It was, after all, a celebration.

At such moments it might have been almost possible to forget that 1890 was not a good time to be born a Jew in Russia. Historically Jews had even been denied residence in Kiev, although the city had been within the Pale of Settlement since 1835. Indeed, Jews had been denied residence in Russia from the 1400s, but the empire's extension into Eastern Europe after the annexation of Poland in 1772 meant that it had had to accept a large Jewish population within its borders. In the 1790s laws were passed that allowed Jews to continue to live where they were already settled and, to encourage colonisation, in underpopulated areas of Ukraine annexed from Turkey. By the 1850s the Pale of Settlement included most of present-day Poland, Lithuania, Belarus, Ukraine, Moldova, Georgia, and the Crimea.

The conditions for Jewish residence shifted throughout the nineteenth century. At times Jews were forbidden to reside in agricultural communities or specific cities and were forced to settle in provincial villages. Soon after he ascended the throne in 1855, Tsar Alexander II initiated reforms. He freed the serfs in 1861 and relaxed restrictions on Jewish residence, allowing certain categories of Jews to settle in previously restricted cities, including Kiev. Its Jewish population then grew rapidly.

Concentrations of Jews in designated areas – in shtetls or towns that grew up outside restricted cities or in districts like the Podil – made them easy targets for anti-Semitic pogroms. From the beginning of the Pale of Settlement, attacks against Jews were frequent, but they increased in number and intensity after the assassination of Tsar Alexander II in March 1881. His son, Alexander III, was much more conservative and in May 1882 introduced new restrictions on Jewish movement and settlement. Intended at first to be temporary, what came to be known as the May Laws remained in effect until the revolution, with further restrictions added throughout the decades just before and immediately after my father's birth. A *numerus clausus* limiting the number of Jews in schools and universities was introduced, and by 1887 quotas allowed only 10 percent of Jews within the Pale to attend university, while outside the Pale the number fell to 5 percent; in Moscow and Saint Petersburg, the restriction was 3 percent. The proportion of Jewish doctors in the army was limited to 5 percent. In 1891, most of Moscow's Jewish population was expelled. In 1892 Jews were prohibited from participating in local government, even within the Pale. The May Laws led to a period of widespread pogroms particularly intense between 1881 and 1884.

Such civil unrest was likely an important factor in my grandfather's decision to leave his native village. One of 12 children, Moses was born in 1862 in Romanovo (today Lenino), a shtetl 200 miles east of Minsk and over 350 miles north of Kiev in a region that is now in Belarus. His father, my great-grandfather Pesach, was a blacksmith in the small town where by the end of the nineteenth century Jews made up two-thirds of the population. Until Russian law required Jews to take surnames in 1844, Pesach had probably only been known as 'Pesach ben Girsh', the son of his father, but since his father was likely also a blacksmith, the family then took the name Koval, 'blacksmith' in Ukrainian. Only sons were technically exempt from service in the Imperial Army, but having several brothers, Moses would have been subject from the age of 12 to military conscription for a period of 25 years, a virtual death sentence. The neighbouring Zil'burgs, however, according to family history, had an only son who died in an attack on Jewish workers at the local mill. To avoid conscription and before their first-born son, whom his parents had called 'Isaak', reached the age of 12, Pesach bought the dead man's papers, and Gregory's father became Moses Isaakovich Zil'burg.[3]

Status as purportedly an only son would not necessarily have protected him, however, for the Russian authorities exploited the May Laws to round up Jews and press them into the army regardless of technicalities, but military service was the least of the threats facing Belarussian Jews. The pogroms of the early 1880s hit the region hard. In large numbers Jews left the countryside for the big Ukrainian cities. At the age of 14 or 15, Moses joined the exodus. He might have walked to the rail station 40 miles to the northwest at Orsha; if he had had the money, he could then have bought a train ticket or looked for work on a boat going down the Dnieper River. But if he had had the money, he would have saved it. As a Jew in flight he headed directly south from Romanovo on foot and walked the 350 miles to Kiev.[4]

My grandmother Anna grew up in slightly more secure surroundings. She was born to Mikhail and Berta Bren in April 1871 in Berdychev, a large town with a rich cultural life 110 miles southwest of Kiev. After Odessa, Berdychev was the largest Jewish community in the Russian Empire with seven synagogues and a high level of literacy – by the 1880s, approximately half of the city's Jewish men and a third of its Jewish women could read the language they spoke – that is, Yiddish. During the pogroms of the early 1880s, however, Jews began leaving Berdychev for Kiev and Odessa. Anna and her family likely moved to Kiev at this time.

It is also likely that Moses met Anna through a Podil matchmaker. Anna had been raised to take on the role of the traditional Jewish wife and mother, while Moses by the age of 28 was a clerk in Kapnik's wholesale grocery and able to offer a wife a measure of financial stability. Furthermore, he was literate: He was able to read and write Yiddish and, with effort, Russian. He was also an observant and philosophic Jew and could read Hebrew – his few years of formal schooling had been with a provincial rabbi and Talmudic in both matter and manner. They might have seemed a good match.[5]

But family life in the apartment where the bris had been celebrated was far from happy. Only 19 when Gregory was born, Anna would give birth to three more children before she turned 27: a second son, Yakov, on 2 September 1892; a daughter Basia in 1894, and another girl, Fera, on 7 October 1897. Affable enough but never a strong character, Anna had her hands full; as the household sapped her energy and limited her conversation to the children and the complaints of local women in the market, Moses distanced himself from involvement in daily matters.

Unlike his wife, Moses was made of tough fibre. Remarkably energetic and amazingly versatile, he set high standards for himself and his children. His character was stern and difficult, but he loved his family and was capable of great kindness and generosity. His apparent hardness was a result of his scorn of vanity and impatience with superficiality, his refusal to accept anything less than perfection. Not a preacher by nature, he would later restrain himself from preaching to his children, but he did lecture them when they were young. He was a philosopher, reflective and concerned about propriety and morality. With the curtains closed against the night, he would read the Talmud by dim candlelight in an attempt to protect his family from notice by outsiders, a fact that the young Girsh would remember all his life. Traditional and deeply religious, Moses had ritualistic propensities and went his own way 'neither too happy about life nor too perplexed about death'. Despite a wide circle of relatives and acquaintances, he was finally close to no one. Gregory would remember him as 'a stranger in his own family'.[6]

Moses Zilboorg, about 1900

In contrast, Anna was very much present but almost completely unreflective, concerned exclusively with what Gregory would later call 'minutia'. Petty matters about which little could be done dominated family life, and an atmosphere of ostentatious tragedy prevailed. By the time he finally began school, Gregory was eager to escape the 'volatility, irascibility, tense self-assertive "I told you so" and peremptory smallness of mind'.[7]

Anna Zilboorg, about 1900

Like many Jews in Kiev at the turn of the century, Gregory would have few pleasant memories of his early years. In her autobiography Golda Meir, born in Kiev in 1898, recalled the 'terrible hardships', specifically poverty, cold, hunger, and above all fear. She described 'the rabble that used to surge through town, brandishing knives and huge sticks, screaming "Christ killers" as they looked for the Jews'. Her father attempted to barricade the entry to their building with wooden boards, small protection against enraged attackers. Beyond their vulnerability was the awareness that 'There was never enough of anything, not food, not warm clothing, not heat at home.' She quickly came to feel 'that life was hard and that there was no justice anywhere'.[8]

Gregory experienced his first pogrom in 1896 and five more between the ages of 6 and 17. He had, like Meir, good reasons to be fearful; pre-emptive tactics and a defensive posture became his response to threats of violence, disenfranchisement, and deprivation. Gregory's interest in psychology and morality as well as his attitudes towards food and dress and money certainly had their roots in these difficult early years. On weekends during my childhood, my father would begin each lunch with a bowl of kasha. He explained to me how to cook it: You beat an egg in a pan, then poured in buckwheat groats and sautéed the coated grains before adding water and boiling the cereal. 'If you are poor and don't have an egg', he said, 'you can do it without.' He paused. I could not imagine being so poor as not to have an egg. He concluded, 'But it's always better with an egg.' Throughout his life he preferred his meat well done; any meat he was lucky enough to get as a child needed to be thoroughly cooked because it was likely to contain worms – perhaps like the meat in Eisenstein's film *Battleship Potemkin*, in which the maggots in the meat are the last straw that provokes the sailors to revolt against the tsar in 1905. There were occasionally no eggs at 32 Kostiantynivska Street; sometimes there wasn't even any kasha. He was always hungry.[9]

By 1897, the year after young Gregory's first memory of a pogrom, there were 32,000 Jews in Kiev, approximately 13 percent of the population. Most were poor; some of them were middle class, like the Zil'burgs, while a few were prosperous, able to build the city's first synagogues in 1895 and 1898, but all of them were under increasing threat from the Russian Orthodox majority populace. While the Pale itself limited Jews' geographical mobility, the *numerus clausus* intended to limit their social mobility was now officially enacted. Earlier reforms, whose intention had been to integrate Jews into Russian society, had portrayed secular education as the path not only to Russification but to progress and modernity. By the 1890s, the imperial government's policy had changed to one of containment, suppression, and even elimination. For Gregory, as he came up to school age, the partially open door seemed about to close.

Despite and in part because of his firm religious convictions Moses would have wanted the best possible education for his children, but financial constraints as well as the quota system reduced the possibilities. Gregory probably began his formal education in the Talmud Torah, the traditional Jewish cheder just a few doors up the street. He would later declare that he had had a Jewish education; certainly his father and the local rabbi would have overseen his religious instruction up until his bar mitzvah.[10]

He began his secular education not at the age of seven, the normal age for entering school in Tsarist Russia, but a year later, having been rejected despite his aptitude because of the limited places available for Jews. Already able to read and write Yiddish and some Hebrew, Gregory was embarrassed at being placed in a class with younger and smaller children speaking a language he could barely understand; he was called 'Girsh' by his teachers, but likely 'Grisha' – the Russian diminutive of the Russian 'Grigori' – by his classmates. Now he also learned Russian – to speak it, to understand it, to read and write in Cyrillic, for him a second alphabet. And despite his initial linguistic dislocation, he embraced Russian as a language as well as the fact of language itself. An impressive linguist, he quickly recognised the importance of words, their elegance and empowering precision.[11]

One of the few Jews in his class, Gregory was at an additional disadvantage: He was left-handed. Throughout his life there were certain things he would do with his left hand – perhaps writing Yiddish was one of them. He cut his food and hammered nails – activities like reading and writing Yiddish that he would have learned at home – with his left hand, and when he later performed dissections, he used his left hand to hold the scalpel, but he wrote Russian and French and German and English with his right hand. At school there were no concessions for the Jewish boy who did not speak the Russian of his younger classmates; the teacher tied his left hand behind his back and he learned to write in neat, very small but clear letters with his other hand.

Moses and Anna's first-born child was not only verbal and determined; he was mentally sharp and indefatigable, energetic, stubborn, and driven with high expectations of himself and others. Gregory sped through the primary curriculum. At the age of ten he had mastered the basics and took the required secondary school entry examinations, passing all subjects with marks of 5 (excellent), but competition was fierce among Jews for the limited places at Kiev gymnasia. He was again rejected and did not get a place even at the local Real School until two years later. He began now to read widely on his own, both Russian classics and contemporary texts. Maturing early both intellectually and physically, he felt painfully out of place in the classroom. He would remember his embarrassment sitting 'with down already on my upper lip … like a fool among kids'.[12]

Gregory's early years were no easier at home, where his education and aspirations put him on a collision course with his parents' experiences and Jewish identity. At 12 he reluctantly endured a bar mitzvah, but he no longer felt comfortable with observances that defined his parents' lives. After this traditional initiation, he refused to attend temple services and informed Moses that he no longer believed in the Torah. The confrontation must have stunned his family. Despite his explosive temper and independent mind, Gregory would not have arrived at his decision to reject observance and confront his father without reflection and anxiety. It would be too simple to see Gregory's rejection of his parents' religious beliefs and practices as conventional adolescent rebellion. Whatever he believed or practised would have no effect on his Jewishness, on his being counted as a Jew in the world he lived in. Being a Jew was written on his body; he had no baptismal certificate that, even had he converted to Christianity or bribed an official, might have allowed him to move geographically or socially in the Russia of his time. He was furthermore still a boy without money of his own and dependent on his parents, whose financial means were limited. He was not happy with his situation in his family or with his situation in Russia, but he donned his school uniform each morning and went off to classes with his brother. If there was a way out or up or over to a better way of life, he was convinced it would be through knowledge and understanding.[13]

Fera, Basia, Gregory, and James Zilboorg, Kiev, 1903

The earliest surviving photograph of young Gregory – perhaps the only photograph from his childhood – is a formal portrait of all four children taken in 1903, when Gregory was not quite 13 years old. The children look solemnly at the professional photographer, who has placed them in conventional positions, girls on the left and boys on the right. Fera, aged five, leans over a table with a bouquet of flowers. Basia, aged eight, stands on a stool in her school uniform with one hand on her sister's shoulder. Yakov, aged 11, similarly has his hand on Gregory's shoulder. The two brothers, Yakov on a high stool and Gregory on a chair, wear their military-style primary school uniforms: leather boots, dark trousers, and jackets with brass buttons. From the stripe on his collar and the ribbons on his cuff, Yakov seems to have achieved some distinction. Gregory's cuff is bare. Their closely cropped hair was very much the style for Russian schoolboys at the turn of the century. None of the children appears particularly at ease, but the boys look more uncomfortable than the girls. Yakov's light colouring sets him somewhat apart, while Gregory's heavy brows, full lips, and large dark eyes make his young face the centre of this photograph. Basia stares straight at the photographer: An obedient child, she was apparently the most content within the family circle. Like her mother, she assumed a dependent female role and devoted herself to domestic minutiae while assuming a posture of complaint, bewailing actual and anticipated misfortune. Basia looks the most like Gregory, but Fera would feel the closest bond with her eldest brother. Their similarities included intellectual promise, determination, and autonomy. Although Gregory and Yakov were the closest in age and their experiences of family and school quite similar, they were awkward friends, different in personality and worldview. As the firstborn son, Gregory was throughout their childhood a step ahead of his brother, who developed a competitive edginess his charismatic older brother never shared. Within the family and in his professional life Yakov would always feel hard done by, at once deserving and cheated. Gregory's tendency to dominate was tempered by analytic retrospection, trenchant humour, and material generosity; he would never feel privileged, and his struggles would inevitably be with forces far greater than his parents and siblings.

The larger geographical and political world with which Gregory would now grapple included not only his city but the empire into which he had been born. Kiev in those days was not the capital of Ukraine but merely one of many cities in a Ukraine that began in what is today Poland and extended as far as Georgia, but Kiev was distinct from other cities in the empire because it held more Jews than any other Russian city except Odessa. In addition to almost the entire territory of today's Russia, the empire in which Gregory came to maturity was larger than what later became the Soviet Union and included most of Ukraine, Belarus, Moldova, and Georgia. To the east Imperial Russia stretched across the Asian continent to Vladivostok, while to the west it covered most of present-day Poland, including Warsaw. To the southeast it extended into what is now Turkey, while to the north it reached into modern Finland. Politically, the tsar took his authority from the Christian God with the support of the Russian Orthodox Church. To be fully Russian, one had to believe in his divine lineage; no Jew could thus be really Russian in the eyes of the majority Gentile population. With his entry into secondary school Gregory would become increasingly aware of his marginalisation as political and social upheaval threatened the empire and his future within it.

In June 1903 Gregory left primary school and in August he entered the Kiev Real School. Denied a place at a gymnasium despite his scholastic promise, he now experienced the marginalisation of his talents. While gymnasia prepared students for university, real schools offered instruction in mathematics, science, modern languages, and applied art as well as practical and commercial subjects. His secondary education prepared Gregory well in three languages and gave him a firm basis in computation and the hard sciences, but it also widened the gap between him and his parents. French and German required the mastery of a third alphabet, and both the Cyrillic and Latin alphabets would be natural to him throughout his life, but while he would continue to be able to speak Yiddish, he later refrained from doing so except with his father and mother; as an adult he could read it only with difficulty and could no longer really write it at all.[14]

His school leaving certificate, dated 5 June 1909, gives his name as Girsh Zil'burg and suggests that he was a competent although not outstanding student. With an indication of excellent conduct, he received the following marks: 'satisfactory' (3 out of a possible 5) in Russian, French, geometry, trigonometry, history, physics, and geography, and a mark of 'good' (4) in German, arithmetic, algebra, natural science (biology), and drawing and drafting. Literature and philosophy are notably absent from the curriculum, but these were areas in which he read voraciously on his own.

Gregory's independent reading was in part an effort to come to terms with the social and political turmoil in Russia during the first decade of the twentieth century. During his six years of secondary school, he could not have avoided the political consciousness that, for many Russians of his generation, displaced or at least sublimated an adolescent sexual awakening. There was no co-education in Imperial Russia before the level of university; Gregory's close companions outside of the family would have been primarily male until his late teens. Never a serious drinker, he would not have been tempted by Kiev's rough taverns, nor apparently was he ever interested in frequenting its brothels, but the city offered him a rich view of life's variety.

Early twentieth-century Kiev was modern by the standards of Imperial Russia. Its Jewish and Gentile poor included not only factory and dock workers but domestic servants, petty criminals, drunkards, and prostitutes. Members of the aristocracy as well as Jewish and Gentile industrialists made up Kiev's substantial wealthy class; while peddlers and pickpockets frequented the marketplaces and alleys, fashionable men and women strolled the boulevards or rode in horse-drawn carriages. With ornate, mostly nineteenth-century architecture, the city boasted impressive monuments, numerous theatres, and an opera house. Police patrolled shop-lined streets and open squares featuring grand public buildings. A sophisticated medical community served the populace in several large hospitals, while the Kiev Commercial Institute, the Kiev Polytechnical Institute, and Saint Vladimir University (the University of Kiev) supported the city's academic and intellectual life. It was not difficult for the young Gregory to spend much of his free time with books. Tea rooms, many of which had reading areas, offered an alternative to boisterous street and tavern culture as did the Troitsky People's Club, finished in 1902, with its large auditorium and library. Public lectures and local newspapers were important sources of information and ideas. The city's parks provided greenery and vistas over the Dnieper for children and families as well as a bit of independence for courting couples, but the open spaces also offered students the opportunity to discuss politics, and there was much for the young Gregory to discuss and to try to come to terms with.[15]

His first year at the real school was fraught with political and social strife. Despite state efforts to foster industrialisation, in 1903 80 percent of the population remained agrarian while the urban working class expanded to fill the new factories. Tsar Nicolas II began to seek a port in the east that, unlike Vladivostok, could be used year-round. On 8 February 1904, the Japanese navy fired on the Russian fleet at Port Arthur (today the Chinese port of Dalian). The Russo-Japanese War that followed lasted a year and a half and involved enormous casualties. Public opinion, initially supportive of the tsar, quickly turned against him, and increased discontent with the Romanovs led to protests throughout the empire.

During Gregory's second year at secondary school, the turmoil intensified. Unions called on workers to strike, and by December 1904 the capital and much of the country was without public transportation, electricity, and newspapers. Shortly after his 14th birthday, on 22 January 1905, imperial guards outside Saint Petersburg's Winter Palace fired on protestors attempting to present a petition to the tsar, a peaceful crowd of thousands that included women and children. The day that became known as 'Bloody Sunday' increased civil unrest while strikes crippled the country. Peasants turned against aristocratic landowners and burned their property while mutinies broke out in the army and the navy. The revolt quickly became the first Russian revolution.

As Gregory began his third year of secondary school, on 5 September 1905 Russia was forced to accept military defeat, a humiliation that exacerbated the widespread protests against the intransigent autocracy. Throughout the Pale of Settlement a wave of anti-Semitic pogroms began as the populace, often incited by police and soldiers, attacked Jews in the streets and in their homes, blaming them for the civil unrest. Other minorities as well as students and intellectuals were also targeted, but Jews bore the brunt of the backlash. Thousands of people were killed and injured. In mid-October the Podil suffered three days of savage violence. As many as 100 people were murdered and at least 300 seriously injured; nearly two thousand homes and shops were plundered and three thousand Jews were afterwards without places to work. At not yet 15, Gregory witnessed the turmoil with horror. He would remember the rain that fell during the days of the pogrom; in Kiev's streets he saw 'mud mixed with human brains'. For 15 roubles a Jew could pay a policeman and the Jew would be safe, but he did not have 15 roubles and feared for his own life and that of his family, whose home and livelihood were threatened.[16]

On 30 October 1905, attempting to quell the rebellion and to retain power, Nicholas II issued a manifesto that ostensibly granted basic rights such as self-protection, freedom of speech, and freedom of assembly. This proto-constitution also introduced universal male suffrage and created a Duma, an elected senate empowered to propose and confirm laws. The tsar retained, however, the power to veto any proposed legislation as well as the power to disband the Duma as and when he wished. The manifesto ended the strikes and violence as the people rejoiced in the idea of a responsive and representative government, but the calm was short-lived as the government reasserted its power, executing protestors and suppressing political activity.

During Gregory's third year of secondary school much of Russia was under martial law while political reaction to the regime divided itself into several factions. Prominent among them were the moderate Octobrists, who supported the manifesto as an important first step towards a constitutional monarchy. The less naïve Constitutional Democrats (known by its initials 'K-D', 'Kadets', pronounced in the French fashion) also supported the Duma as a representative body, applauding the declared principle of free speech despite its patent unreality. More sceptical than the Octobrists but reformist rather than revolutionary, the Kadets were predominately educated men: university professors, students, lawyers, and other professionals. They championed workers' rights and lobbied for full citizenship for all 'minorities', including Jews. A third important political faction was the revolutionary Social Democrats, which saw the Duma as a weak entity and recognised that the freedoms declared in the manifesto were in fact severely compromised. Among the more militant Social Democrats were the Marxists, who themselves comprised various factions, the majority ('Bolshevik' in Russian) being more radical than the minority ('Menshevik').

During the spring of Gregory's third year at secondary school, the tsar redefined the Duma. In February he decreed that his advisory council would become a second chamber with powers equal to the Duma's. In April the government issued a constitution which made no mention of rights and freedoms. When the elected Duma met for the first time on 27 April 1906, its powers were even more limited than those set out in the October manifesto. Many Duma members resigned in May and, just after the end of the academic year, on 8 July, the tsar dissolved the Duma.

A second, more conservative Duma was elected and in session from 20 February until 2 June 1907, during the spring of Gregory's fourth year of secondary school. Yet a third Duma, dominated by aristocrats, landowners, and businessmen more willing to serve the tsar's interests, served from 7 November 1907 until 9 June 1912. The third Duma's duration is evidence of its cooperation with the tsar and the government's repression of dissent rather than of the state's stability. In fact, turmoil persisted throughout the empire, and the last two years of Gregory's secondary education were far from calm. The 1905 revolution had no clear end. Despite some agrarian reforms, the lot of urban workers did not improve; protests and strikes as well as local revolutionary uprisings persisted in the cities and the countryside while political terrorism became an increasing threat. Thousands of civil servants and police were killed throughout the empire between 1906 and 1909, the year Gregory's first phase of secondary education concluded.

Political philosophy, economic theory, social ethics, and personal morality were dominant issues for young Russians in these difficult times. Confined by his curriculum to concrete subjects, Gregory would not have been intellectually satisfied by mathematics that privileged computation or by art classes limited to mechanical drawing. He admired craft as well as practical precision and enjoyed working creatively with his hands, but he would come to maturity outside the classroom as a reader of books and newspapers and as a witness to the uncontrolled emotions, political protests, and mob violence in Kiev's streets.

Notes

1 Ernest Jones to Sigmund Freud, 13 June 1932, Paskauskas, 701.
2 School certificates give GZ's date of birth as 23 December 1890 OS (4 January 1891 NS).
3 JZ to GZ, 25 March 1942. In 1874, when MZ was 12, compulsory military service was reduced to six years.
4 FZ, Orkin interview.
5 FZ, Oskow and Orkin interviews; MZ to JZ and EZ, 11 May 1915, 27 September 1927; GZ to JZ, 16 November 1942.
6 JZ to GZ, 2 November 1942; NM, 'Rencontre avec …', 4; GZ to JZ, 1 April 1940.
7 GZ to JZ, 2 November, 8 September 1942.
8 Golda Meir, 11, 12.
9 GZ, NYPSB, 28 November 1941, 323; email from Adelaide de Menil, 23 September 2013.
10 GZ to 'Très Saint-Père', 31 January 1953, APD.
11 Official certificate, 23 July 1899; GZ, NYPSB, 21 December 1941, 744.
12 GZ, NYPSB, 21 December 1941, 744.

13 MSZ, Dar interview.
14 Nathans, 269; Natan Meir, 102, 349; GZ to JZ, 2 October 1940.
15 Hamm, 153–166.
16 Hamm, 191–192; GZ, 'Apologists of the Russian Reaction', 55.

Chapter 2

The struggle for education

1909–1914

At the age of 18, Gregory already knew that neither commerce nor industry interested him professionally, but two more years at the Kiev Real School still lay ahead. In August 1909 he began advanced classes. A tenuous camaraderie with his brother a year behind him probably encouraged Gregory, but Yakov was likely more satisfied with the curriculum.

These years gave the two brothers increasing independence from the family as they explored the city on their own and attended concerts and theatrical performances, the latter particularly important to Gregory because of the acting out, interpretation, and representation of both literary texts and human psychology; drama seemed to him the exposure of what was normally hidden, a linguistic and aesthetic revelation of what was usually secret, inchoate, inexpressible. Russian novelists were often also playwrights, and Gregory now read and saw performances of Ostrovsky, Turgenev, and Tolstoy as well as the more contemporary Gogol, Chekov, and Andreyev. The significance of a rich literary heritage for young Russians at this time cannot be overestimated. It offered them a view of their culture and themselves, allowing them to escape an often hard life limited by poverty, class, and tradition; it offered them alternatives and posed important moral questions.

Tolstoy's death in November 1910 would galvanise socialists, but young Russians took for granted that they should strive for social justice, freedom, and liberation of the people. Ideological principles were not abstractions for them, and radical activities were common. The 1905 revolution had provided a precedent, and Gregory attended 'self-instruction circles' that had been traditional vehicles of propaganda for liberal movements since the early nineteenth century. Usually lead by a university student or professor and officially aimed at instruction in literature, history, and culture, these groups met at schools and factories under the guise of innocent reading clubs. Forbidden books and revolutionary leaflets encouraged discussions of Russia's political regime. Gregory, soon joined by Yakov, became politically active in an underground of intellectuals who printed and distributed subversive material and participated in secret meetings and public demonstrations. Their social circle also widened, and in the spring of 1910 Gregory began a relationship with Sonya Beizman.[1]

DOI: 10.4324/9781003190936-2

During one school holiday, Gregory and Yakov retreated to the resort of Chernobyl to study for their exams. Fera was sent along to cook for them. The three young people must have enjoyed the independence, but such a holiday was rare despite the relative financial security Moses had managed to achieve. Regularly promoted, he was now a manager in charge of exporting nuts and spices from Persia, while at home a servant helped with the housework a few days each week. At school Gregory continued his classes on the subjects he had already studied along with a new course in law, and his results suggest increased focus and application. On his diploma, dated 4 June 1911, he received a mark of 3 (satisfactory) in trigonometry, probability and statistics, and mechanical drawing; a 4 (good) in Russian, German, arithmetic, algebra, history, natural science, physics, geography, and law; and a 5 (excellent) in French. His achievement in Russian and German and fluency in French was a testament to his extensive independent reading in these languages. His strong performance in law as well as in history and science suggest that he was beginning to consider two possible career paths: law and medicine.[2]

It is difficult to evaluate these advanced courses. In 1925 Gregory stated that the secondary school certificate he received at the age of 20 approximated a bachelor of science degree from an American university. Certainly the eight years he spent at the Kiev Real School provided a solid basis for further academic work, but lacking a gymnasium diploma and thus disqualified for study at a university, he enrolled at the new Psycho-Neurological Institute in Saint Petersburg 800 miles north of Kiev.[3]

Gregory's choice could not have been easy. He would have needed to rely on his father to pay the tuition semester by semester. Moses would have anticipated the further education of his first-born son, but his means were limited. Gregory himself likely spent the summer of 1911 giving lessons to younger students for small sums to help him through his first year, and he also likely continued to tutor while he studied, but his earnings were meagre and he was not careful with money. Distance was challenging; by train, when the railway workers were not on strike, the journey from Kiev to Saint Petersburg took over 40 hours. For a young man with restricted and ill-managed funds, the trip was expensive as well as lengthy and time consuming. Additionally, as a Jew Gregory needed a permit to travel outside the Pale and was barred from lodging within Saint Petersburg's city limits. Perhaps, like other Jewish students, he bent the law and paid a factory worker on the night shift to let him use his bed while he was out, or he may have found accommodation in the countryside west of the Neva River and walked a distance of several miles each day. But because many of Bekhterev's students were Jews, the laboratories and libraries were open at night, and Gregory certainly did what many Jews did: In the daytime, he would sleep in accommodation rented by friends – either Christians or fortunate Jews with residence permits – and at night, he worked. Gregory economised by often foregoing food. Student life would have been uncomfortable at times and financially as well as legally precarious, but because the Psycho-Neurological Institute was a private institute as opposed to a state university, it was liberal. It admitted male and female students from all classes, Jews and Christians, and it was open to those who had finished not only classic gymnasia but teachers' colleges, commercial institutes, and technical high schools. In many ways Gregory's decision was both logical and fortunate, and he felt lucky to have been granted a place.[4]

Founded in 1907 by the neurologist Vladimir Mikhailovich Bekhterev, then head of the Department of Nervous and Mental Diseases at the Saint Petersburg Military Medical Academy, the Psycho-Neurological Institute was a scientific and research establishment for broad interdisciplinary study. Students' first two years were devoted to the natural sciences and the humanities; specialisation only began in the third year of the five-year course. Bekhterev felt that the scientific and practical work of a physician, teacher, or lawyer required a philosophical education so that the future specialist could 'understand mutual relations and dependences between separate scientific disciplines'. In the autumn of 1911, Gregory attended lectures on subjects some of which he had never formally studied before: physics, inorganic chemistry, geology, general biology, anatomy, physiology, general and experimental psychology, logic, history of philosophy, sociology, general history, the history of Russian literature, and theology. The scientific subjects involved experimental work in laboratories more sophisticated than those at his real school, while discussions with fellow students and his professors encouraged his creative thinking about ethical, philosophical, and historical issues.[5]

Gregory was excited by the facilities and atmosphere at the Institute as well as by its academic offerings. He had left behind the tensions at home and was living independently, albeit in straightened circumstances. He now decided on medicine as a profession while maintaining a foundation in law, careers open even in Imperial Russia to Jews who achieved the required qualifications. Thriving and expanding rapidly, well supported by private and government funds, the Institute had started only four years earlier in makeshift accommodation with staff who divided their time between the new Institute and the Saint Petersburg Medico-surgical Academy, where psychiatry had been a faculty since 1857. Bekhterev's institute now had its own facilities, including a building just inside Petrograd's Nevskaya Gate, and there were plans for a clinic on the city's outskirts to study the effects of alcohol. Construction of psychiatric, surgical, and neurosurgical clinics was under way. In autumn 1911, when the medical faculty first admitted students, Gregory was among the Institute's 1,142 students, at last in an environment that would welcome his dynamic personality and help him to achieve his professional goals.

Tuition fees were a pressing concern, but Gregory followed the basic course with enthusiasm. He would have again spent the summer of 1912 tutoring in Kiev. Back in the capital in the autumn, the topics of his second-year lectures included higher mathematics, physical geography, organic chemistry, general biology, anatomy and histology of the nervous system, physiology, psychophysiology of sensory organs, comparative psychology, history of philosophy, history of economic theories, statistics, general history, history of world literature, history of art, and cultural history. This rich curriculum had a powerful impact on his ideas, but Gregory's energies were not entirely spent on academics. The traditional European system of advanced study meant that most work, with the exception of laboratory science and clinical work, could be carried out independently. Attendance at lectures was optional; there were no reading lists or designated accommodation; even residence in the community was neither required nor verifiable. Competence was tested only at the end of a semester or academic year.[6]

Gregory continued to read independently and voraciously, but also visited the capital's art galleries and attended concerts, the opera, and the theatre. His contemporary Pitirim Alexandrovich Sorokin, who came to know Gregory at this time, described the experience: The Institute's young men and women had an intense intellectual life through concentrated study and hearty discussions with professors and other students but did not pretend to have too many virtues and tried not to have too many vices. They felt morally obligated to be politically engaged and sought out educational opportunities among the city's workers, activity regarded as subversive by the government and involving the risk of arrest and imprisonment. Through his political engagement as well as the curriculum, Gregory now developed an interest in morality as well in 'the problem of religions and of Christianity'. Serious concerns were mixed with conviviality, however, and Gregory earned a reputation as a dynamic young man nicknamed the '"director of the corps de ballet" because of his engrossment in the organization of various dancing parties of girl students'. Sorokin mentions 'flirting' as one of the students' extracurricular activities, and certainly Gregory spent some of his enormous energy on flirtation, but he continued his relationship with Sonya from a distance while the substance of his courses as well as the entitlement a qualification would offer were his top priorities.[7]

Gregory's life was diverging from his brother's. Yakov had decided on a career in engineering and applied himself assiduously, earning a prestigious gold medal – signifying that all of his marks were 5s – but even outstanding achievement did not open doors for a Jew in Imperial Russia. Much is made of the status of a student with a gold medal in Sholem Aleichem's *The Bloody Hoax*, a contemporary novel that indicates the difficulties both brothers faced. In this extraordinary book, set in Kiev in 1911–1913, Grigori Ivanovitch Popov, a Gentile student with gymnasium marks of 3s and 4s, exchanges places with Hersh Movshovitch Rabinovitch, a Jewish student with a gold medal. Grisha argues that Hershke's medal will overcome any problems a Jew might encounter, but Hershke maintains the gold medal means nothing for a Jew in the real world. Grisha (as Hershke) is eventually accused of murdering a child in order to use his blood in the making of matzos, and the real Hershke is only able to save him by revealing their true identities.[8]

Aleichem's plot is based on a case that dominated the news in Kiev, where anti-Semitic feeling was agitated by the discovery in March 1911 of a brutally murdered young boy. On 21 July 1911 Mendal Beilis, a Jewish factory clerk, was arbitrarily arrested and imprisoned by the authorities, who viewed the youth's death as a ritual crime. Ample evidence indicated a Christian gang was responsible for the murder and protests occurred throughout Russia, provoking international outrage against the corrupt prosecutors, who were supported by the imperial government, but the case did not come to trial until September 1913. Gregory would have been aware of the increased tensions in Kiev during his final months at school and would have followed the case from Saint Petersburg; he would have read Vladimir Korolenko's passionate appeal against the trial, signed by scores of fellow writers, Duma members, university professors, and 184 students at the University of Saint Petersburg, as well as his essay 'Call to the Russian People in Regard to the Blood Libel of the Jews'. Yakov lived with the controversy throughout his last year of school as the family worried about the continuing revolutionary unrest. Political activity was not restricted in either Saint Petersburg or Kiev to mere consciousness raising. In September 1911, Pyotr Stolypin, the tsar's prime minister as well as minister of the interior, was assassinated while attending the Kiev opera.[9]

A more serious and focused student than his spirited intellectual brother, Yakov had by the spring of 1912 begun courting Eugenia Gel'fman. A year younger than he, she came from a prosperous family. Her father, eager that she marry well, was willing to fund Yakov's education and offered to lend him the money he needed to study abroad. Moses's earnings had recently enabled the family to purchase a small dacha, a wooden holiday cabin in Pushcha-Vodytsya just north of central Kiev, but his resources could not stretch to funding years of study at a foreign university. Embarrassed by his dependence but overwhelmed by Gel'fman's generosity and very much in love with Eugenia, Yakov accepted the loan, paid various authorities for the requisite visas, and packed his bags. At the end of the summer, he left Russia, his family, and his fiancée to begin his studies in electrical engineering at the Institut Electro-Technique de Grenoble in southeastern France.[10]

The Kiev newspapers recounted not only the Beilis case but the unsettling revolutionary activity manifesting itself in protests and terrorism throughout the empire. Moses and Anna continued their life in the apartment on Kostiantynivska Street, but with both their sons away, their attention focused on their daughters. At 18 and 15, Basia and Fera were still at school, but their academic opportunities were unclear. Basia was an unremarkable student, but Fera, like her brothers, excelled in science. It was easier for girls than boys to attend gymnasia and Fera was studying at a gymnasium, so university could be hoped for. What the family probably hoped for Basia was that she would marry well. What they all hoped for was a measure of political and social calm and financial security.

In Saint Petersburg Gregory finished the second year of his basic course, including a class in Latin. Specialisation now lay ahead of him. The Institute's new alcohol clinic as well as psychiatric and neurosurgical clinics were completed in 1912. Gregory was particularly interested in psychiatry, but he was as yet unsure whether to pursue law or medicine professionally. On returning to Kiev in the early summer of 1913, he got special permission, granted only to a small percentage of Jews, to take the terminal Latin examination at the Kiev

Pecherski Gymnasium, an exam set for its own students after eight years of study. He received a mark of 'good'. Latin would be useful in the medical and legal studies that lay ahead, but certified Latin competence was essential for what he later called 'a legalistic trick'. He intended to enrol in law at the University of Kiev because, as a Jewish university student, he would gain the right to spend a number of weeks each year in Saint Petersburg, where he wanted to continue his medical education. Gregory's understanding of the system's loopholes may make him appear devious here, as indeed he was, but he was sincere in his desire to study both subjects and determined to find ways through a system stacked against him.[11]

The photograph attached to his Latin certificate offers a stark contrast to the group picture taken ten years earlier. No longer an adolescent, Gregory looks directly at the camera with a solemn and rather proud expression. His long wavy hair and fulsome moustache are stylish, at once typical of the time in Russia and bohemian. His dark brows and large, deep-set eyes hold the viewer's attention, while his pince-nez suggests intellectual seriousness as well as myopia: Despite his formal dress and careful pose, he does not take off his spectacles for the photographer. If the studious 22-year-old was not in control of his destiny, he desperately wanted to be.

Gregory Kiev, 1913

Gregory likely spent the rest of the summer in or near Kiev and would have seen his brother before returning to Petrograd in September. Because of his status as a medical student, Gregory had avoided the military examination which most Russian men were obliged to undergo at the age of 21, but Yakov – who had returned during the holidays to see his family and his fiancée and to earn what he could working in the engine room of a Dnieper river boat – had no such exemption. The authorities imposed a heavy fine on families whose sons didn't show up when called, so shortly after his 21st birthday on 2 September 1913, Yakov dutifully presented himself for the exam that would determine his military eligibility. He and Eugenia and her family as well as his own hoped the doctors would disqualify him because of his weak eyesight, but the Russian military made no exceptions for young men with spectacles. Militarily fit but unwilling to serve in the tsar's army, he immediately returned to France, this time not only as a student but as a political exile. Needing funds for his tuition, Gregory probably continued to tutor local students in the city or in the holiday towns to the north or the west, but by the end of the summer he also must have been thinking of his brother's plight and the different life Yakov was leading.[12]

In the autumn, his third year at the Institute, Gregory began specialising in psychiatry with lectures in general psychology, psychopathology, social and child psychology, criminology, and neuropsychology. Indeed, individual faculties gave lectures in all the subjects included in state university curricula. Gregory continued practical work in experimental psychology while looking forward to the clinical experience offered to fourth-year medical students.

The Institute offered medical training of the highest order, but its students' revolutionary tendencies were becoming a concern for the government. In 1912, the mayor of Saint Petersburg had reported on political activity among the capital's students. In the margin of the section on the Psycho-Neurological Institute, Tsar Nicholas II had written, 'What benefit does Russia derive from this Institute? I wish to have a well-founded answer.' In the spring of 1914 the minister of public education presented an additional report on the anti-governmental attitudes of Bekhterev's students and recommended the Institute's closure. But by the spring of 1914, Gregory was no longer in Saint Petersburg.

The Institute's records offer little to explain his absence. Under the name 'ZILBUR Girsh Movshevich', the only surviving documents are certificates for the payment of tuition in the autumn semester of 1912, the spring and autumn semesters of 1913, and a document indicating the suspension of his studies. Normally a student's file contained an application to enter the Institute, a gymnasium or other high school diploma, a baptismal certificate or another official document certifying the student's name and date of birth, a student card, and other documents such as records of exam results. Marina Akimenko, the Institute's archivist, supposes that all of the required documents – including documents related to his first year and those placed in the file in or after 1914 – were at some point removed, but why and by whom are unclear. It is unlikely that political activity regarded by the government as subversive would have caused his suspension – the Institute's reputation as a hotbed of revolutionary ideas provoked the concern about the Institute as a whole rather than action directed towards individuals. A student's activity regarded as revolutionary was a matter for the police and would have resulted in arrest and probably imprisonment rather than suspension. That Gregory was a Jew possibly somehow prevented his completing the 1913–1914 academic year, yet perhaps the explanation is simpler and more painful: He may just have been unable to pay his tuition. The circumstances of his leaving are vague, but his feelings were clear: He was deeply upset, frustrated, and angry, yet undeterred in his desire to continue his education.[13]

Gregory would later attribute the gloom and pessimism he felt at this time at least in part to the general political reaction that had followed the 1905 revolution, a reaction that 'depressed and suppressed the last forces and hopes of the intellectuals'. There were, however, more personal and immediate reasons for his distress even beyond his forced departure from the Institute. After a year and a half in Grenoble, Yakov had suddenly decided out of 'sheer pride' that he could not continue to live on money borrowed from his future father-in-law. Without any definite plans beyond the idea that Eugenia would at some point join him, on 13 December 1913 he sailed from Bremen on the *George Washington* for New York. Not only was Yakov rejecting the 'free ticket' for his education, he was setting out on an adventure to 'the promised land' that America represented for many Russian Jews.[14]

There is no evidence that Gregory was jealous of his brother's opportunity, nor did he resent his good fortune, but Yakov's impulsive choice must have made him all the more aware of his own situation. In throwing away the opportunity of an engineering degree from a prestigious European institution, Yakov was also continuing the process of reinventing himself. On the ship's register he gave his profession as 'student' and his address as 'Kostyantynivs'ka 32, Kiev, Russia'; in the space marked 'race or people', a clerk wrote 'Hebrew', yet Yakov left Germany as 'Jakob Silburg', son of 'M. Silburg', masking at least nominally his Russian identity and the Jewish implication of his father's name. When he arrived in New York, Yakov became 'James M. Zilboorg', and soon after 'James Morris Zilboorg'. To Gregory he was still 'Yasha' or 'Yonya', though occasionally and jokingly the francophone 'Jacques', but to Yakov – now James – Gregory remained 'Grisha', firmly fixed in his own difficult Russian circumstances.[15]

When Gregory left Saint Petersburg, he went to Kiev, but life there was changing, too. Many Jews who could were leaving Russia. For some, emigration was a question of money; for others it was a question of where, with Palestine and the United States being the primary alternatives. One and a half million Russians immigrated to the United States between 1900 and 1910; between 1911 and 1914, 868,000 more arrived. Over 40,000 Jews left Russia for Palestine during these years. Eugenia was naturally hoping to join James as soon as she could. The Zilboorgs had relatives, neighbours, friends, and acquaintances who were considering the journey or had already left. Moses's sister Faige Etka had travelled to America via Antwerp and London in 1905, where she had been welcomed by relatives in New York before joining family members already prospering in the Midwest. Most Russian Jews, however, had no one to vouch for them in the New World. The Hebrew Immigrant Aid Society (HIAS) was the largest group helping Jews to flee Russian anti-Semitism, and many emigrating Jews would need help. Aided by the Galveston Plan, an assistance programme that diverted Jewish immigrants away from east coast American cities already crowded with poor European Jews, the Levitas family, whose eldest son Shloime was Basia's age and the cousin of one of Fera's friends, left in August of 1913. Like James, they made their way to Bremen, then sailed for Texas and finally settled in Chicago. Fear about a future in Russia was an undercurrent in daily life; Gregory's personal worries about his future could only have been intensified by the flight of fellow Jews and general atmosphere of anxiety.[16]

When James was in Grenoble the two brothers had begun a correspondence apparently important for both of them, creating a bond Gregory had not felt when they were growing up. James had written in detail about his life in France and Gregory had responded in kind, sharing confidences and nourishing the relationship. Gregory was now eager to know about life in America. His first surviving letter, written from Kiev on 15 February 1914, reveals his mood and character and above all his voice. Gregory found that geographical as well as temporal distance made it difficult to respond to James:

> How can one 'answer' words spoken so long ago … words that have reached me across the waves of the ocean from a place so distant and remote, so foreign and enticing, and, at times, as precious and unattainable as the Promised Land?

Characteristically philosophical, Gregory wrote with psychological insight that he understood and accepted James's decision:

> I have noticed that certain solutions in life are not reached by systematic 'consideration' or pondering. One can consider a mathematical problem, the style of a dress or *façon de parler*, but not a dramatic situation. The solution to the latter comes about on its own, from the sum and substance of life; all you have to do is follow your heart and conscience in each individual case and the time suddenly comes when what you need to do and how to proceed become clear to you. This solution was born in your heart and ripened naturally together with your heart.

Gregory also addressed his own unsatisfactory situation: 'I am working. I am moved along by the current, wherever the wind blows. Like on a sailboat. I am carried by the wind, but I handle the sail so as not to allow the elements to capsize me.' He continued,

> I don't want to think about tomorrow today since I will be thinking about it tomorrow. I think about the future only in schematic terms. I know one thing

> only: higher education is in my future. I will not remain a disenfranchised Jew. I will try one last time this year and that will be enough. If nothing comes about here, I will close up shop and begin to get ready for the long journey. I will not perish. This thought is beginning to possess and embolden me more and more.

Strongly determined, Gregory was not entirely disheartened: 'I know languages (I am studying English, too) and they say I have a good head on my shoulders. Surely this counts for something!'

Gregory was trying to earn money, but philosophically he felt justified in being impulsive in material matters: He enjoyed possessions yet ultimately felt that what money could buy was unimportant, and the insignificance of anything material meant that he could indulge himself. He told James, 'I try not to deny myself most of the things I desire.... If I want to go to the theatre, I go. If I want a suit – I get one; if I want a book – I buy it.' Gregory had made economies – he had stopped smoking in October – but while James had marriage ahead of him, Gregory was unsure about settling down and certainly did not have the means.

What he now wrote to James about Sonya and his own mental state suggests that the relationship might not actually have been serious for either of them. 'Sometimes life gets complicated', he wrote,

> I am now 23, Sonechka is too. What am I waiting for? Here is the rub: she is the delicate, spoiled daughter of her deceased father – it is difficult to draw her into the whirlpool of life's struggles, to pull her away from a life of peaceful happiness. But more recently she is beginning to understand this, and her heart is more and more willing to be found by my side.

Gregory seemed uncommitted to the reality of a relationship:

> Don't think that I am happy in all of this, Yonya. I am always sad in a focused sort of way and I am ever in search of solitude. I love to walk about the city alone for an hour or two – to walk, meander, look around and push my way through the crowd – alone with my thoughts, yearnings, dreams and melancholy, alone in my love for my beloved. I feel good then. I am simply mad about this solitude.... My melancholy and solitude pacify me.

Gregory insisted,

> I am more happy than unhappy in my love relationship. Sonka is a good woman. She knows how to be tender, loving and attentive. I think she will fully understand my new passion for solitude and things will then be truly fine.

He appears naïve here in his portrait of a possible marriage with Sonya, and being 'more happy than unhappy' in the relationship does not seem like a promising basis for a union.

In any case, he had practical and pressing issues to deal with and told James that he intended to compete for admission to the Kiev Polytechnic Institute and to submit his papers for admission to Saint Vladimir University in August, but

> If nothing comes of this, I am getting married and will begin to prepare to leave. I don't know whether I will take 6 months or a year or two to prepare, but prepare I will and then I will leave.

Finally, Gregory turned to his immediate situation as if incidentally: Sonya had appendicitis and he was about to head off to the Jewish hospital, where she would soon undergo surgery. He wrote that her illness 'has generated a stream of worries and cares in my life, but I think that everything will come right in the end'. Gregory concluded in the despondent tone dominating this letter:

> You have written me with all your news, but I cannot cheer you with anything new. Things are very difficult for me sometimes and they are very difficult right now. Something has stirred up a pang of melancholy in my chest: whether it is melancholy about the unknown or sadness about the senseless and lost years of the past, I don't know.[17]

Living at home again, Gregory was sucked back into family tensions his solitary walks did little to appease. He continued to study both medicine and law on his own and somehow managed to obtain the funds and permissions he needed to complete the academic year at the Psycho-Neurological Institute. In April 1914 he travelled to Saint Petersburg to prepare for the year-end exams, which he took in early May. He then returned to the challenges of life in Kiev, where the female members of the family grew increasingly frustrated with him. Fera wrote James that their brother had become 'intolerable': Gregory was buying expensive theatre tickets for 16 roubles, having a summer coat made for 75 roubles and claiming 'some kind of deference to himself'. She reported that their mother was ill and wanted to go to a Black Sea spa, but Gregory gave their mother 'absolutely no money', and when she reminded him, he didn't come home 'for two days at a stretch' or showed up at one o'clock in the morning. Fera went on,

> I had been getting along fine with him, but I can't anymore. There was a terrible scene … when I troubled him with the fact that we wouldn't have even a kopeck from him for a trip to Odessa.… He wanted to throw a bottle of perfume at my head, but he must've felt bad about wasting the perfume and he restrained himself.

Fera admitted that Gregory was better these days at controlling his temper, but she saw his behaviour as an affront: He had enjoyed himself at a local air show and even paid to go up in an airplane – in her view 'out of spite'. She asked James – thousands of miles away geographically and weeks away in time from receiving this news and responding – to scold their brother because the situation had become 'simply awful'.[18]

Fera's adolescent complaints finally reveal as much about the pettiness that Gregory confronted in the family as they do about his self-indulgence, and the situation at home was becoming particularly challenging. Although they had no right as Jews to reside in Kiev, visiting relatives – Gregory's Aunt Chaika and her daughter – were staying in the apartment while anxiously waiting for visas to go to America, where his Uncle David, Anna's brother, had already emigrated. There was a great deal of squabbling and crying and fretting as Chaika became frantic. Informing James that Anna had been diagnosed with 'severe gout' and that Moses was working through the night in order to earn an extra 200 roubles – some of which he intended to send to James and some of which would fund the spa trip – Basia pleaded with her brother to ask their Uncle David to send his wife the necessary documents 'so that there may be an end to her suffering and ours'.[19]

Given all this stress, it is unsurprising that Gregory, as well as his father, who often travelled on business, chose to spend time away from the apartment. When Anna and Fera returned from Odessa, they did not find Moses at home and 'only happened to run into him and see him in Kozyatyn', a town 130 miles southwest of Kiev through which Anna and Fera had probably passed on their way back from the Black Sea. Gregory was not at home either: With Basia in charge of the household while Anna and Fera were away, he had decamped to the dacha. While he longed for a fraternal bond with James and was closer to his youngest sister than to the rest of the family, Anna and above all Basia drove him mad. When he wrote to his mother in Odessa about minor surgery on his foot, Basia reported the incident to James in detail:

> You would think it was something serious, but here he had a little piece of nail removed that had grown into the toe. That's all, but he wrote Mama in such a way that she's very worried and today I received a card from her that's full of alarm about him. Well, it would appear this is just another of his stunts. This is the way he always rewards us, only with his troubles.

After telling James about a relative who was preparing for a course in Paris, Basia concluded rather bitterly, 'Now there's someone who will make something of himself. Unlike our Grisha.' She finally confided that she found Gregory 'contemptible': 'There isn't enough contact or paper, ink or pens to describe Grisha's antics. Never mind him or, better yet, to hell with him.'

Basia was not relieved by Gregory's absence, however, but complained to James that the brother she thought so little of 'comes home only once a week and then only to take care of business. As a matter of fact, he's like a stranger at home.' Basia continued in frustration, 'Well, whatever you say about him, you can't put a stop to any of it.' It would seem that with Basia, as with Anna, one couldn't win. Basia was particularly possessive and controlling, and her posture of complaint – she found Fera 'impossibly impudent', relatives rude and ill-tempered, and life in general 'monotonous' – was only matched by pathetic incompetence. Since leaving school she had been unable to find employment; nothing ever seemed to work out because she was at each turn hampered by others or by her own aches and illnesses. Gregory felt understandably besieged by whining females whose concerns appeared to him inconsequential in the grand scheme of things and especially insignificant when compared with his own struggles for an independent personal and professional life, neither of which they seemed to understand.[20]

Rather madly trying to keep open all of the avenues he had indicated to James, in early June Gregory took an overnight train from Kiev to Warsaw, where he spent several weeks preparing for law exams at the University of Warsaw, an institution with an almost entirely Russian staff and student body. The nature of these exams is unclear, but successful results would evidently allow Gregory to register in the autumn of 1914 for advanced study in law at the University of Kiev. At the time, the prestigious university in Warsaw, unlike universities in the rest of Russia, apparently granted European diplomas on the basis of such examinations, which Gregory was permitted to take because of his independent study and formal coursework in Saint Petersburg.[21]

Gregory spent June and July between Warsaw and Kiev focusing on law. Alone for most of the summer in a shabby hotel in the former Polish capital, he doubted he could complete his medical course; he simply didn't have money for the fees. He was, however, also thinking about his brother in New York. James had written that life in America wasn't going well for him; he hoped to pass a difficult driving test and could only earn small sums through private tutoring in French while working on his English. As Fera had asked, he had risen to the occasion and scolded his brother for selfish behaviour and extravagances. It seems likely, although ironic, that James also resented what he saw as the steady progress on two fronts that Gregory was making towards a professional life, something he had given up on leaving Grenoble. In America James hoped to earn an engineering qualification by taking night classes; specifically, he now wanted his brother to send him money and a Russian encyclopaedia.[22]

On 9 July Gregory took a break from his studies and responded from Warsaw. As evidence of his impressive early competence in English, the letter is worth quoting at length:

> My dear James, yesterday I have send you Pavlenkov's dictionary. As you have writes to me in english, I want to do the same in order to make you understand my progress in the English language. I think you can not laud my writing, but you can say I do not lose my time unfruitly studying this language.
>
> I was very anxious to know your bad state and I regret my impotence for this while in 'a certain question' as yo say.
>
> In your letter I have be movend by your allusion of my behaving, witch you do not approve. I would not say you are in the right, because you must know I am not an avaricious and my heart is not made of stone or sand.

> When you have be in Grenoble I have not refused? Yes? And now do not think I do not want. I am not. Steel one or tow daies it can be than I schall do something.

This ambitious effort to express himself in English reveals Gregory's sense of language, its malleability and sound as well as its precision. 'Steel' and 'yo' are examples of aural transcription – this is likely how Gregory pronounced 'still' and 'you' in 1914. Other spelling mistakes are probably a result of natural confusion ('witch' for 'which' and 'than' for 'then' or 'that'), while his use of elevated language ('laud', 'impotence', and 'allusion') was a result of his serious reading and use of a dictionary. He was also drawing on the languages he had mastered at school: Some orthographical errors are Germanic ('movend' for 'moved' and 'schall' for 'shall'), while making a noun from an adjective ('an avaricious' for a greedy person or even 'behaving' for 'behaviour') is common in French, as is the use of a small letter for words normally capitalised in English ('english'). Gregory was also translating literally from Russian ('my heart is not made of stone or sand'), but the most interesting linguistic element of this first example of his use of English is the ease he obviously felt in using language – as in 'unfruitly' (a word he has coined here and not felt the need to check) and in his elegant parallel constructions, a characteristic stylistic tendency he would employ all his life.

The intense emotions of this letter finally got the better of the linguistic exercise. Gregory continued briefly in English – 'I was surprised and very affected by your words among witch I hear a bad mind' – then shifted to Russian to defend himself and explain his current circumstances. Resenting his brother's demands and criticism while he was doing his utmost to make his way under challenging circumstances beyond his control, he felt as if called on to 'justify myself in the Old Kiev police station'. Gregory was willing to do what he could to help James, but it was difficult to control his emotions:

> Since I received your letter, I haven't found a moment to think about anything other than 'rearranging things' and sending you money. But I will talk with you at another time, when I am a bit calmer and less tired. I am on my way to Kiev now and perhaps I will write you there once I rest up and collect my thoughts.

Yet he could not restrain himself: 'to be honest, I admit that I would have liked to receive your letter sooner and to have known … that there was no hidden malice in these words of yours.' He urged James to continue to write to him as his brother and wished him 'All the best', but reminded James that his own situation in Russia was precarious: 'Life is difficult for me. It is growing more and more difficult all the time, and I would be happy to run away somewhere. I don't know what is going to happen.'[23]

What happened was that Gregory continued his legal studies and took the university law exams in Warsaw in July. On 28 June 1914 Archduke Franz Ferdinand, the heir to the throne of the Austrian-Hungarian Empire, had been assassinated while visiting Sarajevo in Serbia. A month later, on 28 July 1914, his uncle, Emperor Franz Joseph, declared war on Serbia, a Russian ally. On 31 July, the last day of Gregory's exams, the tsar called for the mobilisation of Russian troops. Like falling dominos, declarations of war followed rapidly throughout Europe: Germany declared war on Russia on 1 August; on 3 August Germany declared war on France and invaded neutral Belgium, compelling Britain to declare war on Germany on 4 August; two days later Austria-Hungary declared war on the Russian Empire.[24]

Gregory later wrote of the shock and conflicting emotions experienced by all his contemporaries:

> the Great War came for the Russian thinking individual like an unexpected and tragically destructive blow. He would not support it because of his opposition to the Czarist régime; he could not deny it because of its fatal inevitability.... The war only added to the general confusion of the minds and hearts.

There was now a national sense of helplessness and hopelessness that went far beyond Gregory's individual feelings as a disenfranchised Jew in Imperial Russia, and his despondency deepened in the face of what he saw as a cataclysm: 'A dark shroud of uncertainty and purposelessness enveloped human existence.'[25]

Notes

1 FZ, Orkin, and Oskow interviews; AZ interview; GZ to JZ, 3/4 October 1914, 15 February, 10 September 1915, 22 August 1919.
2 Email from Gloria Levitas, 14 October 2013; FZ, Oskow interview.
3 BIO.
4 GZ, NYPSB, 21 December 1941, 733.
5 For the Institute's history, see www.bekhterev.ru/en/history/index.php
6 Sorokin, 67–69.
7 GZ to 'Très Saint-Père', 31 January 1953, APD; Sorokin, 71, 72.
8 JZ, CV, 30 October 1936, JEZB.
9 GZ to JZ, 29 November 1915.
10 JZ, CV, 30 October 1936, JEZB.
11 GZ, NYPSB, 21 December 1941, 731–732, 738.
12 FZ, Orkin interview.
13 Email from Marina Akimenko, 8 October 2013.
14 GZ, 'The Russian Man', np; JZ to Edward Fiess, 8 August 1940, Schaeffer.
15 Ship's records; 1915 New York state census; U.S. federal census, 1920.
16 Orkin, family history.
17 GZ to JZ, 19 November 1915; quotations, GZ to JZ, 15 February 1914.
18 GZ to JZ, 29 September 1914; FZ to JZ, 11 May 1914.
19 BZ to JZ, 11 May 1914.
20 BZ to JZ, March–August 1914.

21 GZ to JZ, 15 February 1915; GZ, NYPSB, 21 December 1941, 732.
22 This letter has apparently not survived.
23 GZ to JZ, 9 July 1914.
24 GZ, NYPSB, 21 December 1941, 739.
25 GZ, 'The Russian Man', np.

Chapter 3

War

1914–1916

The Eastern Front stretched from the Baltic Sea in the north to the Black Sea in the south along the entire western edge of the Pale of Settlement. The first Russian battles occurred in what is now Poland and resulted in devastating defeats for imperial troops. In late August 1914, the Russian Second Army was almost completely destroyed at a battle north of Warsaw; the commanding general committed suicide. Fifty miles to the east in early September, the Germans destroyed most of the tsar's First Army. The Russian military would not begin to recover until the following spring, and morale, initially supportive of the tsar, quickly fell among the military and civilian populations.

The war brought changes not only to Gregory's plans but to the nation. On the first of September even the capital's name was Russified to 'Petrograd' and rather than staying on for his results, Gregory left Warsaw as soon as his exams were over and returned to Kiev, which quickly found itself just behind the front line. By early October over 310,000 Russian troops had been captured, killed, or wounded, and Kiev's hospitals were filling up with casualties. Throughout the city Gregory saw 'red crosses, crutches, bandages, death notices for those who have fallen in battle'.[1]

Hoping to carry on with his study of law, he submitted his papers to the University of Kiev, but despite his qualifications he was refused admission. Prepared psychologically for rejection, he was nevertheless acutely disappointed. He continued to study, however, and hoped to take an external examination in Warsaw in May, on the basis of which, with a dissertation, he would be granted a law diploma. He also continued to work on languages and to think about America, where James was earning a living as a translator while waiting for Eugenia. She and Gregory met three times a week to study English. He wrote his brother that he was already conversing 'fairly well' before adding that he had also begun to study Italian and wondered what he could do with his languages in America. Unable to establish a professional life in Russia, Gregory told James, 'I have to get out of this rut somehow. Will I ever get out of this horrible situation of "seeking and finding not what I am seeking?"'[2]

Gregory's distress soon intensified. Laid off from his menial job at a chemical factory that had depended on German contracts, he felt 'completely miserable' and

DOI: 10.4324/9781003190936-3

began to consider immigrating to America or even travelling to Harbin in Manchuria, where he imagined using French and English in the offices of the Trans-Siberian Railroad. Both plans, however, depended on money and he had none and no prospects of earning any. Relatives and friends, including Eugenia, were volunteering their services at local hospitals, 'lazarettes', where even untrained help was welcome. Constantly reminded of the 'living nightmare' of war, Gregory decided in November to enlist as a nurse in the new units heading for the Ottoman battlefront in order at least to contribute to alleviating the grief around him.[3]

The Russian army, however, was more impressed than Saint Vladimir University was with Gregory's qualifications and more willing to overlook his Jewishness, but they did not need him in the Caucuses. As a medical student, he was assigned to work with doctors on active service behind the lines. Thus, during what would count as his fourth year at Bekhterev's institute, Gregory unknowingly started what became his first clinical placement, not formally in Petrograd but informally in Kiev under the aegis of the imperial forces. Now, in addition to continuing his independent studies, he worked regularly at a lazarette that treated wounded and shell-shocked soldiers.

Exactly what his responsibilities were isn't clear. His studies at the Institute had included anatomy and physiology. He had done dissections and read extensively in general and experimental psychology, but he had had no supervised clinical training. Bekhterev believed that psychology was a matter of 'associative reflexes', of 'stimulus-and-response', and the curriculum presented a materialist rather than a psychodynamic model of human psychology. Bekhterev, who had trained with some of the greatest medical scientists of the nineteenth century, had experimented with human beings from 1912, but his teaching, as in his course 'Objective Psychology or Reflexology', stressed materialistic understanding, and his psychiatric work was closer to behaviourism than to analytical psychology. Under Bekhterev Gregory had studied the European psychiatric, psychological, and neurological tradition embodied in the work of Flechsig, Du Bois-Reymond, Meynert, Westphal, Charcot, and Wundt. Psychology as one might understand it today was left in early twentieth-century Russia to literature, to Dostoyevsky and Chekov and Andreyev, but Gregory's reading would not have prepared him to treat hysterical soldiers or amputate limbs. His medical education had also been shaped by Russian culture, however, and was informed by 'a spirit of high humanitarian social aspirations for reform combined with a spirit of revolutionary struggle against the bureaucracy and the autocratic cruelty and stupidity of Russian political and economic absolutism'. Inspired with the ideal of building mental hospitals and abolishing constraints for mental patients, Russian psychiatry's strictly materialistic approach meant that in 1914 it functioned on a purely somatic and neurological basis. Russian psychiatry at the time was thus finally 'not psychological but administrative, custodial, descriptive and neurological'. Perhaps what Gregory did at the lazarette involved enlightened management of psychiatric patients rather than surgery or psychotherapy.[4]

Whatever his responsibilities, he was technically on active military service and could not return to Petrograd. In Kiev, the horrors of war weighed heavily upon him. Many friends and relatives were serving at the front. At the end of September the family had heard from Samuel, a cousin whose letter, Gregory told James, was

> full of the indescribable terror of war; he took part in a terribly bloody battle the likes of which he hadn't seen in any of the twenty battles he has fought in. His letter consists solely of a cry and plea for prayer on his behalf. He was lucky: he came out of the battle alive and well. The poor man! He talks all the time about his two little girls for whom he wants to stay alive.

The Russian army was meanwhile defending Warsaw against German attack while in southern Ukraine, the tsar's soldiers had taken Lemberg (Lviv) and were holding eastern Galicia against the Austrian-Hungarian army along a front of 170 miles. Casualties came into Kiev daily by train while recovered soldiers, new conscripts, provisions, and munitions were sent from Kiev by rail to the front. The impact on the city was overwhelming.[5]

As winter closed in Gregory found the war increasingly incomprehensible. He struggled to understand the soldiers as well as the men and women with whom he worked who patched them up only to send them back to the front. He felt not only that 'We, Russians, were fighting to defend our country, to help the tsar's government to win a victory', but a real antagonism towards the tsar and the government. He was simultaneously aware that 'not to fight meant to give up many of our beloved ideals and hopes for Russia's ultimate future – to turn her over to another autocracy of the same kind, but one speaking a different language'. Amid these contradictions and the evidence he witnessed of war's horrors, any enthusiasm for war seemed to him a psychological abnormality. One incident would stand out in his memory. Coming home from work at the hospital one afternoon in 1915, he found a tall soldier in the family apartment, 'a real giant of the Semenoff Imperial Guard' who, having recovered from his wounds, had come to say goodbye to a maid in the household before returning to the front. Gregory listened to the soldier recounting his battlefield experiences:

> You do not see anything, even in daylight.... One would say you had lost your eyes. You do not even see *him*. You are just going on, with rifle and bayonet – the firing is sometimes so strong and the confusion so terrible that many of our own people attack each other as enemies. All are screaming!

The soldier looked like a wild animal, his eyes gleaming with cruelty and his hands clenched as if he were back on the battlefield. '"Suddenly there is silence"', the soldier continued, his body relaxing as he recounted what he saw after the melee: '"one of our men with a hand gone ... an Austrian, with his nose shot away ... a long-bearded Jew with a torn face."' The man broke down and burst into tears. On the basis of such experiences, Gregory concluded that soldiers did not hate the enemy but were simply fighting because they were ordered: 'Among all the thousands of wounded, sometimes mad, soldiers' he met, he was unable to find a single one who seemed to grasp the war's 'true significance'. Caught in the maelstrom, Gregory could only feel that the entire world was 'on the verge of a great moral collapse'.[6]

Gregory meanwhile found himself in personal and professional limbo. He also felt increasingly cut off from his brother. Infrequent correspondence from America could only be partially attributed to the disruption of war. By February 1915, he complained to James that he had only received three letters from him since his departure from Grenoble over a year earlier. Indeed, James had only recently acknowledged the encyclopaedia Gregory had sent from Warsaw, and Gregory struggled to bridge the widening gulf between them. Desperate for a confidant, however, he tried to explain himself to his distant brother:

> I have sat down at the table numerous times and picked up a pen only to set it aside without writing anything. Many times I felt sad to the point of tears – I wanted to write you so badly, to tell you so many things. But the words got stuck in my head the same way they get caught in your throat when you are very upset. Life around me is too kaleidoscopic and I play too small a part in it (hardly by choice!) It is difficult sometimes, but it is impossible to control the emotion I feel when I think about you.

Gregory's professional prospects were even worse than before: He had somehow found the 50 roubles for the year's tuition fees at the Institute – enrolment on which his special military status depended – and he was studying biology in the hope of returning to Petrograd for examinations in the spring, but obtaining the right to residence and money for travel seemed enormous obstacles. The idea of returning to the Institute helped him to justify what he felt was otherwise a senseless existence. He told his brother that his failures to establish himself professionally made him feel that there was nothing he could do to make a life for himself in Russia, and that everything he did would always be wrong.

He was continuing his study of English, however, and now reading Oscar Wilde. No longer interested in 'old writers' like Poe, Byron, Dickens, and Shakespeare, he asked James to recommend contemporary British and American authors with the stature of Russians like Kuprin, Artsybashev, Andreyev, and Bunin. As for the war, he told James, 'I am not going to write about it. It's a difficult and tortuous ordeal. It is horrific and there is no way to speak of it calmly or dispassionately.' The family, he reported, were well except for Samuel, who had been taken prisoner of war.

Gregory had begun to feel like an impotent automaton. He described his emotional state to James as 'lifeless':

> This does not mean that I have lost hope or that I am depressed or without energy. No. It means that life goes on, but it is all meaningless. True, I am

> working enthusiastically at the lazarette with a clear and fraternal sense that I am doing *something* (which happens so rarely). True, I am also preparing for the examinations and somehow managing to occupy my time. I always seem to be busy and yet none of this satisfies my soul.

Not having lost his sense of humour, he found a sardonic simile:

> Regardless of what you are doing, you will never be satisfied when the main thing, the most important thing is lacking. It is like when all the holes in a window are filled with rags or sealed up with paper, but this does not mean that a window pane has been installed.

He felt the clock ticking: He was 24 years old and his life was not in his own hands; he saw himself drowning 'in the darkness that covers our poor, sad and downtrodden nation'.

Physically he was well, but he was obviously suffering considerable psychological distress. A few weeks earlier he had consulted a doctor, who had diagnosed diabetes, but Gregory understood his state as 'probably actually the result of acute neurasthenia'. His symptoms – which included impaired memory, headaches, blurred vision, and lethargy – were the result of his emotional state. He saw himself rather harshly as a Jewish intellectual spoiled by 'needs', constrained by anti-Semitic laws and a personal sense of failure, consumed by melancholy, sadness, and worry. In contrast, Gregory presumed that James had found 'spiritual, legal and personal freedom'. He was certain his brother was forging his own happiness in America, 'unhindered by any deprivation of rights or outcast status'; 'no contempt or abusive political obstacles' stood in James's way. Becoming maudlin, Gregory contrasted his brother's situation with his own:

> You alone are responsible for the steps and actions you take, and if you cry, it is perhaps because you stumbled at takeoff or damaged your wings and not because your wings are chained down and the stronger you become, the thicker the chains.

In addition to his reading in French and German, Gregory's work on English and Italian was a way of reminding himself that he might eventually have a future outside of Russia, that he might one day escape the constraints limiting his life but not his aspirations. He told James,

> I can only explain my love, even my passion for languages to myself by the fact that I want to break free so badly. I no longer want to live this way, think this way or speak this way. I want everything to be clearer, *more free*.

Gregory's frustration was mixed with determination: 'The war, pandemic tension, nervousness and uncertainty about the near future don't allow me to think or speak of my plans, but I sense that what I am now doing and pursuing is not my ultimate or established undertaking.' Lonely and eager for understanding, he pleaded with his brother to write to him. After all, he pointed out, 'we are children of the same environment, the same melancholy and sadness, but you have already made it abroad whereas I have not – or not yet, I should say.'[7]

Eugenia's preparations to join James were coming together as Gregory poured out his heart to his brother. Conventional routes out of Russia – east through present-day Poland and north to Bremen – were impossible because of the war. Thinking that she might leave as early as the end of the month, Gregory held onto his desperate letter in the hope that she could deliver it in person. On 23 February, he added a few lines in English written quickly without a dictionary. He wanted to show James his progress: He still had 'the same pain and the same suffering in my heart', but 'I wish you be very happy, that your life has nothing beyond good and satisfaction.' For the first time he now signed his name 'Gregory' in the English handwriting that would be recognisably his throughout his life.[8]

In fact, Eugenia was unable to leave Russia until early April. She managed to get to Copenhagen and onto a ship that arrived in New York on 11 May. James was likely at the dock to meet her and took her to his boarding house in Upper Manhattan. On 6 June 1915 they were married in a civil ceremony. James was still working as a translator and private tutor and Eugenia had as yet no job, but they were able to make ends meet and they were together.

Life now began to change for Gregory, too. In the letter to James begun in February but still unsent, he added a second note in English before giving it to Eugenia to take with her to America. He wrote that 'two events of very great consequence' had recently altered his 'interior' life, although his external circumstances had not changed. The first Eugenia would tell him because it was delicate and painful – and he was too embarrassed to put it in writing; the second was that he had obtained permission to return to Petrograd to take examinations in medicine. The residence permit on which his studies at the Institute depended had been granted in a roundabout way because of his outstanding work at the military lazarette. Despite everything he had revealed to James and his real frustration and dejection, he was working with committed zeal at the clinic and his superiors had recommended him for an 'Imperial' decoration for excellent and dedicated service to the state. On that basis he was released from his military obligations at the hospital and admitted to the quota of Jews permitted to study law at the University of Kiev … and as a university student, he could travel to Petrograd and reside there for several weeks at a time. Before the end of the month Gregory set off for the capital to prepare for the end-of-year exams in May, but aware that he would need to enrol in law at the University in Kiev in the autumn.[9]

The painful and embarrassing event was the end of his romantic relationship with Sonya, apparently his decision. All their friends had expected them to marry, but Gregory was neither passionately in love nor ready emotionally or financially to settle down. His agenda was his intellectual and professional life. He could imagine leaving Russia but not married life. Eugenia and James would hold the break-up against him for years, feeling he had led Sonya on then failed to honour his commitment and abandoned her. For his part, he continued to be upset throughout the spring and summer, but he did not doubt that breaking off had been the right thing. He tried to explain the situation to James in subsequent letters. Initially he had been afraid of the effect of his rejection on Sonya, worrying that she might even consider suicide, but he had calmed down after the confrontation. He insisted that his decision turned out to have been 'not so bad' and Sonya had recovered relatively well and quite quickly. He continued to be sad about it; the rupture had left 'a scar, a deep wound'. The relationship that had seemed to him to be love had lasted for five of his 'earliest and tenderest years'; he could not 'simply go on living with a peaceful heart, smiling, moving on and forgetting it all', but his education demanded his emotional and intellectual energy. He put his romantic life aside, once more accepted money from his father, and boarded the train for the capital.[10]

As Gregory took his exams, the war was going badly for the Russians. Although their troops were well trained and equipped, the inadequate transportation infrastructure was unable to supply soldiers in the field. In the spring of 1915 the Germans had taken over command of the Eastern Front, and on the first of May they attacked the Russians at Gorlice, between Krakow and Lviv. Within two weeks the entire Russian southern front collapsed. Only 40,000 of 250,000 retreating troops escaped; by the time the Germans retook Lviv on 22 June, Russian casualties were enormous. By July the Germans were pushing north towards Warsaw.

But by July Gregory was in Boyarka, 15 miles southwest of Kiev. This predominantly Jewish community – the basis for the fictional village of Boyberik in Sholem Aleichem's stories – contained many students interested in the lessons Gregory offered throughout the summer. From an inexpensive rented room he wrote James that he was determined not to 'live on Father's shoulders or anyone else's'. Away from the social circle that had included Eugenia and Sonya, he missed his brother more than he had anticipated and was lonely:

> I have no friends or acquaintances, not even nodding acquaintances. I am working and studying, and I think of you very, very often.... If only you understood this without my explaining it and if only our correspondence were as regular as it could be, I would be more than happy.

Gregory had heard nothing directly from James since an acknowledgement of the encyclopaedia in February, although news had been relayed through Eugenia, but since her departure in April, he had heard nothing. The brothers had agreed that it was foolish to take offence at the imbalance of their correspondence, but Gregory now wondered why Eugenia had not written to him. Aside from feeling abandoned, he wanted his brother to send him an English dictionary and a Spanish grammar:

> Not having these books is a palpable obstacle to my plans. I cannot write about the latter, nor do I wish to. I am sick and tired of plans, sick and tired of

> unfulfilled intentions, and I think it best to be silent about them for the time being.

Having done well on his May exams he was in good spirits, even energetic and optimistic about the future, but

> the events of the last months which brought an end to all the senseless and rashly naïve ways of my youth have come crashing down on my head. And my heart aches terribly. I am sad and fearful all the time since there are many difficult and sad things behind me that I am unable to forget – many moral failures and blunders – while ahead of me lie insurmountable obstacles over which I have no control because of the war. I will probably be unable to undertake anything until it is over.

Again he implored James to write:

> You are the one person who is farthest away from me while being the closest to me at the same time, i.e., someone who understands me and who recently became easy to talk to. Ever since you left for Grenoble, we have been distant close friends.

Invariably passionate, Gregory's emotions sometimes overwhelmed him and he became hyperbolic. Even thinking about James was difficult, made him

> feel such grief as if I were crying when I think about you. It is truly crying – real crying – only without tears. It is so difficult – unbearable! … I am overcome by such anxious melancholy that I cannot even write to Eugenia.[11]

At the end of the summer, having earned as much as he could, Gregory left Boyarka, but once again the rug slipped out from under him. The Battle of Warsaw had not gone well for the Russians. In early August the Germans had taken the city that Russia had counted a part of its empire for nearly a century. Any plans Gregory had once entertained about returning to the University of Warsaw for a diploma in law were abandoned. At the end of the month, the tsar decided to take over command of the Russian army, an act with disastrous consequences. Meanwhile the Germans advanced steadily. By late September the Eastern Front had been pushed back to Riga in the north and Czernowitz near Moldova in the south. At its closest, the front was now only 200 miles west of Kiev, to which Gregory had returned at the beginning of the month. He resumed his work at the lazarette and paid off a number of debts as well as the first semester's tuition at Saint Vladimir University. His theatrical representation of the instability of his world was more accurate than melodramatic, however: Just as he was finally ready to start his course, the university decided to evacuate its faculty and students to Saratov, a city on the Volga nearly 800 miles east of Kiev and over 1,000 miles from Petrograd, where he also intended to enrol at the Psycho-Neurological Institute for the 1915–1916 academic year.

With the war going so badly for the Russians, demand for medical care in Kiev was intense and Gregory returned to his work at the hospital where, as an experienced medical student, his skills were needed. Exactly what his status now was isn't clear. Ten years later, he mentioned in a biographical statement having received his decoration 'for valour and service' while working in 1915–1916 in a military hospital 'at the front'. When his credentials were listed in his publications during the Second World War, at a time when military experience in wartime lent extra weight to whatever an author wrote, it was sometimes claimed that in 1915–1916 he had served as a physician at a Russian army base hospital. There was certainly government pressure to rush students through medical programmes in an effort to send more doctors to the front. In the spring of 1915, in response to pressure from the Ministry of Public Education, the Institute began special training courses for medical students so that they could take on field responsibilities. Fifty-six students already in their last year qualified as acting doctors; 200 in their fourth year qualified as auxiliary doctors. More than 300 other students – some with minimal medical training and others studying to be lawyers and teachers – were drafted into military service and sent to the front before the end of the academic year. Perhaps the exams that Gregory took in Petrograd in May 1915 in combination with the clinical work he did in Kiev between late 1914 and May 1915 qualified him as an 'auxiliary doctor'. He never claimed to have been working as a physician during the 1914–1915 academic year, though he probably participated in relatively sophisticated medical treatments during this time; it seems unlikely he was awarded the Imperial decoration as a nurse. The historian of medicine Daniel Todes is aware of at least one Russian who completed a medical degree at the front with only occasional leave at home. The exams for which Gregory prepared so assiduously on his own must have counted for a great deal; certainly his commitment to medicine was unwavering.[12]

Yet his intention to continue to study both law and medicine simultaneously would be nearly impossible. He planned to stay in Kiev until October, then travel to Saratov to begin his studies in law, then from there travel to Petrograd. But money had already proved a deciding factor in his education, and Gregory anticipated that it would continue to be a key element. He explained to James that despite

> this horrible and nightmarish war … I will not be dropping out of medicine at the Psycho-Neurological Institute, and I figure I will graduate from both the law and medicine programs.… It will probably be difficult only financially, but I am not afraid of that and I do not wish to be afraid – I will somehow manage to do what is required.

He intended to spend what he had earned in Boyarka on the two tuitions and the travel, adding that even his relationship with his parents had improved because of his 'independent' existence and 'totally independent appointment to the University'. He told James, 'Our parents have seen that I am not totally frivolous or irresponsible and that I was capable of moving forward.'[13]

Gregory enclosed with this Russian letter to James a letter in English to Eugenia. Without opportunities to converse with native speakers or even to hear the spoken language and without a teacher, Gregory had made remarkable progress. Eugenia had apparently sent him a letter in English indicating that she didn't understand why he hadn't written. Gregory explained he was not 'indifferent' to her life but had been unable to write to anyone after breaking up with Sonya because 'I was plunged in a very great grief.... And for writing one must always be quiet at any rate and not so busy as I was.' He continued,

> Now all is changed in my life. In such a short time I must to endure very much and now I am entirely another Grisha: yes till now I am lonesome. And I think that is the end. I have now very much to do, to work, to do not remain in an inactivity.

He reiterated plans he had shared with James, insisting, 'I do not renounce the medicine in Petrograd, where I shall go in one month. As you see it is much to be done and I am on a very good and clear way.' He felt that his life was more coherent after the challenging months in Boyarka:

> till the last days I was very anxious. I did not know if I'll be received in the university or not. All the summer I lived alone, without company nor friends. From morning till the evening I was at my lessons.

Eugenia had written a bit about her life in America and Gregory responded that he was pleased to know that his brother was 'the same young and energieal "Jonia" he was before America.' Gregory then turned to his immediate life in Kiev: 'I work till now in the hospital and I am very glad. And it is thanks to him [the hospital] that I was received in the university. All is changed there: other phisyshans, other sisters' – only a few of their friends were still there – 'But all is better, the personal is so kind and good and so simple in the same time that it is a great pleasure to work.'[14]

Gregory's sophisticated vocabulary is here enlivened by linguistic freedom: The invented word 'energieal' ('energetic') suggests his increasing ease with English, while misspellings ('phisyshans' for 'physicians' and 'personal' for 'personnel') indicate that he was writing confidently without relying on a dictionary. His irregular use of articles, infinitives, pronouns ('him' rather than 'it' for 'hospital') and impersonal phrasing ('it is much to be done') reveal his native Russian model, but tenses are more or less correct and he uses rather elegant and literary phrases (he has been 'plunged in a very great grief'; he was 'without company or friends'; 'From morning till the evening I was at my lessons'). Gregory's growing linguistic competence would stand him in good stead in the challenging days ahead.

At the end of September, the financial difficulties he had anticipated suddenly became pressing far sooner than he had imagined. He wrote James in desperation, 'I am trapped in a situation with absolutely no way out. Not only am I without money, but I have no coat, no boots.' He preserved his sense of humour – 'I may be a long way off from a 3000-meter [feature film] tragedy, but I am only a millimeter away from a horrible 1600-meter drama' – yet his situation was truly serious: 'My "2 universities" have taken everything I had in savings, and I am in Kiev, unable to travel either to Saratov … or to Petrograd.' Gregory continued ironically:

> In terms of dress, autumn is palpable in the extreme. I am at risk not only of losing a semester both here and there; I am also at risk of losing the most important thing: The hair on my head and what remains of my civilian clothing.

He rightly saw his medical studies as his only way out of a likely death at the front.

The problem came down once again to money. He told James,

> I have not accepted two kopecks from Father since April, i.e., the time I left for Petrograd for the examination, and I DO NOT WANT to and will not accept anything more than that: He has nothing to spare, living expenses are terribly high and I cannot take a thing from him. While I had some money, I gave whatever and whenever I could myself. True, Father has been earning something 'on the side', but there still isn't enough.

He felt embarrassed and defensive – 'I think it is probably unnecessary to say this: nobody is to know about my request' – but James had recently written the family that fortune was turning in his favour and Gregory now asked him to wire him $50 to an address in Moscow. A committed socialist, Gregory was not ashamed about being in financial need or asking for money from someone who had some. He told James, 'I don't doubt that you will not take offense at my request. If this is difficult for you, you don't have to do it. I will not be offended.'[15]

Offense aside, Gregory needed to find funds somewhere, but he would have called upon his brother as a last resort: He knew that James was barely earning his own living and had educational aspirations of his own, while distance meant that money – arranged via letter from Russia and then wired from America – would take at best weeks to arrive at the same time that the conversion rate and the wire itself would mean that much-needed dollars would be lost. Obviously aware that he could not count on James, he likely borrowed again from friends, humbled himself to ask for something from his father, and begged the authorities at the Institute for patience. In October he even managed to arrange an appointment with the education minister in the capital to plead for a transfer from law to medicine at the University of Kiev. Giving up his psychiatric studies was simply not an option.[16]

The importance of medicine to Gregory cannot be underestimated, for it was the same commitment to values that led him to support the revolutionary cause. He later wrote about his dedication not only to medicine and specifically to psychiatry but to the historical context of medicine:

> the dynamic, psychological force of medicine springs from the silent, implicit, but very real sense of social responsibility and inner need to fight for someone else's life.... This human, personal, ardent, and withal so impersonal striving to heal, to save, to safeguard ... is neither understood nor cultivated nor attained by purely technological advances, by empirical acquisition of knowledge, by pragmatic successes or other real or imaginary emoluments, natural or made to order by our culture.

He continued:

> The physician, whether he knows it or not, is sustained by the cultural tradition, and the ever-changing but ever deepening ethos of the medical profession. In a formalistic or ritualistic way this is reflected in the tradition of the Hippocratic Oath, and otherwise in a thousand and one little things which set medicine apart from any other occupation. The deeper substance of medicine cannot be maintained by abstract principles or formalistic traditions; it is maintained by the very history of medicine.

The historical moment in which Gregory found himself in the autumn of 1915 only intensified his commitment to his professional future, and he clung to his place at the Institute.[17]

Fearing that his September letter to James might not have reached him, in mid-November Gregory repeated his request. He summed up: 'I am now in my second year in the Medical Faculty at the Psycho-Neurological Institute and my first year of Law at Kiev University.' By his 'second year in the medical faculty', he meant that he was in his second year of specialisation, his fourth of the five-year program. Having started at the Institute in the 1911–1912 academic year, he had apparently lost a year as a result of financial difficulties, problems with travel and residence, his studies in law, and the vicissitudes of war, and he was still struggling with all of these contingencies. He told his brother that he had just returned from Petrograd and his plan was to remain in Kiev, preparing for several theoretical exams, until January 1916, then travel to Petrograd, where he would work until May in the laboratories and autopsy room. But everything depended on his getting funds for tuition and travel. He explained to James, 'All men born the same year I was have been called up for service.' The matter of money was urgent:

> I am not referring to such small things as a coat or boots, which I cannot yet address, of course. The issue is larger than that: due to my various shortcomings and deficiencies of the past, I have not yet paid the tuition at the Institute

(I paid off all my debts and then there were the trips ...). If I don't pay 150 roubles within the next 5–6 weeks, I will be expelled from the Institute and also 'Goodbye, medicine'. I will lose my deferment as a medical student – and I will be drafted as a law student along with all the other students in 1–2 months.

In order not to worry them, he had kept the situation from his parents and felt he could not ask his father yet again for help. Gregory no longer had a kopeck from his teaching in Boyarka, and he was apparently continuing to work at the lazarette, where he hoped to earn what he needed for the January trip to Petrograd and living expenses during the spring term of 1916, but paying his tuition was critical; in short, he emphasised to James, 'I have to live and study.'[18]

Gregory repeated his request for $50 a third time in a letter in early December, but he underestimated how long his desperate correspondence took to cross the battlefields, the Baltic Sea, and the Atlantic Ocean, where German U-boats cruised. This letter was only stamped as officially received in the United States nearly two months later. By the end of November, however, he finally had a long letter from his brother. James had apparently sent the dictionary and grammar Gregory had requested in July, but James failed to address the financial problem. Gregory immediately thanked him for the books, although he had not yet received them, and reflected on his brother's life in America.

James account of his own situation frustrated Gregory, who was eager for a first-hand report:

Your letters always create the impression of a sort of hectic preoccupation, not so much empty hustle and bustle as being overly busy; it is always difficult to tell from the letters what exactly it is that you are doing. I know that you are working, that you are occupied with something and aiming for something, but what exactly that is (this would be very interesting to know) seems to be enshrouded in the unknown.

James's tendency to become preoccupied with minutiae and to grumble about what seemed to his brother finally petty or simply inevitable was at odds with Gregory's concern with metaphysical and ethical questions and political and social issues. Gregory wrote, 'Sometimes, when I think about you, I am happy for you and pleased. It was very sad for me to read in your last letter where you complain about battered nerves.' Although America would not enter the war for another year and a half and James was under no immediate personal threat, Gregory generously attributed his complaints to a shared temperament, implying that his brother's emotional state was, like his own, at least in part influenced by the state of the world. Gregory continued,

America impresses me as a country of iron energy that knows no 'overheating' or pressure that would be too high. It seems to me that Americans rush

> in their brief lifetime to exhaust not only all of life's pleasures, but also the entire supply of one's individual potential in life.

It was difficult for Gregory to imagine that James was in real distress even as an impecunious immigrant:

> Life in such a country is perhaps a great deal of work and greatly challenging. It seems to be the first country that aims to use the spiritual strengths of the individual as broadly and completely as electric and steam energy.

He pointed out philosophically the enormous possibilities James now had:

> To live a full life, to have just one opportunity to live a full life is a great gift. It is a shame that you are so busy that you don't have time in your infrequent letters to paint a picture of American life from the point of view of her spiritual essence, her boundless energy and ideal staying power, of that America where there is neither spleen nor *dolce far niente* [indulgent laziness], where people rush to live not because they are thinking that life is short, but in order to do as much as possible, to attain the maximum in life.

Gregory moved on from consolation to philosophy: 'Sometimes I think that if people were no longer divided into separate nations and were blended together into one cosmopolitan whole, life would become easier and more interesting.' On the basis of what he had read and heard, he thought, 'America serves as a living illustration of this concept; the nation's style is anational in that it consists of the most heterogeneous immigrants representing all countries and peoples.' He wanted to know James's 'inside view': 'I have only scanty "theoretical" information or the impressions from [Bernhard] Kellermann's [1913 German novel] *Der Tunnel* to go on.' Gregory was obviously thinking a great deal about America, an alternative as both an idea and a reality to the Russia in which he was trying so hard to make a life for himself.

Increasingly committed to a career in medicine, Gregory told James, 'I now see a clear road ahead of me: Medical education.' Preparing for practical work he would begin in Petrograd in the new year, he hoped in May to transfer into the medical programme in Kiev, but failing that, he told his brother, 'I would prefer to drop out of the law programme in Kiev and continue to work at the Institute.' He was still tempted to combine the two programmes but realised that doing so was becoming impossible given his limited material resources and the distance from Petrograd to Kiev to Saratov and back. Gregory was being realistic: 'I made that trip this month and I am convinced that in addition to the monetary cost, it amounts to a tremendous loss of time and energy.' Always philosophical, he continued,

> Regarding the latter, I have just enough to prevent me from falling into despair in the face of 'obstacles' and I am calm now in that respect. As for the question of time, the thought of irretrievably lost time is oppressive to me.

He added, 'Much of what I could have done earlier, perhaps without effort and in timely fashion, I now will have to take on with great strength of will.'[19]

Mortified, Gregory had asked Moses for money to go to Saratov for a few days in late November but now focused on his studies in Petrograd. The medical faculty had refused to allow him further absences, and he was clear where his future lay. By January 1916 his father had given him the money he needed for the rest of the academic year. Moses was understanding, generous, and patient with his eldest son who, in contrast to James, was not financially independent. Reflecting on the hectic pace with which both young men struggled to make their way, Moses shared his philosophy with James: 'for simple life balance', he felt it was necessary to live well, for 'a man is like a tear-off calendar whereby the dates that are torn off will never change and fewer pages remain in the calendar.' Stressing the importance of tranquillity and patience, he pointed out that it would be impossible 'to reach the highest step without spending time on the lower steps. Everything is obtained gradually.' While Moses earned a sufficient income at what he humorously called 'the old university' (that is, at Kapnik's shop), he admitted to his second son that the family's expenses were enormous:

> Grisha takes a lot, but he needed to go to Petrograd, then to Saratov and now again to Petrograd. He is there at the Faculty of Medicine, after all, and he will definitely have to stay for about 3 months. We had to give a guarantee, and although that didn't cost me too much, his expenses now include travel and housing.

Moses told James with characteristically wry wit that he had become a translator, translating 'money into everyday capital'. His financial and emotional support for his eldest son did not waver, but he hoped that 'God will grant that it all comes out right, and he will begin to earn a decent living', confessing to James that the family felt they had been waiting a very long time. Moses likely counselled his eldest son in the same terms, and Gregory, who had a great deal in common with his wise father, attempted to focus his energies. In Petrograd, far from family and friends, he was solitary but not lonely. Although avoiding details, he wrote James with typically trenchant humour, 'While on the one hand there is nothing new with me personally, there is also a lot on the other.'[20]

Indeed, there was a great deal on the other hand. From autumn 1915 into spring 1916, Russia held the long Eastern Front but focused on revitalising its military and rousing patriotism. The fierce battles and enormous casualties of the summer had taken their toll on support for both the war and the tsar. With Nicholas II in command of the army and frequently absent from the capital, political intrigue was rife. With her four daughters and her haemophiliac son close by, the German-born Tsarina Alexandra held the reins of power under the influence of the peasant mystic Grigori Rasputin; both the court and the people were uneasy, suspicious, and fearful. With over two million Russian soldiers captured, killed, or wounded by the beginning of 1916, new recruits – many of them from the far north and east of the empire – as well as seasoned veterans grew discontented with war and distrustful of their commanders. On the home front production had turned from butter to guns, and there were food shortages, breadlines, and strikes. The consciousness-raising groups of the pre-war years had done their work well, and unions and students joined protests across the country. On 9 January 1916, shortly after Gregory's return to the Institute, enormous labour strikes began in Petrograd and spread south to the Black Sea. They were soon quelled by imperial troops, but throughout the empire social unrest continued just beneath the surface of daily life.

Notes

1 GZ to JZ, 21 November 1914.
2 GZ to JZ, 27 September, 3 (quoted), 4 October 1914.
3 GZ to JZ, 21 November 1914.
4 Mora, 'Early American Historians', 59–66; GZ, 'Russian Psychiatry', 715, 719, 726, and 'Some Aspects of Psychiatry', 563.
5 GZ to JZ, 27 September, 3, 4 (quoted) October 1914
6 GZ, POOE, 3–4, 5–6.
7 GZ to JZ, 15 (quoted), 23 February, 6 April 1915.
8 GZ to JZ, 15, 23 February (quoted), 6 April 1915.
9 GZ to JZ, 15, 23 February, 6 April (quoted), 10 September 1915.
10 GZ to JZ, 10 September, 19 July 1915.
11 GZ to JZ, 19 July 1915; MZ to JZ and EZ, 11 May 1915.
12 BIO; GZ, 'Ambulatory Schizophrenias', 149, and 'Masculine and Feminine', 257; email from Daniel Todes to Joel Howell, 11 November 2013.
13 GZ to JZ, 10 September 1915.
14 GZ to EZ, 12 September 1915.
15 GZ to JZ, 29 September 1915.
16 MZ to JZ and EZ, 17 October 1915.
17 GZ, 'Medical History', p. 6.
18 GZ to JZ, 14 November 1915.
19 GZ to JZ, 29 November 1915.
20 GZ to JZ, 29 November, 5, 6 December 1915; MZ to JZ and EZ, 17 October 1915, 10 January 1916.

Chapter 4

Revolution

1916–1917

Petrograd in winter is cold and dark. Even if it isn't snowing, the city on the Gulf of Finland is humid, and the Neva freezes over from the Winter Palace across from the Peter and Paul Fortress in the north past the eastern bridges and inland as far as the eye can see. The sun doesn't rise in January until 9:30 in the morning, and by 3:30 in the afternoon the sun is setting. In the first months of 1916 Gregory made his way in the dark to Bekhterev's laboratories. Daylight hours were spent with cadavers in dissection rooms or with alcoholic and psychotic patients in the Alcohol Clinic. He then made his way back to his rented room by the light of street lamps. Having decided to focus his attention on medicine, he was not traveling regularly either to Kiev or to Saratov and invested his emotional and intellectual energies in the here-and-now of his present life. The isolation and loneliness he had felt since breaking off with Sonya dissipated with his involvement in social and socialist activity. He participated in political reading and discussion groups with both students and workers and capitalised on his abiding interest in drama with paid reviews. His amateur days as the 'director of the corps de ballet' were over, and he soon found employment directing local plays. In the capital's small theatres he probably occasionally acted as well; he discovered how to fund productions and stage a dramatic work. His interest in words, literature, and psychology all figured as he directed and reviewed, but so did his charismatic character, his ability to speak and charm and hold the listener's attention in conversation. In Petrograd that winter he reanimated his social life, engaging with fellow students and professors and taking part in the vibrant political and intellectual whirl of the city.[1]

Sheltered from the snow and wind outside, Gregory's work absorbed him, while his involvement in theatre activities and contact with other students and with workers in labour unions served as a distraction from events beyond the city. Gregory now apparently stopped writing to James. He had told his brother he would not be offended if he could not or simply did not want to send the money he had asked for, but Gregory's life was so vastly different from his brother's that maintaining their correspondence was evidently too challenging for both of them. James and Eugenia had different attitudes and values, and their situation in a country not yet at war made Gregory's life as unimaginable to them as America was to Gregory.

DOI: 10.4324/9781003190936-4

The war continued to affect daily life. After the Allies withdrew in defeat from Gallipoli in early January 1916, the Russians turned their attention to Turkey and initiated an eventually successful offensive that lasted into the spring on the southern coast of the Black Sea. South of Riga in March, however, Russian troops failed to push the Germans back at Lake Narach in Belarus; whatever territory they gained was lost when thaws and heavy rain turned the area into a swamp and forced a retreat. In Petrograd evacuated soldiers were a constant reminder of the carnage occurring at the empire's borders. A ward in the Alcohol Clinic was given over to wounded and shell-shocked men, while throughout the city new hospitals opened in royal and public buildings. Large portions of the Winter Palace, the tsar's official home, were converted into a sophisticated hospital with extensive Russian staff, while the Dmitry Palace on Nevsky Prospect became a base hospital under Anglo-Russian Red Cross administration. Anti-war feeling exacerbated revolutionary tensions as the economy broke down. Waiting to buy bread of deteriorating quality took hours each day. In response to the stresses in his own life, Gregory was smoking again, but he now ate less and less – it took too much time to buy food, and the cost not only of food but of the coat and boots he also needed was rising: By the end of the year the price of milk and potatoes was four times what it had been in the summer of 1914; bread, cheese, butter, meat, and fish were five times higher. There was no longer any coal for heating and, with trains struggling to supply frontline troops, wood was brought in from the countryside by horse-drawn sledges and river barges. Inadequate and mismanaged transport infrastructure was unable to meet the need for provisions and material at the front much less stock Petrograd's shops. Gregory worked and studied, went without meals and began, like soldiers at the front, to suffer from scurvy.[2]

The government wanted doctors at the front and in base hospitals and perceived students as a revolutionary element: Their socialist ideas fostered anti-war sentiments and encouraged workers' protests; the more quickly they finished their programmes, the less trouble it was thought they might cause and the faster they could enter the army. In 1916, with the dual goals of certifying more doctors and limiting socialist ferment, the Ministry of Public Education inspected the Psycho-Neurological Institute and decided to grant it the status of a private university with the same rights as all other government institutions of higher education. It could now award diplomas to qualified medical students, while its other students were permitted to take examinations at the University of Petrograd.

This change had immediate implications for Gregory. His military deferment depended on his being a student of medicine and a university student. The Institute's new status meant he no longer needed to maintain his enrolment at the University of Kiev. His studies in law had so far counted for frustratingly little: He had no diploma from Warsaw despite having taken exams there in 1914, and his enrolment at Saint Vladimir University had drained his finances. He now saw a way to make something of his reading in the history, theory, and practice of law and apparently decided to take final exams in philosophy at the University of Petrograd at the end of the autumn semester. At the conclusion of the academic year at the Institute, he set out on the long journey to Saratov. There, on 16 May 1916, he withdrew from the University of Kiev.[3]

Gregory probably went to see his family at the end of the month, but he felt he could no longer stay except as a visitor in his parents' apartment. In Petrograd the theatre season continued, and there he could earn more than his teaching in Boyarka during the previous solitary summer. He had his philosophy exams to prepare for, and the possibility of a revolution must also have drawn him back at a time when a wave of protests was occurring throughout the country in response to a new military offensive.

In early June the Russian army launched an attack on a long stretch of the Eastern Front between Pinsk, 250 miles northeast of Kiev, and the Romanian forests south of Chernowitz. The goal was to retake Kovel and Lviv. Under General Aleksei Brusilov, the offensive continued until the end of September, inflicting heavy losses on both the Russian and Austrian-Hungarian armies. Despite recaptured territory, however, military morale fell as casualties mounted. Wounded soldiers as shattered mentally as physically poured into base hospitals, and Brusilov's successes met with protests against the war by peasants, workers, and students. The government's response was swift and brutal: The tsar's police and Cossack garrisons arrested thousands of people in Petrograd alone.

The political situation grew increasingly unstable over the summer. The tsar dismissed the Duma at the end of June, and it did not reconvene until November. Politicians and students discussed what could or ought to be done and by which political parties or possible leaders or individuals. The novelist and social critic Maxim Gorky opened his Petrograd apartment to Bolsheviks and others sympathetic to the possibility of revolution. Gorky's friend Leonid Andreyev, known for his psychological fiction and plays, had turned his attention to politics; dividing his time between Petrograd and his country home in Russian Finland, he wrote for the city's newspapers, advocating social equality and arguing against capital punishment and war. Vladimir Korolenko, on the staff of the Petrograd socialist magazine *Russkoye Bogatstvo* (Russian Wealth), wrote not only literary reviews but articles against the regime's injustice. In private homes and public meeting rooms some groups debated the idea of a peasant revolt; others championed urban workers as the most likely to organise. Archdukes and Duma members emerged as possible figures to replace the tsar and transform the government; intellectuals argued about Marx while party leaders on the right and on the left proposed coalitions.

Gregory was inevitably caught in the maelstrom of social debate, an eager participant in discussions and protests he hoped would change the world he was struggling with and give all Russians control over their lives. His primary agenda continued to be his medical studies, but students throughout the autumn of 1916 discussed politics in the Institute's corridors and courtyards and assembled spontaneously and under the direction of student leaders to deliberate and rally. They marched with workers and peasants in Petrograd's streets, and in early November, they crowded into the grand assembly hall of the Tauride Palace to listen to the Duma's increasingly fraught debates.

The political parties now represented there included the liberal intellectual Constitutional Democratic Party (the Kadets, prominent among them Prince Georgy Lvov); the Labour Group (the Trudoviks), representing the peasants; the traditional 'Octobrists'; the reactionary Union of Landowners; the moderate Socialist Revolutionaries (led by Alexander Kerensky); and the radical Russian Social Democratic Labour Party (dominated by the Bolshevist Marxist-Leninists). Important political figures were absent, but their ideas continued to influence the volatile discussions. In exile since 1907 for his part in the 1905 revolution and advocacy of violence and robbery as politically justifiable, Vladimir Lenin had moved about in Switzerland, France, and England in the years before the First World War; he was living in Galicia when the war broke out, and from early 1916 he was in Zurich, but throughout the period he remained in close contact with Russian politics and individual politicians, rabble rousers, and friends. Although differing with Lenin over the degree to which violent acts were defensible, his fellow Marxist Leon Trotsky urged cooperation with other political parties, but he, too, had been in exile after 1905, living in Vienna until August 1914 before moving to Switzerland, France, Spain, and finally the United States. Like Lenin, he continued to publish in both foreign and Russian newspapers, and pamphlets by both men were widely circulated.

When the Duma reopened, the fervour intensified. Conservatives continued to argue that constitutional reforms should wait until after the war. Some members railed against the war, while others, convinced the war could be won, declared their confidence in the Russian military. Criticising the government in a passionate and courageous speech, Kerensky called the war a '"bloody whirlwind into which the democracy of Europe was drawn at the instigation of the ruling classes"' and accused the government of destroying the spirit of the Russian people; he argued that before concluding '"this fratricidal war"' with '"a peace worthy of international democracy"', Russians had to have '"the right to direct and participate in the affairs of state"'. He then stunned the chamber by calling for the overthrow of the government: He reproached the tsar for heeding '"the whisperings and instructions of irresponsible circles, guided by the contemptible Grishka Rasputin"' and told his audience they were obligated to destroy '"the power of those who are not conscious of their duty"'. But there were mitigating voices, and the focus of the Duma shifted to criticism of the tsarina and support for the army and the Allies.[4]

There had been nearly two million Russian casualties over the summer, and the Imperial Army was fighting in a difficult campaign in southern Moldavia and Transylvania. Romania had entered the war on the Allied side in August and was initially aided by Russian troops in the Carpathian Mountains, but once again poor transport meant that the Russians and the Romanians were soon hampered by a critical lack of supplies. By the end of November, the Romanians had been pushed back to the plains. By early December they could no longer count on Russian support. The Austrian-Hungarian army took Bucharest on 6 December. The Russians sent what reinforcements they could in an attempt to prevent an invasion of southern Ukraine as Romanian and Russian forces began a humiliating retreat that continued into January as far as the Danube Delta south of Odessa.

With the Eastern Front pushed westwards, however, Saint Vladimir University had returned to Kiev in September, but its location no longer mattered to Gregory. He studied law, ethics, and sociology in preparation for the philosophy exams scheduled for December and worked at the Institute while preparing for his medical exams now set not for May 1917 but for January. Under pressure to push medical students through their programmes, the professors supervising his research at the Alcohol Clinic decided that Gregory's contact with patients there and work at the Kiev lazarette should together count as his clinical placement.

Compromise measures were arrived at both within the Institute and in the official halls and personal chambers of the city now poised to overthrow the tsar. Shortly after Gregory finished his final exams in philosophy at the University of Petrograd, on the night of 30 December 1916, Grigori Rasputin was murdered by a Duma deputy and two members of the nobility. His death did not bring about the changes anyone hoped for, but it moved the country closer to revolution. Early in 1917, just before the Duma reconvened after the Christmas recess, Gregory took his final exams and qualified as a medical doctor, but the last thing he wanted was to head to the front in uniform.[5]

On the anniversary of Bloody Sunday on 9 January a 100,000 workers struck in commemoration. Food lines grew even longer, and ten days later the government announced bread rationing, provoking still more protests from crowds that included men, women, and children. On 24 January mass arrests followed a workers' demonstration outside the Tauride Palace, where the Duma was not yet in session.

In the 17 months since the tsar had taken direct control of the military, Russia had four prime ministers, five ministers of the interior, three foreign ministers, three war ministers, three ministers of transport, and four ministers of agriculture. Competent men were unable to fulfil their responsibilities, and the mismanaged government became increasingly unstable. In cafés and private homes politicians discussed plans for a coup. When the Duma reconvened in mid-February, its members inveighed against the chaos as police and soldiers held back protesters outside. Ministers shouted that the government was sabotaging Russia's economic, social, and political life, and Kerensky urged members to unify despite their differences in ' "the destruction of the medieval regime" '. His open commitment to revolution was unassailable, but questions still remained about when the coup would occur, who would lead it, and if and how military support could be organised and the masses controlled.[6]

On 23 February, International Women's Day, thousands of hungry female workers filled Petrograd's streets. By evening, joined by working men, the crowd had swelled and become unruly, but the patrolling soldiers did little to stop them. The next morning 200,000 striking workers marched down Nevsky Prospect clamouring for bread and an end to the war. The Imperial Guard was authorised to fire upon demonstrators, and the minister of public education issued an instruction to close universities, including the Psycho-Neurological Institute. But Gregory was no longer in either the dissection rooms or the Alcohol Clinic; he had joined the protests and, when he could, he made his way into the Tauride Palace to follow events there. As a freelance journalist, he had published drama reviews in newspapers, but nothing could have been more dramatic than the events he was now witnessing. He put himself at the centre of the action, in the streets and barracks and hospitals and meeting rooms, probably intending to write about what he saw and hoping to publish reports, to earn enough to eat, to contribute what he could to creating the Russia he had hoped for from childhood. He was on the *qui vive* and available, eager to make connections, to be useful, waiting for an opportunity to offer whatever of his knowledge and many talents might be helpful to the cause.

On 25 February the Duma opened with noisy discord. Kerensky and the Menshevik Matvey Skobelev – a friend of Leon Trotsky's since their co-editing of *Pravda* in Vienna in 1908 – called for the overthrow of the tsar. In the streets, protesters shouted 'Down with autocracy' and attacked policemen while Imperial Guard Cossacks looked on. Nicholas II – who since Christmas had been near the front near Mogilev in Belarus, 500 miles from Petrograd, and at army headquarters near Pskov, 200 miles to the southwest – now ordered General Khabalov, commander of the Petrograd Military District, to suppress the riots by force, but his troops refused to fire on the hungry men and women. Gregory was in the mass of protestors facing Cossacks on the city's outskirts on 26 February as the soldiers joined the people and distributed arms, casting their lot with the revolution in the face of 'the onslaught of the workers of the Obuchow and Putilov plants'. Among the tsar's last acts was an order that day dismissing the Duma, but the deputies continued to meet in the great hall under their own authority.[7]

Gregory spent the next morning on a Red Cross relief tour of Petrograd but returned to the Tauride Palace before noon. He continued to hear shots through the palace's thick walls. Police headquarters, the court of justice, and other governmental buildings were in flames. Twelve hours before there had been doubts about a revolution. Now he was certain the moment had arrived. 'The red lights of the burning houses, the dark spots of blood on the white surface of the snow' were clear evidence. He felt with his companions 'a divine madness of freedom'.[8]

In the early afternoon, with a marching band playing and led by a sergeant, the Volinsky regiment joined the protesting workers, students, and intellectuals outside the palace and pushed their way in. Seeing that the army would support them, the deputies at last moved forward. They formed a provisional committee to restore law and order and, leaving the large hall, Kerensky began writing notes to jail the bureaucrats the soldiers brought in while representatives were sent to persuade the tsar to abdicate. The Petrograd Soviet, a city council of predominantly Menshevik politicians, was in charge of governing the capital but would soon develop into a second governing body. The Georgian Nikolay Chkheidze would be elected chair of the Soviet's Executive Committee – a group of 14 original members, increasing to 90 members over time – while Skobelev and Kerensky would become vice-chairs. The Soviet rapidly decided to publish a newspaper to be called *Izvestiia* with Lenin's friend and fellow Bolshevik Vladimir Bonch-Bruyevich as editor. Everything was suddenly moving ahead more quickly than anyone had thought possible.[9]

Gregory followed events closely, speaking with friends and deputies in corridors and meeting rooms. On the evening of the revolution's first day, like many other revolutionaries, he was suddenly overcome by doubt, by a sense of unreality and lack of confidence. Taught that the masses believed the tsar was a symbol of holy power, the representative of God on earth, he 'feared the critical moment which would follow his overthrow'. Stopping him in a corridor, a soldier asked when 'Kolya' – that is, Nicholas – would be brought out. Gregory shook his hand and assured him falsely, ' "Very soon" '. But the tsar was not brought out, was still hundreds of miles away. Gregory reflected, 'While we intellectuals were fighting, and fearing ... what might afterwards evolve from the brain of the Russian muzhik in his military uniform, that brain was already busy working out its own quiet, sober, practical theories of the revolution.' The revolutionaries had no intention of murdering the tsar, but of course – as the soldier understood – that would inevitably happen.[10]

Perhaps because of his competence in languages, probably because of his background in law, and certainly because of his availability, persistence, and sheer presence, his youth and obvious intelligence and force of personality, Gregory found himself at the heart of the political turmoil, willing and able and implicated and finally involved as an amanuensis, an emissary, a representative of those assuming power. He accompanied Kerensky almost everywhere during the revolution's first week, even to a room on the palace's top floor where the leader ate and slept, visited occasionally by his wife and likely more often by his mistress. Gregory attended general government and cabinet meetings, helped the set designer Aleksandr Golovin cover the Gobelin tapestries on the palace walls, and descended to the basement with other young men to bring up the simple furniture the new leaders needed. He conversed with Kerensky's wife, who spent the days directing relief work from the palace before returning to the children at home.[11]

Leaders quickly began to assemble their personal staffs, but nothing could be formalised until the fate of the tsar was decided. Kerensky objected to appointing a regent but also to violence, and argued passionately with more radical revolutionaries advocating a rapid trial and execution. But as news of the revolution reached troops at the Eastern Front, garrisons began to mutiny, and Nicholas realised that he had lost the army's support. On 2 March he officially abdicated in favour of his brother, who refused the throne unless it was offered to him by a freely elected Duma. The new government rapidly formed and democratic soviets – local councils – were put in place, under the aegis of the Petrograd Soviet, at all levels throughout the huge expanse of Russia.

The Constitutional Democratic Party leader Prince Lvov became the titular head of the government while his fellow Kadet Pavel Milyukov was chosen as minister of foreign affairs and Kerensky as minister of justice. Milyukov, the party's founder, had advocated a constitutional monarchy and supported Russia's current wartime alliances. On 4 March he informed the anxious Allies of Russia's almost unconditional support. With popular feeling strongly against the war, this declaration created the first crisis of the Provisional Government and the remaining ministerial posts were given to more radical socialists.[12]

The next day Gregory, now probably a member of Skobelev's staff, took on his first official duty. With an authorising letter from the Executive Committee, he travelled by train to Yamburg and Narva – Baltic cities 100 miles west of the capital – to coordinate the activities of their military garrisons with those of the Petrograd Soviet. He soon became Skobelev's personal secretary, an assistant and representative charged with everything from greeting officials to accompanying the minister on missions and speaking to external groups on the government's behalf. Gregory took on his responsibilities with enthusiasm. His own politics were not those of the Kadets, who found themselves on the far right of the revolutionaries, nor those of the Marxists on the far left. He was against monarchy and for democracy; he was for the inclusion of all people – Jew and Gentile, female and male, poor and ignorant, or lucky and wise; he was for peace.[13]

In February 1917 Gregory at the age of 26 was at once a lawyer, a philosopher, and a doctor by virtue of his exams, a young and passionate man of some accomplishment and great energy although without a settled present or future. He had grown up in Kiev but come of age in Petrograd. He had heard Chaliapin sing in *Boris Godunov* at the Petrograd opera, attended concerts in both cities, been moved by dramatic productions of works by classic and contemporary Russian authors at the Mariinsky Theatre and the smaller venues where he produced and directed and acted. His leisure activities had not, however, been especially different from what he had done at school and for his exams: He read, he wrote, he thought, he spoke, and he discussed history, philosophy, literature, and music with friends in private and public spaces. He did not regularly drink vodka and could not afford wine; he counted himself fortunate when his tea came hot and strong from the samovar. He was not a large man despite his forceful personality. At five feet seven and a half inches, his presence commanded attention because of his deep brown eyes and his bohemian moustache, his long hair, and the suit that seemed dapper even if it was his only suit. He wore stylish hats, used a cigarette holder, had soft gloves in his worn coat pockets, and made sure there were cufflinks in his cuffs.

But he had never climbed a mountain or put on skis; he had never ridden a horse or milked a cow or chased chickens in a farmyard. There must have been athletes among his friends, boys who ran races or climbed trees, but he hadn't been one of them. He had never learned to swim in the Dnieper in the summer or to skate on its frozen inlets in January; he had not kicked or caught a ball for fun in city parks. He must have seen children squaring off outside of school; he had certainly seen brawls in Kiev's streets and experienced pogroms and now riots, but he had never been a boxer. Somewhere, he knew, were Russians who fenced well with sabres, but he was certain they weren't Jews. He had no desire to join a team or the army;

sport as sport was beyond his experience. He played chess and turned to books and music and the recited word for pleasure and leisure. Romance and sexual desire had not yet animated him; he was not yet awakened to love.

The revolution was the most exciting experience of his life. It thrilled him to be at the centre of things, part of something larger promising more than even he had ever dreamed. The revolution allowed him to hope and imagine and participate, captured his emotions, pushed him to physical extremes, ripped at his heart. Easily and justifiably fearful of larger and stronger men with weapons, he did not believe in violence on principle, but he had just seen police firing into crowds and met soldiers who had killed their officers. As if having finally found his calling, he spent his days with politicians giving speeches; he wrote official letters, attended meetings, met emissaries ... and began carrying a gun.[14]

The Provisional Government was also for peace, but its liberal principles – including expansion of civil rights and freedoms, release of political prisoners, abolition of capital punishment, and organisation of democratic elections – were difficult to achieve in the face of continuing unrest. As members of the nobility fled to Western Europe, the government deliberated what to do with the royal family, under house arrest at Tsarkoe Selo south of the capital, while tensions among conservative, liberal, and Marxist parties hampered both policy and action. A committed Socialist Revolutionary, Gregory saw Kerensky as 'that most honest Socialist and patriot', a 'consistent anti-Bolshevist', and 'the soul' of the revolution, but Bolshevist influence was increasing by the day.[15]

On 24 March (6 April NS) the United States declared war on Germany and Russia's support of the Allies assumed strategic importance: If Russian troops could continue to hold the Eastern Front, France and Britain felt they could maintain their positions on the Western Front until American troops and supplies arrived. It would, however, take the United States months to train the conscripts it needed and to transport its army and supplies across the Atlantic, while the Russian military was in disarray and anti-war feeling even more volatile than before the revolution. Germany saw its opportunity. Hoping to negotiate a separate peace with an anti-war leader, Germany offered Lenin a special train to travel from Zurich to Sassnitz on the German coast. There he took a ferry to southern Sweden, then a train to Helsinki and finally to Petrograd, where he arrived at the Finland Station on 3 April 1917. Welcomed by fellow Bolsheviks, he gave a speech denouncing the Provisional Government and calling for a proletarian revolution. Over the next weeks he continued to write for *Pravda*, published in Petrograd since 1912, publicly attacking both Mensheviks and Social Revolutionaries; in speeches he rallied workers, peasants, soldiers, and sailors to the Bolshevik cause and called for an end to Russia's involvement in the war.

Amid divisive political differences, the Provisional Government was still committed to the war. On 20 April Milyukov wrote to France and Britain indicating that Russia would honour its obligation for the duration. When news of his pledge was reported, mass protests broke out in Petrograd, but Skobelev's attention was directed as much to the provinces as to problems in the capital. With invitations from various Soviets of Workers' Deputies, Gregory was sent south in April to speak on behalf of the government in Kiev, Poltava, and Kharkov in the Ukraine, in Rostov-on-Don near the Black Sea, in the Georgian capital of Tbilisi, and finally in Baku on the Caspian Sea. In Kiev, where Basia and Fera sold tickets to the event and the entire family attended, all the auditorium seats were taken; hundreds of people stood in the aisles and corridors and still others had to remain outside in the street. Gregory spoke masterfully as an eyewitness to the revolution, reporting on the Provisional Government and memorialising those who had perished during the inevitable violence.[16]

The new administration, however, was still struggling for stability. Anti-war resentment forced Milyukov to resign on 2 May while Gregory, en route back to the capital, was in Moscow for a meeting of a soviet of student deputies. Gregory arrived in Petrograd shortly afterwards, perhaps even on 4 May, the day Trotsky returned from New York – via Nova Scotia, England, and Denmark, and then – like Lenin a month earlier – through Sweden and Finland to Petrograd's Finland Station where, again like Lenin, he was met by a cheering crowd. The reappearance of yet another dynamic Marxist revolutionary would further complicate political divisions. Deliberating briefly which party to join, Trotsky cast his lot with the Social Democrats, now riven by Bolshevik and Menshevik factions. On 5 May, the moderate Mikhail Tereshchenko, previously minister of finance, replaced Milyukov as minister of foreign affairs; Alexander Zarudny, one of the defence lawyers during the Beilis trial in 1913, took over as minister of justice; and Kerensky was named minister of war. The mollified Mensheviks now joined the Provisional Government. On the same day, Trotsky's Menshevik friend Skobelev was made minister of labour and his personal secretary took on yet more responsibility.[17]

Within a month of declaring war on Germany, the United States had in place a conscription programme requiring the registration on 5 June 1917 of all men between the ages of 21 and 31. In New York James registered with his local draft board in the Bronx. On the same day in Chicago, Shloime – now Solomon – Levitas also registered, but inspired by news of the revolution he returned to Russia before the end of the summer – by train to the west coast, then by ship to Vladivostok, finally via the Trans-Siberian railroad to Kiev. James deliberated: He had no desire to fight with Americans on the Western Front; he was making a life for himself as a translator, supporting a wife, and taking correspondence courses in engineering. Meanwhile the revolution, whose epicentre remained in Petrograd, had spread. Locally elected soviets mirrored the capital's party politics, and arguments over the war, civil rights, and the use of violence pitted the conservative-liberal right against the Marxist-Leninist left. Matters were only complicated by international pressure to continue to support the Allies.

Matters were complicated for Gregory, too. He was earning a generous salary of 600 roubles a month, but revolutionary tensions as well as hectic travel and pressures associated with speeches in cities throughout western Russia were taking their toll on his health. Probably suffering from anaemia and vitamin deficiencies as a result of a chronically poor diet, he began to have trouble with his eyesight in late May. Overburdened with work, unable to see clearly, and without intimate friends, in early June he asked a colleague to write to Fera on his behalf. He wanted her to come to the capital to take care of him.

The family, however, were occupied with their own lives and reluctant to make changes to accommodate the son and brother they had come to see as unnecessarily busy with his work and excessively emotional about whatever plight he found himself in. Having completed two years of study in natural sciences at the University of Kiev, Fera was planning on accompanying her mother on their annual summer holiday to Odessa. She decided not to go to Gregory. She and their mother had booked berths on an overnight train and a beachside apartment so Anna could have mud baths and Fera could swim in the sea. The letter had given them 'a bit of a fright', Fera wrote James, 'we all nearly lost our minds.' She wired Gregory to ask whether he really needed her, decided she wouldn't go to Odessa, then changed her mind when he didn't respond immediately. She set off for the south, apparently not for a moment imagining that no response might mean that Gregory was gravely ill or even dead. A week later, she told James, she received a telegram saying he had recovered, followed by a letter explaining that he had been devastated by his inability to see and pleaded again with Fera to come.

Melodramatic emotionality was a family characteristic, while impatience with the feelings of others was mutual. Fera informed James that now that Gregory was 'moving up in the world', it was time for him to cease 'tormenting himself ... with his pitiful reproaches', to stop being too busy to pay attention. There is no indication of their father's feelings, but the rest of the family including James resented what they saw as Gregory's sense of superiority. Gregory certainly did not see himself as a superior being, but as he moved up in the world, it became difficult for others not to feel resentful towards him. Still, Fera decided to visit Gregory 'for a month or two' as soon as she returned to Kiev. Tired of living at home and longing to be more independent and among other young people, she was in fact 'ecstatic' at the idea of Petrograd, imagined transferring to a university there and coming 'home with Grisha only for Christmas'.[18]

Later in June, having recovered from the worst of his illness, Gregory attended the All-Russian Congress of Soviets, which created a Central Executive Committee with Chkheidze as chair and Skobelev as vice-chair. In the middle of the month, the Root Commission, a group of Americans lead by the diplomat Elihu Root, arrived in the capital. With promises of trade deals, international aid, and good will, they hoped to encourage Russia's commitment to the Eastern Front. With his competence in English, Gregory served as the liaison officer between the government and the commission, meeting its members both with Skobelev and independently, and speaking at several times at some length with the socialist journalist Charles Edward Russell, who was convinced that the 'whole crux of the war' depended upon 'the action of Russia'.[19]

Gregory was occupied not only with diplomatic matters in Petrograd but with activities that took representatives far from the government's passionate rhetoric and political wrangling. Ukrainian nationalists were clamouring for independence, and on 23 June Kerensky and the other Socialist Revolutionary cabinet members travelled to Kiev, leaving Prince Lvov to charge in the capital. It is unlikely that Skobelev, with his strong allegiance to the Petrograd Soviet, was among the group that went to Kiev. Lvov sent Gregory to Finland at the end of the month, but on his return, he was sent to join Skobelev, by then at the front on a special mission to evaluate army morale. On 1 July Gregory set off by train on the 350-mile journey to Dvinsk (today Daugavpils in Latvia). The next day a compromise negotiated with Ukrainian leaders was announced in a heated cabinet meeting that provoked the resignation of the Kadet ministers. Nationalists, unhappy with the agreement, marched in Kiev's streets, while rumours that the Bolsheviks were receiving German support for anti-government activity disturbed everyone.[20]

As minister of war, Kerensky had been compelled to do something to assure the Allies of his ability to command the Russian army and had prepared throughout the spring for an offensive in the south. At the end of June, with Brusilov again in command, Russian troops attacked the Austrian army along an 80-mile front in Galicia with the goal of capturing the Drohobycz oil fields and the city of Lviv. Despite initial success, the Germans launched a counterattack, pushing the Russians back to Tarnopol 80 miles east of Lviv. With the tsar deposed and the death penalty abolished, Russian commanders had lost their authority over battle-weary troops. Some soldiers now refused to fight; others shot their officers, while many men simply began walking home. With the entire Eastern Front weakened, the Germans pushed their advantage not only in Galicia but along the northern front towards the Baltic Sea.

At Dvinsk in July Gregory experienced directly the horrors of war under battle conditions. He spent nights in the trenches and days under fire between the front line and medical clearing stations 'surrounded by hundreds of wounded and mutilated men'. In the disorder and confusion that followed an infantry attack, he saw a very tall, evidently healthy German apparently dying in hysterical convulsions. Two Russian soldiers brought him water, but he kept on crying and shivering until he lost consciousness. Gregory followed as the men carried him to the nearest Red Cross tent, but he was not in fact wounded and, when he had recovered a little, Gregory asked him, '"How long have you been at the front?"' In utter despair, he answered, '"Three years"' and resumed crying hysterically. Gregory was understandably shocked and appalled. As a doctor trained in psychiatry, he observed with precision and felt particularly helpless as a mere bystander. As an intellectual suddenly in real corporeal danger, he recoiled from the reality of war. His personal experience at the front would make him a pacifist in spite and because of his awareness of the history of war and its possible inevitability. He would insist, 'Never has it brought any solution of our problems. Never has it helped civilization a step forward.'[21]

Helping civilisation a step forward or even working for Russian democracy proved increasingly difficult that summer and, physically tired and worried about the future of both the war and the revolution, Gregory returned to Petrograd with Skobelev and Vladimir Lebedev from the Naval Ministry. On the train the three men discussed the atmosphere of mistrust among revolutionaries because of agents provocateurs. Exhausted from sleepless nights and long days with the troops, they wondered about the Russian army's capabilities, shared their doubts, and worried about Petrograd and the reactions to the Ukrainian compromise; they spoke about the resignation of the four Kadet ministers and the government's instability. They must finally have slept but woke just before the train pulled into Vitebsky station, its ornate arches shining in the early light, the city stretching out before them under a rose and blue dawn.[22]

A great deal had happened since they left the capital. On the day Gregory had set out for Dvinsk, thousands of armed soldiers, sailors, and workers, encouraged by anarchists and Bolsheviks, began demonstrating against the government in Petrograd, Moscow, Kiev, and other Russian cities. Kerensky, on a fact-finding mission to the Eastern Front, was recalled from Minsk and, supported by the Mensheviks and Socialist Revolutionaries, finally ordered troops to control the demonstrators. Over 700 people were killed and wounded. The government quickly put in place punitive measures, ordering the arrest of Bolshevik leaders and authorising attacks on the editorial offices and printing presses of *Pravda*. The mass protests, the resignation of the Kadet cabinet members, Bolshevik antagonism, and German advances at the front brought the government to crisis point. At the end of the first week of July the mild-mannered and elegant Prince Lvov resigned as the head of the Provisional Government and Kerensky, while retaining his post as minister of war, became prime minister.

Kerensky ordered the arrest of Bolshevik leaders. With the Russian army pushed back and demoralised on the Eastern Front, Brusilov called for the reinstitution of capital punishment, something the idealistic Provisional Government refused to allow. On 18 July Kerensky replaced him with his deputy Lavr Kornilov. These changes calmed but did not eradicate military, civil, and political tensions. Trotsky and other Bolshevik leaders were arrested and imprisoned, but Lenin fled to Finland. Along the Eastern Front, the Russians held their positions, but no one pushed them to advance. Kerensky threatened to resign in response to conflicts within the government, but when his resignation was refused, he reformed his cabinet, appointing men who were closer to him politically and personally. Skobelev continued as minister of labour, but Kerensky gave himself as prime minister additional authority in an effort to limit both the power and the influence of the Petrograd Soviet. The offices of the Provisional Government moved west from the Tauride Palace to the Winter Palace while those of the Petrograd Soviet were relegated to the Smolny Institute, a former school nearly three miles away at the city's eastern edge. Political intrigue persisted, however, and at the end of July, fearing an attempt to restore the monarchy, the cabinet moved the tsar and his family to Tobolsk 1,500 miles east of Moscow in Siberia.

By the end of July 1917 Gregory was working from early morning into the night. He had little time to eat and his busy schedule would not have allowed him to buy much rationed bread, but he was used to kasha and had no objections to cabbage soup. He regularly saw the Belgian ambassador Jules Destrée and his secretary Richard Dupierreux, a young man his own age, and he would have eaten better fare at the consulate or at meetings with British and American officials, although the days of grand receptions with unlimited caviar and rich sour cream were long over. Indeed, Petrograd was no longer the city of his first days at Bekhterev's institute. Its water was polluted and its population – which, with the influx of refugees and soldiers, had doubled from one to two million since 1914 – suffered from typhus, tuberculosis, and scurvy. People were hungry, and looting of shops and ordinary as well as royal residences was common. As a result of protests and riots, buildings were pockmarked by bullets while the opulent trappings of empire – statues, ironwork, and gilded facades – had been defaced or destroyed. Revolutionary posters were pasted on kiosks, palaces, and public edifices while red flags appeared on street corners, lamp posts, and bridges. Kerensky left his family and moved into an apartment in the Winter Palace with his mistress, whose baby was due before the end of the year. Gregory concentrated on his work and did not record his impressions of the changed city or how little personal life he now had in the letters he did not send to his brother in America.[23]

Probably, however, he shared his feelings with Sonya. At the end of July he received a letter from Kharkov, where she was studying. Addressed to the Secretary to the Minister of Labour, the Marble Palace, Petrograd in response to a letter from him, Sonya revealed her willingness to rekindle their relationship. She called him affectionately 'my darling friend', but burdened with matters of state and disturbed by his visit to the front, Gregory was more in need of a confidante than a lover. He had told her that he was 'searching about in vain' for someone close to him whose views were not necessarily the same but were 'in harmony' with his own. Accusing her of being a Kadet who understood 'democracy in a tuxedo rather than at a machine or workbench' and denigrating her perceptions as methodical and tactical yet ideologically incorrect, he confessed the probable reason for his writing evidently for the first time in two years: Amid his intense revolutionary activity, he felt lonely. Sonya was disturbed by both Gregory's sincerity and criticism; she called him 'my young, hot-tempered friend' and admitted that she had reread his letter with considerable pain 'many, many times'. She reminded him that she used to be his kindred soul, then apologised for revealing how much she missed him, for disrupting his 'tireless activity' with her 'moans'. Her moans, she informed him only somewhat snidely, 'are so insignificant, so meaningless' compared to what was happening to him, to 'the nightmare' that he was living through. She pleaded with him to do what he felt he must for the revolution, but to return to her, insisting that she wasn't really a Kadet and still shared his perceptions. She concluded, 'I long for you so much.'[24]

Gregory likely felt unable to respond to Sonya's letter. The 'nightmare' he was living through continued, and with each passing day the revolution was becoming more dangerous and the Provisional Government less stable. In early August he probably set off with Skobelev to Baku, Skobelev's birthplace, in an attempt to quell a strike of 60,000 oil workers. The journey would cover 2,000 miles to the west coast of the Caspian Sea, but en route, with or without Skobelev, Gregory detoured briefly to Kiev.

He had not seen his family since April. Basia was now 23 and Fera nearly 20, and both sisters and his parents were well aware of the challenges facing the government. Beyond what they read in the newspapers and the privileged glimpses in the letters Gregory had sent home, the war and the revolution were happening all round them. Food shortages were as stressful in Kiev as in Petrograd and protests frequently filled its streets. Soldiers passed through Kiev on their way to the front, and wounded men continued to crowd its hospitals, but the city was also the centre of the volatile Ukrainian independence movement. The family was impressed with Gregory's work at the hub of political power, but they were likely anxious about his personal safety as well as their own. Solomon Levitas had by now returned to Kiev, and his visits to the apartment would have made Fera especially concerned about revolutionary news. A committed socialist, Sol was reporting for the local papers and paying special attention to the family's youngest daughter. Anna and Basia as well as Fera may have complained to Gregory about the quality of the bread, the cost of cabbage, the dangers of the streets they had to walk to the market, but Basia was in her turn being courted by a soldier whose fate at the front was a constant worry. The family was shocked to discover that Gregory had a gun in his coat pocket, terrified that the weapon would bring the wrath of the police down on the household. Fera viewed him not as a successful political emissary but a wild young man, and his passionate nature did indeed sometimes make him rash and impulsive, easily angered, and quick to judge. The revolutionary son and brother the family knew was after all the same young man whom Sonya had ten days earlier called 'hot-tempered'.[25]

Perhaps at the family's suggestion, perhaps on his own initiative, out of a desire to recover a personal life or from the same impulse that had made him write Sonya after his return from Dvinsk, on 4 August Gregory wired James at the American Bureau of Foreign Trade in New York. The family would have told Gregory that his brother was now working there, given him the address and encouraged him to resume contact. Gregory must have deliberated how to start after the long hiatus, yet with characteristically trenchant humour, he began, 'I haven't lost any time, am Secretary to the Minister of Labour.' Giving his address at the Marble Palace, he tried to communicate his situation succinctly: 'I am working too much, revolutionary and state work.' Having probably seen Sol at the apartment, a Russian willing to leave the land of the free for the sake of the revolution, he then continued, 'I would like you to return to Russia.' Gregory's distress, loneliness, even anxiety seem evident between these brief lines. He concluded by telling his brother he was in Kiev for only two days to take care of ministerial business and to visit the family 'whom I see rarely'. James did not immediately respond.[26]

From Kiev, Gregory took a train north to join Skobelev in Moscow, where Kerensky had hastily called a state conference for mid-August in an attempt to rally support for the government. In the month since his appointment as commander-in-chief, Kornilov had convinced Kerensky to restore the death penalty for disobedient frontline soldiers, but subsequent requests for greater authority over and for the military – demands that if met would have resulted in a military dictatorship – were more difficult for the idealistic politician to accept. Kerensky vacillated. In retrospect it would seem that Kornilov intended to try to save the Provisional Government from the leftist Petrograd Soviet through the exertion of military might, but Kerensky and many of his supporters began to see the general as a rival for socialist power. Kornilov's supporters – including Kadets and others on the political right – were certainly considering a military coup. The political centre on which Kerensky depended was becoming increasingly fragile.

When Gregory returned to the capital, he helped Skobelev prepare a formal statement on factory workers' rights. The visit to Baku had convinced them that without cooperation between workers and management, it would be impossible to control strikes or provide necessary supplies to the front. The Petrograd Soviet and the Provisional Government were at odds; the minister of labour – and Gregory with him – were caught, as it were, between two masters. Skobelev's position provoked Bolshevik scorn, but his statement was among the least of Kerensky's problems.

The state conference had failed to strengthen the government: The delegates crowded into the Bolshoi Theatre had been spilt between the traditional conservatives on the right and the soviets' workers, soldiers, and peasants on the left. Amid the complicated vying for power that followed the Moscow meeting, Kornilov was openly accused of preparing a coup and Kerensky finally acted: He persuaded his cabinet to resign and then, on his own authority, dismissed Kornilov as commander-in-chief. Misunderstanding what was happening and thinking the government had been taken over by Bolsheviks, on 27 August Kornilov ordered troops to march on the capital. What began as support for the Provisional Government suddenly became a counter-revolution.[27]

The Bolsheviks now rallied to support the centrist government. The Petrograd Soviet set up a special committee made up of Menshevik, Socialist Revolutionary, and Bolshevik representatives. With impressive efficiency they organised the defence of the city, arming factory and railroad workers and deploying local garrisons as well as sailors from the nearby naval base at Kronstadt. But in the end no fighting took place. As soon as it became clear that the Bolsheviks were defending the Provisional Government, the advancing soldiers joined the people; on 1 September Kornilov and other officers were imprisoned.

Kerensky's position, however, was even weaker than before the crisis. The right, dominated by the Kadet faction, had sympathised with Kornilov's conviction that only a stronger, more dictatorial government could control the military and address the country's economic difficulties. The left was less inclined to cooperate with a leader they saw as feeble and indecisive, and the Bolsheviks capitalised on popular response, winning support in hundreds of local and regional soviets throughout Russia. After forcing the resignation of his cabinet, Kerensky put in place a frail 'directory' of five men: He was the chief director as head of state aided by directors for foreign affairs, war, the navy, and posts and telegraphs.

The result of the Kornilov affair was an unstable situation that Lenin would term 'dual power', with the Provisional Government and the soviets (especially the Petrograd Soviet) competing for legitimacy, the former a government in name with more or less legal authority, the latter with more actual control by virtue of political as well as popular support.[28]

News from the front did not bolster the failing government either: At the end of August, under heavy bombardment, the Russian navy had abandoned the port of Riga; the city itself fell soon after and the Germans prepared to push on towards Petrograd. After Kornilov's failure, the Russian desertion rate dramatically increased as tens of thousands of disillusioned peasants left their military units and returned to their villages to help with the harvest. Throughout the country there was growing scepticism on all sides – among politicians and ordinary people as well as disheartened soldiers – that the war could be won, that the front lines could be held, that there was any point at all in Russians continuing to fight.[29]

On 16 August, at the height of the Kornilov affair, James had finally responded to Gregory's telegram. As if he had been invited to a garden party, a week after he had received the first message from his brother in nearly two years, James wrote that he would be happy to return if there were a possibility he could serve Russia and asked Gregory to wire 'definite details' immediately. But Gregory had no definite details, and there is no evidence that he answered this telegram or that James ever seriously considered following the example of Sol Levitas and returning to Russia to join his brother in working for the revolutionary cause.[30]

Gregory no longer even had an office in the Marble Palace. As of the cabinet's resignation at the end of August, Skobelev was no longer a government minister and he and his personal secretary moved into a converted classroom at the Smolny Institute, where as vice-chair of the Executive Committee of the Petrograd Soviet Skobelev now concentrated his attention. In acknowledgement of Bolshevist support in resisting Kornilov, the Provisional Government released Trotsky and other Marxist leaders on 4 September, but throughout the autumn social unrest escalated. Encouraged by Marxist rhetoric, workers struck in unprecedented numbers and took over factories, while peasants turned on estate owners, destroying property and claiming land for themselves. Politicians from all parties were beginning to feel that only a socialist government which took into account the soviets would have any legitimacy and control. Coalition and compromise were discussed not only in the corridors and staterooms of the Marble Palace but in the large ballroom and former classrooms of the Smolny Institute, where Gregory, in support of the Executive Committee, prepared for the Democratic Conference scheduled for mid-September in Petrograd's Alexandrinsky Theatre. This large meeting of representatives from soviets throughout the country was called to decide the nature of Russia's government; its delegates would vote to replace the Provisional Government with a permanent government whose composition and character would reflect and be determined by a democratic process.

Personal life was subordinated to critical public concerns, and Gregory was likely unprepared to receive a second letter from Sonya in early September.

Although she had not received a response to her July letter, she was apparently intent on proving that she was indeed a kindred soul. She confessed that she was unable to concentrate on her law lectures because everything she experienced was coloured by him and quivered 'in the rays of light' emanating from him. She then waxed florid about the autumn sun, which spoke to her 'of love, of a caress, a kind glance that warms the heart, a soft whisper penetrating a sleepy consciousness, awakening and bringing it to life again'. She was desperate to see and talk with him, but evidently accepted their separation; it seemed painfully cruel, but she knew 'this is the way it will be forever, my whole life'. She called him her 'darling, kind, young friend' and insisted in closing that he was always in her thoughts. Sonya's letter is at once sweet and affectionate, tender and sad. Gregory was certainly also capable of great affection and sadness, but the autumn of 1917 left him little time for private feelings, little energy for matters beyond revolutionary business. He attended unruly meetings of the Executive Committee and ate when he could with the hungry soldiers and workers who crowded the Smolny Institute's refectory, but he probably did not answer Sonya's letter.[31]

Gregory did not have much time either for Fera, who had arrived in Petrograd at the end of the summer. She had managed to transfer her two years of study in Kiev to a university in the capital and wanted to specialise in bacteriology, but her months in the city did not make her 'ecstatic'. Food shortages and sporadic violence made academic progress difficult, and she could offer little companionship to her brother, who was seldom available. For his part, while he admired his sister's sense of adventure, her intelligence and academic purpose, he no longer needed nursing and could not give her the attention she must have wanted. Fera struggled as long as she could, but there wasn't even distilled water for experiments in the unheated laboratories and, when the cold weather swept in from the north, the students had to work in their overcoats, making precise scientific work almost impossible. Before the end of the academic year, Fera would not only leave Petrograd, she would be forced to give up her university education entirely.[32]

While Fera settled into her new surroundings, Gregory continued to be an informal ambassador for the Provisional Government. The Democratic Conference offered an opportunity for networking on a grand scale. During four days of heated debate, he shared a loge box with Alexandra Kropotkin (daughter of the anarchist Prince Pyotr Kropotkin), Alexander Zarudny (until two weeks earlier minister of justice), and Vladimir Bekhterev himself. During the conference Kropotkin introduced Gregory to Major Raymond Robins, a representative of the American government and the Red Cross. Robins had recently arrived from Vladivostok with medical supplies and a group of 40 Americans, including doctors prepared to help in the Petrograd's overcrowded and under-provisioned hospitals. From the theatre box over the next four days Gregory listened as resolutions were proposed and passed and amended and defeated. At its conclusion, the Democratic Conference elected a 'pre-parliamentary' council but failed to define Russia's future government. The result was political crisis.[33]

Kerensky immediately called upon the elected council for advice and again reformed his cabinet on the basis of partisan compromise, giving posts to moderate Socialist Revolutionaries and conservative Kadets but excluding the Bolshevik left, creating a government that was still 'provisional', dependent for its authority on a new constituent assembly, scheduled to convene in early November. Real power continued to rest with the soviets.

By the end of September 1917 Gregory realised that the revolution for which he had worked so hard and hoped so much was turning into something else entirely. Strikes and protests continued in Petrograd's streets, on the nation's railways, and in the Baku oil fields, while the German navy attacked Russian ships near Riga, then pushed on towards the Gulf of Finland. In the wake of the Democratic Conference, the Executive Committee deliberated Russia's future. Skobelev, now a pre-parliamentary councillor as well as a member of the Executive Committee, was elected to represent the soviets at an Allied military conference planned for Paris in late October, and Gregory began to prepare for their trip, but exactly what they would be explaining on Russia's behalf was unclear. On 8 October Trotsky was elected chair of the Executive Committee. Still in Finland, Lenin called for an armed revolt in articles in *Pravda* and in daily letters addressed directly to the Petrograd Soviet. Under its direction Bolsheviks who had come to Kerensky's aid during the Kornilov affair organised a Military Revolutionary Committee. Intellectuals were disheartened. The months of revolution had aged Gorky: His gaze, which to Gregory had always seemed 'frank and level', was now shadowed by physical and moral pain, while his bearing, though still straight, suggested a concentrated sadness. No longer voluble, he seemed to be trying to master constant worry. In mid-October, in a corridor of the Mariinsky Palace, where the pre-parliamentary council met, Gregory saw Andreyev for the last time. Although he occasionally spoke to fellow Kadets, he was walking alone, 'wearing a black shirt, as if in mourning'. Coalition, compromise, moderation, even peace began to seem impossibly idealistic goals.[34]

Notes

1 BIO.
2 Rappaport, 18; GZ, NYPSB, 21 December 1941, 735.
3 BIO; university form, 16 May 1916.
4 Kerensky quoted, Abraham, 112, 113.
5 BIO; GZ to Frederick van Beuren, 10 June 1931, ASCCU.
6 Kerensky quoted, Abraham, 122.
7 Abraham, 126, 127; GZ to HES, 8 September 1941.
8 GZ, 'Behind the Screen', 916.
9 Abraham, 132–133.
10 GZ, POOE, 7–8.
11 GZ, 'Against Kerensky', np.
12 GZ, POOE, 100.
13 Letter from Executive Committee; BIO; Chautauqua pamphlet, c. 1920.
14 Email from Gloria Levitas, 14 October 2013.

15 GZ, POOE, 100.
16 Invitation, Tbilisi Soviet of Workers' Deputies to GZ, 21 April 1917; MZ to JZ and EZ, 10 April 1917; FZ to JZ, 30 June 1917.
17 Minutes, Moscow meeting.
18 FZ to JZ, 30 June 1917.
19 GZ to JZ, 14 December 1918; Russell, 37–38.
20 Pass from Prince Lvov, 27 June 1917; travel attestation, 1 July 1917; BIO.
21 GZ to JZ, 4 July 1922; GZ, POOE, 74, 75, 149.
22 GZ, 'Behind the Screen', 920.
23 Rappaport, 234–237; GZ to JZ, 18 December 1918.
24 'O.S.' to GZ, 23 July 1917.
25 Email from Gloria Levitas, 14 October 2013.
26 Telegram, GZ to JZ, received in New York 17 August 1917, passed by censor 22 August 1917.
27 Figes, 442–453.
28 Lenin, *Pravda*, 9 April 1917: www.marxists.org/archive/lenin/works/1917/apr/09.htm
29 Figes, 454–455.
30 Telegram, JZ to GZ, 29 August 1917 (16 August 1917 OS).
31 'O.S.' to GZ, 6 September 1917.
32 FZ, Irvine interview.
33 GZ to JZ, 14 December 1918; Abraham, 292–294; Figes, 466–467.
34 BIO; GZ, 'Maxim Gorky', np, 'Leonid Andrieyev', 489.

Chapter 5

Escape

1917–1919

Gregory rushed between palace corridors and meeting rooms, made phone calls to offices from one end of the capital to the other, ran errands, scribbled notes, took messages, and tried to respond to questions, both practical and philosophical, whose answers in these troubled times he didn't know. He observed the frustration of disturbed politicians, the distress of intellectuals, the resentment of hungry men and women protesting on the city's wide boulevards and along the canals. In the Smolny Institute and the Mariinsky Palace he listened to diatribes and tirades, impassioned speeches and heated arguments; he was privileged to confidences, overheard private conversations and whispers.

In early October, likely under the cover of darkness, Lenin returned to Petrograd. Kerensky had ordered his arrest, but he was finally back in the capital, a lurking presence who snuck in and out of private homes for secret meetings and through a side door into the Smolny Institute. At least once Gregory saw him enter, his bare head bowed and his shabby clothes dirty. The Bolshevik leader didn't notice anyone watching in the dim light; without glancing around, he descended directly to the basement. While Trotsky made a speech that lasted into the small hours, Gregory marvelled in horror at the power Lenin wielded even when 'invisible'.[1]

As the Bolsheviks veered towards armed revolt, Gregory could not have been aware of the sequence of events that history has managed to put into chronological perspective. His loyalties, such as they were, belonged to the hopes and ideals of the first moments of Kerensky's leadership back in the early spring, but he wasn't naïve either then or now. By the autumn of 1917 Gregory was a sophisticated opponent of the Bolsheviks. He felt Kerensky and Lenin were correct in their rejection of 'the formulas of the Russian bourgeoisie' and 'the aspirations of European capitalism', and he recognised that the Provisional Government's fatal weakness was its inability to compromise with either the Kadets or the Bolsheviks, both of whom accepted that a revolution required force and violence. When the Military Revolutionary Committee ordered its armed volunteers – the Red Guard – to occupy railway stations, the telephone exchange and state bank, Gregory understood that the Bolsheviks represented 'the real spirit of national and revolutionary unity', yet he was powerless to do much but look on.[2]

DOI: 10.4324/9781003190936-5

With the Red Guard on the move, Kerensky ordered the arrest of all members of the Military Revolutionary Committee, closed down the Bolshevik presses, and cut the phone lines to the Smolny Institute. He also sent government soldiers to the Kshesinsky Palace, which Lenin's supporters now occupied, then borrowed a car and drove south out of Petrograd towards the army's general headquarters to rally the troops he needed.

On the evening of 24 October Gregory and Skobelev left the Smolny Institute, where Trotsky was loudly addressing the Executive Committee, deriding Kerensky for his refusal to set up a dictatorship, and made their way in freezing rain to the Winter Palace. This night would mark for Gregory the passing of the old order and the beginning of a new one he already detested, and he was at once stunned and conscious of the historical moment. Streetcars were erratic, and he and Skobelev likely made their way on foot over a distance that would normally have taken a little over an hour, but barricades had been set up and groups of men with machine guns crouched around small bonfires on the large boulevards. Skirting the Tauride Gardens and following the riverbank, the two men would have passed milling crowds, heard shots and sirens before they finally arrived, probably a little after 8:00 pm.[3]

Notified that the Bolsheviks intended to take over, the members of the pre-parliamentary council had sought refuge in the Winter Palace. Essentially under house arrest, the representatives of the Provisional Government deliberated into the night how they might defend themselves and the Russia they believed in, vacillating, trying to think up and put in place a final plan. Cossacks stood guard while soldiers still ostensibly faithful to Kerensky walked about in the entry hall and lounged in the corridors. Even from the Malachite Hall upstairs, where Skobelev rejoined the other councillors, Gregory could hear sirens and everyone repeated rumours.

Just before 10:00 pm the crew of the *Aurora*, a cruiser anchored near the Nikolaevsky Bridge, fired a blank round, a signal for the Red Army to attack. Possibly an hour later, maybe less, two sailors from the ship arrived at the palace and insisted on seeing Kerensky. Sent downstairs to deal with them, Gregory was still capable of being polite, of choosing his words carefully; he would remember that he said, 'Perhaps I can help you, comrades. Kerensky is at the headquarters of the General Staff.' To his surprise he found the sailors were resolved to support the Provisional Government, but nothing was predictable that night. Gregory must have been aware before leaving the Smolny Institute that Lenin's plans were no longer on schedule. At the Winter Palace he was privy to the representatives' inconclusive deliberations, and partial reports, hearsay, and private messages passed over the barricades outside; he probably guessed that discussions were also occurring among those deserting Kerensky, between the Kadets and the British Ambassador, Sir Georges Buchanan, whose concern was invariably Russian support for the Allies.[4]

Sometime after 2:00 am Bolshevik soldiers arrived to arrest the councillors, and Gregory watched as they were led away over the Neva to the Peter and Paul

Fortress. At some point he, too, was briefly arrested, perhaps with the council members, but at 4:00 am Gregory was still in the Winter Palace, still awake, watching in despair as a mob stormed in, pulled down the wall-hangings he had helped to cover eight months earlier, smashed crockery and chandeliers, looted whatever remained of the tsar's richly stocked wine cellars, pillaged the books in the library.[5]

Early on 25 October, with the Petrograd Soviet and the Bolsheviks in control of the capital, Gregory must have left the Winter Palace alone for his rented rooms, where at last he slept. By the time he woke, a new government was in place, and it would be impossible regain his bearings in a city ironically at once so changed and so much the same. Despite the looting, the barricades, the sirens and shots in the night, the coup had occurred with astonishing speed and very little bloodshed. The Petrograd Soviet and the entire soviet structure were firmly in place as democratic governing bodies. There would be transformations – the Executive Committee would soon be replaced by the Council of People's Commissars; Lenin no longer snuck around in dirty clothes – but the Smolny Institute continued to be filled with vociferous politicians and the streetcars resumed their daily routes. Almost all Gregory's Russian friends in the capital were either in prison or in danger of being arrested or re-arrested. His foreign acquaintances were, as they always had been, more worried finally about Russia's continued commitment to the war than about how left or right or dictatorial or democratic the government was.

October's last few days belonged to the Bolsheviks. There were rumours of Kerensky's imminent return with an army, but neither he nor an army appeared. At the Smolny Institute Lenin addressed the Executive Committee, but Gregory would probably not have been there to see him. Throughout the city small groups of soldiers and sailors, like those who had declared their loyalty to Gregory, offered pockets of resistance: Army cadets briefly took over the telephone exchange before being arrested, while Red Guards rounded up boys in military uniforms and shot them on their academy grounds and along the Moika Canal.[6]

Such scenes of brutality and barely organised violence, like the plundering of the Winter Palace, would have reminded Gregory of the pogroms of his youth: disordered law enforcement, uncontrolled cruelty, roaming groups of thugs and robbers. Already hungry people grew hungrier amid reports that the Germans were preparing to attack the capital from the west. The Bolsheviks could do little immediately to address possible starvation or the threat of invasion, but Lenin quickly had declared an end to the freedoms so important to Kerensky and his followers: The days of free speech and freedom of the press were over. News from elsewhere in Russia wasn't heartening: In Moscow it took ten days for the Bolsheviks to take over, and there was a great deal more violence; thousands were reported dead in Moscow's streets as the winter's first snow began to fall. Fearful, unsure, disheartened – like foreign nationals in both cities – Gregory now packed the few possessions he owned, left the rooms he shared with Fera, and set off with his sister on the long journey home.

He was exhausted. Sleepless nights and political upheaval had taken their toll on his body and his spirit. By the time he left Petrograd for the last time, he was physically and emotionally depleted and suffering from 'moral depression'. Malnourishment had drained his energy and weakened his teeth, but there was little he could do about either in Kiev. His mother's chicken soup likely helped, but accepting soup and living once again under his parents' roof would embarrass and frustrate him.[7]

Family dynamics remained the same as during Gregory's childhood despite the changes brought by the revolution. Fera put aside her hopes for a university diploma in science and, like Basia, found work in an office. The idea of leaving Russia weighed on everyone's mind, but such a prospect required money, and daily needs in these difficult times took priority over saving up for future possibilities. Moses had taken on more responsibility at work, but Anna was hard pressed to keep food on the table; there were days when no one could leave the apartment because of intense fighting in the streets. Food was an even bigger challenge now that Gregory and Fera were back at home, for there was also an additional mouth to feed. Not only soldiers but refugees from the north flooded Kiev as revolutionary factions clashed in Petrograd and Moscow. People in apartments with three or four rooms were required to take in soldiers or other transients. To avoid accommodating often boisterous strangers, the family now offered one of their rooms to Sol Levitas.[8]

The months that followed the Bolshevik takeover did not allow Gregory to recover from his experiences at the centre of the revolution. He had fled the capital for numerous reasons. He was most immediately afraid of being arrested and imprisoned – and understandably worried about what might happen to him in either case. Petrograd had offered him an education and an opportunity to work for ideals he still believed in, to participate in a historical moment in a grand way. He had continued as Skobelev's secretary during the weeks of pre-parliamentary meetings even as the older man's differences with Trotsky had become pronounced and his position in the Petrograd Soviet tenuous, but with Lenin's rise to power, Gregory had lost his job and become an enemy of the Bolsheviks by association as well as on principle.

Gregory's immediate concern was to find work and keep a low profile. He could have sought employment as a qualified lawyer or doctor, but both options would have placed him in visible and vulnerable public positions. Law would have put him on a collision course with the Bolsheviks, while medicine would have kept him so busy that he would have had little time to work against them.

Kiev posed special challenges as the seat of Ukrainian separatism, and after the October Revolution the Ukraine's large Jewish population would be subject to intense persecution. Theoretically Marxism was against anti-Semitism, but it was also against any expression of religious belief. Under the new government, synagogues as well as churches would be suppressed, and religious Jews identifiably different in physical appearance, dress, diet, or behaviour continued to be targeted. Gregory was an assimilated Jew, but his parents were not. Ukrainian separatists perceived the Jews as Bolsheviks and the Bolsheviks – in their encouragement of assimilation – as Jews. The Red Army now fought fierce battles with the nationalists; generally unsophisticated Marxists, Bolshevik soldiers saw Jews as the bourgeoisie, fair game for attacks, reprisals, and organised military pogroms that would result in the murder of thousands of Ukrainian Jews.

Shortly after Gregory's return to Kiev the troops that Kerensky had sought in vain to mobilise in support of the Socialist Revolutionaries rallied behind Kornilov, who had escaped from prison in early November. Cossacks loyal to the Provisional Government as well as former officers from the Imperial Army joined forces with Kornilov to organise a volunteer force, denominated the White Army, to fight the Bolsheviks. The result was a civil war in which various factions, including the Ukrainian nationalists, battled the Red Army in a struggle to determine Russia's future.

In November 1917 Gregory found himself at loose ends in a city no less tense than Petrograd with violence approaching literally from all sides. For the new government, disengaging from the war that had drained Russia's resources and devastated the morale of its citizens was a strategic priority: Peace with the Central Powers would garner popular support, but more importantly Lenin needed Russian troops deployed on the Eastern Front for battles on their own soil. With the capital threatened, the Bolshevik government began negotiations at Brest-Litovsk. The Soviets declared a ceasefire on the Eastern Front in December, then launched military offensives against Ukrainian separatists. Gregory now turned his attention once more to drama and journalism. Performances in Kiev theatres were inevitably coded commentaries on Russia's power struggles, while local newspapers would pay him for drama reviews and articles on the political situation convulsing the country. Words would for a while boost his spirits and keep him relatively safe while allowing him to earn a meagre living in ways coherent with his principles and ideas.[9]

Neither Skobelev nor Gregory would represent Russia at the Allied Conference that, like so much else Kerensky's supporters had planned and hoped for, never came into being. As most foreign nationals left the capital, many Russians sympathetic to the Provisional Government fled south to or at least through Kiev before heading to wherever in Russia their homes happened to be. Andreyev retreated to his country house on the Finnish border. Despite his political objections to the Bolsheviks and several weeks in prison, Sorokin, who had been Kerensky's personal secretary, managed to stay on for a while as a professor of sociology at the University of Petrograd, but on his release from prison, probably passed through Kiev on his way home to Baku. Marc Slonim, a dedicated Socialist Revolutionary, served briefly in the Soviet government as an elected deputy from the Bessarabian region near his native Odessa, but by the end of January he had joined Gregory in Kiev as a fellow journalist. Gregory tried to maintain contact with people he had met in Petrograd. Until they, too, fled, he corresponded with the Belgian diplomats Destrée and Dupierreux, but post was erratic and letters sent to and from Russia during this chaotic period often did not reach their destinations.[10]

Gregory characteristically wasted no time in becoming an active participant in the familiar community in which he found himself. He joined the Kiev Artistic Club, and by 20 January 1918 was a member of the editorial staff of the Kiev newspaper *The Call*. By 28 May 1918 he was a regular contributor to another local paper, *The Russian Voice*. On 2 June 1918 he was a delegate from *Theatrical* to the All-Ukrainian Congress of Press Workers. On 17 July 1918 he was asked to substitute for the editor of *The People's Cause*. He attended the opera and the theatre, reviewed the productions he saw, and again took on the complex responsibilities of producing and directing plays not only in Kiev but in other Ukrainian cities, including Kharkov and Odessa.[11]

Gregory and a friend in a soldier's uniform, Kiev, 1918

Amid his subversive journalism, political reports, and historical, philosophical, and psychological analysis of current events and plays, Gregory began to be seriously interested in morality, in ethics, in religious issues broadly understood, in what would or could or should be the right thing to do. He was still devoted to the revolution and understood it had offered him 'a marvelous education', but his experiences in Kiev in 1918 made him feel that 'a very tender and beautiful tie had been broken' between himself and 'the masses'. Instead, he saw in the Bolsheviks and their supporters 'the spirit of war rampant'. It seemed soldiers and workers were no longer thinking of a new social order; he felt they weren't looking for comrades and friends, saw only enemies and sought revenge.[12]

Gregory struggled both intellectually and emotionally to come to terms with the instability that surrounded him. The Soviet government announced on 24 January 1918 that there would be no first of February that year; 31 January would be followed by 14 February as Russia moved from the Gregorian to the Julian calendar. Three days later, the Central Powers broke off peace negotiations with the Soviets while signing a military treaty with the Ukrainian People's Republic, which was participating in the talks as an independent nation. Under attack from the Red Army, the Ukrainian government moved its seat from Kiev to Zhytomyr, 90 miles to the west. As the Bolsheviks struggled to take Kiev, the Germans launched a new offensive along the entire Eastern Front and advanced rapidly, capturing Dvinsk on the first day and Narva by the end of the month, both strategic cities Gregory knew from his visits on behalf on the Provisional Government. After a week, using Russian trains on Russian railway lines, the Germans were within 100 miles of Petrograd and Lenin transferred Russia's capital to Moscow. On 2 March, the Germans took Kiev. The next day, despite divisions among the Bolsheviks, Lenin persuaded the Soviet government to accept the terms proposed by the Central Powers, which now included recognising the independence of the new Ukrainian state.

Eager to exploit its resources in order to bolster its position on the Western Front, Germany had offered the Ukrainians military support against the Soviets in exchange for recognition of its independence; the result was a period of German occupation. In April 1918, the Germans arrested the Ukrainian prime minister and disbanded the new government, essentially making Ukraine a protectorate as part of its plan to create a series of puppet states to serve as geographical buffers between Germany and Russia. By the end of April the Ukrainian government was once again in Kiev, but conservative Ukrainians were put into positions of power while Ukrainian activists were driven underground and into the countryside. There was much to disturb Gregory and his Socialist Revolutionary colleagues in the cities, towns, and villages throughout the expanse of the Ukraine. When the puppet government attempted to restore land nationalised by the Bolsheviks, it provoked peasant uprisings and terrorist attacks. On 30 July the German military governor Hermann von Eichhorn was killed by a bomb on a street in central Kiev.

Gregory would read the details of the Treaty of Brest-Litovsk in the newspapers, but he would experience first-hand the violence of Russia's civil war. From his parents' apartment windows he saw clashes between Bolshevik and Ukrainian soldiers as well as fighting that followed two months later between the Red Army and the invading Germans. The city was the site of physical conflict as well as ideological tension, and although no longer anyone's secretary but his own, he found himself at the centre of the Ukraine's complicated battle for freedom and autonomy.

The civil war and struggles for independence in regions beyond Kiev would take their toll on the whole country as Russia moved towards a unified Soviet state. South of Rostov in mid-April Kornilov was killed in a battle between his White Army and Bolshevik forces at Ekaterinodar near the eastern coast of the Black Sea. Gregory could only have understood his death as a blow for a socialist Russia, although his feelings were mixed: Many of the White Army's supporters were remnants of the imperial past or mavericks unsympathetic to Socialist Revolutionary ideals, so while they were anti-Bolshevik, they were also fiercely nationalistic and anti-Semitic. He was repelled but not surprised to hear in mid-July that the tsar had been executed at Yekaterinburg, and probably doubted the Bolsheviks' public assurances that the rest of the Romanov family had been sent to 'a secure place'.[13]

When the editor of *The People's Cause* returned, Gregory decided to take some time off of his own. Typically, this would be a working holiday. Ukraine's treaty with the Central Powers had opened a western corridor for travel over lands that had been battlefields until the spring. Perhaps under the auspices of contracted articles and certainly out of his commitment to continuing revolutionary activity, Gregory set off for Vienna. En route he would see for himself fought-over Galician territory, but his main purpose seems to have been to maintain connections with revolutionary contemporaries.

As the train passed through the western Ukraine in late August, he saw for the first time the ravages of war on the countryside. The destruction and carnage he had witnessed in Petrograd and Kiev had not prepared him for desolate vistas where aged peasants gathered the scanty harvest. In the fields were great holes made by Russian and Austrian shells, while in the towns and villages not a house stood intact. He passed through settlements reduced to piles of bricks, to broken walls beside an occasional chimney; wire entanglements and trenches ran across the low hills where instead of armies of men, Gregory saw 'armies of crosses'.[14]

In the late afternoon the train arrived at Pidvolochysk on the Austrian-Galician frontier. Historically a town through which goods and travellers passed from one empire to the other, Pidvolochysk had traditionally outfitted Russians for the West. Often arriving in boots and heavy shirts belted outside baggy trousers, they could leave in a contemporary European suit and tie. The once-thriving commercial centre was a shell of its former self: Gregory saw no brick warehouses or upscale shops or anyone engaging in the once common under-the-counter exchange of tobacco and vodka for woven goods and pottery. Walking through the town on a street paved with Jewish gravestones, he was unable to find a single undamaged house and read on the remaining walls Russian inscriptions written in charcoal: ' "The second battery, dirty Austrians" ' and ' "The 21st battery kill Jews." ' In the twilight he followed the sound of children's singing to the edge of the town where the fields began and there he saw ditches of foul water, large pieces of metal, skeletons of horses, and human bones.

The solitary hours on the train enabled him to analyse his psychological state. He felt melancholy, depressed, and far more fearful than he had been under fire at Dvinsk, afraid not of physical violence but of 'the shadows' of his own 'exhausted brain and nerves'. Despite his philosophic commitment to revolutionary ideals, he now began to ask himself difficult ethical questions about the nature of conflict and the future of humanity, the value of work, and the psychic impact of war. Faced with so much destruction, he wondered if it were only the material products of human labour that were burned and shattered and buried and realised it was impossible to emerge from the experience without 'moral or spiritual loss'. He concluded that brutalisation was inevitable: 'he who has engaged himself to the work of killing, if only for a little time, must lose his reverence for human life. He must lose his consciousness of the value of seeing eyes, beating hearts, speaking lips.' Reverence for life was at the core of Gregory's commitment to medicine, while beyond deposing the tsar, the revolutionary struggle for a just society seemed to have provoked, like the ongoing World War and the Russian civil war, only destruction. Gregory spent the night alone in the Pidvolochysk station, pondering what he had seen and waiting for the train that would take him for the first time beyond Russia's borders.[15]

He arrived in Vienna in early September and would spend the next three weeks in the Austrian-Hungarian and German Empires during their final moments. As in Russia at the time of the February revolution, political turmoil, food shortages, labour strikes, and general unrest were in the process of bringing about the downfall of monarchies weakened by war. Both empires were facing many of the same challenges as post-revolutionary Russia, primary among them the desire for independence of the various ethnic minorities once held together under imperial rule. Czechs, Slovaks, Yugoslavs, Italians, Serbs, Croats, Bosnians, Ukrainians, Romanians, Hungarians, and Poles wanted autonomy as separate nation states. Their representatives in the Viennese Reichsrat that September argued heatedly for recognition and debated both inside and outside the chamber the forms of government autonomous states might choose. As in Russia, the liberal and leftist parties considered themselves internationalist rather than nationalist, while many of the politicians saw themselves as revolutionary and spoke with Gregory as one of their own. Each day during his visit he attended sessions of the Reichsrat, listening from the balcony to impassioned socialist speeches. The Polish Social Democrat Ignatz Dashinsky's words seemed to Gregory 'a strange combination of terrible despair and undying hope', while the Czechoslovak Agrarian Frantisek Stanek told him that the world importance of empires composed of different nations was over. Gregory must have felt as if he were back in the Duma in Kerensky's early days, but he was now a seasoned revolutionary, had witnessed the demise of experienced statesmen with hopes no less passionate or admirable than those of the leaders he now met. He would later decide that, although the politicians in Vienna might not have recognised it, the most pressing question was how to reconcile democracy with 'the desperate reaction of nationalism'. Gregory realised that at a certain moment 'nationalism passes its climax of community solidarity and enters a stage of chauvinism' he understood as 'the egotism of a community asserting itself'. He equated this egoism to pernicious 'personal or family egotism on an enormous scale', an assertion that reveals his psychological understanding of his own family's dynamics as well as his astute sociological understanding of the aftermath of revolution.[16]

From Vienna Gregory travelled north as far as Berlin, where he was astonished that politicians were still hopeful about the war's outcome despite the intense suffering of the people. He was forced to accept the ironic contradictions of his journey as he headed south and then east into Hungary. He had witnessed 'the ravages of the war in the very heart of the Central Powers', but when he now saw exhausted soldiers returning from the Italian front, 'weak, hungry, pale, and ill, walking shadows of human beings', he realised the Allies were going to win. Rationally he felt glad because he saw an Allied victory as the lesser of two evils, but he also felt a deep sorrow and above all a terrible and terrifying apprehension for the people. On his arrival in Budapest, he saw 'on the shores of the beautiful Danube some four or five hundred Magyar and Croatian soldiers lying in the hot sun, eating with avidity rotten watermelons that had been thrown away as unfit for food'. Asking himself what made them willing to suffer 'hunger, misery, illness, unspeakable wretchedness, and still continue to fight', he could only conclude that they fought because they were not individuals but a mob who attributed to the physical enemy 'the terrible frustration of their spiritual life'.[17]

Yet in Budapest, as in Vienna and Berlin, Gregory found the national mood as hopeful and enthusiastic as in Petrograd and Moscow under Kerensky. In a coffee house in the Hungarian capital he met a hussar colonel who told him he had nothing against the Russian people but only against the tsar; together they discussed Dostoevsky and Tolstoy, yet Gregory was finally repelled by the soldier's glorification of fighting and killing. The trip had given Gregory vivid impressions of the panoply of war in the countryside and in three sophisticated European cities, but his contacts with statesmen and intellectuals had not managed to justify the conflict or to give him confidence in the future. On one of his last days before heading home he walked alone along the Danube, past Budapest's elegant Elisabeth Bridge, then wandered for several hours among the ruins of a sixteenth-century fortress. He felt in need of regeneration.[18]

Gregory with a Hungarian soldier in Budapest near the Elisabeth Bridge, 26 September 1918

Kiev in the autumn of 1918 offered little to affirm its beleaguered population psychologically or spiritually, and for Gregory personally Russia was becoming increasingly dangerous. His writing was provocative and seditious, and he would remember even years later the risks he took and his awareness of his own vulnerability as he stood with his friend Slonim one dark night on 'a much-bombarded street in Kiev'. They had just 'put to bed' the final issue of 'a paper that made the Germans angry and the Communists more angry and the Ukrainian separatists most impatient'. After his late summer trip, he was discouraged and depressed. It seemed to him that the revolution he had worked for had given way to a period of terror whose end he could not imagine. As the days grew cooler and leaves began to fall in the city's parks, Gregory must have begun to feel that he was living on borrowed time.[19]

There are two stories about Gregory's departure from Kiev, both told to me by my mother, who must have heard them from my father. In the first, my father and two friends were transporting a printing press down a Kiev street. Perhaps one was Slonim, but Slonim nowhere tells this story. There was a sudden gunshot and one of them (not my father, not Slonim) fell dead on the sidewalk. I have wondered how my father would have instantly known that the man was dead. Perhaps he was shot in the head. Perhaps the bullet went straight through his heart. Gregory immediately ran home to 32 Kostiantynivska, gathered a few things and some money, and left his parents' apartment, Kiev, and Russia without looking back.

In the second story the family was at home but Gregory was at work. A boy came to the apartment and informed Anna that men were coming in the morning to arrest him. As soon as Gregory returned, he realised that he would need to leave his family, the city, and the country. He took a few belongings and a few roubles and left immediately.

Both stories have a variant: My father was afraid that he might be recognised, so he decided to wear a disguise. Since the age of 14 he had sported a distinguished moustache. For the first and only time in his life, he shaved it off. He had no dress-up clothes in the apartment – my mother must have told me this story when I was quite young, perhaps to point out how fortunate I was to have dress-up clothes or to illustrate how deprived my father had been in Russia – but he did have an idea: My father quickly went to the local hospital, where he was known because he was a doctor, and dressed up as a female nurse. It has always been hard for me to imagine my father as a woman, but given his love of the theatre, his ability to mesmerise an audience, it is certainly possible he at least considered leaving Kiev disguised as a nurse.

Both stories also have an epilogue: The next morning, soldiers came to the door of my grandparents' home to arrest my father. Informed that he wasn't there, the men entered the apartment and insisted on arresting Sol Levitas. The family protested that Sol wasn't Gregory, they were arresting the wrong man, but the soldiers wouldn't listen. Sol went to prison in Gregory's place and the following day was taken into a courtyard to face a firing squad. Just as the men were cocking their rifles, one of them shouted, 'Wait a minute! That man isn't Gregory Zilboorg! I know Gregory Zilboorg and that man isn't he!' (My mother was always a very strict grammarian, so this Russian soldier said grammatically, 'that man isn't he' rather than 'that's not him', in retrospect a much more likely equivalent of what a Russian soldier in a firing squad might say). Sol Levitas was released.

I have often thought that there must be another epilogue. Surely Sol must have been relieved; the story must have ended with the family's joy when he returned to the apartment. Perhaps Sol was angry, having almost been killed in Gregory's place. And wasn't the proper conclusion to the story Gregory's enduring gratitude to Sol for having almost died, for having – however unwillingly – provided him with a cover that likely allowed him to escape? But I never heard this story from Sol or Fera, nor did my father tell it to me in any version nor did he ever seem particularly grateful to Sol.

I know of no other versions of Gregory's departure from Kiev, no comments on his decision to leave, no letter or document that substantiates the stories my mother recounted or offers evidence to the contrary. Something certainly propelled him to leave Russia, and despite the occasions when in frustration he told James that emigrating might be in his future, Gregory loved Russia; he had expended a great deal of time and energy thinking about ways to change it; he had spent nearly two years as an active revolutionary both as Skobelev's secretary in Petrograd and as a journalist in Kiev. He would not have left easily or without deep and lasting sadness; he would not have left unless compelled.

What is certain is that, when Gregory left Russia at the end of October 1918, he took with him only what he could find quickly and carry easily. He took his two school leaving certificates and official photographs as well as all his Petrograd passes and Kiev identity cards and documents. The only personal items he took with him were three photographs – the one of the four Zilboorg children taken in 1903, the one of himself with a friend in a soldier's uniform, and the one taken in Hungary a month earlier – and the two unanswered letters from Sonya.[20]

At Kiev's central station Gregory begin to retrace the route he had taken two months earlier, but this time he had no newspaper assignment and no foreseeable income; what money he had with him he spent almost entirely on his train ticket. He had no programme except to escape, no fixed destination, no travel documents, and no resources beyond his wits.

On his arrival in Vienna, he immediately went to the Spanish embassy. As a neutral country, Spain had accepted responsibility for protecting the interests of citizens whose nations were without diplomatic representation in the Austrian-Hungarian Empire. On 6 November Gregory received from the Spanish ambassador an official passport in both French and German authorising travel in Austria, Germany, and Switzerland. He signed the document 'Grégoire Zilbourg' as if he were French, dropping his patronymic and, unlike his brother, making no gesture towards it; the man who would become Gregory Zilboorg would have no middle name. The next day Gregory was able to secure a letter from the German-Austrian State Office for Foreign Affairs, identifying him in German as 'Dr. G. Silburg', a Russian lawyer pursued by the Bolshevik regime, and stating it was impossible for him to return to Russia.[21]

Gregory's plan was now clearer: He wanted to get from Vienna to New York, but the route through counties at war with the Allies would be geographically as well as politically circuitous. The German letter permitted travel to Switzerland or Holland via Munich. Even leaving Austria, however, would be a challenge without money, while getting to the United States was another matter entirely. Gregory could not afford to spend much time in the Reichsrat – where ten days before his return to Vienna ethnic German deputies had renamed the lower house 'The Provisional National Assembly for German-Austria' – but he contacted everyone he could think of in the city, meeting not only with statesmen and officials but with journalists; drawing on his fluent French and German and functional English, Gregory would write his way out of war-ravaged Europe.

He had understood in September that the Central Powers would lose the war, but could not have imagined he would be in the Austrian capital when the armistice was signed on 11 November, the same day that Charles I of Austria abdicated, leading to the proclamation of a republic in Austria on 12 November and in Hungary four days later. What he continued to imagine for all of Europe was an ideal socialist union of republican states – 'The Imminent Realisation of Socialisation', as he entitled the article 'by a Russian Socialist' that appeared in the weekly pacifist newspaper *Der Friede* ('Peace') on 12 November 1918. Calling on whatever reserves of hope he still nourished for political transformation, he declared, 'We are most certainly standing on the threshold of a new era.' He called the Russian revolution a 'dark experience' for which he had worked and suffered, but insisted that 'the great task of democracy around the world is above all the resurrection and reinforcement of democratic forces which are at the moment half exhausted and whose intellect has been debilitated by the war.' Drawing on his own half-exhausted and debilitated energies, he wrote in German, railing against revolutionary violence while arguing passionately for democratic socialist ideals. He signed his article 'Georg Silburg'.[22]

Gregory was kept in Vienna by his need to earn enough to pay for travel elsewhere and by his desire to secure permission to go to the United States. Newspaper articles allowed him to earn his train fare, but official permission to cross the Atlantic was impossible to arrange in Vienna in the days immediately following the armistice. Gregory made contact with other journalists, among them the American Nellie Bly, resident in Vienna throughout the war, who had reported from the Russian front in 1914 and who worried, like many Americans, that central Europe would follow Russia's path to revolution and Bolshevism. On friendly terms with a number of officials, Bly did her best to get him letters of safe passage at least to Holland in the hope that from there he could get to a 'happy haven' in 'the Land of the Free', but more than that she could not do for the young Russian she addressed as 'Dr. Zilboorg'.[23]

On 20 November Gregory left for Munich where, in the Ministry of Foreign Affairs, he met with Kurt Eisner, the Bavarian revolutionary who was now the region's first republican premier. Gregory would have had a great deal in common with the elderly Jew who had been a journalist and drama critic, and he was cheered by the wise man's wonderful smile, 'his venerable gray hair, his slow and tender voice'. As Gregory walked the streets of the Bavarian capital, he felt 'all the time' as if he were back in Petrograd in March 1917. He found the 'enthusiasm for the new life ... and the hatred of the old' were 'patent in the tone and gesture of the city', but his few days in Munich were merely a pause on his journey north.[24]

He was quickly once more in transit on trains that took him through Germany. In Frankfurt the retreating soldiers told him, ' "We are a people of order. We will maintain order. The Kaiser did not succeed, therefore he is down, but we will maintain our stability without him." ' Gregory was shocked and could only conclude that they spoke with 'the voice of the wonderful militaristic German machine with its implacable negligence of personal aspirations'. Changing trains in Cologne, he again found German soldiers in the station, 'with set faces, looking as if deeply troubled by newly mobilized thoughts'. It was strange to be walking in his civilian clothes among the grey-coated and grey-capped men, and he felt he was witnessing 'the silence of a defeated nation'.[25]

But Gregory could not finally come to terms with his intense emotions merely intellectually through historical understanding. In the Cologne station, his response was more personal and elemental. He would remember,

> It was cold, it was drizzling, it was a foreign land. I was away from home, never to get back home. It was dark, pretty near a black-out.... I was on my way to what I hoped might turn out to be America. I had exactly nothing in my pocket. In my hands I had a cane which someone had left in the car of the train, and I had picked it up. Shadows of soldiers were passing by. It was about two o'clock in the morning.

Inside the station, 'in the semi-darkness', he saw 'hundreds of men in uniform'; women in white were distributing hot water that passed for soup. From time to time he heard the semi-cracked dissonance of a mandolin.

> Otherwise there was silence. Every few minutes an officer would come out and murmur figures, and people belonging to those units, apparently, would silently get up and walk out. There were no chairs in the waiting rooms. People were lying on the floors.

Stepping outside, he saw the spires of Cologne Cathedral. As his eyes became accustomed to the darkness, he could make out bunting on the parapets and houses. In the morning he could read the message: '"Willkommen unbesiegte Helden"' – 'Welcome home unconquered heroes'. The short sentences here and the starkly recorded impressions of sounds and silence, darkness and faint light reveal Gregory's psychological efforts to process the ironic incongruences of his experience. He had left home, but he hadn't yet arrived at a chosen destination. He was safe, but travelling through the wreckage of war. He was a revolutionary, but the revolution was over. He was a German-speaking Russian in what had been enemy territory and was now simply a defeated land. He hoped to get to Bly's 'happy haven', but he hadn't heard from his brother in months; he had no passport and no money and couldn't conceive of what lay ahead of him or of who he would be when he got there.[26]

On 24 November 1918 Gregory arrived in The Hague. As in Vienna, he needed to find ways of earning money and he needed to get documents that would allow him to immigrate to America. Without Dutch, which he began to study, he could less easily work as a journalist, but he could use French, and there was a Russian consulate in Rotterdam to which he certainly went soon after his arrival. Probably the first thing he did after descending from the train, however, was cross the street to a large green park, where he sat on a bench to get his bearings. He was dislocated, emotionally drained and virtually if not literally penniless, but he was at last in a country where he could stay until he had solved the problem of getting to the United States. Then one of those coincidences occurred that seem unbelievable except in fairy tales but actually do sometimes happen in real life: Gregory overheard two men speaking Russian. He got up and introduced himself, and the Russian engineers befriended him, lent him money, and put him touch with contacts who would invite him to speak and pay him for doing so. He walked up the street and checked into the Park Hotel, one of the city's best and most elegant. This would be his base for the next four months.[27]

Gregory's mood vacillated as he prepared lectures and filled out forms, went from consulate to consulate, met with officials, and explained his situation. The Russian revolution and the Bolsheviks were fascinating topics on the minds of many Europeans and Americans, who were curious about the Soviet state and apprehensive that amid the political turmoil following the war radical socialists might prevail in other countries. On 5 December 1918 he spoke for the first time in Holland, on 'La Russie et la Catastrophe Mondiale' ('Russia and the World Catastrophe'). This and subsequent lectures were widely reviewed in local papers in which he was referred to as 'Gregorius Zilbourg' ('Gregorius' being Dutch for 'Gregory'), 'Gr Silburg', and more often as 'Grégoire Zilbourg'. On 14 December, probably thanks to the kind engineers, he was invited speak on the current state of affairs in Russia to members of the Society for the Development of Industry and the prestigious Industrial Club in Amsterdam. Over the coming weeks Gregory would polish and expand 'La Russie and la Catastrophe Mondiale' and prepare a second lecture, 'Russian Literary Destinies', for presentation in French and Russian to various groups in Amsterdam, Rotterdam, The Hague, and Leiden.[28]

By mid-December, with speaking engagements on his calendar, Gregory at last felt able to write James for the first time since his abrupt departure from Kiev. Speaking, writing, and thinking mostly in French since his arrival in Holland, he chose to write his brother in French because it was natural for him and because he was apprehensive that a letter in Russian might not pass whatever censorship he presumed was still in place. He reflected on what he called the 'sad and interesting odyssey' that had followed his 'long and fierce struggle with the Bolsheviks and the Germans'. He informed James that he had finally decided to leave Europe 'for a certain period of time in America', but he needed help with formalities. Specifically, he asked James to contact authorities in Washington on his behalf, indicating that he was coming to visit his brother and then going to Vladivostok to join the anti-Bolshevik government being formed there. Gregory was probably not seriously considering returning to Russia, but he wanted to keep his options open and to persuade the authorities that he was not himself a Bolshevik. Thinking of Americans he had met in Petrograd and hoping they would remember him, he enclosed a calling card and asked James to give it to Senator Root, who he had heard was still in New York and not in Paris with President Wilson at the Peace Conference. Gregory revealed to James that he was in a kind of sad and stressful limbo: stuck in Holland without the documents he needed to go to America, but also cut off from the world he had left behind in Kiev. Because of the civil war, all communication with Russia was interrupted; he was no longer in touch with his parents and sisters, and knew they must be nervous not to have heard from him.[29]

On 17 December Gregory finally received permission to travel to the United States in a document signed by the consul general of Russia, by the American vice-consul and by the British vice-consul, but he still did not have the required documents to allow him to enter the United States or to stay there. He spent his 28th birthday and Christmas and New Year's in The Hague; by early January he was becoming desperate. He cabled James with a list of Americans he hoped would help him, among them Charles Russell, the journalist who had been a member of the Root Commission, and Major Raymond Robins, who had led the American Red Cross expedition to Russia. Gregory followed up with another letter in French. He told his brother that he was almost too sad to write and more and more nervous since he still had no passport. Although his lectures were going very well, he felt 'completely alone in desperate, horrible solitude, as in a prison which is apparently open, but which is in fact narrow, stifling, oppressive'. His sadness was different from 'the melancholy of childish weakness'; it was 'an anxious synthesis of years spent in activity and intensity'. He analysed his shattered emotions: His anxiety didn't destroy his energy, but it disturbed him more and more. Earlier he may have been a romantic solitary dreamer; now he gave himself to life with full knowledge of what he saw as its potential wickedness and cruelty.[30]

At the end of February Gregory still had no visa or passport, but he was immeasurably happy to have finally received letters in Russian from both James and Eugenia. Having realised that 'the mail' was as 'slow as a sick turtle', he responded in Russian, admitting their words made a deep impression on him. After not having heard from either of them in such a long time, the impact was especially powerful since he was 'all alone, abandoned in the small, emotionally satiated and lonely Netherlands', cut off from the home he had left four months earlier. Gregory was a passionate man with a tendency in personal communication to dramatise his situation and emotional response, but he did not exaggerate facts and what he wrote seems an accurate reflection of his feelings at the time. Despite his distress, he had not completely lost his characteristic humour and capacity for self-mockery: 'It is difficult', he wrote,

> to describe or tell you about the heaviness, the torment and unhappiness I have had to suffer because I have not abandoned the hope I will see you soon and will be able to share this with you in person. Besides, I think that you may actually receive this letter after my arrival in New York, and for that reason it would lose some of its meaning.

Gregory then explained why he wanted to go to America and what he hoped would be possible for him. He felt that there was nothing left for him in Bolshevist Russia, which he characterised as full of 'blood and bigotry, emotional decline and handwringing'. Besides, he felt that he had already given Russia everything he possibly could, 'my health, my temperament, my creative impulse'. He had been 'prepared to give even what remained of my "I"' – that is, his very self, his life – but realised that would have been useless, while his willingness to die for a new Russia was emotionally difficult for him to contemplate. America represented for him the possibility of the regeneration he craved. He had ambitious plans and imagined that 'at Harvard or the Great Columbia University' he would get to work on material he had 'in the form of documents and personal memories and experiences' from his time with the Provisional Government. He announced to James,

> Within 3–4 months I plan to publish a book about this as well as a collection of articles I wrote which were published in various journals over the past two years. In addition, I intend to make money on the side giving lectures, as I am doing here in the Netherlands.

Gregory's confidence must have astonished his brother, who had been hard put to make a living during his first years in America. James was still employed as a translator, and his English was competent only because he had been living and working in New York for over five years. Like Gregory in Russia, he had earned meagre sums giving private lessons, and only after two and a half years had he felt able to support Eugenia. James must have been appalled at Gregory's idea that in three or four months he would learn English well enough to write a book and that his memories and experiences would be sufficient to make him money 'on the side' by giving lectures. Gregory probably seemed to his brother at best a fool, a proud greenhorn who would soon learn the realities of life in the new country. At worst, James must have been resentful and felt his wild brother was lording over him his achievements and capacities. James must have found Gregory arrogant when he confided, 'Whether by a stroke of good luck or because of my youth or unusual fortitude, I have come out of social and political upheavals and personal unhappiness (particularly great) rather energetic and full of ideas.' Since arriving in Holland, he continued, 'I have managed to give about 15 lectures in various cities – rather successfully, I might add. They are always warmly received by audiences and the press alike.' Gregory reflected,

> Perhaps the reason for this productivity is the unexpected moral victory I have achieved here: You know that I am abroad for the first time and yet I am capable of giving an impromptu lecture in French or German with no difficulty – without any notes or papers – and just as easily as in Russian.

Gregory had no one other than his brother with whom he could share his satisfaction in his successes and likely thought James would be proud of him. Gregory told him that it might be surprising but he was considered in Russia 'one of the best speakers and a very good lecturer'.

Gregory was indeed a dynamic and mesmerising speaker and lecturer, but he probably realised that his description did sound like boasting and hastened to add,

> this is not important. Russia is no better for it, nor am I: It cannot truly be considered a moral accomplishment. Your name appears in large print on posters and in the papers. A sea of heads is before you.

Confessing it was nice to imagine that their old friends, who hadn't expected much of him, would be impressed, he returned to his main point: He had had nothing, had gone his own way and found himself.

The purpose of this significant letter was to prepare James for his brother's fragile emotional state. Gregory clearly did not want James to feel he would be a burden, so he also confided his achievements and dreams, stressed his independence, his capacity to function in languages other than Russian, his ability to earn money and make something of himself even when starting from nothing. Gregory finally became specific. Aware that relatives and acquaintances would be curious, he asked James and Eugenia to

> tell a lie or make up a story, but see to it that I don't see anyone ... because I am wrung out emotionally, because I am shattered by the many painful and trying things I have experienced, and I dream, as if about the impossible, about not seeing any of our so-called loved ones for several days except you, who are dearer to me than you realise. I dream about seeing you with deep emotion.

Sincere and naïve, Gregory expected a happy reunion with the brother he hadn't seen in nearly six years, had no idea he was preparing James and Eugenia for other than his high hopes and his psychological condition.

Eager as he was to leave for the United States, Gregory was making a name for himself in the Netherlands and found it difficult to refuse invitations to speak. In early March he finally received his passport and held off sending his February letter until he could confirm his date of arrival. In a postscript he explained that he could have travelled as early as the following week but felt he could not refuse a request from Destrée, now the Belgian minister of arts and sciences, and the Belgian minister of justice Emile Vandervelde, both delegates to the Paris Peace Conference, who had asked him to lecture in Brussels at the Maison du Peuple, where the renowned French socialist and pacifist Jean Jaurès had spoken two days before his assassination in 1914. Deferring his departure until the end of the month, Gregory also accepted additional invitations to speak in Liège and Antwerp.[31]

On 29 March Gregory at last left Holland. Most of his earnings since arriving in The Hague went to pay for his hefty hotel bill and his first-class ticket on the *S.S. Rotterdam*, one of the most luxurious ships then crossing the Atlantic. Gregory adored doing things in style: ordering a pricey summer suit in Kiev with his last kopeks, splurging on the thrill of a flight in an air show, buying any book he wanted if he had money in his pocket, travelling first class as soon as he could afford to. He knew how to starve, how to put up with privation and work hard all day and into the night, but if he had money, he spent it. He dressed for dinner on the ship in expensive clothes he likely bought for his lectures. He read in the ship's library and, on deck and in the smoking rooms, he smoked cigars as well as a pipe and cigarettes in an elegant holder. He discussed the past, future, and Bolshevism with Samuel Gompers, the American labour leader en route home from the Peace Conference, who was sufficiently impressed to arrange for him to lecture on board.[32]

Gregory on the deck of the S.S. *Rotterdam*

Gregory in the ship's library

On 4 April 1919 for one last time Gregory would speak in French on 'La Russie et La Catastrophe Mondiale', a lecture at the core of his *ave atque vale* for Europe. Never again would he act in such a small part on such a grand stage as during his time as a young revolutionary. In future his stages would be smaller, his own roles larger and more significant.

Notes

1 GZ, 'The Invisible Lenin', 81.
2 GZ, POOE, 117, 118.
3 GZ, 'The Invisible Lenin', 80.
4 GZ, POOE, 115–118.
5 Figes, 486–487, 488, 491–492; Reed, 100–102; Rappaport, 290, 293; GZ, POOE, 116–118; BIO.
6 Rappaport, 298–299.
7 GZ, 'The Invisible Lenin', 80, 81.
8 FZ, Oskow interview.
9 GZ, 'Ambulatory Schizophrenias', 149; GZ to 'Très Saint-Père', 31 January 1953, APD.
10 GZ, 'Thirty-five Years', xix–xx; GZ to JZ, 18 December 1918.
11 GZ's Artistic Club card, 1918–1919; pass, Congress of Press Workers; newspaper letters acknowledging his status; GZ to JZ, 18 December 1918.
12 GZ to 'Très Saint-Père', 31 January 1953, APD; GZ, POOE, 187, 188.
13 GZ, 'The Death of Nicholas II', np; Slater, 153.

14 GZ, POOE, 144–145.
15 GZ, POOE, 145–149.
16 GZ, POOE, 87, 88.
17 GZ, POOE, 71, 72, 73.
18 GZ, POOE, 70, 169–172.
19 GZ, 'Thirty-five Years', xix.
20 'Declaration, Alien about to Depart for U.S.', 18 December 1918.
21 Official documents.
22 GZ, 'Die Unmittelbare Verwirklichung', np.
23 Nellie Bly to GZ, 20 November 1918.
24 GZ, POOE, 136, 134.
25 GZ, POOE, 128–130.
26 GZ, 'The Psycho-Social Paradoxes', 1, 4–8.
27 'Declaration, Alien about to Depart for U.S.'; GZ to JZ, 14 December 1918.
28 GZ from Society for the Development of Industry, 14, 27 December 1918, 6 January, 22 March 1919.
29 GZ to JZ, 14 December 1918.
30 GZ to JZ, 5, 6 January 1919.
31 GZ to JZ, 28 February 1919; postscript, 3 March 1919.
32 GZ POOE, 173–175; lecture notice; passenger list.

Chapter 6

Embracing the New World

1919–1922

New York was mild and sunny on 11 April 1919, and although James was likely at work at the New York Board of Trade, it is nice to think Eugenia welcomed Gregory at the dock. He would take public transport the length of Manhattan to their rooms on the upper west side in an old brownstone building north of 'the Great Columbia University' about which he had heard so much. There he would live with his brother and sister-in-law for the next few months while he tried to recover from the revolution and adjust to post-war America.

He was, as he had anticipated, 'shattered, suppressed and depressed' and badly in need of 'mental and moral recovery'. He had eaten well on the boat, but ten days of *haute cuisine* on the high seas was insufficient to sustain either body or soul. The first days with James and Eugenia were likely affirming, but James would have let him know he was an extra mouth to feed in a space better suited for two than for three. He was soon again feeling hungry as well as exhausted and isolated. My mother recounted what followed: James informed his brother that he would need to get a job as quickly as possible. Gregory proposed that James allow him to live with them for six months while he improved his English and wrote his book; Gregory would pay him back once he was on his feet. James countered that Gregory needed to start contributing sooner than that and suggested he go out and dig ditches. There were plenty of ditches to be dug in America in the spring of 1919, but Gregory didn't feel called to dig them; the fact was, he felt called to do other things.[1]

Years later, in analysing the psychology of 'the typical intellectual immigrant', Gregory would reveal the emotional situation in which he found himself. The intellectual immigrant arrives 'downhearted and disappointed. His early ideas failed at home, his early hopes at home were shattered.' He is not a working-class immigrant who can peddle needles or sweets or newspapers and wonders if he can peddle his democratic ideals. Gregory continued: 'The market for such merchandise seems oversupplied, or for some other reasons there appears to be little demand for these wares.' Soon

> a very singular and paradoxical transformation takes place ... the intellectual immigrant feels most secure in the street and in his room: no one spies

DOI: 10.4324/9781003190936-6

> on him, no one threatens him with imprisonment – he does not have to look furtively about him before he says what he has to say. Yet he feels lonely – not at home.

Although he can speak English and express himself freely, 'he does not yet know the language well enough to understand easily when spoken to. There are so many busy people around, so many cheerful people, so many strangers.' He feels 'that state of silent despair' which makes him a critic of American life. He feels that everyone in America is too cheerful while the rest of the world – in Gregory's case Russia – is so miserable. The intellectual immigrant sees Americans as naïve, their theatre too full of musical shows, their music screechy, their minds limited, their intellectual horizon narrow and provincial; their interests seem materialistic, while they worship bigness rather than greatness. His mood is one of gnawing criticism and he feels an unwelcome surliness. He seeks out other Europeans as sympathetic souls for, Gregory explained, 'no one is a more severe critic of this country than the newcomer during the first months or even years after his arrival.' He feels superior, that he does not belong and that there is no market for his wares – and these feelings in turn feed his melancholy egocentricity.

The fact is, the typical intellectual immigrant misses 'home', and Gregory missed Russia. 'There is the child within', Gregory wrote, 'that longs for "mother"'; the intellectual immigrant longs for the 'psychological and symbolic extension of the mother image', which is his native land. This is, Gregory argued, the source of 'the double allegiance' which will at some level stay with the intellectual immigrant throughout his life because 'It takes a time, a great deal of time and spiritual work before one is able spontaneously and naturally to call a strange woman "mother".' The process of adaptation ahead of the intellectual immigrant involves remobilising his psychic energies, converting them 'into creative work, into cheerful effort and serene contemplation of life'. Earning a comfortable living, having the right to vote and to free speech, or even owning an automobile would be insufficient.

Gregory finally saw language as the most potent factor in assimilation. It was not enough to have the necessary degree of familiarity to order a meal, to read a newspaper, to enjoy a movie; the intellectual immigrant needed to acquire a level of fluency that would allow him to think spontaneously in English. He needed to achieve 'not the purely intellectual understanding of the language … but its psychological flavor', its emotional nuances. Like the typical intellectual immigrant, Gregory would only feel part of America when his inner life could be expressed and reflected in English. Only then would his double allegiance become 'synthesized into an inner harmonious psychology which would make it possible to utilize the cultural values' he had brought with him from Russia with those American values he would adopt.[2]

Gregory felt that writing a book would help him attain the fluent English he craved. Hoping for his brother's support and using his address, Gregory ordered stationary and calling cards and set out to make the connections he needed to work as a journalist and speaker on Russian literature and the revolution – in other words, like the typical intellectual immigrant, he decided to try to peddle his democratic ideals.

The spring of 1919 wasn't a bad time to attempt such a task in America, but it wasn't a very good time either. Fear of Bolshevism was rife, and the entire labour movement was under suspicion. Throughout the country newspapers reported on leftists of all sorts, on anarchists like Emma Goldman and Alexander Berkman in New York as well as labour leaders like Tom Mooney and Warren Billings in San Francisco. Bombs delivered through the post along with protest rallies and union marches provoked distrust of socialists, political activists, internationalists, communists, liberals, Europeans, Jews in general, and Russians in particular. Hostility towards the Russian revolution, seen as having damaged the war effort, was widespread although unfocused, while at the level of local and national government, anti-communist teams of lawyers and police organised to control actual and perceived threats through arrests and mass deportations. The strikes, race riots, and anarchist bombings unnerved and fascinated the public. 'The Red Scare' of 1917–1920 drew on and encouraged xenophobia and paranoia, but there was also great intellectual interest in Russia, curiosity about the revolution and what its implications might be for America and the world.[3]

Gregory probably had no idea he was courting danger when he set out with his calling cards, although James and Eugenia would certainly have warned him. James was sympathetic to socialism, but he had not returned to Russia to fight for it; his feet were firmly planted on American soil, where in 1919 even leftist leanings could cause trouble for a Russian Jew. Like their sisters, James wanted to control his brother, but Gregory would not be controlled by his family or anyone else, although the hazards of socialism would quickly become apparent to him as he sought outlets for his writing and opportunities to speak. He soon met Pauline Turkel, an energetic young anarchist instrumental in organising a mass meeting to protest Mooney's imprisonment, a May Day event in Madison Square Garden Gregory probably attended. Through Turkel he would meet other young socialists, including her friend Eleanor Fitzgerald, a fellow anarchist and the business manager of the Provincetown Players, a group of writers and intellectuals committed to staging innovative theatre. One thing would lead to another very rapidly for Gregory, for whom it seemed that one thing invariably led rapidly to another. He entered the New York socialist melee with all the enthusiasm he could muster, prepared to take advantage of whatever opportunities presented themselves.

Gregory swiftly began writing. He started in languages he knew and began publishing in the Yiddish press in May. He would write articles in Russian for the New York daily *Novoe Russkoye Slovo* into the autumn of 1920, but seven weeks after his arrival he began publishing in English. In June he began to send letters to the editors of English language journals – making points, correcting articles, getting his name in print. By August he was confidently writing pieces for *The Dial* and *The New Republic*. He would continue to write in English on the revolution, on Russian literature, and particularly on drama through the autumn of 1923.

One element of the typical immigrant, intellectual or not, that Gregory omitted in his discussion is the instability of identity as reflected in the immigrant's name as well as profession. Gregory had been aware of shifting identities as his name changed each time he left home for school, as he moved from a Yiddish into a Russian environment and back again. It changed repeatedly as he travelled through Europe to America, the patronymic disappearing, the spelling of both his given and family names morphing with each country. In print and at the podium, he appeared more or less as 'Gregory Zilboorg' ('Gr Zilboorg', 'G.Z.', or German, French, or Dutch variations on both 'Gregory' and 'Zilboorg'), although whether he was referred to as 'Mr.' or 'Dr.' remained flexible for a decade. For the Yiddish daily *Der Tog*, his articles appeared under 'Zvi Zilboorg', a clever pseudonym with roots in 'Girsh' or 'Hirsh', meaning 'deer' in Yiddish, as does the common Jewish name 'Zvi' or 'Tzvi' in Hebrew. Colleagues would call him 'Gregory', but only occasionally to intimate friends and family members would he be 'Grisha'.

Gregory's career was as unstable as his name in 1919 as he struggled to establish himself in the New World. The first months in America defined him variously as a former revolutionary and a historian, philosopher, journalist, dramatist, and literary critic, but not a lawyer (a 'jurist' as he had been in Russia and Europe) or physician. With so many roles to play, although none of them his chosen profession, it is tempting to call him simply a 'renaissance man', but his many talents did not make it easy to be Gregory Zilboorg and his various roles did not settle his career or his life. His psychological state did not help matters, either, but Gregory was busy. He read newspapers and even the New Testament in English, attended dramatic performances, and saw at least a few silent 'movies'. He considered producing, directing, and translating plays. He went to labour rallies, called on editors, and met with patrons of charitable and Jewish organisations. In his spare time he began work on his book, and at least once in the summer was persuaded to go to the beach – perhaps by Eugenia or another woman, whose coat and handbag were captured in the photo she snapped. A beach was definitely alien territory for Gregory, and he lounged uncomfortably on the sand in his street clothes, read a newspaper, and smoked a cigarette.

Gregory, likely at Coney Island or Rockaway, summer 1919

The summer was an uncomfortable time for Gregory as relations with his brother and sister-in-law became strained. The more connections he made, the more successful his attempts at a professional life, the more interest others began to show in who he was and what he might have to say, the more trying life became at home. It is difficult to reconstruct the incident that provoked what would finally be an unbridgeable rift between the two brothers. Women played a part in it, but there is no evidence of any romantic relationship, and it seems more likely that the confrontation involved the dangers of social causes. Likelier still the issue was trivial. Fera had called upon James to scold Gregory for nearly throwing a bottle of perfume, spending money on clothes and leisure activities, and upsetting the family about matters she felt didn't warrant concern. Basia had expected James to sympathise with the family's frustration with a son and brother who alarmed everyone with what she saw as 'stunts' and 'antics', who refused to be controlled and would in her view amount to nothing. Now apparently it was Eugenia who disagreed with Gregory's opinions or behaviour or circle of acquaintances. In mid-August there was an altercation; she asked him to leave and he did.

James followed up with a letter which hints at the basis of the argument but does not clarify it. Evidently a woman was coming to New York to see Gregory and a friend or relative knew and told James. He then confronted the woman who, when 'pressed', confirmed the meeting. James and particularly Eugenia were furious because they had not been informed. James felt it was 'natural' for him to be interested but was aware that Gregory might find his pursuit of the matter 'only undesirable meddling'. James defended himself and his wife, who was feeling guilty. James told Gregory that he didn't think anyone needed to apologise for anything and insisted, 'I have known you for some time now and I don't think you have changed in terms of your disposition. The same is perhaps true of us. For that reason, the particulars of any back-and-forth savagery are not necessary.' With characteristic pomposity, he addressed Gregory as if he were a child:

> Now that you are removed from the heat of the argument, if you can look at things squarely, as an adult (forgive me, this is my old way of approaching your many ways), then you will agree with me that … each of us has our habits and none of us has the right to force the other to change them. What each of us thinks of the other's habits or character is of no consequence at this point. The only thing that matters is the clear realisation that we cannot live together.

He then came as close to an apology as he was capable, 'I feel badly that we cannot get along better – it was only a matter of my youthful forgetfulness that I thought otherwise three or four months ago.' Aware that his brother was still financially strapped, James added that if he ever needed anything, he knew where to find him; James would expect the same of him in a similar situation. He closed by insisting that it would do no good now to talk, but maybe they could meet in some indefinite future.[4]

Gregory was hurt and offended by his brother's letter, which he found 'random and strange' in part because James had not written him honestly or openly or at length or personally for years and did not even address him by name. Gregory wrote that he nevertheless understood that 'psychologically' James anticipated a response. Frustrated and confused, Gregory continued, 'It is apparent that you understand that I am having a difficult time, that I would probably want to share this with someone, but you want no part of that. Are you ashamed or something?' Gregory was angry with the gossipy nature of the issue and his brother's repeated assertion that he could no longer live with them. Gregory had already told Eugenia, after her 'dirty accusation', that he was leaving and not coming back. Gregory then offered James his psychological analysis. The issue wasn't a matter of 'youthful forgetfulness' but 'something else':

> I am alone. My personal life has been devastated.... To a certain extent, a lonely life is to be respected. The two of you, and especially Eugenia, lack that respect. And where respect is lacking, a person's baser nature comes to the fore. The cultured individual always wants to mask this baseness with fine words, but the essence of it doesn't change.

He continued,

> I feel ill at ease about your letter. It would be better if it were written in a hysterical or rude tone. But there is something of a myopic and cold decency about it; it is natural but myopic. It is a cold formula without content – or, to be more precise, no human, humane content. This makes me feel uneasy and somewhat embarrassed for you.

He didn't want either James or Eugenia to be 'nervous' about the situation, however. He reassured them, 'I am calm. That means there is nothing for you to be nervous about either.' In part because of his own hot temper and certainly because of James's rigid and controlling character, Gregory's hope that he would find in James the brother he had imagined and longed for would never be fulfilled.[5]

As the days grew cooler Gregory immersed himself in labour causes and arranged lectures on the revolution in New York and further afield. He was eager for accuracy and honesty about what had occurred in Russia. He sent a letter to *The Evening Post*, which had called him Kerensky's 'Minister of War'. 'That is a mistake', he wrote, 'I was not Minister of any kind in the Provisional Government and acted only as Secretary to the Ministry of Labor.' He wrote *The Globe* to correct *The New York Times* on 14 September 1919, in which a photograph was entitled 'Admiral Kolchak, head of the Russian government at Omsk, seated with his aids in an automobile in front of his palace at Omsk'. Observing that

Kolchak was in 'a secondary place', with characteristic linguistic precision and wit Gregory declared,

> I am able to say that this fact is due, not to the democratic character of the admiral, but to the fact that this picture was taken at least two and a half years ago, when Admiral Kolchak was not head of any government.

After identifying all of the officials – 'None of these three persons is an aid of Kolchak. None of them is in Omsk' – he concluded with dramatic concision: 'If the truth about Russia is misrepresented in some papers in articles they are always open for arguments, but pictures have a very convincing power although there is, as you see, very little truth in some of them.' Sponsored by the Detroit Labor Forum in Detroit in September, Gregory spoke on 'Kerensky and the Soviets' at Auto Workers' Hall. A few nights later he spoke on 'Present Day Russia: Its Role and Significance' at Grace Universalist Church in Lowell, Massachusetts, where he denounced the British blockade of Soviet Russia and described the deprivations and harsh conditions that followed the revolution. He was introduced as having an M.D., a Ph.D., and an L.L.D., the American equivalents of the credentials he felt he had.[6]

Back in New York he had found accommodation only five blocks from James but could not afford to change his stationary or calling cards. He was still quite unsettled, his attention divided between writing and speaking engagements, on which his income depended, and his desire for a professional life commensurate with his qualifications and aspirations. At the beginning of October, he enclosed a hand-corrected calling card in a letter with a hand-corrected letterhead to the pacifist Reform rabbi Judah Leon Magnes. The card identified Gregory as 'Special Correspondent' for *Kievskaya Mysl* ('Kiev Thought') and *Teatralnaya Zhizn* ('Theatre Life'). The letter itself reveals his still imperfect English: He had been unable to call on Magnes, because 'Unfortunately I am all this time very busy', 'Therefore I write' on behalf of 'a first class worker', a woman who is 'a perfect stenographer both in English and in Russian' who has lost her job 'because of disgust'. He hoped that Magnes would help her find work and signed himself, 'Very friendly yours, Gregory Zilboorg'. He had not yet written the book he had described to James, nor was most of his energy going into writing articles for newspapers back in Russia, but he was about to add yet another activity to his scramble for an American identity.[7]

In early October 1919 Gregory enrolled in the Graduate Faculties of 'the Great Columbia University'. On his transcript, the basis for admission is indicated as his medical studies at the Psycho-Neurological Institute, specifically 'M.D. 1917', although this medical qualification is followed by 'LLD 1914', a degree presumably deduced from his description of his exams at the University of Warsaw. He enrolled, however, in basic undergraduate courses: 100-level classes in history, philosophy, sociology, French, and German, as well as 200-level courses in history and philosophy – 16 credits in the winter semester (Oct–Dec 1919), 15 credits in the spring semester (Jan–June 1920), and 9 credits in the 1920 summer session. His attendance was unsurprisingly erratic, and in only one of these courses did he actually receive credit. In History 286 in the spring semester he received a grade of 'P' (pass). In two he received credit for attendance only, and in most no credit at all because he did not take the final exam. He received no credit because of 'irregular attendance' in Philosophy 167 and an 'Incomplete' in French 106.

Perhaps Gregory did not understand the American system of university education. Possibly he enrolled in an effort to improve his English, although if that was so, taking elementary German and French doesn't make sense. Probably he hoped to meet interesting or influential students and professors. At the beginning of each term, he likely intended to attend classes, complete required work, and show up for the final exam – intentions which his other obligations made impossible. Yet it seems bizarre that he signed up for elementary courses in the social sciences, an area in which he was already well read, and in languages in which he was fluent. Maybe all he wanted was access to Columbia's library for both its resources and the private space in which he could write his book. It is probably simplest and kindest to conclude that for more than a year after his arrival he continued to have the 'difficult time' he indicated to James in August 1919. He was also still the same young man he had been before the war and the revolution. He was not so much distracted as overcommitted, not so much unfocused or neglectful as passionately taking on more than he could handle. In America as in Russia he allowed his health, his academic life, and even the human connections he longed for to fall by the wayside as he strove to earn a living and create the intellectual opportunities that would finally define him both personally and professionally.

Despite these academic and emotional struggles, Gregory became increasingly successful as a lecturer. In late autumn James apparently heard him speak and was so impressed he felt called to write. On Columbia University Library letterhead, Gregory responded with the grace and humour of which he was capable. Touched by his brother's flattering letter, he wrote that his frequent absence from New York and 'constant busyness' had prevented his responding immediately. With acute psychological insight, Gregory confided that it seemed to him his brother's letter was not so much about him personally as about a political spokesman and research lecturer whose qualities of speech and thought had had a great impact: 'This is flattering for me and, to a certain extent, for you as well, as you evidently have begun to become pleasantly disappointed.'[8]

This renegotiating of the relationship and re-establishing of connection would need to happen over and over again as these two different personalities clashed. Gregory would inevitably do or fail to do something that exasperated and angered James, who would respond by scolding, rejecting, and insulting his brother – barring him from the apartment, accusing him of misunderstanding, of not helping the family financially or supporting the family sympathetically or of failing to follow whatever moral rules James felt Gregory had broken. For his part, exasperating as Gregory was, he behaved generously after James forced a rupture; he would be magnanimous, unwilling to blame or take responsibility, uninterested in retribution or continuing the discussion. For Gregory, his heart as well as his purse were always open to his brother, though he backed off when offended. Gregory felt with some justification that James wanted to scold him, to hold him to standards he thought were silly or 'petty bourgeois'. James wanted to control his brother, and Gregory was never going to let anyone tell him what to do.

Ten days later, on 11 December 1919, Gregory married Ray Liebow, probably in a religious ceremony. Gregory did not mention his future wife in his wry letter to James and his decision to marry seems to have been rather if not extremely impulsive. Writing again to Magnes, he indicated he particularly appreciated the rabbi's 'friendly kindness' since 'I am in this country almost absolutely alone. At least I was until last week.' Gregory likely informed James of his marriage only in the new year since the solitude he mentioned was in part a result of his alienation from James and Eugenia, but his marriage was no secret. His socialist contemporaries would soon have known of the change in his circumstances; indeed, he and Ray had met through socialist activities, probably directly or indirectly through Pauline Turkel or other mutual acquaintances.[9]

Years later Gregory would contend that he was not 'clear-headed' at the time he decided to marry. Specifically, he was physically hungry, without money or friends, and looking unconsciously for a place to sleep, a home. In December 1919, however, Ray was certainly in love with Gregory. Socialists were being arrested on the city's streets and the threat of deportation hung over all immigrant activists – if Gregory were destined to be deported, she wanted to go with him. Both romantic and depressive, Ray was an attractive and stylish young woman who found her husband a dashing figure, an apparently magical man who at least at first admired her sensitivity to beauty as well as her desire to escape a difficult family situation.[10]

Superficially Ray and Gregory had much in common. Born in Odessa in March 1893, she had left Russia with her parents and two brothers in 1898, before either of the revolutions, but like Gregory she was the first-born child and a Jew from an observant Yiddish-speaking family. Like her husband and many other immigrants, she had also changed her name in the transformative process of becoming an American, as had all the members of her family as they adjusted to their life in the New World. The passenger manifest of the *Pretoria* from Hamburg to New York listed the Liebows as Noah and Rosa and their children as five-year-old Riva, three-year-old Simon, and one-year-old Arie. Soon after their arrival in the United States another son, Morris, was born, and the 1900 census gave Ray's parents' names as 'Nathan' and 'Rose' and their daughter as 'Rebecca', while Simon had become 'Sam' and Arie had become 'Louis'. The census-taker noted that Rose was illiterate although Nathan could read and write Yiddish, but neither could yet speak English; none of them had ever spoken Russian. Ray's father was a butcher in a shop serving the Jewish community in their Bronx neighbourhood.

Rose and Nathan would slowly learn to read and write basic English and could manage in spoken English by the time Ray married. Following the typical immigrant pattern, however, the children would become culturally American and English-speaking, while the Yiddish-speaking community remained the parents' frame of reference. By the time Ray met Gregory, there were four additional offspring: Annie was a mature 17 in 1919, yet Bernard was still a boy of 11, Irving was nine and little Sylvia was only four. Ray must have been glad as Annie grew old enough to help her care for the other children, but by the time she left home Ray had had quite enough of washing nappies and feeding babies, more than enough of little ones pulling at her skirts and asking for milk. She had finished high school and, at 26, felt more comfortable in English than in Yiddish. Having found work in the city's garment district, she could afford to buy herself an occasional new dress and called herself not 'Riva' or 'Rebecca' but 'Ray'. What she really would have liked to have called herself was 'Clara', but such a suggestively Gentile transformation was a step too far.[11]

Gregory's marriage may have involved merely a civil ceremony. Logically this is what Gregory would have wanted, and Ray had little intellectual or personal interest in religion and no interest at all in what Gregory repeatedly referred to in his letters to his brother as the spiritual. Still, whether to please her parents or as a vestige of what seemed only proper, they arranged to have a ketubah. This traditional marriage contract details the husband's obligations to his wife and is not usually signed by the couple but by two male witnesses just before the religious ceremony, and Gregory turned to Magnes for clarification. Enclosing the Hebrew ketubah, with his own name as 'Tzvi son of Moses' and Ray's as 'Chaya daughter of Noah', he explained, 'I did not sign it because I did not know in what language it has to be done.' Gregory was concerned about doing the correct thing, but by the end of this momentous year he had more than traditional matters on his mind and more pressing problems, with a wife in tow, than putting his name on paper.[12]

Gregory with Ray standing beside him in a stylish hat, winter 1920. Gregory looks uncomfortable on the ice: Hands in his pockets and standing somewhat apart from the others, only he and the man with the dog are without skates.

Ray was right to fear the possible consequences of Gregory's lectures and writing. On 21 December 1919, only ten days after their marriage, 249 people were deported to Russia for radical activity, including Goldman and Berkman. Gregory now concentrated on his book on the revolution. Although not particularly literary, Ray likely helped him with his English, and it was probably in consultation with her that he went over his article 'Another Plan to Smother Russia'. On a copy of the published version, which appeared in print in early 1920, Gregory carefully noted grammatical and stylistic mistakes. He underlined 'friendly' (incorrectly used here as an adverb, as in his letters to Magnes) and the conversationally acceptable 'pretty' ('a pretty large report', 'the Jewish population is pretty thick', and 'The latter understand it pretty well'). He marked the absence of an article when he wrote that 'Petlura, the Ukrainian leader, is far from being innocent in bloody events of the last few months', while in 'the Kaiser would be able to exploit Russia easier', he underlined 'easier' as well as two sentences that began with 'but', his statement that 'New and new wars will go on', and the awkward 'Bethman-Holweg offered to the Czar peace.' Such attention to articles, adjectives, and adverbs as well as stylistic conventions and word order would shape the elegant and perceptive book that finally appeared in March 1920, nearly a year after Gregory arrived in America.

It had taken longer than he had hoped, but *The Passing of the Old Order in Europe* turned out to be larger in scope and more emotional than the book he had imagined in Holland. Themes and topics that would interest him and define his work throughout his life emerge clearly here: war and peace; state authority and the individual; psychotic responses to violence; political science and philosophy; ethics; nationalism; religion; the significance of art.

At once sincere and pretentious, raw and sophisticated, the book also reveals Gregory's continuing struggle to come to terms with his revolutionary experience. Despite his attempt to process the turmoil he had witnessed, he was still unprepared to understand the man who had emerged from his Jewish family in Russia, from his studies of law and medicine, from the stress and violence of war and revolution. He was not yet ready to see or accept the person who had crossed the boundaries of continents and cultures and languages, not yet psychologically or spiritually capable of synthesising his experiences and feelings. Thus, *The Passing of the Old Order in Europe* contains a great deal of abstraction, a broad discussion of history, philosophy, political theory, ethics, and morality – but little self-examination, few specifics about events Gregory witnessed and participated in and even fewer personal details – and his treatment of his subject is often jumbled, non-linear, non-narrative, confused, and oblique. In recounting and analysing recent Russian and European history, Gregory hoped that his readers would learn from the anecdotes, memories, and facts he shared, but he was concerned they might not, and a tone of harangue pervades his analysis of the contemporary political, economic, social, and psychological state of the Western world. Yet the book is not without insight or wisdom, and it appears in many ways prescient as well as informed and intelligent; despite its prevarications, it is honest and characteristic of the author who was attempting to right the wrongs of the world at the age of 29.

Gregory dedicated *The Passing of the Old Order in Europe* to Romain Roland, Friedrich Foerster, and Maxim Gorky, and to 'all those who in the darkness of hatred held fast their lights of love'. Already presented in fragments as lectures in Russia, the Netherlands, and America, this book shows Gregory's efforts to analyse the psychological as well as moral issues of the First World War and its aftermath. Drawing on his own experiences, the nascent psychoanalyst was convinced that 'humanity has developed a very serious disease', a 'mob psychosis' he attempted to define and describe: 'The contagion was carried by the war, by revolution, by political lying, by diplomatic betrayal, social disturbances and moral suppression.' Citing Roland's *Jean-Christophe*, the novel for which he received the Nobel Prize for Literature in 1915, Gregory declared that mediocrity was the disease which caused the war and described the illness as a 'contagion of clamorous, hazy half-ideas, half-words' in which 'minds are submerged' and temporarily lose 'their governing forces, their process of criticism and independent reasoning'. Significantly, Gregory's focused on psychology and language; 'mob psychosis' and 'half-words' had brought about the current state of crisis. Key concepts here are 'lying' and 'betrayal'; the solution was a matter of sound intellect and ethics.[13]

The book is at once a compendium of everything Gregory had ever read and his attempt to define himself as a moral philosopher and political historian. He discussed the American and French revolutions, Napoleon and Bismarck, the role of the state, and popular political consciousness. Following his medically informed psychological analysis, Gregory argued, for example, that a true and principled majority rule embodying the people's will had, throughout Europe, 'committed suicide'; centralised mechanical states had 'hypnotized' the populace. Similarly, people's 'instincts' and 'impulses' had been directed towards utilitarian rather than moral ends, while economic imperialism was 'merely one of the most acute forms of the general disease'.[14]

Gregory's legal and psychiatric training is evident in both his language and his analysis: Medical as well as scientific analogics and metaphors abound, while political analysis reveals the author's historical and personal awareness of partisan rivalry and internecine conflict. With youthful passion Gregory discussed Christianity and the Versailles treaty, Marxism and Bergson in the same breath, while his point of view as well as his national identity remained rooted his own immediate experiences. He wrote, 'We in Russia' and 'to me as a Russian', praised 'Russian and French psychoanalysts' who drew on literature with sensitivity and understanding, insisted that 'Literature is the last refuge and asylum of life', and saw 'no line of demarcation between scientific thought and artistic creation'. The incipient psychoanalyst wrote of 'neurotic impressionism which seeks relief from the impact of reality'. He disliked contemporary cinema because it was silent and declared that its popularity demonstrated that 'Words were worn out to such an extent, had become so banal, so dull, that there was no longer any need of them.' He insisted that war and revolution were inevitable because of cultural and artistic dissolution: The

> vital forces of individuals were dying, smothered into oblivion by the stolid weight of a mechanical society. Life could not go on in that fashion without losing its driving force. Society itself was suffering from a sort of elephantiasis which slowed up its motions and threatened to prostrate it by the effect of its own weight.

Indeed, 'This condition could not last any longer.... The channels of life were blocked. Destruction in one form or another, war or revolution ... was necessary to open them.' Similarly, 'The war was a fungus that drew nourishment from the dead tissue of the European spirit', while 'The Congress of Vienna ... with its absolute disregard and violation of national principles, opened the way for the diseases and abnormalities of our day'. Invariably ethical, Gregory finally argued that the Western world in the early twentieth century found itself 'in the mechanical state of world civilization spiritually'.[15]

The crux of Gregory's sophisticated understanding of the both the First World War and the revolutions he experienced comes in the middle of *The Passing of the Old Order in Europe*. Revealing his dual understanding of the Provisional Government's failings and the Bolsheviks' successes, he developed his ideas with precision and insight, with the rhetorical authority and charismatic voice that fascinated his lecture audiences. He declared,

> a revolution should not be considered as a mere shifting of political gears, for the purpose of speeding up the state machine toward social or political maximalism. A revolution is essentially something much more deeply human and personal than that. It is primarily a protest against traditions, policies, and prejudices that have been accumulated in the growth of a state. It is a new effort of life to break through the stifling envelope that was created originally to protect it.

Gregory deftly moved from simile to metaphor: 'A revolution cannot accordingly be made – it must spontaneously grow. It is born in the womb of the nation itself, and it makes its way violently into the light of day, under a baptism of blood.' He insisted,

> A revolution has the unique feature of attaining its highest point of creative effort at the very first outburst of destruction. A revolution without violence can have no creative power, at least during its first period. Its value is in proportion to the thoroughness with which it is able to sweep away a clotted mass of dead theories and archaic institutions.

Gregory developed his argument carefully:

> the old order was based … upon a kind of mechanical solidarity, upon chauvinism, upon a fanatic belief in the divine mission of the state.… The notion of moral solidarity, a solidarity conscious of its responsibility for the structural soundness of society, was completely lacking.… The old European order did not acknowledge any responsibility except that for carrying out the plans of groups which dominated it.

However, Gregory quickly moved on once more to metaphor:

> The masses were in the same relation to the state as a factory is to its owner. The owner is interested in the efficiency of his factory, and in trying to obtain a maximum output he will usually keep his machines in good order: but if he finds it possible to increase production at the cost of the machine's life he does not hesitate to do so.

This unenlightened attitude was, Gregory argued, typical of European rulers: 'The war came. The machines went to pieces. The organization broke down' and 'The upholders of the old order discovered that the instruments which the state had been treating as machines were in fact conscious human beings with ideas of their own about the lives they proposed to live.' Gregory finally arrived at his point: 'The revolution was, in a comprehensive sense, a release from machinery – the political machinery of the ballot, the social machinery of classes, the religious machinery of ecclesiasticism. Life unlocked the armor of machinery, and breathed freely and moved nimbly.'

Gregory next focused on the 'bitter paradox' of revolution: Its value had to be measured by the extent of its destruction. He explained,

> While a revolution is a protest against violence, brutal force, mechanical constriction, and human oppression, it is compelled to use violent means against the elements which made it possible. Benevolence cannot be its primary characteristic; it cannot wish the old order well, for its very nature forces it to the repulsive task of extermination.

As if at the lectern, Gregory exclaimed his conclusion: 'The tragic dilemma of a revolution is that it can clear the ground for its ideals only by using methods that undermine them!'

Gregory then continued calmly and philosophically. It was 'useless to deny the necessity for destruction', more important 'to discriminate between the sort of havoc revolution brings in its wake and that which war produces'. Skilfully again using metaphor to move his readers, he hit his stride and hit home his point:

> Essentially, both war and revolution work with the same instruments. There is, however, as much difference between international wars formally declared

> by governments and civil wars begun without declaration by peoples as there is between the knife of the murderer and the knife of the surgeon.

Specifically,

> The murderer kills in the act of gratifying revenge or seizing loot. His victim dies perhaps without pain. The surgeon's knife, on the contrary, may cut with exquisite torture, but the surgeon uses it on his patient, regardless of the shock, the loss of blood, and the discomfort, in order that he may remove a tumor and save a life.[16]

Gregory was justifiably proud of his book: He had written the wide-ranging history that he had hoped to write and had done it in English. The book was positively noticed. In his popular *The Revolt Against Civilization: The Menace of the Under Man*, the white supremacist historian Lothrop Stoddard quoted the book at length, using its anti-Bolshevik arguments while dismissing its revolutionary views as 'Menshevik'. The *New York Tribune* reviewer declared that although Gregory was sometimes 'lured away from the hard path of strict scientific accuracy in his eagerness to establish political and literary analogies', he wrote 'with fire, eloquence and scholarship'; he was 'a thoroughgoing pacifist' and his book 'An interesting philosophical consideration of various material and spiritual weakness in modern European culture'. The reviewer in *The Boston Post* was similarly impressed. He found *The Passing of the Old Order in Europe* 'stimulating and eloquent'. Despite his judgment that Gregory was 'more specific in destructive than in constructive criticism', he declared that the young author was persuasive because he 'knows conditions and history and he writes so well and so logically'.[17]

Gregory would earn enough money from his book to support himself and his wife for the next little while. The subject of Russia – the revolution, current events, Russian literature and especially drama – would be Gregory's bread and butter, the only source of his precarious income well into the 1920s. Amid a hectic lecture schedule, in late 1919 he had directed Andreyev's *Beautiful Sabine Women* at the Neighborhood Playhouse on the Lower East Side. Translated as *The Pretty Sabine Women* by Thomas Selzer and first published in English in *The Drama* in 1914, the play was well received and continued to be performed into the spring. Gregory changed 'Pretty' to 'Beautiful' and may have polished Seltzer's translation in other ways in a production based on his staging of the same play in Kiev in 1918, but Seltzer was sufficiently impressed to publish *The Passing of the Old Order in Europe* as one of the first books to come out from his experimental firm.

Such networking enabled an intense agenda of lectures and travel throughout 1920. In addition to addressing local audiences in New York City, Gregory spoke in Buffalo in January; in Milwaukee in February; in Baltimore in March; in Boston in May; in Highland, New York, in June; in Pittsburgh and Richmond in October; and in Pittsburgh again as well as in Rochester, Chicago, Cincinnati, and Memphis in November. The groups he addressed ranged from the Men's Society of Pittsburgh's Rodef Shalom congregation to Boston's Twentieth-Century Club. His talks were sponsored by the Russian Economic Relief Committee, socialists and labour unions, business leaders, university clubs, women's groups, and institutes furthering the arts or public education in general. Some venues were simple, others prestigious: He spoke at the Manhattan Trade School for Girls, the Brooklyn Institute, the Brooklyn Academy of Music, Cooper Union, and the Pittsburgh Chamber of Commerce. Sometimes other speakers shared the platform: Nathaniel Schmidt, a Swedish-American Baptist minister and professor of Oriental Studies, joined him in addressing a chapter of the Intercollegiate Socialist Society; the labour lawyer Louis Waldman accompanied him in Milwaukee. Gregory was one of 16 featured speakers during the 1920–1921 season of New York's Fine Arts Guild, whose impressive list included, among others, the English writer John Cowper Powys, the socialist writer Max Eastman, the historian and philosopher Will Durant, the political journalist Lincoln Steffens, and the birth-control advocate Margaret Sanger.

Generally, however, Gregory was the sole attraction. A newspaper account of his visit to Rochester offers a vivid portrait. The able lecturer appeared as 'Distinctly a foreign type' with 'a dark complexion ... long black hair, a long black moustache and penetrating eyes'. He seemed to have an 'extremely nervous disposition', pacing 'up and down the room rapidly' while speaking 'with great fluency' in 'perfect English'. He addressed the Century Club in the morning, then in the afternoon 'was entertained by prominent citizens', while in the evening the dinner in his honour in a private home included 'members of the faculty of the University of Rochester, leaders of the Chamber of Commerce and representatives of other organizations of the city'. His audiences found him fascinating. Even in what for him were certainly new and unusual situations, Gregory rose to the occasion. When the Intercollegiate Socialist Society adjourned a series of meetings on the shores of the Hudson River north of Poughkeepsie, students and speakers alike gathered 'for a marshmallow roast' on a nearby hillside. There they told stories and 'listened until past midnight to the Russian folk songs, led by Gregory Zilboorg'.[18]

There is no mention of Ray in the many newspaper accounts of Gregory's lectures, and his limited family life was generally quite separate from his work at his desk and on the lecture platform. Ray probably occasionally attended local talks, but she was already familiar with their substance and Gregory was probably unable to afford an extra train ticket when he travelled. Rather, Ray stayed at home in their small apartment in the Bronx, where she had friends as well as family. Despite the tensions between the brothers, however, by the spring Gregory had introduced Ray to James and Eugenia, who by the autumn of 1920 was heavily pregnant. James was now in his final year as a full-time post-graduate in mechanical engineering at Columbia, although he continued to work part-time as a technical translator and spent vacations as an intern in metal factories in both New York City and Pittsburgh. Through James and Eugenia, Gregory heard news of family still in Kiev, but he had not written since telling them of his safe his arrival in Budapest over two years earlier, just as he had not written to James until he was on his feet in Holland and organising his departure for the United States. Gregory's escape from Russia had also been also an escape from family. As he indicated to Magnes, his impetuous marriage to Ray was to some degree a result of loneliness, a complicated longing for home that was both conscious and unconscious as well as fraught. Since Gregory could not return to the Russia he had fought for and continued to love, the Russia that would be a significant part of his intellectual and emotional life for years after he had said goodbye to Fera at the Kiev train station, he tried to create an alternative, an American family. The effort to do exactly this had failed with his awkward attempt to reunite with the brother James never had been and could never be, to become part of the fragment of family that James as well as Eugenia had represented to him from the time of their departures in 1913 and 1915. The fact that he was frequently on the road was not conducive to a conventional married life nor was Ray's aversion to the idea of children, but neither seemed to bother Gregory deeply in 1920.

Gregory was more upset by his brother's attitude towards him, which continued to be disparaging and dismissive. With the publication of *The Passing of the Old Order in Europe*, Gregory had hoped for approval and enthusiasm, but James had failed to notice its publication, and when Gregory presented him with a copy, he set it aside without even opening it. During a visit to James and Eugenia's apartment, Gregory was accused by one of his brother's acquaintances of having been bribed to write the book by a Soviet publishing house, yet James said nothing in his brother's defence; indeed, he remained silent. When another acquaintance then quoted James as always repeating 'Please don't confuse me with my brother', James merely blushed. Gregory felt understandably wounded and rejected.[19]

In Gregory's absence, however, Ray forged a fragile link between the two couples, and the Kiev news that passed from James and Eugenia to Ray and Gregory wasn't heartening. Eugenia's parents were considering immigration to Palestine. Fera had fallen in love with Sol Levitas, who was still living with the family and still writing for the anti-Bolshevik press. Periodically policemen arrested him, then released him – a regular and disquieting routine. Basia was engaged to Semel Berdychevsky, a slender young medical officer in one of the many battalions based in the city, and she worried about her fiancé's health and safety. The price of cabbage was going up, but sometimes there was no cabbage; it was often unsafe to go to the market in any case, even for wood for the stove. When they burned the sacks of nutshells Moses brought home from work, the apartment stayed warm overnight.[20]

The New York newspapers reported daily on Russia's suffering and the Bolsheviks' struggles. In February 1919 General Symon Petlura had become head of a Ukrainian state fighting both the Red and White Armies, but before the end of the year his forces had lost control of most of the region, including Kiev, and withdrawn to Warsaw. Negotiating with the Poles, he had agreed a Ukrainian border that ceded Galicia to Poland in exchange for military support. Petlura's army attacked Kiev in May 1920 but was again compelled to retreat. While the

Soviets controlled most of Ukraine from early 1919, throughout 1920 and most of 1921 the Red and White Armies continued to battle each other as well as Petlura's forces for control of western areas from the Crimea to Chernobyl. Both in *The Passing of the Old Order in Europe* and in his lectures and journalism, Gregory addressed current events in Russia as well as the revolution, but he no longer had much first-hand information. Surely he worried about family and friends caught up in the power struggles and ensuing pogroms – neither White nor Red generals nor Petlura could control the anti-Semitism of their troops – and he was well acquainted with the physical deprivations that followed the breakdown of infrastructure as food supplies, clean water, and communications all faltered, but there was little he could do about Russia's problems except to throw himself completely, whole-heartedly, even nervously and defensively into his work.

The last performance of *The Beautiful Sabine Women* occurred in April 1920, but Andreyev and drama generally continued to occupy Gregory's attention as he began to widen the topics on which he was prepared to speak. At New York's Labor Temple in the autumn he was billed as 'Eminent Author, Dramatist and Lecturer' for a series of lectures on 'Voices of Social Hope and Despair', talks not only on Russian authors but on Guy de Maupassant ('Victims of a Civilized World') and Romain Rolland ('The Voice of a Prophet'). Before the end of the year he also began a new project: a translation of Andreyev's last play, the tragicomedy *He Who Gets Slapped* (1922).

It is not surprising that Gregory would choose this work for his first translation. 'Heir of Schopenhauer, Dostoevskii and Nietszche', Andreyev was a modernist sceptic whose subjects were the power of irrational impulses and the flaws of social institutions. Formalistically traditional, he had achieved by 1920 a wide popularity in English. American translators and critics Herman Bernstein and Thomas Seltzer had championed Andreyev in modernist and mainstream presses as early as 1909, while in 1914 Emma Goldman had grouped him with Shaw, Maeterlinck, and Gorky in *The Social Significance of Modern Drama*. Gregory was drawn not only to Andreyev's anti-tsarist, pro-revolutionary politics and concern for civil rights for Russian Jews and an end to violence, but to his interest in human psychology. Andreyev's popularity in America additionally meant that this play had the potential to earn its translator much-needed funds.[21]

Translation was also a portable project he took with him and worked on in hotel rooms and trains as he lectured on the Eastern Seaboard and in the Midwest. By the time James finally became an American citizen on 4 January 1921, Gregory had become familiar with large swathes of American geography and culture. Eight days after his brother's naturalisation, Gregory also began the process by declaring his intention to become a citizen in the Supreme Court in the Bronx. By the time Eugenia gave birth to Natalie on 25 January, however, Gregory was in St. Paul and received the news from Ray by telegram. From Minneapolis Gregory wrote James to congratulate him on the following day. Contextualising his reaction with a reference to Levin's passionate response to the birth of his first child in *Anna Karenina*, Gregory wrote,

> In such instances, people typically feel something and consider it their duty to convey that, while they actually may not feel a thing. I feel something. After all, you are wiser than me now. You now know exactly what Levin felt as he stood outside the door to Kitty's bedroom, but I don't. I send my greetings and very best wishes.

Gregory's note is sincere, generous, elegant, and typical. It is also a bit wistful. James would never actually be wiser than his brother, but in embarking on fatherhood, he was taking on an experience that Gregory, too, hoped to have. James was, however, on the brink of launching a professional career in his chosen field. Gregory was as yet in no position to take on the responsibility of children even had Ray wanted them. He was not quite living hand-to-mouth, but as soon as the money came in, it tended to go out, and the demands of lecturing were taking their toll. He closed by giving James a glimpse of his current life: 'I am traveling on tonight or setting out to Omaha, Nebraska tomorrow morning. I'll see another couple hundred old maids – damn!'[22]

Gregory continued to cobble together an intensive schedule of lectures throughout the winter and into the spring of 1921, but in March his translation of *He Who Gets Slapped* appeared in the modernist *Dial*. Gregory described Andreyev at the time he wrote the play in 1916 as on 'the last step of the pessimistic ladder which he was ever descending into the abyss of hopelessness'. The action occurs in a circus, a symbolic world 'full of spiders, champagne and human outcasts'. A highly educated intellectual feels he has no alternative but to become a clown, performing stunts and getting slapped, but 'the public laughs, unaware that this laughter is a mockery at itself, at its culture, at its thought, at its achievement'. Relations between individuals as well as groups are such that He is forced to efface himself. Andreyev treats his characters with 'bitter sarcasm and unfriendliness', yet he does not blame the clowns, jugglers, and bareback riders who finally collapse under the burden of 'fate, accident, and cowardly slander'. This powerful play is at once disquieting and poignant, and Gregory's masterful translation would enable opportunities that he could not have imagined.[23]

Lecturing, however, remained Gregory's primary source of income, and in the spring of 1921 he got lucky: He was invited to join the circuit of the Swarthmore Chautauqua, one of the travelling tent groups that sponsored educational lectures as well as dramatic and musical performances in small towns and farming communities throughout America in the days before radio and television brought information and entertainment to the masses. Throughout the summer he would follow a tight schedule organised by experienced administrators; he would move from town to town with at best a day between lectures, but he would meet other sophisticated performers – among them college professors, politicians, writers, and actors – and he would be well paid.

Already on the circuit in Woodstock, New York, in May, he wrote his brother of the changes in his fortune. James had apparently asked for money, which Gregory was unable to send. He confessed, 'I am simply in no physical position to do anything':

> The brother of one of my friends came to America recently. I owe this friend virtually everything I have, for without him I would have starved somewhere in Germany or Austria.... his brother has ended up in an extremely difficult situation, and I have helped him out a bit. About 6 weeks ago he suddenly fell dangerously ill: acute appendicitis, peritonitis....

Gregory had already sent James $100 from Memphis, which James had never acknowledged. Gregory nevertheless now told him,

> If you had turned to me before his illness, I could have done something. There is nobody I can borrow from. All of my friends here are *Americans*, orphans or penniless – or people with millions from whom I couldn't ask a kopeck.

With the signing of the Chautauqua contract, his current situation was relatively secure, he admitted, then offered his view of their fractured relationship. Gregory had often mentioned to Ray that James would likely need money now that he had a child and wanted to be in a position to help, hoping that things were not so bad for James as they seemed. He reflected,

> you and I practically never saw each other, we didn't know about each other and we showed no obvious interest in each other. That is the essence of all swinishness. We lived and live like strangers, and for that reason we are not prepared and not up to it when the occasion presents itself to help one another out – so we do nothing. This,

he concluded, 'is bad.' He now admitted that he had been wounded by his brother's disparagement, his evident indifference to *The Passing of the Old Order in Europe* and unwillingness to counter the accusations of bribery – in sum, his concerted separation of himself from Gregory's achievements and values. Having expressed his frustration in an angry tirade, Gregory typically put aside his hurt feelings and concluded with characteristic cleverness and humour,

> Believe me, I would give away all of my trousers now in order to help you, but as if to spite me (I mean this literally) all my trousers have split except my tuxedo trousers, and I had to order a suit specifically for the road. All of my suit coats have been left behind in the city without the trousers.[24]

With his new suit Gregory cut an elegant figure under the enormous Chautauqua tents. Off stage, he relaxed a bit with the other 'talent', as the circuit performers were known, while on the platform in the summer heat, he addressed farmers and shopkeepers, vicars and local officials, housewives and teachers on holiday, all of whom had put aside their normal activities for a week of educational entertainment. The Russian revolution, Bolshevism, and classical and modernist European drama may have been topics far from their daily experience, but in both substance and manner, Gregory was a hit. A North Carolina reporter summed up the reaction: 'Dr Zilboorg was easily the greatest speaker brought to Elizabeth City by the 1921 Chautauqua and made a profound impression.' When the season ended, Gregory had in his bag not only his tuxedo and plus fours but names and addresses of people who would invite him to speak in the coming months at civic and arts clubs and on university campuses. Perhaps even more important, he also had a signed Chautauqua contract for the following summer.[25]

GZ 'relaxing' with 'the talent', summer 1921

Meanwhile American newspapers reported worsening conditions in Russia. Severe food shortages in the Ukraine had gained world attention, and in August 1921 the U.S. Congress passed the Russian Famine Relief Act, authorising over $20 million in aid. The American Relief Administration began food distribution in the autumn in an effort that would continue for over two years. At its peak, the ARA, supported by Jewish and Christian agencies, fed over ten million Ukrainians on a daily basis. Kiev itself was outside the famine area; indeed, the surrounding fields were producing a surplus, but the Bolsheviks shipped the harvest elsewhere. American food, medical supplies and personnel, as well as trainloads of Ukrainian grain passed through Kiev's depots as did refugees fleeing stricken areas. By the end of the year typhus, influenza, small pox, and diphtheria posed problems not only in the eastern Ukraine but in Kiev and Minsk. In the winter, the situation became dire.[26]

Gregory worried about Russia but did what he could in speaking about its history and culture. While he had appreciated the enthusiasm of the Chautauqua crowds, in the autumn he began to seek more sophisticated audiences. In September his article 'Reflections on a Century of Political Experience and Thought' appeared in *Political Science Quarterly*. In November he spoke to the New York City Civic Club on 'Traveling Through the Gopher Prairies', a title that suggests with caustic humour his frustration with naïve listeners – those he had termed 'old maids' – and with his own life as a lecturer. In the same month his translation of *He Who Gets Slapped* was performed by students at Swarthmore College in Pennsylvania, a Quaker institution where the founder of the Swarthmore Chautauqua Paul Martin Pearson taught public speaking and Jesse Holmes, with whom Gregory had lectured over the summer, taught philosophy. Before year's end, Gregory's article 'Chautauqua and the Drama' appeared in *Drama*. Here he declared with some measure of pride,

> This season I visited nearly one hundred towns with the Chautauqua tent, beginning with North Carolina through the Virginias and Pennsylvania to New York State. The Swarthmore Chautauqua with which I traveled has in all about eight hundred towns and it undertook to present at least one drama or comedy and one opera in every town.

He came down hard on popular media, the 'banality' of jazz, vaudeville, and the movies ('a sliver sheet platitude') – all, in his opinion, inferior to drama in depth, emotional range, and psychological understanding.[27]

Drama weighed on his mind in the autumn of 1921, for he was networking in charismatic fashion and seizing the day to champion *He Who Gets Slapped*. The Swarthmore production was gratifying, but for the sake of Andreyev, Russian drama, and his own pocket, he hoped to see the play on Broadway. By December the Theatre Guild had decided to produce it, the Russian-born designer Robert Milton had agreed to direct it, and the accomplished Richard Bennett had been persuaded to accept the title role. Gregory would be credited as the translator in the programme and was involved less officially in the staging. There were meetings to attend and legal contracts to negotiate, but the play would open at the prestigious Garrick Theatre just after Christmas – in good time, depending on reviews, to make a splash for the 1922 season.

The play was, however, not the only thing that weighed on Gregory. James had received his degree in mechanical engineering in June 1921 and accepted a job at Westinghouse supervising the assembly and installation of steam turbo-generators in Philadelphia, Pittsburgh, and New York. He would never be rich, but his financial needs would be met by work in his chosen profession. While Gregory's own situation looked promising in December 1921, his income remained tenuous, dependent on whatever opportunities he could cobble together from week to week and month to month. He had always understood lecturing as incidental, not a career in itself. He wanted to continue to write, but he didn't want to be a professional writer any more than he wanted to be a professional translator. He saw his brother achieving professionally what he had always wanted, but apparently without envy or jealousy, neither of which were part of his character. Rather, liberated by James's success, Gregory felt that it was now his turn to realise his own aspirations.

He must have spent at least some of 1921 reflecting on his financial situation and professional goals. The ongoing process of inventing and reinventing himself was physically as well as psychologically exhausting. He was tired in all ways of living by his wits, moving about, never arriving at what he wanted to become, selling himself as this or that or something else again. He had not been free to define himself in Tsarist Russia or during the revolution. In America necessity had been the wind that had blown him hither and yon. Before the end of the year he decided (again) to commit himself to medicine.

The choice was a reprise of decisions he had made in Russia several times over, but it was quite a different path from the one he had been following since joining Kerensky's government. It was not what he had started when he enrolled as a graduate student at Columbia in the autumn of 1919, and it was a world away from the speaking platforms of provincial America, where he was generally introduced as Mr. Zilboorg (the former revolutionary, the literary man) and only occasionally as Dr. Zilboorg (the historian with a Ph.D. in law from the University of Petrograd and an M.D. from the Psycho-Neurological Institute). Three years after leaving Russia he still wanted to save the world and exalt the individual. An American medical degree would require a narrowing of focus, discipline, and commitment, but first he had to persuade the authorities at Columbia that he was up to the challenge, prepared and apt and dedicated to the work that lay ahead.

On 14 December 1921 Gregory attended an interview for admission to Columbia University's College of Physicians and Surgeons. As with anything he really wanted, he threw himself whole-heartedly and with all of his energy into the task of exceeding whatever standards were required, whatever the task necessitated. 'Overkill' does not begin to describe what Gregory was capable of on any front, and he pulled out all the stops. The interviewer's notes paint quite an extraordinary picture of a quite extraordinary applicant.

The interviewer began with the nuts and bolts of filling in a standard form with information most candidates would have found it easy to provide (Name? Home address? Present address? College? Average grades? High school? Extra-curricular activities?) but increasingly difficult for Gregory as he attempted to describe his educational and life experiences. Under 'Name', the interviewer wrote 'Dr. Gregory Zillbooweg', which he then corrected by crossing out one of the 'L's but still capturing phonetically what Gregory's pronunciation must have been at the time. Under 'College', the interviewer put 'Realschule, Kief, Russia'. 'Average Grades' was left blank, while after 'High School' and 'Extra-curricular Activities', the interviewer drew a black line suggesting irrelevance or his or Gregory's inability to approximate a suitable response. Under 'Financially OK', the interviewer, evidently assured by Gregory's confident response, wrote 'O.K.' Under 'Entrance requirements completed', the interviewer wrote 'All except English'. He left blank 'Oath of allegiance' and 'Letter of admission requirements', while under 'Psychologically', he was evidently nonplussed and put merely a question mark. Under 'Remarks', however, the interviewer indicated that he was impressed. 'Has been a member of Kerensky's cabinet. Speaks excellent English. Is taking a Ph.D. at Columbia in the Faculty of Political Science', and finally 'Is evidently a man of brilliant mind. Wants to study medicine to apply psychopathology to social problems.' Nevertheless, Gregory up close and engaged in private conversation revealed inadvertently tensions and contradictions invisible to his lecture audiences. Despite his excellent English, he was still an aspiring immigrant; despite elegant accoutrements and confidence, he remained financially pressed. The faculty member concluded with a few observations on the candidate's physical condition: Gregory had 'long black hair with what appear to be nits in it and lots of dandruff on his sealskin collar.'[28]

Gregory in his coat with the sealskin collar, 1921

Gregory's decision to pursue an American medical degree at the very moment he was coming into his own as a drama critic and translator is perhaps ironic but unsurprising. The young man who had studied under Bekhterev wanted to be a doctor as well as a lawyer, a psychiatrist as well as a revolutionary. He was a student of human beings in their social context, an advocate for those he saw suppressed by the tsar and the Bolsheviks in Russia and by mass culture, conformity, and commercialism in America. Gregory's writing and lectures had stressed the psychological impact of war and revolution on the individual, and *The Passing of the Old Order in Europe* had been the expression of everything he thought and felt on those subjects. The book completed, he had turned his attention to the nature of the theatre, to the psychology of both playwrights and their fictional characters, and to the psychological dynamics of Russian but particularly American plays and audiences.

Between 1920 and 1922, Gregory wrote regularly for *Drama*, offering everything from 'A Course in Russian Drama' to his opinions on individual plays and productions. Above all, however, he used his articles to expound his theories of art in general and the theatre specifically. In each case, his point of view was ethical and psychological. He declared, for example, that Russian theatre was historically 'a social and moral institution', while 'its point of departure, its premises, were psychologically deeply rooted in the social aspirations and moral ideals of a given period'. He abhorred the contemporary American 'star system', which he saw as 'anti-individualistic' since it prevented 'psychological harmony and consistency'. Drama's substance, he contended, was the 'interplay and interstruggle of emotions and ideas' in which every actor was given 'the full possibility of self expression'.[29]

Arguing both psychologically and philosophically, Gregory theorised that 'Art must not estrange itself from suffering', from depicting characters under stress, but he was simultaneously interested in the sociological as well as psychological relationship between audience and play. Thus he contended that *Hamlet* 'was in Russia almost a national play, because the Russian intellectual, his hesitation, his head of a *raisonneur*, his heart of an impulsive rebel and his tiny willpower found himself in Hamlet'. Using explicitly psychological language that was not yet Freudian, he posited that drama 'is essentially the artistic expression of our social ego in its conflicts with our other egos'. Because it was 'a complex synthetic phenomenon', theatre would fail as theatre if one of drama's many elements was 'deliberately given a predominant part to the detriment of others'. Seeking an appropriate metaphor, he looked to music rather than to psychoanalysis: 'Theatre is symphonic – a compound expression of interrelations and interactions among individuals, masses, principles, traditions, initiatives, personalities and conventionalities.' Ethical concerns were characteristically as central to Gregory's thinking as his understanding of theatre as a psychological phenomenon. He went so far as to call the principle of artistic freedom his 'religion', insisting that art must be unhampered and unimpeded, not 'interfered with by any authorities legal or moral': 'The lawmaker or politician has no right to interfere with the freedom of the theatre any more than he has the right to prescribe the use of certain manners of yawning or sleeping', while 'The official moralist has no more rights than the politician.' As in *The Passing of the Old Order in Europe*, in his drama criticism Gregory looked at the relationship between the masses and the individual, and always came out in favour of the latter: 'Since freedom is the essential part of any art and especially that of the theatre, the drama must be free of the mob spirit which is slavish by nature' and cruelly absorbs 'the creative initiative of the individual.'[30]

As Gregory began garnering recommendations for his admission to medical school, he continued to write for *Drama*, employing language that was increasingly psychiatric. In 'The Theatre of the Past in Soviet Russia', he wrote, 'Russia, being in a state of revolution, lives on mass psychosis and on compulsion. Therefore the theatre as a whole is inevitably made subservient to the abnormal psychic state of the people' and 'there is a certain retrogression toward primitive pageantry, spontaneity of mass emotions, the disintegration of intimacy and lyricism, which always are the characteristic traits of dramatic art even in dialogue and mass movement.' He concluded, 'what we have in Russia is the theatre of the long lost past, which came back to us quite naturally just as many of our slumbering primitive instincts awake in us in time of distress and moral exhaustion.'[31]

Given obligations to which he had already committed himself and his determination to take up medicine once more, Gregory was emotionally divided. *He Who Gets Slapped* debuted to rave reviews in January 1922 and Brentano's published the play in the spring. With a reputation as an accomplished translator, he began to consider projects that might sustain him through the medical studies he hoped lay ahead. He began to translate Ilya Surguchev's 1915 play, *The Violins of Autumn*. Years later, however, he revealed the personal significance of the choice he was making, declaring, 'medicine contained and carried within itself the eternal values of mutual assistance, preservation of life, alleviation of suffering, and rendering man a useful member of the community.' He chose psychiatry specifically because of its commitment to 'man as a living value in himself, man as a living unit who in addition to his obligations to God and society has rights which he may assert, man as a functioning unit of mankind', because of psychiatry's commitment to 'the concept of the human personality and man's value as a social particle, as a living individuality, as a moral unit, and as a carrier of life'.[32]

Admission to Columbia was not yet assured, however, and he had hoops to jump through to complete his application. Before a notary public on 17 February Gregory swore to the accuracy of official translations of his school leaving documents. On the same day, the director of admissions sent a letter to Dr. Frederick T. van Beuren at the College of Physicians and Surgeons stating formally, 'the education certified to by these credentials covers fully the requirements for admission.'[33]

Gregory lined up recommendations by seeking out eminent members of Columbia's faculty who might be willing to support his candidacy. Despite the unusual transcript of incomplete coursework, it seems that Gregory was indeed a doctoral candidate in political science. William A. Dunning of Columbia University's Department of History readily agreed to write to William Darrach, dean of the College of Physicians and Surgeons, calling Gregory 'a gentleman of wide culture, high character and great zeal in the cause of scholarship and the practical application of knowledge'.[34]

When Gregory discussed his intention to return to medicine with Columbia's bacteriologist Hans Zinsser, he made such a positive impression that the renowned professor suggested he apply for advanced standing. After careful consideration, however, Gregory decided against it: 'I do not want to make a fool of myself by attempting to pass examinations for which I am not prepared.' He reflected honestly, 'I have been out of touch with Medicine for over five years. I am busy now and shall remain busy until next fall and therefore will be unable to look over my medical books.' He nevertheless anticipated that soon as he started, it would

> easily be seen how far advanced I am as compared with the regular beginner and although technically I will not be exemted [sic]. I hope I will actually enjoy a certain freedom of work and shall be busy not so much with segregating the *musculus sartorius* as with serious study.

Gregory's main worry was not advanced standing but the fact that the medical school would not make a decision until July. He explained to Zinsser, 'It would be [a] rather painful situation if they should reject me. I therefore want to ask you to be kind enough to pull all the strings and press all the buttons you deem necessary and possible.' He detailed his predicament:

> I want to point out to you that I am now busy with thoroughly liquidating many of my present activities and connections in order to have my time free next fall for medical work. Imagine my connections disconnected and my doings undone and … for some reason or other a negative reply to my application.

Having been encouraged by the dean to apply to more than one medical school, Gregory declared his reluctance:

> I have a sentimental attachment to Columbia University. I am there a candidate for a Ph.D. in the Faculty of Political Science. After a short while I shall therefore be a Columbia alumnus and I would hate to leave an institution to whose liberal spirit I owe a great deal.

Gregory closed with profuse thanks, then characteristically added a cheeky postscript: 'Am sending[,] under separate cover, some of my printed works.'[35]

This significant letter indicates Gregory's confidence as well as his clearly fraught and worried state. His English is at once elegant and not quite perfect:

He occasionally omits necessary articles and commas, yet tenses and even modal verbs are correct and precise; word order is only occasionally unnatural. His use of repetition and sensitivity to the sound of his sense results in powerful phrasing ('Imagine my connections disconnected and my doings undone'), while his balancing of long with simple sentences is stylish and dramatic. The capital 'M' in 'Medicine' suggests its importance to him, while his use of Latin ('*musculus sartorius*') is both consciously humorous, professionally accurate, and typical bravado. He appears a bit desperate, emotionally honest, even confessional, and grateful to the point of fawning at the same time that he vaunts his impressive achievements. The letter also reveals his sense that he might only be able to get what he wanted by pulling strings and pressing buttons, relying on influence and being seen as an exception to the rule, a uniquely worthy case. This sort of behaviour enabled him to survive as an intellectual Jew in Tsarist Russia and to escape across wartime Europe; it helped him to negotiate immigration to the United States and to earn a professional living even while struggling to master English and adapt more generally to American life – and it would help to get him admitted to Columbia's medical school.

Zinsser forwarded this letter to William Darrach on 23 February, explaining that he really didn't know Gregory and thus didn't feel able to make a recommendation, but pointing out that 'The quality of this letter will perhaps give you a better idea of his really considerable intelligence.' On 2 March the dean received yet another letter on Gregory's behalf – from Edward Alsworth Ross, professor of sociology at the University of Wisconsin, who claimed to know the candidate better than Zinsser:

> I regard him as a brilliant and highly gifted man who has already demonstrated his intellectual power as well as his quick mastery of the English language.... I consider that Doctor Zilboorg is so highly gifted that he will make a name and a career for himself in this country and that he will rank eventually among our most valuable citizens.

Such fulsome praise was generous as well as prescient. If Darrach had any doubts about admitting Gregory to Columbia's College of Physicians and Surgeons, this recommendation must have assuaged them. Ross made clear that in his opinion Gregory was no ordinary immigrant to the land of the free and reflected perceptively, 'Every such great social upheaval as that which occurred in Russia has cast into foreign countries types that otherwise never migrate and that may greatly profit the country which gives them opportunity. Doctor Zilboorg is one of this kind.'[36]

Notes

1 GZ to Hans Zinsser, 22 February 1922, ASCCU; GZ to 'Très Saint-Père', 31 January 1953, APD.
2 GZ, 'The Vicissitude', 393–397.

3 Powers, 15, 23.
4 JZ to GZ, 21 August 1919.
5 GZ to JZ, 22 August 1919.
6 'Mr. Zilboorg's Position', np; 'Concerning a Kolchak Picture', np.
7 GZ to Judah Leon Magnes, 1 October 1919, Magnus papers, Central Archives for the History of the Jewish People, Hebrew University of Jerusalem.
8 GZ to JZ, 1 December 1919.
9 GZ to Magnes, 22 December 1919.
10 GZ to NM, 26 January 1953; email from AZ, 18 September 2013.
11 Email from AZ, 18 September 2013.
12 Marriage record 6419, New York City Municipal Archives, the Bronx; GZ to Magnes, 22 December 1919.
13 GZ, POOE, 9.
14 GZ, POOE, 22–26.
15 GZ, POOE, 36, 46, 47, 50–51, 55, 63, 64–65, 66, 84, 85.
16 GZ, POOE, 139–143.
17 Stoddard, 142–143, 183–184, 194; 'The Old Order Passes', *New York Tribune*, 21 November 1920, Section VII, 11; Alfred S. Clark, 'What Are the New Books Saying?' *Boston Post*, 2 December 1920, 18.
18 'Russia Can Be Saved by Trade with America', *Democrat and Chronicle*, 19 November 1920, 27; Clum, 12.
19 GZ to JZ, 5 May 1921.
20 FZ, Oskow and Orkin interviews.
21 Rischin, 53.
22 GZ to JZ, 26 January 1921.
23 GZ, 'Introduction', *He Who Gets Slapped*, 7, 8; Rischin, 51.
24 GZ to JZ, 5 May 1921.
25 *The Independent* (Elizabeth City, North Carolina), 10 June 1921, 1.
26 Fisher, 29, 442–443.
27 GZ, 'Chautauqua', 17, 18.
28 GZ, interview, 14 December 1921, ASCCU.
29 GZ, 'The Star', 95, 96.
30 GZ, 'Intellectual Ice Cream', 336; GZ, 'The Theatre of the Past', 195.
31 GZ, 'The Theatre of the Past', 195, 196.
32 GZ, 'The Changing Concept', 446.
33 Director of admissions to Frederick T. van Beuren, ASCCU.
34 William A. Dunning to William Darrach, ASCCU.
35 GZ to Zinsser, 22 February 1922, ASCCU.
36 Zinsser to Darrach, 23 February 1922, ASCCU; Zinsser to GZ, 8 July 1936; Edward Alsworth Ross to Darrach, 2 March 1922, ASCCU; Ross, 8.

Chapter 7

'The Great Columbia University'

1922–1923

In the spring of 1922 Gregory and James began to send food and clothing to Kiev. Basia had married in late 1919 and had been right to worry about Berdychevsky, who died not of wounds but of a ruptured appendix two months before their daughter Nadia was born in July 1920. Basia as a young mother and widow continued to live in the family apartment where the addition of a baby didn't make difficult life on Kostiantynivska Street any easier.

Basia, Fera, and Nadia, Kiev, 1922

There was certainly plenty of room for a child. In summer of 1921, when his repeated arrests became too dangerous, the family had scraped together enough money to enable Sol Levitas to escape to Poland. By the spring of 1922 he was in Danzig, a 'Free City' under the protection of the League of Nations. Sol's absence didn't apparently bother the Russian authorities, but they no longer wanted to board people in the Zilboorg apartment; they wanted the apartment itself. Threatened with eviction, Moses sold the parcels from America in order to bribe officials to allow the family to remain. When Fera thanked her brothers separately for their help, Gregory advised her to leave; she should join her fiancé and together they

DOI: 10.4324/9781003190936-7

should leave Europe for the United States. For the first time since Budapest, he also wrote to his parents.

Fera was torn: She felt obligations to her widowed sister and to her aging parents. She loved little Nadia, but she loved Sol, too, and they had been separated for nearly a year. The Emergency Immigration Act of 1921 made it more difficult for Russians to enter the United States, yet Sol had family in Chicago and the right to residence; he had started the citizenship process by filing his declaration of intention in 1916. James had just become a citizen and Gregory had written a book in English and translated a play. She felt sure these achievements would count for something but realised her departure would mean less income for the family left behind. Sol told her one could get along in German in Danzig, but despite the war, the revolution, and its continuing aftermath, Russia was home, and no one she knew stayed for long in Danzig; Danzig was where, after Poland, Russians went en route to somewhere else.

Gregory wasn't sure what part to play. He could send parcels through aid agencies and money when he had money to send, but as matters were coming to a head, he was on the road again. Without his work on the lecture circuit, there would be no money to send abroad, but with medical school on the horizon, he was also translating at a hectic pace. He found the work tiresome and was distracted by worry about his family. James had told him before he set out that, in his opinion, the best plan might be to bring the entire family to New York. James was on the road himself between Westinghouse factories and reminded Gregory that he had a family of his own to support. Worried about Gregory's finances as well as his own, James wondered if Gregory could return to Kiev to supervise the exodus, asked if he knew someone influential who could go on their behalf. In his opinion, they needed to do something, but Gregory should do it; he reminded his older brother, who didn't need reminding, that Gregory was older and more familiar with circumstances, while James hadn't seen the family in nearly a decade. James repeated what their sisters had written to him and Eugenia: Basia was worried for the child; Fera didn't know what to do. James had never met Levitas: Was he the right man for Fera?

Gregory did not take kindly to this sort of badgering, to unproductive worry and unanswerable questions, but he was concerned himself, felt a degree of responsibility and an abiding affection, especially for Fera and his father. Gregory did what he could over the summer. He spoke to acquaintances in Washington while he was there in June, and on a brief trip back to New York he received the first letter from his father since his departure. A letter from Fera was also waiting for him as well as one from James, telling Gregory again what he felt best while reiterating his own inability to do anything practical beyond the sending of yet another parcel. Gregory responded at length to James from Pennsylvania, enclosing the letters from Moses and Fera so his brother could read for himself how things stood. James's point of view had troubled Gregory so much that he had spent a night walking in the fields outside Carlisle and had been unable to shake off the ensuing exhaustion for a week.

His thinking, however, had crystallised upon reading his father's letter. He felt it reinforced his point of view and gave him so much joy that the fatigue caused by his sleeplessness had immediately disappeared. He arranged to send his parents $200 through the ARA, then reassured James,

> Everything is clear. From Firka's letter you will understand that I invited her one and a half months ago now. It is possible that she is already abroad or that she will be soon. In any event, I hope that she will be here no later than the end of September. As an American citizen, you will have to help with the affidavit.

He reassured his brother, 'Don't worry about the rest.'

Although James thought the entire family should come to the United States, Gregory felt only Fera should come and summarised the situation as he saw it. Pointing out that they had always viewed their parents' situation differently, that without consulting him or against his advice, James had been encouraging the family to emigrate, Gregory had decided to act 'personally and independently'. He knew James would be offended, made clear that of course James had the right to do things his own way, but he in his turn had to proceed as he saw fit. He hoped James would now stop worrying and fussing, for his own sake but also for the sake of the family. He wrote, 'Firka's trip, helping our parents materially and monetarily, Firka's wardrobe, et cetera, is going to cost me about 1,500 dollars – our poor sister is extremely tired and in need of sympathy and peace.'

Well aware that he would be earning nothing during the upcoming winter because of his commitment to medical school, Gregory needed to be financially careful at every turn and did not feel he could accommodate the entire family in a small apartment near Columbia, where he hoped to move as soon as he heard about admission. With less travel on his schedule, he must have hoped for a conventional married life with Ray, but as a student he anticipated regular lectures and long hours working in laboratories. If he took in family, he told James, 'That would mean ruining not only my life, but theirs as well, since they will hardly be happy if they have to live with us, on our shoulders, at a time when my means are insufficient.' Furthermore, Gregory felt that it would be painful for the family to leave the apartment for which they had just paid a very high price. He explained his reasoning:

> If with my help they manage to breathe freely this upcoming year or two, they will relax and perk up. If I spend on them and for them, let's say, another thousand dollars this year, and yet another thousand the following year, then my plan will succeed.

In sum, he reassured James, his threefold responsibility – to Fera, to his parents, and to Ray – was 'an exceedingly difficult although tolerable combination'.

In closing, Gregory typically changed the subject. Once he had said what he had to say, expressed his deeply felt convictions, unburdened himself of his irritation and frustration, even anger and exasperation, Gregory was always ready to move on even if his audience was stunned or hurt or outraged. Moving on was, for Gregory, closure: He had expressed himself and unreasonably expected others to feel as he felt, to feel that the storm had passed for them as it had for him. He asked James if Westinghouse made accessories for a wireless telegraph and, in case it did, if James could get such things for him at a discount. If his brother could send him a catalogue, Gregory would let him know what he needed. Such a request, at the end of such a letter, was not for Gregory offensive, but he probably suspected that James might find it so. Despite his egotism, Gregory was not a selfish man nor was he insensitive to other people's feelings; he could be extremely blunt, but he was also capable of great kindness. With respect to finances, money was something one earned and then spent. What things cost was a practical matter about which he had no scruples. If he wanted something, he asked. If someone needed something he had, he would give it if he could. Money was no deterrent to asking or giving, although reality did enter the equation, so if one could get something at a discount, all the better. Sensitive to his brother's psychology, Gregory explained what for him was merely a practical matter: The items he was requesting were not for him personally 'but for a very sick boy who has taken up wireless telegraphy. I promised him I would help set him up with everything he needs so that it does not cost him a lot of money.'[1]

The events that followed as Fera left Kiev would define the relations among the siblings for the rest of their lives. Just as the altercation in the summer of 1919 had been a defining crisis in the relationship between Gregory and James, the practical and emotional dynamics of the summer and autumn of 1922 would define the relationship between Gregory and Fera. Unrealistically, Gregory had expected to find in James the ideal brother he had longed for. He had similarly unrealistic expectations of Fera and misunderstood her aspirations. He nevertheless had an abiding respect for his oldest sister and felt a measure of responsibility for her.

Fera's escape from Russia was more difficult than Gregory's four years earlier. For Fera, there would be no simple train from the Kiev station. By 1922 one needed an exit visa, and because she could not legally get one, her escape was a classic refugee story that began with finding someone to smuggle her across the border. In late June she travelled west with an agent and another woman in a horse-drawn cart as far as a village on the Russian frontier, sheltered in a peasant hut while the man who had brought her drank vodka with the guards. Under the cover of darkness they crossed on foot into Polish fields. When they heard barking dogs, the agent spread a fur coat on the grass, told his passengers to lie down, then covered them with branches. There they hid for the rest of the night while the man went to find another cart and horse. They drove off quickly before sunrise; if stopped, the women were to say they were going to a wedding. At dawn they arrived at a town with an office staffed by the Hebrew Immigrant

Aid Society, where the other woman's husband was waiting. With false papers provided by HIAS, Fera next took a train to Warsaw, then another to Danzig. At the free state frontier she was roughly searched by a guard, but a HIAS agent intervened, grabbed Fera's small suitcase and together they ran through the station to the street outside, where Sol was standing behind a barrier. The guard who undressed her had failed to find the only things of value: two 20-franc gold pieces she had carefully sewn into her garter belt. The coins, Moses had told her when he gave them to her, were for wedding rings. By the end of June, as Gregory was justifying himself to his brother and as James was fretting about his own as well as everyone else's finances, about what might happen and what anyone should and could do about it, Fera was in Danzig, settled in a rented room, waiting for Gregory to send money for the boat and to arrange the papers she needed for the voyage to America.

Still on tenterhooks about Columbia, at the end of June Gregory was in Ashland, 100 miles northwest of Philadelphia, where he addressed 'an audience of 1,200 coalminers'. Knowing his brother was truly emotionally distressed, he had recently telephoned him from Birdsboro, a steel factory town on the Schuylkill River in western Pennsylvania – not exactly a Gopher Prairie, but a similar distance from the urban sophistication of New York or Petrograd. The call had cost Gregory a pretty penny, and he must have felt it was important. In addition to immediate family, concerns pressing upon James included Eugenia's parents, who like the Zilboorgs were suffering in Kiev, and his own finances: Finishing his degree had put him $600 in debt, and his job at Westinghouse was not generating enough to pay it off. He asked Gregory for money.

Gregory mastered his impatience with his brother's morose focus on trivialities and tried to comfort him, to persuade him to see the future more optimistically and to pay attention to life's positive elements rather than indulge in complaints Gregory saw as 'childish nonsense'. Gregory wrote bluntly,

> I am having a difficult time, my brother, and you know it. You are having a difficult time, and I know it. Truly, why worry oneself, why intensify the sadness? You know very well that your situation does anything but make me happy. You also know that thinking about the old folks and their cruel life is becoming even more frightening now with Firka's departure.

He reminded James that their father had been very happy with Gregory's progress in America and had thought his letters sensible. Putting aside the tensions between the two brothers, Gregory informed James of the actions he had taken: He had wired Fera $150 and followed up with a bank transfer of another $150. He had then sent Fera a telegram telling her a letter would follow.

His summary of this letter to Fera and his directions to James detailing what part he should play reveal Gregory's attention to detail and managerial efficiency, his ability to see the big picture, to put wheels in motion, to take charge and cope. He was once again the director of the *corps de ballet*. He had advised his sister 'to leave for Berlin, put on her shoes, get dressed, freshen up and not worry about a thing'. He told James to send Fera an affidavit of his citizenship and a copy of his naturalisation papers. 'Be so kind', he wrote,

> as to arrange all this and try to see to it that the letter goes out on the *S.S. President Arthur* headed for Danzig from the Port of New York on Saturday at 3 o'clock in the afternoon. Letters are probably picked up only before 10 or 11 o'clock in the morning. If you drop a letter in the mailbox at or near City Hall on Friday after 12 o'clock noon, that will work out nicely.

Gregory enclosed a check:

> Cash it and arrange for the following: Send out several 50-dollar parcels – two in Father's name, two in Mother's and one in Basia's. Keep the remaining 50 for yourself; it will probably come in handy before the first of the month.

James still thought an American citizen should go to Russia and bring Fera to the United States. He did not volunteer to be that citizen, but Gregory would not be eligible for citizenship for another two years and neither of them was financially or otherwise in a position to make the trip. Since January Gregory had thought that someone should travel to Kiev, and he imagined returning to see his parents himself once he and Ray were both American citizens, but all this was now moot. He told his brother his priority had to be earning money. 'Firka is costing me about 1,000 dollars', he told James, and imagined that 'she will cost a good deal more' since, he presumed, she was committed to finishing her university education. He wanted to be able to fund that once she crossed the ocean.

Dealing with family concerns was sandwiched between Chautauqua engagements, and Gregory's characteristic energy is impressive. In Washington earlier in the month he had spoken to Congressman Albert Johnson, chair of the Committee on Immigration and Naturalization; in St. Louis he had met with Dr. Max Aaron Goldstein, founder and director of the Central Institute for the Deaf, who was planning a summer trip to Europe with his wife. Perhaps, Gregory thought, the Goldsteins could bring Fera back with them, ostensibly as a private servant. Gregory was pulling out the stops for Fera as he had for himself in Holland, making political, professional, and personal connections and calling upon anyone he felt might help. He pleaded with his brother as he tried to console him: 'please, Ionya, don't be nervous and don't imagine unnecessary nonsense. Whom God helps, nobody can harm. After all, we are accustomed to standing up to grief.... It is not worth getting upset about small things. Life is difficult enough'. Gregory needed to get on with his own life, but despite his numerous responsibilities and impatience with his brother, he had not lost his sense of humour. He was writing James with only a few minutes to spare before his lecture. Obligated to pass through Philadelphia between two provincial cities, he had not slept for 76 hours; his hands and feet were swollen and his head was splitting, but he had downed a shot of whisky and said to himself, ' "Workhorse! Off to plow Shakespeare!" '[2]

At the beginning of July Gregory at last received confirmation of his acceptance at Columbia with fees partially waived or at least deferred for the first year. This must have been reassuring, but Gregory had already counted on it, planned for it, anticipated the four years of study that awaited him. He also received yet another anxious letter from his brother. Nearly at the end of his patience, Gregory replied characteristically from Middleburg, Pennsylvania. He told James emphatically that he was not going to respond to his nervous irritability. He did not want to put further strain on their relationship, but he did want to address some of his brother's doubts and statements.

James was sceptical about Gregory's financial resources. Gregory reassured him: He was still earning royalties from *He Who Gets Slapped*; he was getting $250 a week for this year's 19 weeks of lectures on the Chautauqua circuit, and had just been invited to speak during the summers of 1923 and 1924, so he felt his needs were more than met for the immediate future. James had, in Gregory's view, gotten himself 'all worked up for nothing' about what Gregory had said about his inability to help him repay his debt. James had indicated the amount and Gregory had openly and honestly told him that he simply could not send him such a large sum of money now. He then begged James not to share doubts about his means with Fera: 'You don't even know what they are', he wrote, 'and the poor girl will lose her mind with worry and anguish now that all her hopes and dreams are focused on the help I can give her.'

James was suspicious of what he saw as the 'secretive nature' of Fera's arrival. There was nothing at all secretive about it, Gregory informed him. He confessed that Fera's predicament had 'tormented' him terribly, and he had been as surprised as James by the suddenness of her plans. He was concerned above all about the impact her departure might have on their parents and in his letters to them had suggested diplomatically that Fera's departure would not be 'a final separation' but only a temporary period of study to finish her degree in bacteriology. However, he explained to his brother, 'Firka had become so miserable and exhausted that she immediately responded to the invitation herself and left the country right away.' Gregory, while feeling badly for his parents, was glad that Fera was coming. He understood his brother but felt he was 'too uninterested in the facts and too interested in imagined and presumed relationships' and 'ulterior motives'. With a good grasp of everyone's psychology including his own, Gregory was on top of the situation. Despite limited patience, his own egotism and tendency to tell others what to do, he was reasonable and responsible. He had taken charge and was diplomatic but clear, understanding but firm.[3]

Never one to let anything go easily, James followed up with yet another challenging letter, which Gregory answered from Berwick, 60 miles east of Middleburg but 120 miles north of Philadelphia, where the itinerant lecturer had to go to change trains. Gregory had now reached the end of his tether. 'I would be hard pressed to say I derive much pleasure from our correspondence', he told James. Gregory was distressed that Eugenia had only added a brief note to her husband's letter, the first he had heard directly from her after a long silence, and that his brother apparently couldn't see the forest for the trees, but found it ridiculous to quarrel. Indeed, he felt the situation would be funny were it not so sad. Eugenia had evidently reproached her brother-in-law with some rumour she had heard, and Gregory told her the gossip was absurd: 'if you are not contradicting it but merely mentioning it, then you should be ashamed of yourself.'

In short, Eugenia and James wanted to return the $50 he had told them to keep. This Gregory also found silly, evidence of conventional bourgeois morality. He analysed the situation: He himself was well acquainted with difficult times, want of money, and the anguish of deprivation. He had suffered physically and been nervous, but poverty had never humiliated him; he had never been ashamed of it. The whole trouble, he told James and Eugenia,

> is that you are *ashamed* that you lack money. For you, receiving help seems a *disgrace*; that is why it is twice as difficult for you and why you have conjured up this monstrous nonsense regarding my alleged fears that you would expect my help as if you were slaves of some kind.

He felt their distrust and suspicion isolated them from people and the world. Such alienation was not only foolish but, in his opinion, 'unsafe, not only from an intellectual and cultural standpoint', but from the standpoint of 'moral hygiene'. Gregory's psychological perspective was penetrating. 'Don't be suspicious', he advised, 'don't be distrusting, and much of what you are now "sure" of will lose its verisimilitude.' While James claimed that his view was a result of age and experience, Gregory in fact discerned in his brother 'a very real immaturity seasoned with a subconscious yet obvious bourgeois conventionalism'. While James had claimed to be unsentimental, it seemed to Gregory his brother needed to become a bit more sentimental for, he chided, 'sensitivity is clearly born of sentimentality'.

Gregory concluded by returning to the practical problem of enabling Fera to come to America. The Goldsteins couldn't bring her with them as they were returning via England and if Fera were to accompany them, another set of complicated visas would need to be negotiated. The doctor and his wife had, however, seen Fera and were still in Danzig. He was sending them 150 German marks to give to her. In an effort to conclude this phase of his correspondence with James, Gregory informed him that he would be in New York for a week later in the month; they could see each other and discuss matters then.[4]

Gregory's letters to James during the summer of 1922 reveal a competent man of wide experience, insight, and good judgement. He was managing an intensely busy life on practical, financial, and emotional fronts: lecturing hither and yon over a hectic summer, arranging his sister's immigration, and preparing to shift identities yet again, this time from a highly regarded lecturer and translator to a rather lowly student. Ray was holding down the fort in New York, there to welcome her busy husband home when he returned and supportive of his decisions. She herself saw James and Eugenia from time to time and reiterated Gregory's view of Fera's pending arrival. Gregory's marriage had adapted itself to the rhythms of his life, and the fact that he and Ray were often apart was a tolerable necessity, although both of them must have looked forward to the relative calm and stability the autumn would bring.

Not yet a medical student but no longer the young revolutionary just off the boat, Gregory concentrated his energies more and more on understanding not the history and future of the modern world but the inner life of the individual human being. Throughout the rest of July and into August, he lectured in upstate New York. His polished performances typically began with establishing a combative relationship with his audience. He would warn them, 'I am not a pleasant talker. I make it my business to be unpleasant. I dislike the word "pleasant" and the word "future".' Some of what followed derived from his book, but his lectures suggest an increased emphasis on human psychology and spiritual life. In 'The Emancipation of Liberty' Gregory told his listeners that emotions on their own were not spiritual but animal, that human psychology was not spiritual unless enlightened by human ideals. He observed that in speaking about feelings, people try to explain them away rather than explain them and pointed out, 'Humanity would be better off if we adopt the view that the future is in the present if we try to do right and act in accordance with spiritual ideals.' Too easily people followed leaders rather than thinking for themselves so, he announced, we lack liberty and suffer 'a spiritual death'. Somewhat bitterly he declared that he did not apply his analysis to any particular country but to the whole world.

The lecture is full of such sweeping statements designed to startle. Gregory told his listeners, 'The one thing the world has too much of is leaders.' Typically, he then refined and explained, 'Leadership should be the expression of accumulated spiritual forces, and not that of the man who leads the sheep. The only thing the public does not need is rest. Today we must be restless.' He then softened his tone, revealing the kinder, gentler, more vulnerable man. Another thing people needed was mutual understanding and he offered Jesus as an example, pointing out, 'Christ … had no utilitarian idea but talked alike to the sinner and the rich man.' He concluded, 'Today we are suffering from the spiritual degeneration of the world.… I do not like to be the prophet or the physician. The patient must know his cure if he feels it.' In his lectures Gregory was at once provocative and accommodating, antagonistic and comforting. He painted a picture of the world in dire straits and told his listeners what he saw as uncomfortable truths, bullying them, then insisting they were capable of doing right, acting in accordance with spiritual ideals, imitating Christ, and promoting mutual understanding.[5]

Much as Gregory may have declared that he didn't like being prophet and physician, those were indeed the roles he assumed, and his lectures were simultaneously jeremiad and consolation. 'The Emancipation of Liberty' finally reveals as much about his own spiritual, emotional, and intellectual state as it does about his techniques and convictions. The techniques would be useful to him in speaking and writing throughout his professional life, as would many of the conclusions he had arrived at by August 1922. That patients would know their cure if they felt it would become an underlying principle of his psychoanalytic practice, while the restlessness he urged was certainly something he had felt most of his life. He still felt restless as the summer drew to a close, but spiritually he was beginning to feel he might have found the right path.

Gregory was specifically thinking a good deal about Christ, and he may have discussed spiritual life with some of his Chautauqua colleagues when he wasn't exhausted by travel or busy sending funds and parcels to Danzig and Kiev or writing letters to his nervous brother. At home in the new apartment with Ray, he certainly discussed family matters, but he probably kept his spiritual life to himself. Spiritual life must have seemed less immediate than dealing with the practical problems of monthly rent, university responsibilities, and Fera's continuing plight.

By August Fera had managed to secure a visa to enter the United States, but she and Sol still didn't have enough money for their tickets. She had taken Gregory at his word and spent a good deal of what he had already sent. She cheerily informed James, 'I am brand new from head to toe – from my underwear and stockings all the way to my winter coat.' She was planning to spend a little of the remaining funds on a parcel to Kiev while waiting for additional funds from her generous elder brother, but she was eager to cross the ocean, for what she thought of as 'a normal life' after the privations of war, revolution, and the Soviet regime. Despite relatively peaceful life in Danzig, Fera was not a flibbertigibbet; she was an intelligent and capable woman who was also bored, tired of shopping and doing nothing. Nevertheless, she and Sol had mixed feelings about emigration. Leaving Europe had a finality about it for a Jew. She wanted to see America and her brothers, and Sol wanted to see his family in Chicago, but Fera already missed the family she had left behind in what she told James was 'our Russia'. For their part, she wrote, 'Our family misses me terribly. Papa writes such teary letters – they are painful to read.' Deserted by three of his children, Moses had put aside his characteristic detachment and reserve; he had become 'a sentimentalist'. Maybe, Fera now thought, she and Sol might go to Germany; maybe they would visit America, then return 'home' to Russia.[6]

With his lectures finally over, Gregory sorted his finances: so much for Fera and Sol, who married in Danzig on 22 September; so much for regular parcels to Moses and Anna and Basia and her daughter in Kiev; so much for rent and living expenses for him and Ray; so much for tuition for Columbia. The summer had ended well. He had been invited to serve on the Chautauqua Drama Board along with Paul Pearson, Sam Hume (a professor at the University of California at Berkeley), Winthrop Ames (a New York theatrical director), George P. Baker (dean of the School of Dramatic Art at Harvard University), Theodore Ballou Hinkley (editor of *Drama*), and Charles F. Warner (director of the Redpath Chautauqua). Pearson and Hume would become good friends, while the others would be helpful contacts in the theatre world that Gregory continued to care so deeply about.

As he finally began his first semester at Columbia University, Gregory's status shifted, but that wasn't the only thing changing in New York. James's position at Westinghouse wasn't so secure as he had imagined. The company could move young men about as it wished, and what it wished was to move him to their new plant in Monterrey, Mexico. In September Eugenia's parents, like Fera, paid an intermediary and left Russia for Danzig, undecided about their terminus but with similarly mixed feelings about America. For the Hel'fmans it was Palestine that beckoned, but the bars to getting there were as challenging as those to the United States, while the funds they had drawn upon for the education of their future son-in-law were by 1922 severely depleted. As James reluctantly prepared to relocate, Eugenia decided not to stay in New York nor to follow her husband to what they hoped would be a temporary posting but to travel to Europe with little Natalie. By the end of October she would board a ship to join her parents for an indefinite period in Danzig.

In contrast, for the first time in a decade Gregory would remain in the same city for an uninterrupted and extended period. His new apartment close to Columbia's main campus was a bus ride from the College of Physicians and Surgeons south of Central Park. Gregory had little time to stroll Manhattan's streets or watch trees from bus windows, however, as he focused with characteristic intensity on coursework in anatomy and vertebrate morphology, biochemistry, histology and embryology, physiology, and neuroanatomy. He spent most of his days and evenings indoors in lecture halls, laboratories, and libraries, listening more than he spoke, taking his place in the audience and following his professors' instructions.

Unsurprisingly Gregory had little in common with his classmates. At nearly 32, Gregory was several years older than most of the other medical students and most if not all of them were American born and bred, too young to have served during the war or participated in a revolution. He had little time for socialising in any event, but he did meet men at Columbia who would become life-long friends, among them Abram Abeloff, specialising in surgery, and Ralph Brodsky, specialising in orthodonture – men with Russian Jewish backgrounds – as well as Johnny Kilroe, a cheerful Irish Catholic who would specialise in obstetrics. Abe even swam for him. A normal part of the first semester's first week was the swimming test. Columbia didn't want any of its graduates to drown accidently. Gregory had no intention of drowning, but thought it absurd that he would be expected to learn to swim, so persuaded Abe to swim for him, to give his name as Zilboorg, swim the required length, and get Gregory's name checked off as a qualified swimmer. When Gregory found a rule preposterous, he didn't feel circumventing it compromised his moral standards. Others might jump through such hoops, but when he found rules he didn't feel should apply to him, he would inevitably find another way of jumping.

With swimming out of the way, Gregory concentrated on dissection and observing cells under microscopes, putting Russia at last to one side, finally on a path towards Americanness, towards integration. The past would always be part of him, but his childhood and youth and the country in which he had forged his identity would weigh on him less now that he had a professional direction and medical career before him. He would later confess that a yearning for Russia had persisted throughout his first years in America, but he was now able psychologically as well as practically to move on, to embrace the present (medical school) and the future (psychiatric work).[7]

With Gregory's coursework came attendance requirements, unit tests, final exams, and personal evaluations, but such humbling strictures – against which he had previously sometimes squirmed – he now accepted as part of the American medical education to which he was committed. Towards the end of October his irregular preparation was formally approved: A Medical Student Qualifying Certificate from the State Department of Education at the University of the State of New York indicates that, as of June 1913, he had 'satisfactorily completed the preliminary education that is required by law and by the Regents' rules for admission to any medical school in the State of New York'. He must have been gratified.[8]

By the time Fera and Sol arrived at the beginning of November, they had no one to turn to but Gregory. In the end HIAS got Fera a job as a guide for 50 Jewish orphans with relatives in the United States. Fera and Sol travelled with the children as third-class passengers – not quite steerage but a far cry from the luxury Gregory had splurged on when leaving Holland. They certainly arrived tired, in want of baths and not especially happy to find themselves in the New World. Gregory for his part wasn't particularly happy to have them in his small apartment and did not welcome them so warmly as they had hoped, made it clear they could not stay indefinitely. Just because he had contributed so generously of his time and energy as well as his money did not mean that he wanted them to live with him. He was rude and they were imposing, and once again there were unmet expectations and muddled communication. By the time Fera and Sol left for Chicago in early December, no one was happy. Fera felt understandably rejected and hard done by while Gregory felt deeply guilty and defensive. One can only imagine what Sol and Ray felt, he with his Marxist convictions ('to each according to their need') and she with her loyalty to Gregory but not much else; the only common language all four of them had was Yiddish.[9]

The last thing Gregory wanted that autumn was to communicate with anyone in the language of what throughout his life he called 'Kostiantynivska Street' – that is, the literal and psychological language of his Kiev family. He didn't want to be dragged back into the old tensions and pettiness he associated with his mother and Basia but also fought in James and Fera. Gregory wanted another way of seeing the world and resolving differences. English rather than Russian would become the literal language that would allow him to communicate what was most important to him, but his current studies would give him a medical language which went beyond the mastery of new vocabulary. The language of his medical career positioned him in a particular psychological relationship not only with future patients but with the other people and with the historical and political world in general. Yet even as a first-year medical student at Columbia, Gregory was aware that normal language and the language of his medical career would finally be insufficient for his emotional needs.

On 12 November 1922 Gregory was received as a member of the New York Monthly Meeting of the Hicksite Quakers. If he was at last at home with Ray on a daily basis, he now formally began a journey on which Ray would not accompany him. Later he would claim that she was actively hostile to the idea of God and the practice of any religion. She was at least indifferent, had no interest in religion nor in her husband's beliefs, but joining the Friends was an important personal and cultural moment for Gregory, a logical extension of his deeply held principles, of his commitment to peace, equality, and the individual, a result of his search for community, affirmation, and love. Friendship with Pearson and Holmes was instrumental in his decision, which had little to do with Fera and Sol's arrival, although possibly the sudden presence of the Old World in his New York household was a tipping point. Just as he had sought with both Sonya and James a sympathetic attachment anchored not only in affection but in shared politics and moral principles, he formed with Quaker colleagues a special bond. His spiritual life would remain private, not a matter he would share with friends and unfortunately not even something he would be able to share with his wife. While offering him a community and the literal, psychological, and spiritual language of silence, his decision to join the Friends would in many ways separate him from his family, his Jewish past, and future medical colleagues. His spiritual life itself would remain for years an exclusively private matter he would allow others to glimpse only in passing.[10]

In Chicago Fera and Sol settled reluctantly into immigrant life in the Levitas family household. Their mixed feelings about America had been exacerbated by Gregory's reception, but they were less bothered by what had happened in New York than he was. They found manual jobs in a workshop using heavy industrial machines. Fera was paid $12 a week and Sol 25, but Fera reported to James that she had quickly caught a cold and been obliged to rest in bed for four days: 'My neck hurt so badly I couldn't move my head. The doctor came and saved me', but 'Everything is fine now and tomorrow I go back to work.' Fera could complain dramatically like Basia, but she was more resilient and enterprising. She also had a sense of humour and a thicker skin than her easily wounded siblings.

If Fera was ready to pick up the pieces of her life and move on, with his deep sense of responsibility and attendant guilt Gregory remained concerned about everyone's feelings and wrote a long letter in an attempt to explain what had happened in New York, to justify and exonerate himself, to apologise in his way to Fera and Sol. However willing he was to support his family financially when he could, contributing money was not the same as emotional generosity, the giving of self and selfless giving, which were more difficult for him to manage. Fera didn't have much patience with him and reported sardonically to James that she had received 'a very "kind", "philosophical" letter from Grisha' which deserved attention 'by virtue of its absolutely beautiful handwriting, spelling, length, etc.' Complaining that he wrote 'on one theme only – about how we are displeased with Ray and him, and he with us, and so on and so forth', Fera was finally dismissive: Gregory 'generally just talks nonstop and offends Sol – and me just a bit more – but I pay no mind and didn't respond to it at all.'[11]

In the crowded Levitas apartment, Fera and Sol were adjusting to immigrant life but unhappy with their lot. Sol imagined they might one day return to New York, uncomfortable in a country he found 'foreign and cold', while Fera felt life had been 'a thousand times better in dear, nice Danzig'. They wouldn't have hesitated to go back if they had had the money.[12]

During the Christmas break Gregory finished an article that reveals as much about his concern with transcendent values and his view of the American present and the Russian past as it does about its ostensible subject. In 'The Russian Invasion', he discussed the upcoming arrival in New York of the Moscow Art Theatre, using the opportunity not only to analyse the dynamics of the actors and their Russian repertoire but to condemn Broadway's advance publicity, its 'wholesale praising machine', its 'bacteria', and the 'baseball noise-making' of local audiences. In contrast to American commercialism, materialism, and superficiality, he admired the Russian troop's 'self-abandon through the expression of the profoundest substance of the human Self', claiming that the 'intimate' and 'religiously solemn' actors compelled even the average person 'to feel the complex spirituality of life'. As the year drew to a close, Gregory was thinking a good deal about what really mattered, not only about medicine but about reality and identity and the inner person. He also regretted that the Art Theatre had not included comedies in its tour. One of the things that galled him about his Russian family was how seriously they took themselves, their apparent incapacity for humour when humour was called for rather than commiseration or pettiness. In mentioning the Art Theatre's capacity to provoke laughter, he recalled Stanislavsky's performance as 'the sick crank' in Molière's *Le Malade Imaginaire*, a recollection that had made him laugh out loud.[13]

The holiday must have provided occasions for convivial laughter as well as respite from his studies. Ray had no desire to see her family, but with James in Monterrey, Eugenia and Natalie in Danzig, and Sol and Fera in Chicago, only Uncle David, now an insurance broker in Queens, would have invited Gregory and Ray to any family celebrations. They probably did not cross the city in the winter snow to attend. Perhaps he attended the theatre with Ray or met Abe and Johnny to celebrate his birthday with a whisky, although Gregory would not have felt celebratory about the news from Russia, recently renamed the Union of Soviet Socialist Republics with Lenin at its head. More personally, he reflected on all Fera had reported about his parents and worried about how they were managing without her. He continued to send parcels and small sums, but eventually something would need to be done. Given his experience with Fera and Sol, he couldn't imagine accommodating his parents along with Basia and her child. Always fascinated with new technology, Gregory may well have treated himself to a radio and listened to the classical concerts and operatic performances just starting to be broadcast on New York stations.

The new year brought Gregory's exam results and the first formal evaluation of his academic progress. On his preceptor's evaluation at the end of January he was marked as 'Above' for 'Intelligence' and 'Pleasant' for 'Personality', while he received the highest evaluation ('good') for 'General information', 'Interest in his work', and 'General health'. For 'Desirability as an intern' he was given an 'O.K.' Discussion of his promise may have occurred in an interview, but the section of the report entitled 'Further remarks' was left blank.[14]

Adapting to medical school routine had been even more difficult than Gregory anticipated. The plan was to concentrate on his studies during term time, then write and lecture during the summers in order to earn what he needed to pay his university fees and support himself and Ray during the rest of the year. This meant a tight schedule and careful budgeting not only of finances but of intellectual and emotional resources. By the end of the academic year he was staying up late and getting up early, cramming and worrying as he prepared for the decisive final exams. Surely the fact that he would need to write in English weighed on him in addition to the responsibility for course content, but he passed them all, then packed his evening clothes and plus fours, and set out in late May for the Midwest under the auspices of the White and Meyers Chautauquas.

Throughout the summer of 1923 Gregory would work even on Sundays. He found the midwestern heat debilitating and the entire experience 'dirty and disgusting all about – both physically and spiritually', yet hectic lecturing would seem to him like 'a blissful vacation' compared to what he thought of as his more intellectually challenging 'winter work', which drained him not only physically but emotionally. What he would do with a medical degree was, however, becoming clearer.

During the winter, under the direction of the prominent neurologist Frederick Tilney, he had reconstructed two brains (those of a chimpanzee and an orangutan) and performed several clinical experiments whose results Tilney would draw upon in papers on the auditory pathway in the central nervous system and on reflexes. Gregory found Tilney 'a true researcher, a European style man', and Tilney had been sufficiently impressed with Gregory's work to invite him to teach on the neurology course during the 1923–1924 academic year. Gregory would not be paid, but he saw the teaching as valuable in helping him to achieve the autonomy he hoped medicine would offer. He was now certain he wouldn't be a general practitioner who made 'house calls'; he wanted to lecture at a university or research institute, work in laboratories, and write papers for professional journals. He wanted to establish himself even while in medical school so that by the time he began to practise, he would be independent.[15]

With characteristically philosophic introspection, he explained his feelings to James: As a result of his experiences in Russia, he felt he had failed to achieve anything 'either qualitatively or quantitatively'; emotionally, he had gained experience in 'commonplace pain, heartache, discontent and an endless series of sufferings and face-to-face encounters with unwelcome death', but had not attained any of his goals. Certainly capable of his own sort of melodrama, Gregory declared his life so far had left him with few things of any value. Specifically, 'my social and political ideals have been thoroughly stained with blood and stamped meaningless. My philosophical convictions are lost to the personal tragedies I was forced to endure.' He saw his only hope at this point as a diploma in medicine, which he felt would afford him intellectual, emotional, and material independence from 'people, society and a "power structure" ' he found 'altogether loathsome'. And, he insisted to James, he wouldn't forfeit this hope even if it meant saving his own wife.

Gregory was on the defensive again, declaring his principles and justifying his choices and commitments once more because he felt threatened to his core by what he saw as the rock and the hard place ahead. Very simply, the family's situation in Kiev was becoming critical. Fera had meagre resources. Despite being unhappy in Mexico and separated for the time being from his wife and child, James had an adequate salary. Gregory had the possibility of a comfortable income as a lecturer, but only if he gave up medicine. In short, Gregory told his brother, he would help as he could, but he point blank refused to take on the official, financial, and practical responsibility of his Russian family; he would not give up medicine.[16]

Notes

1 GZ to JZ, 23 June 1922.
2 GZ to JZ, 28 June 1922.
3 GZ to JZ, 2 July 1922.
4 GZ to JZ, 4 July 1922.
5 'Dr. Gregory Zilboorg', 1, 2.
6 FZ to JZ, 23 August 1922.
7 GZ to JZ, 6 March 1932.
8 Qualifying Certificate, 24 October 1922, ASCCU.
9 FZ, Irvine interview.
10 NM to Emmanuel Suarrez, 27 July 1951, APD
11 FZ to JZ, 18 December 1922.
12 FZ and Sol Levitas to unidentified recipients, 28 December 1922, JEZB.
13 GZ, 'The Russian Invasion', 127, 128, 129.
14 Preceptorial Sheet, 29 January 1923, ASCCU.
15 GZ to JZ, 17 June 1923.
16 GZ to JZ, 29 May 1923.

Chapter 8

'Complete *moral* independence'

1923–1926

Gregory began his summer travels in Chicago, where he saw Fera and Sol for the first time since they had left New York. He was disappointed in both of them, finding Sol still preoccupied with Menshevik Marxism, as if he had learnt nothing from the revolution, while Fera seemed 'an ordinary overweight petty bourgeois woman'. Gregory suddenly saw his sister and brother-in-law rather clearly: Fera had no intention of pursuing an advanced diploma in biological research; Sol was a committed socialist through and through. Neither was fundamentally very much like Gregory, much as he might have imagined them differently. Peacefully discussing their parents' plight, Fera found nothing more intelligent to say than ' "I don't recognize you, Grisha. You have either changed beyond recognition or someone has had a terrible influence on you!" ' With humour that could not have been taken kindly, Gregory retorted, ' "Forgive me, but it must be Ray." ' The consummate showman, he then smiled and lit up his pipe. For his part, Sol proposed borrowing the money required to get the family out of Russia, but he wanted Gregory to sign a promissory note. Gregory refused, fearing that if Sol defaulted on the repayments, he would be liable. Sol taunted him: ' "If it happens that we are unable to pay for two or three weeks, then you will have to pay, Grigory Moiseevich – whether you like it or not." ' Sol may have felt such terms were fair, but Gregory responded with outrage: 'Like hell I will!'[1]

Gregory found James more sober and humane, but everyone agreed that something needed to be done. In his most recent letter Moses had confessed that the family had nothing left, having used and spent everything. From Merlin, Tennessee, in June Gregory sent him a small sum in American currency and wrote to James about the other issues uppermost in his mind.

Beyond the difficulties facing the Kiev family and the money Fera and Sol and James were insisting he contribute were two matters that pressed upon Gregory in the summer of 1923 and would continue to press upon him throughout his life. The first was independence: his desire for the freedom to be who he was and wanted to become, his insistence on his autonomy, his liberty to think, say, and write what he wanted and to make decisions without being beholden to others or held to standards, rules, or regulations he felt unnecessary, unjust, or immoral. Money was a factor in the independence he wanted but ultimately merely an enabling

DOI: 10.4324/9781003190936-8

element. More important was political, social, and individual freedom, freedom from bourgeois conventions, bureaucracy, and the risk of censure. His Russian past had made him both contentious and apprehensive, at once suspiciously self-protective and always on guard, easily menaced, primed to attack first whenever he thought he might be accused. A large presence on the literal, professional, and personal stages he acted upon, he cherished privacy; despite his characteristic swagger, he knew he was vulnerable. The flipside of his desire for independence was the perception of threats – generally more real than imagined – and a consequent fear and defensiveness.

Because Columbia now recognised his status as a graduate of the Psycho-Neurological Institute, Gregory was eligible to take the New York State Medical Board exam in June, but he chose not to. The licencing exam was offered again in September, but again he held off. He was, of course, occupied with lecturing, but felt he didn't need to worry about licencing at this point. Once he had established himself through research and writing, as he had explained to his brother, he would take the exam and receive a licence as he started in private practice.

The plain fact, however, was that Gregory didn't want any state involved in his life. His real motivations for deferring the exam may have been unconscious, but he was quite conscious of the threat he perceived from the notoriety he had already achieved in America. James had urged him to write to the new U.S. consul in Riga on behalf of his parents, but he refrained from doing this, too, explaining to his brother that he was trying to avoid contact with American officials in all of his affairs because his name appeared in several government documents reporting on Russia, socialism, and immigration. Additionally, Lothrop Stoddard had mentioned him in his recent book about the death of civilisation. Gregory felt he now needed to be especially careful because the anti-socialist, anti-immigrant Coolidge, who had just become president following Harding's death in early August, had written three 'idiotically pogrom-like, purely Romanov articles' for a popular journal, and specifically named Gregory as a leader of 'the Third International movement in the U.S.' He was making a conscious decision to '"sit tight" and maintain a low profile'.[2]

The other matter that pressed upon Gregory was spiritual life. He did not discuss his religious choices with his brother any more than he discussed them with Fera or Ray or his Columbia classmates or mentors, but spiritual life was connected to his desire for independence as well as to his concern with the workings of the brain, both ape and human, a fascination that would lead him quite naturally from neurology to psychoanalysis. He told James he saw medicine as the final step on his path to 'complete *moral* independence' and explained that whether working over a cadaver, a test tube, a dead brain under a microscope, or a live brain in the operating room, he was satisfying his intellectual curiosity 'without serving or answering to anyone', an attitude of 'contemptuous solitude' he recommended to James out of concern for his brother's psychological and spiritual well-being. He pointed out perceptively that the modern civilisation to which James was tethered as an engineer – emblematised by the Westinghouse conglomerate that had sent him so blithely to Mexico – would inevitably slow him down, for it demanded everything of him without allowing him to think about anything extraneous or giving him 'the opportunity to develop spiritually or become spiritually free'.

Moving quickly from generalisation to specific analysis, Gregory saw his brother's lack of spiritual development as the reason he 'thrashed about' and took so much onto his 'spiritual shoulders'. Revealing both psychological and spiritual understanding, he philosophised that people often consider whatever they are doing as the most important thing, even though they have to do it, so they struggle like caged animals because they do not want to live and work under compulsion. But, he insisted,

> You can strip a man of his shirt, you can even skin him, but nobody can take away his creative inner 'I'. And the more well developed this 'I' is, the more independent, the more free and active the individual personality.

Gregory felt James was allowing his inner, spiritual needs to flounder 'in the corners of his soul' without addressing or stifling them, a way of being that was causing him anxious discontent, heaviness of heart, and loneliness.

It was wrong, Gregory pointed out, to think one could find fulfilment in others, in a wife or family, a tragic mistake to suppose life together as two was the same as the single life: 'There is no such blending of personalities and lives.' Instead, spiritual freedom must be sought apart from others. He was concerned about his brother's 'unmet and partially met needs' – whether they were reading books or solving mathematical problems or drawing up plans for a new invention or even a flirtation or infatuation with someone else's wife or daughter. He urged James to give into and meet these needs, admitting that he was judging from his own 'precisely tested and even suffering-filled experience'. He confessed that he never allowed himself to suffocate in the measured life of the most pressing needs regardless of what they might be. In the name of 'duty', he told James, 'people too often multiply those needs which are imposed on them from without and which they are afraid to dismiss for even a minute.' Drawing on his medical training for metaphors, Gregory considered needs and so-called duties and obligations as physiological realities: People needed air to breathe, but it did not follow that air should be one's religion. People had certain metabolisms, but this did not mean that digestion should become the cornerstone of their lives. People also needed to earn a living and consider external conditions in the world. Yet he placed all these needs in the same category as physiological functions and stressed that he took them no more or no less seriously than micturition, digestion, or respiration. He recognised those functions as hugely important, but they were natural and would follow a normal course on their own; 'I remain aloof.' Thus, he explained, his brother sometimes found him coarse. He was not as he was out of stupidity or cruelty but because he consciously shrugged off everything that encroached on his 'inner freedom'.[3]

While partially self-explanation, Gregory reveals in this important letter both his pastoral concern for his brother and his capacity for psychological insight, yet he also offers a glimpse of his own continuing preoccupation with what he called the 'spiritual' and his frustration with 'unmet needs' which are not at all a matter of the physical body that followed its natural and normal course come what may. Joining the Society of Friends had by no means ended his spiritual searching, and he was obviously still struggling to align his moral independence and contemptuous solitude with his concern for the psychological well-being of both others and himself.

This letter also hints at the nature of Gregory's marriage to Ray. He had obviously not found nor probably had he sought more than companionship in their marriage, and because of financial and professional considerations as well as Ray's personal aversion, children at least at this point in his life were out of the question. Although Gregory was repelled by their circumstances and what he saw as their acceptance of conventions, Fera and Sol were looking forward to a baby, due in the new year. Part of the problem in Kiev was the fact that Basia had a child, and Nadia must have been a solace to her grandparents and widowed mother during trying times. For their part, James and Eugenia had a much-loved little girl, and when Eugenia's parents finally left for Palestine, she and Natalie returned to New York in August, where they saw Gregory and Ray briefly en route to Monterrey. James had missed his wife and daughter, and the reunion was surely sweet, but Gregory was clearly sceptical that his brother's family would satisfy him psychologically or complete him spiritually. Emphasising what he saw as the limits of marriage, he had pointed out that he, too, was married, while adding somewhat defensively 'and quite happily'. Gregory could joke with Fera that his wife had been the bad influence on him, but the clever riposte suggests a degree of bitterness. As for his own career, he was brutal in stating that if it came down to it, he would sacrifice his wife for a future in medicine. Yet Ray was certainly helpful to her husband and a practical support at home, running errands on his behalf, mending torn trousers. She knew from her own family how to make ends meet and manage a household. She had carefully cultivated good manners and taste; neither intellectual nor literary, she liked what things looked like and dressed well. English was not her mother tongue, but it was natural to her as it would never at some level be to Gregory; surely her fluency must have been a resource. Despite her emotional vulnerabilities, Ray was attractive, supercilious but also elegant in public. Gregory in his turn had a sense of marital obligation, but there had been no 'blending of personalities and lives', while his mentioning to James on the basis of his own experience the attractions and pain of flirtation or infatuation with someone else's wife or daughter doesn't suggest satisfaction. He may not have expected more of Ray or their marriage; he may not even have been disappointed, but he certainly does not seem to have been fulfilled.

With so much on his mind, this summer on the road was particularly taxing. Life for Gregory was always a matter of determination and choice, opportunities created and will exerted, and he embraced each day with dramatic intensity. Despite external forces, be they social, political, economic, or personal, he was the principal actor in charge of his fate, demanding a great deal of himself, striving to meet his own high standards with tremendous energy and concentration while resisting whatever limits might be imposed upon him, but he was always also ultimately a realist. Funds did eventually run out. People could and did bleed and die or break down emotionally in wars and revolutions. Trousers ripped and needed replacing. Hotels and trains were often dirty and money could only buy what money could buy.

The elegant lecturer

What money bought in 1923 was dinner jackets and radios as well as kasha at home with or without the occasional egg and potatoes on the road. For the man with the elegant cigarette holder and distinctive moustache, there was no mention in his letters of Ohio's orchards or the lush fields of Illinois and Iowa, of the June strawberries and August apples, the chicken and pork chops on country tables in summer, and the crackers and lox city peddlers sold from carts and stocked in shops throughout the year. Yet determination and will, ethics and philosophy, however forcefully argued in words that never seemed to fail him, were finally insufficient to carry him through. He fell ill in Missouri in July, recovered and pushed on, but before September had to cut the lecture season short and return to New York. Gregory was compelled to draw on his summer funds even before paying his Columbia fees, using his carefully calculated earnings for consultations with specialists for a throat ailment and related intestinal problems that required three weeks in hospital.

The diagnosis of possible tuberculosis was not reassuring. Nervous and worn out, Gregory treated his symptoms with Listerine and gentian violet and struggled to get the rest and fresh air his doctors recommended. He would start the new academic year with financial and health worries compounded by the inevitably distressing news from Kiev, but decided to keep from Ray the seriousness and specificity of whatever was physically wrong. Given her tendency to become depressed, he thought it best that she not know everything, although keeping the details to himself made things personally more difficult. Health and his finances were inextricably related: Without a healthy throat, he felt useless; without financial means, he could offer little support to his parents, who now wanted to leave Russia as soon as they could find a way.

Fera and James continued to press Gregory for the requisite funds. Throughout the autumn he repeatedly tried to justify to them – and perhaps to himself – his decision to continue his studies and research. Forcefully and bluntly, he wrote his brother that he had given everything he could, but he would not sacrifice himself – that is, his future in medicine. He felt James and Fera had considered everything 'except me', and demanded what right they had to devise plans in which their participation amounted to moral support while loading on him a weight that threatened to ruin his personal life. He had given Fera his savings; his help had kept the family from starving. He felt Fera spitefully saw him as a criminal while James expected him to repeat his own sad sacrifices and compromises. In full dramatic mode he told him,

> if it is my fate to die soon, then I must take care of Ray.... And if it is my fate to live, then I want to live rather than eke out a miserable existence. Whether consciously or not, anyone who encroaches on my life path knows not what he does.... there are those things to which the proverbial 'line in the sand' applies.

Well aware of the difficulties their parents were facing, he understood equally well that he could find a way out for them only at the expense of his entire life, at the expense of the few valuable things in life he had managed 'to glean and preserve after storms and sufferings' and 'a year of blood and difficulty'.[4]

It was a rocky start to the academic year in which Gregory was teaching neurology as well as following the prescribed course for second-year medical students. In early October he submitted yet one more article for *Drama*, taking the new Municipal Theatre of St. Louis as his ostensible subject. What he wrote about, however, was the American public's obsession with the off-stage details and gossip of an actor's personal life, attention he condemned, declaring,

> We must respect and value and analyze and try to understand the artistic individuality instead of the bodily person of the actor. Not the degree of his being in the limelight or the degree of his cleverness and skill, should be our measure of values, but the degree of the actor's culture, his depth, his contribution to the art of self-expression and self-impression.

Transparently, it was exactly such respect and understanding that he wanted from Fera and James and longed to earn from future colleagues. When he wrote, 'the actor must be cultivated, not only trained; respected and not only applauded; cherished not only liked', he was describing precisely the stature he hoped to achieve through hard work in his own profession. He was tired of being merely the exotic charismatic performer on gopher prairie stages, tired of arguing with his family who, it seemed to him, were dragging him back into the petty squabbles of their shared Russian past.[5]

Although Gregory concluded his article by promising that he would expand 'next time' on some of his points, there was no next time. With this article he put his direct participation in the theatre world behind him and turned his literary attention to a translation of Yevgeny Zamiatin's dystopian novel *We*. Banned from publication in Russia, a smuggled copy had been sent to E.P. Dutton, who offered the project to Gregory. Overloaded as always, he nevertheless took it on; translation late at night was a way to earn money that didn't involve his throat.

Zamiatin's novel was uniquely suited to Gregory's talents and interests. Set a thousand years in the future in a city of glass buildings enclosed by the Green Wall, the book depicts a mechanical world in which every hour and human act is monitored and regulated by the 'United State', a tyranny headed by 'The Well-Doer' that suggests the contemporary Soviet Union, while Gregory's translation hints simultaneously at a possible future United States of America. The narrator, D-503, is a philosopher-mathematician whose journal records an emotional and creative life that persists despites the state's effort to deny him individuality. In charge of building the spaceship *Integral*, D-503 is seduced by the alluring and rebellious I-330, who plans to take over the project in a revolt. Obsessed with I-330, D-503 begins to dream, according to the United State an indication of mental illness, an experience rich in metaphor and inspiration, destabilising sensations and desires. Indeed, the entire novel becomes increasingly destabilised, a modernist reflection of the protagonist's emotional, political, moral, and spiritual breakdown: Synaesthesia, paranoia, unbridled erotic passion, and the uncanny combine in a series of bizarre events in which the state, the weather, the natural world beyond the Wall, and the characters' psychological impulses hurdle towards political and psychic revolution and inevitable suppression. When his journal is discovered, D-503 confesses everything in a desperate effort to relieve his psychological distress. He then undergoes 'The Great Operation', during which his 'Fancy' (his imagination, his individuality, his capacity to love, his 'soul') is removed. At the novel's end I-330 and her followers are executed, although the potential revolution based outside the Wall continues to threaten the United State. D-503's last journal entry suggests that he has not completely lost his capacity to feel, but like his inner world, his syntax has begun to fracture. He insists 'I hope we win', then 'I am certain we shall win.' His final utterance is appropriately a fragmented, dependent sentence: 'For Reason must prevail.'[6]

The novel appealed to Gregory as a psychological study exploring not only the problem of a human being caught in a revolution but larger issues of paramount importance. One of these was language – the language within the text, through which the agonised protagonist struggled to express his emotions, but also the language of the text itself. In his foreword, he noted the 'tragedy' of Zamiatin's predicament, 'the spiritual loneliness of the artist who cannot speak to his own people' but must rely on words translated into another language and addressed to those outside his country. Gregory assumed the responsibility for mediating between Zamiatin's Russian words and the English words which would be the novel's only embodiment for years to come. Beyond its modernist syntax – whose sentence fragments, ellipses, and exclamations as well as themes echo Andreyev's – *We* appealed to Gregory because, he contended, it examined the most difficult problem in the civilised world: 'the problem of the preservation of the independent, original, creative, personality', the problem of 'the individual versus the mob'. While this issue occupied Gregory explicitly in his lectures and translations and was a frequent topic in his correspondence with James, there are other issues in *We* also on Gregory's mind whether or not he discussed them or was even conscious of their weighing upon him. One was certainly women: I-330 is a *femme fatale*, a 1920s vamp who smokes and drinks, but she is juxtaposed to D-503's assigned sexual partner O-90, a small, round woman who adores D-503, longs for a child, is impregnated by him, then smuggled out of the United State by I-330 in an act of female solidarity. The novel also features two other women: a physically unattractive aging informer, who desires and stalks D-503, and a very old woman, who passively supports I-330's revolutionary activity and represents history, nature, and motherhood. D-503 has understandably mixed and shifting feelings about all these women, but it is possible to read Zamiatin's text as a study of women's roles and power. Sexuality and maternity as well as the larger issue of love are central topics whether one focuses on the women or on D-503 and his black male poet friend R-13. Writing – be it a private 'record' such as the narrator keeps or public verse – is another topic as is science, especially medicine, and specifically – coming back to psychology as the novel's primary subject – the inner workings of the human mind.

Dutton could not have found a more appropriate translator, but neither could Gregory have found a more appropriate project to occupy him when he wasn't putting his intellectual energy into his Columbia coursework. An uncomfortable narrative that pushes against the boundaries of form and language, in its wide sweep *We* overreaches its author's grasp, is simultaneously and in turns jocular and earnest, ridiculous and frighteningly serious, satiric and poignant, relying on what Gregory would characterise, using Gogol's expression, as 'laughter through tears'. In addition to the technical challenge of rendering Zamiatin's modernist text in idiomatic English, Gregory must have found the translation emotionally taxing as it forced him to wrestle with its tonal tensions as well as its subjects and themes.[7]

The next year and a half would be for Gregory a period of translation, months during which he would put aside his identity as a lecturer and establish his reputation as a distinguished translator of Russian, yet on a daily basis he was a mere medical student putting in the expected hours in classrooms and laboratories. At the end of October 1923 Gregory received an evaluation of his progress towards his coveted degree. On his 'Preceptorial Sheet' he again received an 'Above' for 'Intelligence' and an evaluation of 'Good' for 'General information', 'Interest in his work', and even for 'General health', but his 'Personality' was now noted as 'Strong' and his 'Desirability as an intern' had become 'Debatable'. Emphasising that there was 'no question as to his natural ability', his perspicacious preceptor added that Gregory had 'An interesting personality, very self-confident, widely read and versatile', yet he was 'Rather given to self-explanation'.[8]

There was indeed never a question as to Gregory's ability, and he successfully divided his energies between translation and coursework, but despite what he apparently reported to the preceptor, his health wasn't good. The vitamin deficiencies and anaemia from which he had suffered in Russia were again plaguing him. He had not fully recovered from his summer illnesses, and he felt tired almost all the time. He spent evenings and weekends at his desk, economised on food, listened to the radio, and limited his forays to the theatre. His gums continued to bleed despite applications of gentian violet, but he still had months to recover from whatever was ailing him before he resumed lecturing in May.

As the year turned Gregory must have reflected on the world around him. On 9 January 1924 Fera and Sol's first child was born, a little girl they called Nora. Despite the tensions over money, Gregory surely wrote to congratulate his sister in the same generous spirit in which he had congratulated his brother on Natalie's birth two years earlier. In Monterrey, James and his family were settling into a Mexican life he was grudgingly beginning to accept as more than temporary. In the wider world, following Lenin's death on 21 January, Petrograd became 'Leningrad' and Joseph Stalin took the reins of the still foundering nation. Gregory would not have been able to keep his mind off Russia even had he not been translating Zamiatin's satire, while early in the year a new production of *He Who Gets*

Slapped impressed audiences at the Petit Théatre du Vicux Carré in New Orleans, bringing its translator much-needed funds while reminding him again of the world in which both he and Andreyev had defined themselves.

The academic year would end unremarkably, but Gregory must have been satisfied with his progress. He passed all the courses required of second-year medical students: anatomy, bacteriology, medicine, pathology, pharmacology, physiology, psychiatry, and surgery. He was probably aware, however, as spring came to Manhattan, that his summer plans would need to change.

Not only was he constantly swallowing blood, but by April he could push his front teeth back and forth with his tongue; he was in no condition to lecture. Consulting specialists once more, he worried about more than his gums. Throughout the spring the U.S. Congress had debated further immigration restrictions and on 26 May the Johnson-Reed Act, known as the Immigration Act of 1924, became law. It severely limited the annual number of immigrants from any one country, allowing entry to older immigrants over the age of 60 who might be joining relatives but making it more difficult for younger people, especially those from Eastern Europe, including Russia. The news must have disturbed Fera and Sol; James and Eugenia would have been troubled in Monterrey; but in New York Gregory finally followed his specialists' advice and underwent surgery on his jaw. The diagnosis was scurvy and the result was several weeks in hospital paid for by whatever funds he had in reserve and no possibility of a bonanza summer income. His pain, debility, and worry about his health now decreased and presumably he had the luxury, despite a slow recovery, of daily glasses of orange juice, but the experience meant a seismic shift in his negotiation of his future.[9]

If lecturing was no longer on the cards, Gregory was never a man without plans. His teaching on Tilney's course in neurology had pleased his superiors. As soon as Gregory left hospital in the middle of June, he began unpaid but strategically significant work as an assistant in neuropathology to George Hughes Kirby at the New York Psychiatric Institute and Hospital on Ward's Island. A highly regarded Columbia professor who had studied both in the United States and under Emil Kraepelin in Munich, Kirby had worked closely with the Swiss-born psychiatrist Adolph Meyer, taking over the directorship of the New York Psychiatric Institute when Meyer moved to Baltimore to head the Henry Phipps Psychiatric Clinic at Johns Hopkins Medical School. On Ward's Island Gregory would work long days throughout the summer of 1924 with Kirby's other assistants, among them Bertram David Lewin, a qualified psychiatrist who was already beginning to establish himself. An intelligent and vivacious Texan six years younger than Gregory, Lewin had grown up speaking German and Spanish as well as English in a Jewish household. With his finely tuned sense of humour, sensitivity to language, and interest in Freudian ideas, Lewin and Gregory enjoyed each other and shared a mutual respect that would foster an enduring friendship.[10]

By the end of July Gregory began to feel like himself again. He wasn't earning anything, but he was learning a great deal and making important connections that would further his career in psychiatry. Ray had finally become an American citizen in June. His own application would need to wait until he had achieved five years of residence, but the question of his professional career again pressed upon him and once more the issue was financial. From the time he had entered the hospital it had become clear that he would need a loan to cover the fees for his third year of medical school, but by August he was worried about paying for food and rent. Then he received a telegram from Riga followed by a letter from James.

Who sent the telegram wasn't clear, and even its contents were cryptic. The family had already left Kiev, were perhaps in Latvia, on their way to Rotterdam; tickets had been purchased for a transatlantic crossing on a ship whose destination was not New York or even the United States: Moses, Anna, Basia and four-year-old Nadia would soon arrive at a port on Mexico's east coast.

Gregory was stunned; James was even more stunned, while Fera was less stunned and more practical. James's immediate reaction was to accuse Gregory of having advised the family to head for Veracruz, citing myriad reasons that Mexico was a very bad idea. Despite the seriousness of the matter, Gregory had not lost his sense of humour and denied ever offering such advice, informing his brother that he found his letter extremely interesting in that James had given the same reasons against the family's going to Mexico that Gregory had given when James had suggested they go to New York. 'Perhaps now', Gregory told him, 'thanks to the misunderstanding, you will understand me better than before.'[11]

Fixated on blame, James squirmed under the pending responsibility that was about to become his. For her part, Fera defended the family's decision, telling James that he was right about everything and specifically about Mexico yet, she pointed out, they were also right in their own way. While James might know local conditions all too well, the family knew no less well 'all of the inexpressibly difficult weight of Russian life – a half-starved, wretched existence'. In Fera's eyes their approach had been simple: They had chosen the lesser of the two evils. While Fera found Gregory 'obtuse' and told James she had crossed her elder brother off her 'list of people who are capable of interest in anything other than their own careers', James continued to fret and complain until even Sol wrote him in Gregory's defence: He was wrong to think someone had set him up and the family was coming as a result of anyone else's advice. Like Fera, he insisted that their decision was simply 'the result of their despair and the hopelessness of the situation'.

Fera and Sol did what they could. Mexico City had no HIAS office; as far as James knew, there were no Ashkenazi Jews in all of Mexico, no Yiddish or Russian speakers with whom his family would be able to communicate. Sol thought someone at B'nai B'rith might help. Fera sent James addresses she had discovered of Jews who had recently immigrated to Mexico. The Kiev family would be exhausted after a 21-day third-class voyage, but Fera worried that James would criticise them, would welcome them with less than the warmth and affirmation they deserved; he should accept the self-evident if banal reality:

> they are, after all, our parents. And who, if not we, their children, should help them when they are in need? True, each of us has a family of our own now, but it is our duty, and we have an obligation to take upon ourselves its fulfilment.

She was particularly concerned that James would criticise Basia, who had apparently masterminded the impulsive exodus. Fera implored James not to say anything or to blame their sister for having chosen Mexico, reminding him that sooner or later Basia was always easily offended. Over and over both Fera and Sol urged James to write to Gregory and plead for money.[12]

Despite his financial worries, as his Russian family arrived in Mexico Gregory began the 'rotations' which would expose him to every medical specialty. Columbia's programme consisted of two years of basic sciences followed by two years of clinical education in the wards, and Gregory's time in classrooms and laboratories was over. In October his 'Preceptorial Sheet' again indicated good progress. His personality was marked as both 'Pleasant' and 'Strong', while all his other marks were as before, including his 'Desirability as an Intern', which remained 'Debatable'. Under further remarks the preceptor wrote, 'An interesting, versatile and mature personality, a little opinionated and self-satisfied, but likable. He will do best following his own interests under independent conditions.'[13]

It was becoming clear not only to those who evaluated Gregory's performance but to Gregory himself that the most logical way forward in terms of personality and inclination might be an academic career in which his medical knowledge and experience would inform research and writing. A 'residency' – referred to by Gregory's preceptors as an 'internship' – was a period of three or more years of supervised clinical work in one's chosen specialism and served to prepare the new doctor for the independent practice of medicine. Not all students went on to do internships, but at first-rank medical schools like Columbia, the majority of graduates would have welcomed the additional opportunity to develop their expertise before setting up in private practice. Gregory's 'debatable' desirability as an intern was no bar to an academic career, but it would present challenges both to himself and others during a possible internship and in any future medical practice. However 'pleasant' his personality, it was also, after all, 'strong'.[14]

Struggling to solve his own financial problems and concerned about his parents despite and because of the fact that he could not help them, Gregory was sometimes distracted from his clinical rotations at Presbyterian Hospital's Vanderbilt Clinic. As usual, he was juggling issues on various fronts. On 7 November, with Ray as a witness, he filed his declaration of intent to become a United States citizen, giving his birthday as 25 December 1890 and his occupation as medical student and lecturer. Now that he was working on the wards, he had fewer evenings to devote to translation, but his future suddenly became more secure. December 1924 would be a bumper month. Within weeks of finishing his translation, Dutton published *We*, so there would soon be royalty income. Just before Christmas Metro-Goldwyn-Meyer, who had bought the rights to *He Who Gets Slapped* in the summer, released its production starring Lon Chaney, Norma Shearer, and John Gilbert. Produced and directed by Viktor Sjöström, the silent film nevertheless credited Gregory as Andreyev's translator and would generate additional royalties. Finally, thanks to his Columbia professors Thomas W. Salmon and Charles I. Lambert, on the last day of the year Gregory was awarded a scholarship of $400 ($5,500 today). The funds, paid to the grateful recipient in four instalments (in January, February, March, and April 1925), would help enormously, but despite the scholarship and royalties if the novel and film did well, Gregory would need to borrow money to make it through the academic year.[15]

Likely as part of his efforts to secure further financial support, on 4 January 1925 Gregory composed a detailed biographical statement. He indicated he was currently working on two problems: 'Social reactions in psychotics' and 'Puberty psychosis'. He added, with characteristically charming sincerity and humour, 'It is hard to write down a series of facts about one's own self without transgressing the boundaries of discretion. *Fecit quod potui* [I've done what I could] and tried to remain human.' On the same day he wrote to Frederick van Beuren to thank him for his offer to help with a loan, explaining, 'the money I hope to raise will be returned as soon as I can do so. I may be able to do so very soon; it depends upon the fate of my last literary and theatrical efforts.' Compelled to be honest, Gregory closed by admitting, 'And yet I may not be able to return the money soon.' In fact, it would take him over five years to pay back the two loans arranged by the dean, amounting in total to $2,000 ($26,000 today).[16]

Gregory's 'literary' efforts included not only *We* but yet another translation. The journalist Bernard Gerson Richards had offered Gregory a contract for Korolenko's *In a Strange Land: The Story of Every Immigrant*. Based on the author's visit to America in 1893, this 1895 novel, whose title can be literally translated as 'Without Language', tells the story of a simple Ukrainian immigrant without a word of English who struggles to understand the United States. The book is at once a bittersweet satire and a tender psychological comedy that often mocks both the poor peasant and the absurd situations in which he finds himself. Matvai, the protagonist, eventually finds what he has gone to America to seek ('a piece of land, a house, cows and calves … a wife, too'), but also feels 'a poignant sadness press upon his heart … because something new was born in him, while the old died and was still dying'. He longs for the Russia he will never see again and mourns the loss of his native language which his children's children will never know.[17]

Gregory universalises the narrative in his own freely added subtitle, and it is not difficult to understand why he agreed to translate this work even as he was assimilating in mid-1920s' America. He had married and mastered English, was advancing in his medical studies, and could finally imagine financial solvency, but like Korolenko's displaced Russians, he also experienced 'Doubletown', where his background and experiences meant his frame of reference was quite different from that of most people he met. The gulf between Russia and the United States, between Europe and the New World, between past and present, is symbolised in the novel by language, and for Gregory language would always be both personally and professionally the essential issue on which his identity depended. He praised Korolenko in his foreword for his spiritual leadership, moral integrity, and stoic humanism as well as his powers of observation, tenderness towards human frailty, and sympathy with suffering – all qualities that Gregory despite his flaws hoped to embody in his personal life and as a psychiatrist. He decided to translate Korolenko because he admired the author's 'complete disharmony with our modern trends towards revolt, dictatorial self-assertion and concentrated mob action'. Gregory declared,

> we shall soon realize the necessity of turning back to the old and forgotten and perhaps even trite humanistic ideals … which point to the value of Man as Personality, the value of the Individual as the creative bearer of what is best in human nature.

He finally asserted that *In a Strange Land* was important because it revealed the difficult problem of 'assimilating one's mind and soul with the minds and souls of others, who are so much like us and yet so different'. Even with citizenship pending, Gregory would always be an immigrant and found in Korolenko a kindred spirit.[18]

Unlike the peasant Matvai, however, Gregory had a professional life to establish and was beginning to define an area within psychiatry of particular importance to him: the history of what he would call 'medical psychology'. While continuing his rounds at the Vanderbilt Clinic, he started to write. At the end of January he presented his first medical paper – entitled 'Heroes and Crowds: Some Lessons of the Russian Revolution from a Medico-psychological View-point', it would deftly combine his many interests – to the History Section of the New York Academy of Medicine, and at the end of the following month he addressed the Psychiatric Society of Ward's Island, probably on the same topic. With the past and the present, translation and 'medico-psychological' matters on his mind, Gregory was a diligent but inconsistently focused student, yet if he was profligate with his energies, he was economising and looking to economise further, hoping for a psychiatric placement for the following academic year that might allow him on-site accommodation on the grounds of a mental hospital. As he succinctly explained to James, he was not only busy but dealing with 'a whole series of rather complex circumstances'. The 'extremely scant conditions' were becoming more difficult, and he was concerned about covering even basic living expenses, but part of the unspecified 'complex circumstances' was Ray's general unhappiness, her sense of being unappreciated and without direction. He did not complain, grieve, or even feel unlucky to find himself in such straits, recognising that his choices had put him in what he saw optimistically as 'a rather difficult but unavoidable and promising transitional period'. Realistically, however, if he succeeded 'in calmly navigating the reefs', he felt his professional and financial position was bound to improve. It could not, however, have been much worse. When James complained that he was $200 out of pocket from supporting both his family in Monterrey and contributing to the new arrivals settling into life in Mexico City, Gregory could only tell him that if he was asking for money, he should ask outright and Gregory would try to borrow it.

There was little more at this point that Gregory could do for Ray or for his parents and sister and little niece. At the age of 60, Moses was no longer young, but he was a resourceful man in good health and, like his eldest son, admirably capable of making his own way under challenging circumstances. Although James hadn't known it, there were indeed other Russian Jews in Mexico's capital where there was no Ashkenazi synagogue, but there had been no synagogue in Kiev when Moses had first walked into that city. He soon found nine other men with whom to pray – a *minyan* was all that was needed. Drawing on business contacts in the near East, including Eugenia's father in Palestine, Moses began to work independently as an importer of dry goods and foodstuff, the sort of international trading he had done in Russia, and the family soon set up a household. Anna and Basia with Nadia in tow shopped in the colourful markets, and with Basia's help Anna made copious kosher meals, seeking out other Jews who paid for the privilege to eat with them. The family must have appreciated the mild winter; they must have enjoyed the sunshine.

Adjusting to the altitude, Anna sometimes felt short of breath, consulted a doctor, told him her eldest son was also a doctor, wanted the physician to send him a report. On this score, even thousands of miles away, Gregory could be useful. The diagnosis was 'mild myocarditis', a usually asymptomatic condition due to a virus or the difficult conditions under which she had lived in Kiev, and Gregory was genuinely concerned. He worried that the altitude was not good for her and that she was working much too hard, urged James to report his impressions of both their parents, for he could not rely on Basia, who in anguished discontent wrote him an endless stream of complaints about their father, about Mexico, about her own health. If Anna had myocarditis, Basia told Gregory, she was suffering from 'cardioneurosis', which as Gregory well knew was anxious worry about the state of one's heart, an emotional not a physical condition. Basia appeared not to have changed, and if she had, it was for the worse. He found her a 'typical semi-pathological female hysteric'. His insightful reading of the situation was that Basia, perhaps without realising it herself, did not want to work, although she was capable. He felt that something should be done. Perhaps at the end of the academic year he could arrange, probably with Lewin's help, an underwritten trip to mental hospitals in Texas. If he got as far El Paso, he could make a side trip to Monterrey so the two brothers could discuss matters face to face. Perhaps, Gregory imagined, he could then go on to Mexico City to see the family for the first time since leaving Kiev six years earlier. He did not go so far as to tell James that he missed his parents, but he clearly did.[19]

On 2 March 1925 Gregory finally became an American citizen in a standard ceremony during which he forswore allegiance to any other government or state. He must have had mixed feelings, abjuring loyalty to the Russia he loved but also to the Bolshevist Soviet Union he detested while finally gaining the privileges and protection of the country he had come to know from Massachusetts to the Carolinas, from Tennessee to the provincial midwestern prairies. He must have felt wistful but also triumphant.

March was another good month. Dutton brought out a second printing of *We*, and at the end of the month Richards published *In a Strange Land*. Gregory had become a respected translator, but his literary achievements came ironically at a time when he was eager to give up translating and just as he attained citizenship – and what in some ways had both novels been about if not what it meant to be a citizen of a particular state, a member of a community defined by its language and rights? Indeed, milestones in his life as well as many of his achievements would be ironic at the time or in retrospect. Korolenko's novel would be the last Russian translation he would undertake.

He still hoped to travel to Texas, to see his brother and the family in Mexico, although he did not mention the possibility of bringing Ray with him, of introducing his wife to Moses and Anna. He was thinking about how he might improve their situation, about what he might bring his parents from New York and how he might avoid Mexican customs charges. He asked James to tell him 'the number or size of Father's suits'. If he managed to come, he wanted to bring Moses some nice clothes.[20]

By the end of May Gregory had completed all the clinical rotations required of third-year medical students. He received a grade of 'C' in surgery, orthopaedic surgery, and urology and a 'B' in dermatology and syphilology, diseases of children, laryngology and otology, ophthalmology, and practice of medicine. In necrology, obstetrics and gynaecology, and psychiatry, he received an 'A'. He didn't manage to secure funding for a trip to Texas, however, nor did he travel to Mexico in the summer of 1925.

Instead, in June he moved alone into accommodation on the grounds of Bloomingdale Hospital, the psychiatric division of New York Hospital, in White Plains, a suburb 20 miles north of New York City. In principle and even in practice, Ray had no objection to living with her adored husband in a hospital apartment, but she could not imagine anything in White Plains that would be attractive or sociable or even just nice. After what must have involved much emotional discussion, the solution they arrived at was a year in Paris studying art. Ray probably saw this as a romantic alternative. She likely imagined visits to elegant museums, painting in oils, conversations using her high school French. Gregory must have felt that doing what she said she wanted – becoming an artist – would somehow make his wife happier. Perhaps without compunction – what was money finally except money? – he used a portion of his slender means for her voyage and the art classes he hoped would relieve her depression and give her an independent sense of direction and worth.

At Bloomingdale and at Lambert's clinic at Bellevue Hospital in Manhattan, Gregory would complete the clinical work in psychiatry that would conclude his four years at 'the Great Columbia University', but there was concern with his not entirely satisfactory performance, and van Beuren wrote him to tell him so. On Bloomingdale stationery with his own name printed elegantly and professionally at the top, Gregory responded with responsible and anxious abjection. His first thought had been to meet with the dean, but his rotations meant that he wasn't free during van Beuren's office hours and, he told him in his still slightly Russified English, 'I do not want to trouble you outside the office hours.' There was nothing to do but apologise. 'I cannot say that I did my best,' he continued, 'but as I consider the multiplicity of circumstances I at times do feel that *fecit quod potui*, although I want [to] assure you that I know that I am probably wrong in that.' Given 'the multiplicity of circumstances', it is astonishing that Gregory weathered the third year at all, but he didn't defend himself further or offer specifics. He simply told the dean he expected 'to make a great effort to make "the last lap" without difficulty.'[21]

In October Gregory's preceptor marked him much as before, noting his 'Personality' as 'Pleasant' but adding under remarks, 'Forceful personality. More adapted for original research than for a conventional clinical career. Might be a bit difficult as an intern. Interesting, highly intelligent, perhaps a little opinionated.' All this was indeed so, and as Gregory began his final clinical year of specialisation in psychiatry, he was clearly setting out on a path that would be original and creative, that might well focus more on research than clinical work.[22]

Then, in early December, Ray returned. The months abroad had not measured up to her dreams, and miserably homesick, she returned on the ironically named *Homeric* to the husband she had sorely missed. Perhaps Gregory's reports from Bloomingdale had reassured her that there was indeed a social life among the staff, that the simple accommodation was not so bad after all; perhaps she had become as depressed in Paris as she had been in New York; perhaps she simply hadn't had the emotional resources to live without her husband in a foreign country. Ray probably didn't know what would make things better for her, and Gregory didn't know what more he could do than what he had already done and was doing: trying to become a psychiatrist and make ends meet.[23]

Lecturers die hard, and in mid-February 1926 Gregory briefly hit the road again to speak in Montreal. Billed as Dr. Gregory Zilboorg, he chose subjects and themes new to Canadians yet exactly those on which he had been lecturing throughout his Chautauqua years. He praised Andreyev and Chekov, Ibsen and *Hamlet*, but in his provocative way announced there was no Anglo-Saxon drama. He condemned popular culture, calling vaudeville and the movies empty 'shows' which were not individual but mass-produced and anti-humanistic. His audience was impressed, and a local report offers a vivid glimpse of Gregory in full swing. Objecting animatedly to 'the iron-heeled boot of the so-called civilization which has industrialized human souls so long', he

> walked about, gesticulating freely, stopping very suddenly and dramatically, flashing his teeth in a quick smile and delivering epigram and bon mot in lightening fashion. He was equally quick in changing from one subject to another, digressing here, pausing there to examine a point, coming back to the drama or to social upheavals in Russia.

The consummate performer must have found it a challenge to be the cooperative student following a rigid curriculum and the directions of others. His moment in Montreal must have amused him, must have liberated him for a passing hour to be that other self. But he still had several months before the end of his clinical year and plans to make about what he would do afterwards.[24]

On his return to White Plains, Gregory opened an account with the Gotham National Bank of New York – a bank account, like American citizenship, was one more step towards establishing himself, towards security and solvency. Fascinated by the hospital's psychiatric patients, he had embraced life at Bloomingdale and was working hard to get along with colleagues and to satisfy his superiors. In early May, he graduated from Columbia's College of Physicians and Surgeons with a degree in medicine. At last a fully qualified doctor from a first-rate, internationally recognised institution, he could finally practise professionally in his chosen field. He must have been proud; he must have gone out for a drink with his classmates and taken joy in what he had achieved. Never a man to think only of the present, however, he was also thinking of at least the immediate future. His performance at Bloomingdale had been so strong that Gregory was taken on not as an 'intern' but as an 'Assistant Physician', the rank held by most psychiatrists on the staff. He was also offered the opportunity, as a doctor qualified by both his American and Russian credentials, to accompany a patient travelling to Europe in May.[25]

Naturally he accepted, but there was still the matter of money. He would leave Ray what remained in his bank account, but for his own needs, he turned to his brother. Gregory was not insensitive to the irony of his request. 'Apparently we write each other only when we end up in a "tight" situation', he told James, and now 'It's my turn'. He would be gone for six weeks but hadn't even a dime of pocket money and wouldn't have any until his return. 'If you can help me', he wrote, 'then do so immediately.' He did not mention a specific sum because he didn't know his brother's situation, but 'If you can', he asked James, 'send me 100. If not, send less.' He then added a postscript for Moses. Gregory didn't care that Basia found him impossible; he wasn't bothered that Fera had crossed him off her list of people capable of empathy, but he didn't want to be the prodigal son. He still desperately wanted to please his father, to make up for and justify all the requests he had made for money to get him to Petrograd and Saratov, for his fees at the Psycho-Neurological Institute and the University of Kiev. He wanted Moses to be proud of him and wrote frankly in a succinct and touching postscript 'To Father':

> Even from the most pessimistic point of view, things are going outstandingly well for me – I have been appointed to a very important post. And my position in the profession is thereby 'fixed'. I now hope that I will manage to pay off my debts and return to an independent life in the coming year.[26]

Notes

1 GZ to JZ, 17 June 1923.
2 GZ to JZ, 7 August 1923; Coolidge, 66; Stoddard, 183–184, 194.
3 GZ to JZ, 17 July 1923.
4 GZ to JZ, 18 September 1923.
5 GZ, 'About Actors', 18.
6 Zamiatin, second edition, 218.
7 GZ, 'Foreword', Zamiatin, second edition, xiv, xv.
8 Preceptorial Sheet, 24 October 1923, ASCCU.
9 GZ to JZ, 5 August 1924, and NYPSB, 281.
10 Thomas W. Salmon to William Darrach, 18 September 1925, ASCCU.
11 GZ to JZ, 5 August 1924.
12 FZ to JZ, 14, 17, and 20 August 1924; postscript from Sol Levitas, 17 August 1924.
13 Preceptorial Sheet, 13 October 1924, ASCCU.
14 Email from Stephen E. Novak, 19 August 2013.
15 William Darrach to Nicholas Murray Butler, 31 December 1924, ASCCU.
16 BIO; GZ to Frederick T. van Beuren, 4 January 1925; van Beuren to GZ, 8 July 1930, ASCCU.
17 Korolenko, 213, 214.
18 GZ, 'Foreword', Korolenko, v, vi, ix.
19 MZ to Menashe Gelfman, 11 October 1931, JEZB; GZ to JZ, 8 February 1925.
20 GZ to JZ, 8 March 1925.
21 Third-year transcript; Thomas W. Salmon to William Darrach, 18 September 1925; GZ to Frederick T. van Beuren, undated, all ASCCU.
22 Preceptorial Sheet, October 24 1925, ASCCU.
23 Email from AZ, 5 February 2018.
24 *Montreal Gazette*, 15 February 1926, 10.
25 B.W. Griffin to Frederick T. van Beuren, 4 March 1925, ASCCU.
26 GZ to JZ, 28 April 1926.

Chapter 9

Bloomingdale and Berlin

1926–1931

Gregory's trip to Europe was a welcome respite from a challenging clinical year. His financial penury was almost at an end as was his time as a student, while his status at Bloomingdale shifted as he became an official member of staff. Accompanying a patient likely returning home, Gregory fulfilled his assigned duties, then drew on whatever pocket money he had been able to raise and headed to Vienna, a city he now thought of not as the capital of a crumbling empire in socialist ferment but as the centre of psychoanalysis.

What Gregory did in Austria in late May and early June 1926 isn't clear. Certainly he hoped to meet Freud, but there is no record that he did so. He likely called at 19 Berggasse and he probably met Anna Freud there. On several occasions he saw Alfred Adler, who invited Gregory to his home, where he met Adler's wife Raissa, a Russian socialist sympathetic to Trotsky and Soviet communism. Gregory preferred Freud's ideas to Adler's 'Individual Psychology' with its emphasis on consciousness and social influences, but he was cordial and, through Adler, was introduced to other European psychoanalysts. Gregory arrived in Vienna soon after Freud's 70th birthday celebration, an occasion not only for Freud's family but for many of his followers who came to pay tribute to the great man. By the mid-1920s, however, some of Freud's colleagues were developing divergent theories; many who had been in Vienna for analysis had now set up private practices and clinics of their own in their native countries or elsewhere: Melanie Klein had left Austria for London, while Raymond de Saussure had returned to Geneva; Max Eitingon, Franz Alexander, Sandor Rado, and Hanns Sachs were working at the Psychoanalytic Institute and Polyclinic in Berlin; Otto Rank and Rudolph Lowenstein were by the summer of 1926 in Paris. Perhaps Gregory met Heinz Hartmann in Vienna; perhaps he met Ernst Kris and Sandor Ferenczi before heading to Paris and Cherbourg, where on 14 June he set sail for the United States on the *S.S. Majestic*. On board, Gregory was a dynamic presence. He walked the length of the deck discussing Freud with fellow first-class passengers, among them John Cowper Powys. Youthful and elegant, Gregory was full of life and in his element, his dark silky hair ruffled by the sea breezes as he exuded his enthusiasm for psychoanalysis.[1]

DOI: 10.4324/9781003190936-9

By the end of June, however, he was back in White Plains. His weeks in Europe had been liberating: he had been once again a world traveller, a free spirit engaged in open discussions with intellectuals on the cutting edge of exciting new ways of understanding individual human beings. He now resumed his daily work with psychiatric patients in a less stimulating environment among familiar and not always congenial colleagues. From the beginning of his time at Bloomingdale in September 1925, Gregory had encountered men and women who admired him a great deal as well as others who had mixed feelings towards him at best and at worst deep reservations that set them against him from the start. The immediate issue was not his strong personality nor even his debatable suitability for hospital teamwork but the fact that he was a Jew.

William Logie Russell, superintendent of Bloomingdale, had accepted Gregory on the recommendation of Thomas Salmon, who had always held him in high regard. During the 1925–1926 academic year, Russell had apparently not paid much attention to Gregory, and it came as a revelation in the summer of 1926 that he had inadvertently hired a Jew. Gregory soon sensed an uncomfortable tension between them. He was repeatedly assigned to work with psychotic patients regarded as custodial cases rather than severe neurotics or those who had suffered acute crises that might be resolved with immediate treatment. An experienced and diplomatic administrator at the height of his career, Russell was accustomed to keeping his feelings under wraps and covered his anti-Semitism with a suave quietness, yet Gregory sensed that the superintendent never forgave him for breaking the precedent and becoming the first Jewish staff member in the hospital's history.[2]

Gregory's relationship with Mortimer Williams Raynor was altogether different. Soon after Raynor took up his post as Bloomingdale's medical director in September 1926, the two men found they had much in common, including an interest in the unconscious and psychoanalysis, and Gregory would consider Raynor not only a mentor but a supportive friend. Raynor's favourite retreat was the hospital library, the centre of Bloomingdale's scientific life. As medical director he arranged numerous seminars and sponsored lectures by visiting American and European physicians. Bloomingdale was closely associated with Cornell University Medical College and, like many members of staff, Raynor was also a professor of clinical psychiatry. In 1928 Russell, too, would add to his title of superintendent that of professor of psychiatry at Cornell. Gregory logically hoped he might devote much of his vast energy to teaching and research. If Russell reserved judgement, Raynor encouraged Gregory's interest in history and an academic future. During the autumn of 1926, Gregory began to make notes towards a projected history of medical psychology.[3]

At Bloomingdale Gregory also got to know medical men and women who were his contemporaries, among them Raymond Gosselin, who would become a valued friend, and George W. Henry, director of Bloomingdale's laboratory. Stubborn, impatient, and narcissistic, Henry – like most of Gregory's medical contemporaries – had already established himself in his career. Unhappily married, he had begun, nearly a year before Gregory's arrival in White Plains, a torrid affair with Elizabeth Mangam, his assistant technician. When Henry's wife confronted him in January 1926, he abruptly fled. Given the unusual circumstances, he was granted *in absentia* a formal leave beginning in February. The divorce was messy, but after ten months away, Henry returned to his job and a year later married Eleanor Anne Siebert. During this stressful period Henry confided in Gregory. In retrospect, Gregory would regret his response, which went beyond compassionate listening. He found Henry profoundly depressed and withdrawn even after his second marriage, and in order to divert him, suggested before the end of the year that Henry look up some material on the history of organic psychoses and mental hospitals.

Gregory did not need help on his book, but Henry had intimated a competence in several languages and Gregory felt research would give his colleague 'a sort of push'. The result was disturbingly unsatisfactory. Henry knew none of the languages Gregory thought he had, and all the data he compiled came from second-hand sources in American journals. Gregory found Henry's work 'deplorable' and 'extremely inaccurate', lacking in both perspective and synthesis. How to put matters right while dealing with a stubborn, impatient, and increasingly difficult colleague posed practical, intellectual, emotional, and moral problems that would plague Gregory for more than a decade. That Henry was anti-Semitic as well as hostile to psychoanalysis didn't help the situation either.[4]

A sensitive man nevertheless capable of insensitivity, Gregory was discovering that working with colleagues required finesse, and Henry was not the only one to challenge his tolerance as well as his diplomatic skills. As with his family, some of the predicaments in which Gregory found himself were of his own making, although they generally resulted from good intentions anchored in firm principles and from his taking on more responsibility than he could handle. Egoism also played a role as Gregory, often without due reflection, would overreach and then backtrack, but from childhood he had been a master at verbal defence, at the deflection of criticism, at turning an attack upon the accuser. Intellectual denial as well as intimidation often seemed to him the only way out of the holes he dug for himself. Even when aware that he was at least to a degree responsible, he was still deeply reluctant to admit culpability even if (or sometimes because) he felt it disproportionately. Gregory's relationship with Henry was only a case in point, but it was neither the first nor would it be the last.

During the autumn Gregory continued to correspond with Adler, who hoped to include Bloomingdale as part of a lecture tour, but those inclined towards psychoanalysis opposed him and there was also personal antipathy. While their views of human psychology did not coincide, Gregory still felt that Adler deserved a hearing. Working with his colleague George E. Daniels, Gregory tried to schedule a series of talks, but when they discovered other people were doing the same or conflicting things in terms of arrangements, Gregory begged off. He offered Adler an elegant apology that included a characteristic denial of blame: 'permit me to express in my name as well as that of Dr. Daniels my deep regret for the complications the responsibility for which in my opinion does not rest with me.' Before the end of the year Adler did lecture at Bloomingdale on his provocative 'individual psychology' and Gregory was politely collegial throughout the visit, but he would always distance himself from the older psychiatrist's ideas.[5]

Work with patients and his own writing finally absorbed Gregory more than relationships with colleagues. By the end of the year he had an outline for what would become *A History of Medical Psychology*. A good deal of research lay ahead of him, but he was encouraged by men whose support he valued, including Salmon and Raynor; even Russell, who would write a history of New York Hospital's psychiatric service, was sympathetic to Gregory's efforts.[6]

Bloomingdale naturally expected its doctors to keep up with research and advances in medical thought, and with its close connection to Cornell, the hospital had strong academic and scholarly commitments. Most new staff appointments occurred, as in Gregory's case, in July or September (at the end or beginning of the university year), while senior physicians tended to hold academic ranks with teaching responsibilities. Once a week a staff meeting was held at which topics of scientific interest were discussed, while conferences to which outside physicians were invited were held five times a year. A fellowship for study abroad was awarded to a doctor each spring, and staff were encouraged to lecture to external groups and to publish in professional journals. Such opportunities were right up Gregory's alley.

In mid-February 1927 Gregory presented his first psychiatric paper, 'A Psychosis Caused by a Latent Focus of Infection (Ischio-Rectal Abscess)' to a meeting of the New York Academy of Medicine. The paper likely had its origin in the autumn of 1926 at a staff meeting devoted to individual cases, and Gregory probably developed the paper for further consideration at one of the hospital's discussion sessions before presenting it at the Bloomingdale conference on 'Psychoses Associated with Somatic Diseases'. The detailed case study was certainly systematically developed and is worth summarising at length to show both the state of Gregory's training and practice at the time as well as the strongly medicalised, physical, and historical orientation of his approach to psychiatry.

He began with an extensive and ostensibly objective history, noting the health of family members – including a maternal uncle who never married and lived to the age of 90 – as well as a strong family trend of 'Lutheran fanaticism'. He then focused on the patient: an unmarried 47-year-old manager at a textile mill. The patient's vision was slightly impaired because of close work done under bright lights, and he normally drank several glasses of wine a day, becoming 'only mildly intoxicated'. He had contracted a cold four months before admission to Bloomingdale and teeth had been extracted. For two months afterwards, he had felt unwell and had finally taken to his bed. About two months before admission, he showed the first signs of mental disorder: forgetfulness and confusion. He developed a fever a month later and was admitted to a general hospital. He complained of constipation and abdominal pain and had lost 24 pounds during his three months of illness. He soon became 'delirious, sleepless and increasingly restless' and finally 'irritable, disturbed and difficult to manage'. His physician moved him to Bloomingdale, considering this a case of 'alcoholic psychosis' and suggesting that '"the origin of the fever might be in the liver together with obstinate constipation"'. At this time the patient was 28 pounds under his normal weight, pale and dehydrated.

Gregory gave a detailed account of the patient's physical state including his temperature, pulse and respiration rates, blood pressure, the condition of his chest, liver, spleen, abdomen, deep reflexes, rectum, and prostate – all apparently healthy. He concluded his physical examination by observing, 'Both small toes were overriding their fellows – a congenital deformity', then noted that the patient's 'carrying angle' – the angle at which the elbow is held – 'was feminine. Pubic hair of feminine distribution. Genitalia quite small. Little more than the meatus could be seen, the glans penis being concealed by an extreme phimosis' – that is, by a foreskin that could not be completely retracted; the patient in addition reported incomplete and painful erections.

Gregory then described the patient's disorientation and confusion. He was 'restless, distracted, unable to keep up a sustained conversation', thought he was in a hotel in Vienna or Cologne, in a country place, a dark cellar, a taxi. He didn't understand he was ill and hospitalised. Extensive blood and urine tests were normal, as was a chest X-ray. A temporary diagnosis was made: The patient had 'a toxic infectious psychosis with an unknown focus of infection'.

Ten days after admission the patient was circumcised, but his fever persisted, as did his disorientation, insomnia, memory problems, general apathy, and loss of appetite. Six days later his buttocks were mottled with bluish areas, and a slight redness appeared on the right five centimetres from the anus. The patient was then diagnosed with an ischio-rectal abscess and operated on under general anaesthesia. Examination of the exudate revealed a streptococcus infection.

The patient immediately improved both physically and mentally. He started to eat and became more cheerful and less irritable. His memory also improved. Because of his severe weight loss – he weighed 100 pounds at the time of the surgery – he was given a transfusion. Four hours afterwards, he developed a high fever and appeared again psychotic, disoriented, and very active, jumping out of bed and urinating and defecating around the room. Within two days, however, his temperature was normal and he developed severe cold sores on his lips. His mental symptoms disappeared and he had no memory of his psychotic behaviour.

During the following seven weeks, the patient gained 38 pounds. Once the drain from the sinus of the abscess was removed, it began to heal well. Before he left hospital, he had a nocturnal emission without discomfort. Two and a half months after admission he was discharged as recovered. Two weeks later, he got married. At a follow-up meeting six weeks later, he had no complaints and was back at work.

The two conclusions that Gregory drew from this case are particularly interesting. He stated that circumcision 'was indicated as a matter of simple hygiene' but emphasised that the patient's religious background and the fact that at the time of his illness he was unmarried with 'anomalies of development' (his 'deformed' toes, feminine carrying angle, and feminine distribution of pubic hair) made circumcision 'of great medical importance'. Gregory concluded that the sexually disabling phimosis was dangerous because 'conditions of this kind, especially in individuals with a suggestion of feminine makeup, are amongst the causative factors of alcoholism'.

Gregory digressed briefly – his questioning mind was difficult to rein in – and wondered why it took so long for an accurate diagnosis and what the primary cause of the abscess might have been. Today we know that such abscesses are caused by common bacteria that collect for a variety of reasons, although even now diagnosis can be quite difficult, requiring a trans-rectal ultrasound or a pelvic scan. Physicians today do not transfuse patients so readily, and it is certainly no longer common for a responsible doctor to consider the combination of strong religious feelings, overlapping toes, sparse body hair in men, and a tight foreskin as a cause of alcoholism. Gregory's understanding of his information is outdated and his resources were historically limited, but his first conclusion, however wrong-headed it may seem to twenty-first-century readers, was the result of a classic and thorough psychiatric education in America and his own training while working with alcoholics at the Psycho-Neurological Institute.

Gregory contextualised his second conclusion historically. He specifically discussed 'infectious psychosis' – psychotic behaviour as a result of a severe infection – with reference to the German psychiatrist Karl Bonhoeffer's classification of symptomatic psychoses in 1908 and to the work of the German internist Carl von Liebermeister, who in a German textbook in 1875 described three clinical stages of progressive discomfort, disorientation, and hallucination. Gregory then noted the 1906 studies of organic deliria by the Swiss-born American neuropathologist August Hoch as well as earlier work by the seventeenth-century English physician Thomas Sydenham on psychotic manifestations associated with malarial infections. Gregory was now in full historical flow: It was 'of interest to note' that, with few institutions for mental illness in the mid-nineteenth century, psychiatrists of the time – he mentioned Esquirol, Martini, Georget, and Burrows – considered that infectious psychoses belonged to the field of general medicine. Jacobi, he observed, was the first to consider them as within the psychiatrist's competence. Gregory at last arrived at his second and most significant conclusion: It was unwise 'to draw a strict line of demarcation between these two branches of medicine'. Such a dangerous separation deprived general practitioners of concepts they needed and tended 'to turn the psychiatrist away from the use of our medical equipment'. This point – that the psychiatrist must examine the whole person, both mentally and physically, and seek to treat patients' mental symptoms within the context of their physical state by using 'medical equipment' – would be important in both his future practice and in his medical ethics, while his historical contextualising connects Gregory's psychiatric work with his earlier and future writing on social, political, and literary topics. He would never be content to work with individuals in isolation nor with fragments of information. His sweeping mind would always seek a broader perspective, a wider environment, a larger framework. His first professional paper as a psychiatrist was completely characteristic, although it did not yet reflect the Freudian theory that would significantly inform his later work.[7]

Of the four papers presented by Bloomington staff to external groups during the 1927–1928 year, three were by Gregory. 'Psychosis Caused by a Latent Focus of Infection', which appeared in the *New York State Journal of Medicine* in July 1927, was one of only two articles by Bloomingdale doctors published that year. He was off to a flying start that could not help but be noticed by his colleagues, who must have been at once impressed and resentful.[8]

Gregory's writing during his second year in White Plains suggests that he had more on his mind than individual case studies. His second psychiatric paper, 'Malignant Psychoses Related to Pregnancy and Childbirth', was presented at a meeting of the New York Obstetrical Society on 10 May 1927 before appearing in the *American Journal of Obstetrics* in February 1928. In contrast to his first paper's brief bibliography of three items (one each in English, French, and German, between 1906 and 1923), Gregory appended to his second paper a full page of notes listing references in English, French, and German ranging from 1856 to 1926. His research was now obviously scholarly and more extensive, although he made no mention of Freud or psychoanalysis. Having excluded from his sample women with physical problems that might complicate the post-partem period, Gregory focused on psychiatric issues. He suggested that the 'schizoid personality' might be prone to post-partem difficulties, especially after the birth of a second or later child, and connected women's 'psychosexual' difficulties with the risk of psychological difficulties after childbirth. He concluded that, while future studies ought to include a control group, 'The psychiatrist unfortunately seldom has the opportunity to study the normal woman.' During the year he also presented 'Some Mechanisms in Post-Partum Schizophrenia' to the Philadelphia Psychiatric Society. Of the three subjects in which he had earned an 'A' during his fraught third year at Columbia, one had been psychiatry, his chosen specialism, while the two others had been necrology – which must have attracted him for its purely scientific value – and gynaecology and obstetrics. Gregory would continue to think and write about the nature of schizophrenia, yet – given Ray's negative feelings towards the prospect of children – women's psychology and particularly their attitudes towards pregnancy and childbirth were of personal as well as phenomenological interest.[9]

By the end of 1927, however, Gregory had decided that psychoanalytic theory was key to understanding the human mind. In December he contacted Abraham Arden Brill, the founder and president of the New York Psychoanalytic Society, to discuss membership. With Brill's recommendation and the support of Abram Kardiner, one of Freud's analysands, Gregory was accepted in February 1928 as an associate member, the status of a psychiatrist who had not yet completed a training analysis. He attended his first meeting in March, and at the end of April presented a paper, 'Post-Partem Schizophrenias', the first of his writings almost entirely psychoanalytic in nature. He cited two case studies, but now only as illustrative of the Freudian framework, which he established by citing not only Freud but Sandor Ferenczi, Karl Abraham, Karen Horney, Helene Deutsch, and Ernest Jones. The paper is rife with Freudian terminology. With references to the Oedipal and castration complexes, frigidity, vaginal sexuality, and penis envy, 'the unconscious', 'the super-ego', and 'repression', the paper offers evidence of Gregory's wide reading as well as his intellectual preparation for the training analysis he was now hoping to undertake in Germany.[10]

While continuing to work on his history, Gregory prepared his application for the fellowship that would allow him to go abroad. In January 1928 Gregory submitted a 66-page 'thesis' to a Bloomingdale committee, 'Most Common Mechanisms Met with in Psychopathology'. Based on case studies and on his reading especially of Freud and Ferenczi, the essay demonstrates a comprehensive understanding of psychoanalytic principles and practices. The coveted fellowship was competitive and, as the winter snows fell on the hospital lawns, Gregory waited for a decision, spending long hours with patients and his free time in Bloomingdale's comfortable library. A year in Europe would allow him not only to work with Freud's colleagues at the prestigious Berlin Psychoanalytic Institute but, he hoped, to complete the research for his history.[11]

Overestimating himself and the work required, Gregory felt he was almost ready to finish what he thought of as the first volume of a two-volume history. The fact that he found Henry's contributions completely unsatisfactory did not yet seem a serious problem: Gregory could recast them, incorporate them, or put them in a separate section at the end. Indeed, his relationship with Henry remained cordial if occasionally strained, and they jointly presented a paper on the early nineteenth-century French physician Philippe Pinel at the annual meeting of the American Psychopathological Association in New York in early March. Probably with Gregory's encouragement yet perhaps also in a spirit of competition, Henry was one of the few Bloomindale staff who was now presenting papers. In the spring of 1928 Gregory lectured at Swarthmore College on 'Contributions of Medical Psychology to the Philosophy of Life' (a topic after his own heart, broadly conceived for non-medical listeners) and at the National Arts Club in New York City on Russia (his standard subject, still of interest to an intellectual audience), yet his vast energies were increasing focused on psychoanalysis, while Henry scattered his attention, speaking to various groups on topics ranging from 'Medieval Psychiatry' to 'Emotions and Digestive Functions', 'Focal Infection in Teeth', and 'Some Practical Considerations Pertaining to Mental Hygiene in School Children'. Meanwhile, more confident than boastful and more hopeful than mendacious, Gregory told colleagues that the history's first volume was close to completion, spurring himself on in the process of seeking information and support from his many correspondents.

By the time the daffodils bloomed at the end of April, Gregory had received confirmation of his fellowship and gone into high gear. He contacted the American medical historian Fielding H. Garrison, then a bibliographer in Washington, and asked him how he might go about joining the prestigious the German Society for the History of Medicine and Natural Sciences. On 12 May Garrison wrote to his Swiss colleague Henry E. Sigerist, then professor of history of medicine at the University of Leipzig, proposing Gregory for membership as 'well worthy of inclusion' on the basis of 'a very excellent history of psychiatry which will be the first English work of any value on this subject'.[12]

Gregory must have spent the rest of the spring – when he wasn't treating patients or writing letters or working on his history or making presentations – preparing a presentation for the annual meeting of the American Psychiatric Association in Minneapolis in early June. By the time the paper appeared in print as 'The Dynamics of Schizophrenic Reactions Related to Pregnancy and Childbirth' in January 1929, it included an impressive formal bibliography of 82 works in English, French, German, Italian, Spanish, and Russian. The framework was psychoanalytic, but for the first time Gregory proposed his own theoretical addition to psychoanalysis, drawing a metaphor from stereochemistry to elucidate characteristics of women prone to schizophrenic reactions to pregnancy and childbirth. Citing Freud's statement that psychoanalysis is related to psychiatry as histology to anatomy, Gregory posited a new dynamic psychology offering a 'bio-chemistry' of the mind. Less obscurely and more helpfully, he concluded, 'Too little attention has been paid to the importance of sexual frigidity in women.' He finally stated succinctly and insightfully, 'The sexually frigid man is biologically well protected; he becomes impotent and thus avoids what he wishes to avoid. Moreover he considers impotence an illness.' In contrast,

> The prevalent traditional opinion with regard to women is that they are usually frigid; that it is not an illness and that they will 'get over it'; if they do not get over it[,] however, they are not relieved by society from the necessity of functioning biologically as if they were not frigid.[13]

As they packed their bags, Gregory and Ray prepared themselves for the experiences they imagined lay ahead of them. Gregory looked forward to his psychoanalytic training, including his own analysis; he had his history to work on and new colleagues he anticipated meeting in Leipzig, Vienna, and Paris as well as Berlin; he was excited at the prospect of working with many of Freud's analysands. Bert Lewin had spent the previous year at the Berlin Psychoanalytic Institute and been analysed by Alexander; the friends must have discussed what training there involved – not only the personal psychoanalysis but the lectures and seminars as well as the opportunity for 'control analyses', the chance to analyse one or two patients under the supervision of experienced analysts.

For her part, Ray was proud of Gregory's accomplishments and thrilled by the idea of going abroad again, this time with her husband. She had no job, no particular occupation or career or professional aspirations; appreciating beauty wasn't exactly a vocation, in spite of how much beauty mattered to her. Caring for the household and supporting her busy husband had kept her occupied in New York City, and in Gregory's absence she had run errands on his behalf. When he was studying and writing, she had felt and been less necessary, but the city had bustled with activity and people. In White Plains, she was on her own while Gregory worked long hospital hours or stayed up late in concentrated solitude at his desk. Suburbia was definitely not her chosen milieu, although she liked Henry's wife Eleanor, enjoyed having the couple in for drinks with other young psychiatrists on a Saturday evening, liked planning small supper parties, laying a pretty table. She must have wondered if they would have an apartment in Berlin or merely rent rooms and socialise in restaurants. She had heard Germany would be colder in winter than New York. Into her bags that summer she put her coat with the fur collar, Gregory's coat with its fur collar, two scarves, fur hats. She probably didn't feel sad to leave White Plains, was probably happy to be going away for an entire year. Given the papers Gregory had worked on, they must have discussed what having children might mean, but if they had children, would she be going at all? She certainly didn't feel children were necessary; surely children did not complete or fulfil a woman. She must have felt she was complete and fulfilled as things were, despite occasional dissatisfaction and sadness. Perhaps Gregory thought Ray would feel less alone in Berlin, a vibrant city with a rich theatrical and musical life. Ray thought she would find things to do; she might take art lessons, might herself be analysed.

Ray, likely on the Bloomingdale grounds

It was not only the fellowship that allowed them to focus on the trip. Gregory's income for the last two years had been not only predictable but sufficient for their needs despite the loans he was still paying off, and neither he nor Ray needed to worry so much now about either money or family. With a promotion at Westinghouse, James had moved with Eugenia and Natalie from Monterrey to Mexico City. The transfer to the United States that he had hoped for hadn't materialised, but at least all of the Zilboorgs in Mexico were in the same vicinity, while Fera and her family had moved to New York, where Sol had found congenial if not particularly remunerative work on the staff of a socialist magazine. Ray had no compunction about a year away from her own family; by 1928 she had very little contact with any of them, a fact for which she might have held Gregory responsible but which she certainly must have recognised as in large measure her own choice.[14]

By the time they arrived in September 1928, Berlin if not the country seemed to have recovered from the war. Despite ongoing reparations and post-war financial instability, Germany's capital was prospering in Weimar's 'golden twenties', the nation's version of America's 'Jazz Age'. The arts flourished in the decade that in Germany belonged to the bitterly satiric painters Otto Dix and George Grosz, to the Bauhaus architect Walter Gropius, to Bertolt Brecht and Kurt Weil, whose modernist *Threepenny Opera* was performed on Berlin's stages throughout Gregory's analytic year. Wilhelm Furtwängler conducted the Berlin Philharmonic; Mozart's *Zauberflöte* as well as Serge Diaghilev's *Ballets Russes* featured at the State Opera house. Berlin at the end of the decade was a cauldron of political extremism as well as the arts; it was the capital of a threatened republic, the industrial, left-wing metropolis of Christopher Isherwood's *Berlin Stories*.

Gregory's attendance at the theatre and the opera isn't documented, nor is there a record of his presence at concert performances or art galleries nor his consumption of champagne in cabarets, but he couldn't have been unaware of the city's cultural offerings and political tensions, the exciting if also decadent spectacle whirling all around him. His psychoanalytic work would absorb him, demanding energy and concentration as well emotional investment, and he would spend much of his free time on his history, but he was no longer putting in 17-hour hospital days. His training demanded 10 or 11 hours each weekday, a comparative holiday. He spent his evenings and weekends as he wanted while possibilities beckoned on every corner of the Kurfürstendamm between his rooms on Sächsischestrasse and the Psychoanalytic Institute near the Tiergarten. His Bloomingdale colleague Ray Gosselin began two years of study at the Institute at the same time as Gregory, and there were other amiable Americans there as well, among them Ives Hendrick, who would go on to found the Boston Psychoanalytic Society. Gregory would rapidly develop a lively social circle of international contemporaries. He liked good wine; he enjoyed nice restaurants, serious music and drama and art. With American dollars in his pocket, he was for the first time in his life free to partake as he chose of the world around him.[15]

Gregory began his training in a new building on Wichmannstrasse designed by Freud's youngest son Ernst in a spare rather than modernist style: Its bright interior resulted not from trendy interior decoration but from the tall windows overlooking the street. Used to Bloomingdale's spacious buildings with their comfortable furnishings and extensive support staff, Gregory was immediately struck by the simplicity of the premises, which housed not only the Psychoanalytic Institute, the organisation in charge of training, but the Polyclinic offering psychoanalysis to outpatients for free or a minimal charge. In addition to a single meeting room and a lecture hall, there were only six treatment rooms, one for Eitingon, the Institute's director, and another for the doctor on duty. A part-time secretary working on an old-fashioned, portable typewriter was responsible for all correspondence, patient registration, and rota lists, while astonishingly everything managed to function without an official budget or even a bank account.[16]

The Polyclinic was a natural product of the psychoanalytic movement's commitment to social justice. With roots in the pan-European free-thinking socialism that had nourished Gregory's political fervour in Russia, the organisation served two functions: It offered psychanalysis to people from all backgrounds while providing cases for the 'control analyses' integral to the Institute's programme. With 40 new patients in 1928 and 43 in 1929, the Polyclinic had 117 cases on its books by 1930.[17]

Funded by the Russian-born Eitingon, the German psychoanalyst who used his private fortune to shape the organisation he directed, the Berlin Psychoanalytic Institute had attracted many prominent European analysts. In 1928 the staff included Germans (Carl Müller-Braunschweig, Ernst Simmel, and Karen Horney), Austrians (Sachs, Otto Fenichel, and Siegfried Bernfeld), and Hungarians (Rado and Alexander); Horney was the only woman, and except for Horney and Müller-Braunschweig, all of the psychoanalysts were Jews. Most had been analysed by Freud himself or by Sachs or Karl Abraham, who had founded the Institute with Eitingon in 1920 and died three years before Gregory's arrival. The tensions among these figures, however, who were beginning to define their theoretical differences from Freud, would not have surprised Gregory, who had learned a great deal from his time at Bloomingdale about working with people with differing views.

Yet Gregory was confused by his first impressions. Despite his excitement about working with intellectual Europeans, with humanistic individuals none of whom was anti-Semitic, his surprise at the simplicity of the facilities made him aware that he had become – almost without his knowing it – Americanised, while the tension he felt at the beginning of his own analysis added to his confusion. His early uneasiness, however, soon dissipated. He shared the Institute's values and admired its efforts to promote egalitarianism, progressivism, and social conscience. Warmly welcomed by Eitingon, Gregory rapidly surmounted what he came to see as his 'naive astonishment ... at purely external things' as he embarked on the course that would become the model for psychoanalytic training throughout the world.[18]

The Institute offered three modes of learning: didactics (lectures and seminars in theory and concepts), the training analysis (a personal experience of psychoanalysis), and supervision (supervised practical work, the 'control analysis'). The course was flexible and potentially short, while the range of lecture and seminar topics must have reminded Gregory of Bekhterev's institute: psychology, literature, art, philosophy, anthropology, pedagogy, and sociology were all significant areas for psychoanalytic study. Gregory was impressed as the 'huge, all encompassing, synthetic possibilities of psychoanalysis and its current achievements' were scientifically and precisely set out.[19]

Alongside 'didactics', Gregory began his training analysis with Alexander. Born in Budapest as Ferenc Gabor Alexander on 22 January 1891, he was – given the difference between calendars in Russia and the Austrian-Hungarian Empire – almost exactly Gregory's age, but by 1928 Alexander's career was established. An assimilated Jew from a privileged intellectual family, his childhood had been comfortable and secure. Having received his medical diploma from the University of Budapest in 1913, he served as a physician in a Red Cross unit during the First World War and in 1920 had been the first student to enrol at the Berlin Psychoanalytic Institute, where he was analysed by Abraham. After completing the course, Alexander had stayed on to teach and supervise. Physically heavy, muscular and tall, married with two young daughters, Alexander was an imposing presence. Freud had in the early 1920s sent his second son to Alexander for analysis. Alexander's first book, *Psychoanalyse der Gesamtpersönlichkeit* ('Psychoanalysis of the Total Personality'), had appeared in 1927 and he was at work with the German criminologist Hugo Staub on a book on psychoanalysis and the law. There were many reasons Alexander might have seemed like a good choice as Gregory's analyst, and Gregory was prepared to like the man he was also eager to accept as a future colleague, but Alexander could never have functioned as Freud's 'blank screen' that at least theoretically and more or less practically the analyst was supposed to be for the analysand.

The training analysis unfortunately did not go well. The Institute was committed to the 'one-person psychology' perspective in which transfer dynamics were the focus of interest and inquiry. The most important element of any training analysis is the fundamental idea that self-knowledge is essential for the future psychoanalyst, and Gregory's initial discomfort must have stemmed at least in part from a natural fear of what might be uncovered. In addition, Gregory certainly knew about Alexander's reputation as well as something of his personal background both so like his own and so different. Furthermore, in addition to daily analytic sessions, the two men, like all those at the Institute, encountered one another in social as well as professional situations. Transference is inevitably a tricky matter for both patient and analyst. What Alexander felt about transference in Gregory's case isn't explicitly documented, but from Gregory's perspective the transference was negative from the start. That is, he unconsciously saw Alexander as a threat, a figure towards whom his feelings were hostile; his resentment, anger, and fear became the extremely uncomfortable focus of the year-long analysis.[20]

Gregory's control analyses began in November. For the next ten months, under the supervision of Horney, Sachs, and Eitingon, Gregory saw two patients for an hour several times a week. Given his years of clinical work, he was immediately on familiar ground. Nevertheless, Polyclinic outpatients were with few exceptions not so ill as those he had treated at Bloomingdale; they were not suffering from the post-partem psychoses and schizophrenia that had recently captured his interest in the hospital setting. He was required to share detailed notes on each case with his supervisors in order to correct errors and misconceptions. 'One-person psychology' determined the slant that supervision took in the control analysis as in the training analysis itself, and the focus of discussion was again the dynamics of transference.[21]

Seminars and lectures were more comfortable territory, and throughout the year Gregory played an active role in the German Psychoanalytic Society. As early as 9 October 1928, when Alexander lectured on '*Strafbedürfnes und Todestrieb*' ('The Need for Punishment and the Death Drive'), Gregory was a discussant with Müller-Braunschweig, Horney, Simmel, Rado, and the Hungarian psychoanalyst Jenö Hárnik. In June 1929, when the Norwegian psychologist Ola Raknes, a fellow student at the Institute, lectured on '*Gesichtspunkte zur Religionspsychologie*' ('Aspects of the Psychology of Religion'), Gregory was again a discussant with Fenichel, Müller-Braunschweig, Simmel, Rado, Horney, and Eitingon, as well as the Swiss psychoanalyst Gustav Bally and the German lay analyst Erich Fromm. Gregory was making contact with people who would become his psychoanalytic colleagues for the rest of his life, yet his year abroad was also about meeting people with a particular interest in the history of medicine. Research for his book would take Gregory into Berlin's libraries and old bookshops, but also to Leipzig to meet Henry Sigerist, the university professor to whom Garrison had written on Gregory's behalf in May.[22]

Early in 1929 Gregory set out on one of several trips he would make to Leipzig that year. The two-hour train journey was expressly to consult library resources at the university's Institute for the History of Medicine, where he had arranged to meet the director who in 1925 had succeeded Karl Sudhoff, the renowned German historian of medicine and the library's venerated founder. Sigerist's Russian-born assistant Owsei Temkin showed him the vast library before introducing him to Sigerist, whom Gregory found initially cool and pleasant but with a 'friendly smile on his face'. Despite his initial professional formality, Sigerist's 'eyes were keen but not searching, his hand out-stretched in the warmest possible manner'. Gregory was delighted to be welcomed so affirmatively, but there was yet more that drew Gregory to the Swiss historian who had been born in Paris – 'something un-German about his demeanor' and a charming 'touch of the French "r" in his pronunciation'. Sigerist and Gregory quickly relaxed, conversing in a way that was 'free, lively, and full of good cheer', discussing history, Russia, even the American journalist and cultural critic H.L. Mencken. In the end the two men spent the entire day together, finally leaving the Institute to dine in a large, noisy restaurant, where there was music and song, good food, and a great deal of the

German sparkling wine called 'Sekt'. They spoke freely in German of 'the history of the world, past, present and future' and of food, about which Sigerist particularly was passionate. Before Gregory left on the last train to Berlin, Sigerist took out a small notebook and asked him for the addresses of good restaurants in New York, Chicago, and Washington, then dictated the addresses of his own favourites in the German capital. Gregory would remember the day as 'splendid'.[23]

Left to right: Hungarian medical historian Stephen d'Irsay; Swiss medical historian Arnold C. Klebs; Henry Sigerist (with a 'friendly smile upon his face'); Karl Sudhoff; historian of botanical science Friedrich W.T. Hunger; and Owsei Temkin, Leipzig, 1929[24]

Back in Berlin as the snow fell, Gregory's analysis was apparently going fairly well, and his enthusiasm for psychoanalysis remained unabated. He was learning a great deal and felt that analysis might help Ray to overcome her depressive tendencies. Fees were on a sliding scale and he was willing to spend money if it would make his sad wife happy, so whether through the Polyclinic or independently, Ray also entered analysis. The effect of the sessions, which probably addressed her depression, was positive, and she soon became as enthusiastic as her husband about psychoanalysis, although for her the attractions were more personal than intellectual.

At least in terms of the weather, that winter in Berlin was much like those Gregory had known in Petrograd: cold and snowy and long. He spent most of his evenings at his desk and felt he was making good progress on his history, soon considered the first section finished and hoped to complete a draft of the second by April. He had as yet no American publisher, but there was already interest in a German translation. He was also thinking of the work ahead of him when he returned to the United States. He was eager to resume his study of mental pathology in relation to childbirth, this time focussing on depressions. While her husband was content indoors, Ray bundled up and went out, must have liked the look of the city transformed by snow. Gregory wrote to van Beuren, who had urged him to apply for an opening at New York Presbyterian Hospital. After updating his Columbia mentor on his professional progress, he explained his obligation to remain at Bloomingdale until at least 1931 – one condition of the fellowship being two years further service – then concluded on a personal note that suggests the differences between him and his wife: 'The winter here is rather severe – 19 degrees C below zero in Berlin. I do not skate and therefore do not enjoy the wheather [sic].'[25]

Ray probably skated that winter and thus managed to enjoy the season almost as much as she enjoyed her own analysis, which structured her days while Gregory was busy. As she lay on a couch, her analyst listened earnestly to everything she said. Never before had she felt that her words mattered so much; she revelled in the experience and felt understood. She also likely sensed that her gratification was an affirmation of Gregory's profession, a confirmation of his choices, judgement, and future. She must have realised that her satisfaction would please her husband, would help her to be what she wanted to be: the wife he needed and wanted.[26]

As winter turned to spring, Gregory travelled not only to Leipzig but to other university cities in Germany, seeking books related to his history and making connections among psychiatrists and historians of medicine. Some trips were pragmatic, others a form of pilgrimage. He apparently travelled to the Burghölzi Klinik in Zurich to meet Freud's contemporary Eugen Bleuler, the Swiss psychiatrist who had coined the term 'schizophrenia'. There he also met Bleuler's son Manfred, and the two men quickly warmed to one another. Manfred Bleuler would, as a result of their acquaintance, spend the following year as a medical intern at Bloomingdale. Gregory similarly travelled to Paris, where he met the French psychiatrist René Semelaigne. Another physician of Freud's generation, Semelaigne was also the great nephew of Philippe Pinel, the 'great psychiatric reformer' about whom Gregory would write at length in his history. Hoping Semelaigne would endorse the book, Gregory showed him drafts of a few chapters, which they discussed with mutual enthusiasm.[27]

GZ and Franz Alexander on the ship to England, July 1929[28]

If networking was an important part of Gregory's year in Europe, he could not have chosen a better occasion to crown his months abroad than the 11th International Psychoanalytical Congress in Oxford at the end of July. There Gregory encountered men and women with whom he had corresponded, or whom he had met on his travels or at the German Psychoanalytical Society, or whose work he had read, or whom he knew by reputation, psychoanalysts from all over Europe including Anna Freud and Ernest Jones, the head of the British Psycho-Analytical Society. Indeed, of the 186 attendees, 108 were members of the International Psycho-Analytical Association. In addition to the scientific proceedings, participants were given a tour of Oxford and feted at Queen's College with a welcome reception and a concluding banquet. Sándor Lorand had a movie camera and filmed the psychoanalysts walking out a door into a courtyard at Lady Margaret Hall. Many lit cigarettes during the break in proceedings. Alix and James Strachey walked towards the lens with Karen Horney and Melanie Klein not far behind, while a hefty Franz Alexander briefly took centre stage. As the camera panned and swivelled, female psychoanalysts in cloche hats smiled in guarded amusement and bearded male analysts nodded to the filmmaker. Slim and dapper, Gregory suddenly appears, moving from right to left, conversing animatedly with a colleague, then disappears from view only to reappear seconds later, walking forwards before vanishing out of range.[29]

Gregory returned to the continent in August, but by the middle of September he was back in White Plains with Ray, who had left Germany at the beginning of the summer. With the analysts en route to England, there had been little to keep her in Berlin. If she had accompanied Gregory on any of his many trips, she had been a tagalong, not an active presence during intellectual or professional discussions, excluded from meetings and libraries and psychoanalytic conversations. Gregory quickly resumed his clinical work with psychotic patients at Bloomingdale, where there was not much encouragement for psychoanalysis. American life had not stood still in his absence, but it must have seemed in some ways as if he had never left. Having received Bloomingdale's fellowship for study abroad for the 1929–1930 academic year, Henry and his wife were in Germany and Holland, so Ray was a bit lonelier, and Gregory missed Gosselin, who had remained in Berlin, but he greatly enjoyed Manfred Bleuler's presence, a bit of Europe in America. In Gregory's absence, the Republican Herbert Hoover had defeated the Democrat Alfred E. Smith, the Roman Catholic governor of New York, in the 1928 presidential election, and the roaring twenties continued to roar. The economy was still buoyant, and Prohibition continued as the leaves on the Westchester trees turned their seasonal yellow and red and orange.

Somewhat more notable changes had occurred in the life of the wider family. With the economy booming, James and Eugenia had decided they could afford a second child; Lydia's arrival in March 1929 must have pleased not only her parents and eight-year-old Natalie but the Russian grandparents. In a renewed effort to find a job that might allow him to return to the States, James left Westinghouse in October for a position at the Electric Bond and Share Company, one of the conglomerate's suppliers, while, despite Sol's slender income, Fera was also expecting a second child, due in December. Her ailments notwithstanding, Anna arrived in New York on 27 October to help out in the Levitas household. Two days later, after a meeting at the New York Psychoanalytic Society, Gregory saw his mother for the first time in over a decade.

One can imagine the reunion: Anna in happy tears, Fera heavily pregnant, Nora shy before the uncle she didn't remember, soup simmering in the kitchen, hot tea and spicy *pryaniki* on the table. Sensitive and highly emotional himself, Gregory was likely moved, his own eyes filling, the tea and sweets very welcome. But he would also have been uneasy with the very Jewish Russianness of the cloying household so like the one in Kiev from which he had fled not only because of the revolution's political aftermath. In America as in Petrograd, with Fera he generally spoke Russian; with their mother, they spoke perforce the Yiddish of his childhood, which after so many years probably rolled awkwardly even off his fluent tongue. He must have been uncomfortably reminded of his mother's limitations, her conventional tastes and bourgeois standards, her self-absorption and narrow focus. Confronted with motherhood incarnate in Fera (visibly large with her second child, a housewife responsible for a five-year-old not yet at school) and in Anna (her matronly figure and insistent presence, her maternal concern focused not only on her little granddaughter but on Fera and on him), Gregory would have struggled to check his temper.

The negative transference during analysis with Alexander had surely involved his feelings towards his mother. The issue of his childless marriage must have come up. Ray's attitude towards children would have been significant in her own analysis: Female fulfilment through maternity is fundamental to Freud's theories, and Ray had now begun to accept the idea that embracing motherhood would enable her to overcome her depressions. For his part, Gregory liked children, had expected children from the start of the marriage, had felt that as soon as he was on his feet financially, children would naturally come along, but his personal experience of mothers had not been positive. His psychiatric work on pregnancy and post-partem psychoses suggests the matter was on his mind for more than professional reasons, while his continuing interest in 'mental pathology in relation to childbirth' must have had its source at least in part in his concern about Ray's emotional state. His interest in depressions associated with motherhood was also rooted in his own conscious and unconscious struggle – as a psychiatrist, as a psychoanalyst, as Ray's husband and an eager potential father – to cope with a marriage that in some ways frustrated and disappointed him. Anna's presence in New York must thus have discomforted him for myriad reasons and forced him to confront his feelings towards a model of motherhood he violently rejected.

By the time Gregory boarded the train for White Plains on the evening of 29 October 1929, the stunning news of what came to be known as Black Tuesday had made the headlines of all the papers. The stock market crash would have little direct impact on Gregory: His job was secure and he had no financial investments. He had even managed to repay three-quarters of the sum he had borrowed to get him through Columbia. The impact on James and the family in Mexico, however, was immediate: American companies would suffer at home and abroad as the dollar plummeted, quickly affecting the exchange rate and the family's standard of living. In New York the crash only confirmed Sol's socialism, but this satisfaction and the joy he and Fera took in the birth of their second child – Mikhail, known as Misha – on December first did nothing to help pay the rent. Help in paying the rent in the United States and Mexico could only come, as Sol had insisted when discussing the loan his brother-in-law had refused to co-sign, from Grigory Moiseevich.[30]

Juggling personal and professional responsibilities, Gregory had his hands full in typically overburdened fashion. At the end of the year he became chairman of Bloomingdale's 'Monday Night Meetings'. Throughout 1930 he coordinated the programme, drawing on his organisational and diplomatic skills. He personally directed ten general sessions on 'practical aspects of clinical psychiatry', which alternated with symposia on such topics as 'mental nursing', 'psychoses', 'neuroses', 'personality development' and 'the neurophysiological orientation' as well as three reports by Gregory himself on 'the results of one year's application of psychoanalysis'. Three evenings were devoted to 'research problems' – specifically suicide types, homosexuality, and criminal tendencies – but psychoanalysis itself was not given its own evening. Gregory tactfully explained the deliberate decision: 'It is thought that the dynamic and psychoanalytic features of psychopathology, clinical and theoretical, belong to the domain of psychiatry as an integral part of it and should not be considered as something separate'; his programme 'would make it possible to link up the psychoanalytic concepts in psychopathology with our practical problems and avoid placing psychoanalysis in the domain of speculative considerations'. After his year abroad, Gregory became a strong advocate for psychoanalysis, but he recognised that not all of his contemporaries were sympathetic to Freud, nor was psychoanalysis always appropriate to the variety of cases the psychiatrist confronted.[31]

In addition to hospital shifts and institutional obligations, Gregory worked on his history and prepared papers for presentation and publication. At the end of February 1930 he engaged in a revealing interchange with T.H. Weisenburg, editor of *Archives of Neurology and Psychiatry*. Informing him that the journal would be happy to publish 'Affective Regeneration in the Schizophrenias', Weisenburg nevertheless wondered if Gregory wanted to respond to comments he anonymously quoted by 'an associate editor'. Despite the paper's being a clear expression of the author's beliefs, a 'decidedly worthwhile' study of an interesting case, the associate felt it was influenced by Eugène Minkowski's *La Schizophrénie* (1927) – a book influenced in turn by Eugen Bleuler and the French philosopher Henri Bergson – rather than by Bleuler's own thinking, as the paper contended.[32]

Gregory's response was a detailed and spirited defence as he rejected with pointed rhetorical elegance all of the implicit and explicit criticisms. He didn't reveal or even imply that he had intuited that the critic was Adolph Meyer, professor of psychiatry at Johns Hopkins Medical School and a recent president of the American Psychiatric Association. Instead, Gregory opened with general faint praise, a characteristic tendency of his one-upmanship and a technique he certainly knew well from his familiarity with both drama and legal arguments: 'The question touched upon by this comment is as important as it is interesting.' He quickly, however, became specific: He had never read Minkowski's book, although he felt he knew his work through his earlier article in a French journal and considered his own views completely different; his opinion was 'based on the review of the theoretical pathologies of the last 30–35 years' and shared 'not only by the younger generation of psychiatrists' but by most psychiatrists in Switzerland, Marburg, Tübingen, and Heidelberg. Gregory was out to trump his older critic and defended his understanding of Bleuler:

> In addition to the direct study of Bleuler's work, I had the good fortune of going over Bleuler's views and of ventilating them repeatedly with Professor Bleuler himself who made Bloomingdale his headquarters throughout his recent stay in this country. I also followed up the suggestion of your associate editor and talked over the matter with Dr. Bleuler, who was a frequent participant in the conversations I had with his father. Bleuler Jr., like his father, indorsed my understanding of Bleulerian views.

It was regrettable, Gregory pointed out, that Bleuler's recent work had not yet been translated into English, but made it clear that he had read both Bleuler's *Schizophrenie* (1911) and *Naturgeschichte der Seele* (1918) in German as well as his earlier work to which Meyer referred. Gregory neatly implied that the critic was outdated as well as ignorant in his understanding of Bleuler's 'views'.

Gregory then addressed the issue of historiography. Meyer felt the paper's author did not see 'historical development in the truest light'. This argument, Gregory granted, was more or less true about any historical viewpoint – a matter of individual and debatable opinion. Before going on to present his own theory of history, he deftly and not without flattery named Meyer, known for his detailed case studies of psychiatric patients, as 'one of the very first to propound the views of psycho-biological unity and to undermine the classificatory and nosological rigidity', and regretted that neither Meyer nor one of his students had ever published 'any comprehensive, systematic work which would bring together his many valuable concepts and views'. Gregory then explained his own understanding of historiography:

> if we conceive of the historical development of a science as merely the chronological sequence of ideas expressed and investigations made – then there will always be a great deal of argument as to the priority of this or that invention or idea.

He pointed out,

> most of the very original and valuable ideas and even the discoveries which had later become incorporated into our common knowledge had been arrived at several times before they were finally accepted and made use of by the naturally conservative and oblivious humanity.

He then concluded,

> if we are to think of the history of a scientific discipline as of a dynamic process, we shall then have to take cognizance not so much of the chronological priority but of the fact that proved for some reason more potent in influencing the further development of the given discipline.

Bleuler's influence might not be due to his originality or chronological priority but to the accidental fact that he was the first to publish 'a systematic and a more or less inclusive reconstruction of our views of *Dementia Praecox*'.

Gregory elaborated,

> no new idea, no matter how strict the scientific discipline, is ever totally new; many valuable ideas find very few, if any followers and interpreters until some incident or set of conditions releases a sort of a wave of imitation ... and this circumstance always brings up the question of originality, priority and authorship and throws it at times into a state of confusion. Yet as far as historical dynamics is concerned, the one who releases this wave of imitation enjoys the greatest reputation.

Turning from the general to the specific, Gregory clinched his argument while anchoring it in the breadth of his historical awareness:

> Darwin rather than Anaximander is given credit for the concept of evolution, although Anaximander more than two thousand years previously saw man evolve from a fish through a chain of climactic, geologic and biological influences and adaptations.

Gregory closed by thanking Weisenburg for his kindness in sharing the critic's comments, then dismissed their pertinence with more faint praise ('I believe that there is room for an interesting discussion of the points raised or implied') and discounted their importance: 'I really do not think there is actually any divergence of views. It is merely a question as to the methodological approach to a historical phenomenon.'[33]

Gregory's approach here was typical of his way of thinking and arguing, and it repeatedly allowed him to win a dispute or defend himself from an accusation: He outclassed his interlocutor with erudition and verbal eloquence, intimated that his opponent was the victim of ignorance and misperception, and concluded that – no matter what objection or counterargument had been raised – there really was no significant issue; his own perspective had all along been correct.

Meyer would feel that Gregory had missed the point in dealing with 'ideas of priority' rather than with 'the fundamental attitude' towards schizophrenia, but informed Weisenburg that he did not think it would be 'essential' to comment on or even acknowledge Gregory's letter. Clearly, however, Gregory had the power to pique. At the bottom of his typewritten response to Weisenburg, Meyer added in his own handwriting, 'I may say that [the psychoanalyst Paul Ferdinand] Schilder, who read the article, agreed with me.' Meyer had the luxury of avoiding an argument with Gregory; many of his colleagues as well as students, patients, acquaintances, friends, and family members would have neither this luxury nor Meyer's good sense.[34]

Gregory continued to work frantically throughout the spring. His responsibilities at Bloomingdale in addition to his writing took their toll on his health and energy at a time his family also needed him. By the end of March his eyes were so tired that he even stopped reading the newspapers, but when Fera developed an abscess as a result of nursing difficulties, he offered to pay for treatment while probably also suggesting putting the baby on modern infant formula. Despite seeking his advice, neither Fera nor Anna paid much attention to him and the abscess finally had to be lanced. Gregory was exasperated and let off steam by telling James that in his view the women adhered to 'the most uncivilized habits of antiquity', preferring to remain 'uncultured Russians who call the doctor only when they "cannot stand it any longer"'. Yet Gregory tried to help his mother and sister to the degree he was able in ways they were willing to accept. During her five months in New York, he gave Anna nearly $300, funds that certainly helped sustain the Levitas family, and before the end of her visit, he resolved to send his parents $30 a month ($500 today) starting in April. He still hoped to travel to Mexico, but he was working closely with two patients he didn't feel he could leave for the foreseeable future. He was particularly eager to see his father, but aware, especially after his recent encounters with Anna, that 'in a certain sense' both parents were very much like strangers to him emotionally. He felt this was 'totally natural' yet it made him 'a bit sad'.[35]

Gregory was also concerned about Ray. Throughout the autumn he had encouraged her to accept the idea of having children, and early in 1930 she had given in, apparently now convinced that her depressions had their source in thwarted motherhood and the solution was to start a family. She became pregnant in February and during the first three months felt physically well if extremely lonely. Without a circle of friends, she was dependent on her husband, but Gregory was so busy that he rarely had time to spend with her. Then, in early May, she miscarried. The loss of the baby during this pregnancy so heavily laden with mixed emotions was traumatic. Gregory must have been understanding as well as upset, but Ray's psychological as well as physical state remained delicate for several months. He would characterise Ray's reaction as a 'sickness' that was both 'complicated and prolonged.'[36]

In contrast to this emotional upheaval, Gregory's financial situation was increasingly settled and secure. Not only able to contribute to the support of his sister in New York and to his parents' household – which included Basia and Nadia – in Mexico, by July he was finally able to repay the last instalment of the loans van Beuren had arranged. Enclosing a cheque for $619.82 ($8,700 today) in his letter to the dean who had been so supportive, Gregory admitted 'a sense of gratitude and a feeling of indebtedness which cannot be paid by cheque'. Despite his defensiveness, limited patience, and hot temper, Gregory was paradoxically also capable of generosity, gratitude, and grace.[37]

While his hospital duties claimed much of his time, as one of only 43 full members of the New York Psychoanalytic Society, Gregory was eager to become involved in analytic training. Following the Berlin model, the society's members engaged in lectures and seminars, in training analyses of future psychoanalysts, and in supervising their control analyses. After his year in Europe, he was qualified to take on these responsibilities, and in January 1930 Brill had appointed him to the Educational Committee, membership of which made him officially a training analyst; Brill reappointed him in January 1931.[38]

In addition to his work at the society, Gregory lectured to various organisations between the autumn of 1930 and the summer of 1931. Some of his presentations were general, standard addresses to community groups a Bloomingdale physician would be expected to make. He spoke to the New York City Conference of Social Work on 'Mental Hygiene for the Adult', and with his colleague Gerald R. Jameison, the physician in charge of Bloomingdale's Women's Department, he addressed the Medical Society of the State of New York on 'Clinical Methods in the Prevention of Psychoses'. His committed psychoanalytic perspective is evident in presentations to other groups: He addressed the Russian Medical Society of New York on 'Psychoanalysis and Organic Disease' and the New York Psychoanalytic Society on 'Fragments of Transference Relationships'. He was developing a new interest as well – in suicide – and addressed the New York Psychiatrical Society on 'Suicide: Psychological and Sociological Implications' and the American Psychoanalytic Association on 'Technical Problems in the Analysis of Suicides'. When he addressed the Association for Research and Mental Disease, however, on 30 December 1930, he spoke on 'Depressive Reactions Related to Parenthood', a telling title that suggests continuing personal and professional concern.

The Henrys had returned from their sojourn in Europe in September, but Henry's time abroad hadn't made him any more sympathetic to psychoanalysis nor had it focused his mind. His publications during this period ranged from 'Experimental Catatonia Induced by Bulpocapnine in Birds' to 'Root Canal Infections' and 'Gastro-Intestinal Motor Functions in Manic-Depressive Psychoses: Roentgenologic Observations'. With Henry Gregory had an uphill battle ahead of him, but both he and particularly Ray were delighted to have Eleanor back in White Plains.

Gregory's last year at Bloomingdale was a period of transition. With drafts of portions of *A History of Medical Psychology* he approached W.W. Norton, Freud's American publisher. Although he anticipated Semelaigne would write a 'brief foreword', in February 1931 he wrote to Garrison, now in the Department of History of Medicine at Johns Hopkins Medical School in Baltimore, in the hope that he might agree to write an introduction to boost the book. Declaring that 'our History of Psychiatry ... is finally completed', Gregory told Garrison it was slated for publication at the latest in January 1932.[39]

Parental attitudes towards children continued to interest Gregory, and at the annual meeting of the American Orthopsychiatric Association in New York in late February he presented 'Sidelights on Parent-Child Antagonism', contending that, although mediated by culture, antagonism between parent and the child was universal. With characteristic humour, however, he responded to discussants' questions by saying the situation was not hopeless: 'Universality does not mean homogeneity. It is universal that we are all neurotic but we do not all belong in a hospital.' He pointed out that antagonism is variously managed:

> We are all very aggressive, and one satisfies his aggressiveness by answering questions, while another bursts forth and hits someone in the nose. It is a universal phenomenon that the suspicions and hatred of children have many aspects, and it is a question of how a parent manages this hatred. If the parent has not found the proper treatment and busts the psychic nose of the youngster, then it is dangerous.

Gregory didn't go around hitting people in the nose and often satisfied his own aggressiveness by answering questions, but even without children of his own, he was well aware of the problems posed by 'parent-child antagonisms'.[40]

Ray had recovered sufficiently from the traumatic miscarriage and became pregnant again in early 1931. Gregory was delighted, and the couple looked forward to the baby's arrival in October. Gregory also began to look forward to the end of his clinical obligations, to a return to city life and an independence simply impossible at an institution. 'The Deeper Layers of Schizophrenic Psychoses', the paper he delivered at the annual meeting of the American Psychiatric Association in Toronto in June, suggests not only his commitment to psychoanalysis but the ways he worked with individual patients, methods he would continue to use in the years ahead. Examining a particular case, Gregory revealed that he wasn't the stereotypically passive analyst, reserving comment and merely listening. Rather, he guided the patient when she was ready to try an experiment, suggesting she stop masturbating for a while to see if the feelings and ideas so intense and mixed in the autoerotic experience could then be separated and understood. This, he argued, brought about self-understanding and stability. Indeed, it appears Gregory worked in many ways as Freud did, who often expressed his feelings during analytic sessions and, like many psychoanalysts in the first half of the twentieth century, accepted gifts from patients and even occasionally gave patients presents or lent them money. The American poet H.D., analysed by Freud in the 1930s, noted that his beloved dogs were a common topic of conversation, and Freud encouraged her to borrow books from his library. Like her contemporaries, Horney regularly arranged to have her patients accompany her on her holiday travels in order to continue their therapy. When Gregory started in private practice, written and unwritten rules for psychoanalysts were not yet established or clear, and despite the economic depression and his dreams of an academic post, private practice was what lay ahead.[41]

At the end of the summer Gregory concluded his work at Bloomingdale, but he still hadn't finished his history, which hinged on his relationship with Henry. Matters had been strained between them since before Gregory's year abroad and had not improved after Henry's return. On 29 August 1931 Gregory wrote his colleague in an effort to define and resolve their differences. He explained he had been uneasy about the book for a long time. Henry had pushed for publication while Gregory had stalled. Gregory conceived of a 'real' history – 'not a catalogue or list of repetitive quotations', not 'a verbose chronological table, or a dull, second-hand gossip about vague things gone by, or a journalistic compilation of questionable scientific value' – and had needed to consider the nature of medical history, verify facts, and consult original sources. With all this intellectual effort, Gregory was offended when he discovered accidently and indirectly that Henry – during his absence in Berlin and again the previous spring – had delivered two historical lectures without acknowledging Gregory's role in the research and thinking on which they were based. When colleagues had mentioned the lectures, he had been unable to conceal his embarrassment and resentment, but had initially attributed Henry's behaviour to tactlessness.

After Henry's return, tensions had increased. Gregory found Henry's 'usual sour aggressiveness' bitter and even hostile, shaking his confidence in him. Henry had seemed to believe in Gregory's work, but Gregory had heard that behind his back Henry had questioned his competence. Gregory attributed this behaviour to Henry's 'neurosis, to unconscious jealousy, and to suspiciousness', qualities Gregory had learned to accept 'more than any other person on the Bloomingdale grounds'. Recently, however, Henry had lost his temper during a staff meeting, exclaiming that psychoanalysis and psychoanalytic theory were dishonest, and had repeatedly criticised Gregory's psychoanalytic approach. Gregory deplored the situation, had again found extenuating circumstances and attributed Henry's hostility to neurotic aggressiveness and lack of analytical training.

He began to wonder, however, about the book: How could they collaborate if Henry felt Gregory didn't know what he was talking about? Gregory discussed the matter first with Ray, who was naturally partial, and then with Russell, who was not at all partial to him and not impartial to Henry, but when Gregory discovered that Henry had told Raynor that Gregory could not be counted on to verify facts, he wondered if it was even possible to write a book with both their names on it. Gregory then heard that Henry had said that Gregory's word was not to be trusted, that he was an egoist who was only after his own interests, a man without a scientific conscience who manipulated data to suit his own ends, a typical 'damned Jew'. Gregory had finally confronted Henry, confided some of his own experiences as a Jew in Russia. When it was again reported that Henry had called him 'a damned Jew', he was stunned. He now informed Henry that however much he tried to tolerate and forgive, he could not pardon racial hatred, could not forgive Henry's exhibition of 'a Jew-baiting feeling which is so universal, common, stupid and so totally unscientific'.

Henry's behaviour had depressed Gregory. He had lost interest in the book and, despite serious effort, had been unable to bring himself to finish the last chapter, simply could not think of associating with Henry in any social or scientific undertaking. In this important letter he confessed he had tried to come to a decision about the book, but felt they had reached an impasse, and finally asked Henry outright if he could 'volunteer a suggestion'. Gregory was certain that his part of the book could stand by itself since he had collected the majority of the historical information, while abbreviations suggested by potential publishers had concerned Henry's transcriptions from various articles or lists of quotations. Trying as hard as he could to be generous, Gregory told Henry he appreciated the difficult emotions his letter would provoke, for it had taken him several months to master his painful feelings and write. Certainly Henry had worked hard, but collaboration required qualities Gregory felt Henry lacked: cultural perspective, respect for facts, a scientific conscience, and a capacity for loyalty.[42]

Henry's response was immediate, defensive and palliative, although he failed to understand how profoundly he had wounded Gregory. He claimed he was glad to receive his letter, now understood the difficulties that had prevented the book's completion as well as Gregory's 'embarrassing situation'. He apologised for not having credited Gregory when presenting the historical paper in Gregory's absence; the book's publication had seemed remote to him at the time. When Gregory mentioned the issue on his return, Henry realised that he had erred and had since tried to be more careful, basing presentations only on his own research and mentioning the history whenever appropriate.

Henry then considered 'the question of friendship and loyalty'. Having been touched when Gregory had been the only one who openly and spontaneously supported him in his 'domestic troubles of 1925', Henry pointed out that he was the only one who had repeatedly pled Gregory's case and listened attentively to his personal and professional confidences when Gregory had encountered 'difficulties at the hospital'. When Gregory had applied for the fellowship to study abroad, Henry had also wanted to apply but had held off so Gregory might go, generously deferring his own application until the following year.

Having portrayed himself as a loyal friend, Henry shared his frustration with the book. He had estimated it would be completed in a year, then before Gregory went to Europe or at least before he returned. Henry had thought Gregory was spending all his free time on the book, then heard he was translating a book for Alexander; while abroad and on his return, Gregory had continued to publish papers even though the history wasn't yet finished. Henry thought his work would be woven into the book as his contribution 'was never intended as a finished product nor as anything which should remain intact', and insisted he had twice assured Russell the history would be scientific and accurate. Conceding that it was 'unfortunate' that they differed about psychoanalysis, Henry felt psychoanalysis was 'distinctly another subject'.

In response to what most disturbed Gregory, Henry grovelled. His 'experiences with members of the Hebrew faith or race' had been 'largely unpleasant', yet he nevertheless hoped for 'concrete evidence' his prejudice was unjustified in relation to particular individuals. He accused Gregory of unfairness in not revealing how wounded he was when Henry expressed negative feelings about Jews. Henry hadn't realised Gregory and Ray were Jews until he met psychiatrists in Europe who revealed it to him and 'would have been pleased to have known in the beginning that there were at least two of your race who did not merit any of the ill feeling which I have had'. Indeed, if Gregory had informed him, he would have been spared a good deal of embarrassment, implying that the tension between them over this issue was largely Gregory's fault. He then censored Gregory for listening to the reports of others and not confronting him directly. Declaring he didn't remember ever having called Gregory a 'damned jew', and if he had, he regretted it, but insisted the phrase 'is so universal that it seems to have little meaning', and even his wife, who didn't share his prejudice, began to have doubts about Gregory 'with the indefinite postponement of the book'. Henry admitted having been impressed by Gregory's account of his struggles in Russia, and as far as Gregory and Ray were concerned, Henry had tried to overcome his feelings. By obtusely suggesting that Gregory and Ray were exceptionally exempt from his anti-Semitism, Henry clearly felt he was exonerating himself, while Gregory naturally felt just the opposite.

From his perspective, Henry didn't see the issues Gregory raised as impediments to collaboration. He appreciated Gregory's original research but had conscientiously studied the sources to which he had access, including those Gregory had given him. Aware that his work was less substantial and more limited in scope and significance than Gregory's, Henry insisted that now as in the past he was perfectly willing for Gregory to use as much or as little of his contribution as he saw fit.

In the end, Henry was irritated by the tensions between them but by no means so disturbed as Gregory. Henry's failure to understand his friend's anguish would ironically make it easier for both men eventually to move on, but as the summer of 1931 drew to a close, Gregory would put aside the challenge of finishing the book as he turned his attention towards establishing himself in private practice.[43]

Notes

1 Alfred Adler to GZ, 19 June 1926; John B. Kelley to Marshall Field, 7 November 1941, GZB.
2 GZ to Smith Ely Jelliffe, 7 November 1938, GZB; email from AZ, 5 February 2018.

3 GZ to Jelliffe, 7 November 1938, GZB; GZ, 'Foreword', HMP, 11.
4 Terry, 45; GWH obituary; *New York Times*, 24 May 1964, 92; GZ to Jelliffe, 7 November 1938, GZB.
5 GZ to Alfred Adler, 8 November 1926, and to Charles Davis, 21 August 1928, GZB.
6 GZ to Frederick T. van Beuren, 10 June 1931, ASCCU; GZ, 'Foreword', HMP, 11.
7 GZ, 'A Psychosis', 1, 2, 3, 4, 6, 7, 8.
8 *Annual Reports*, 1926, 1927, 1928, 1929, 1930, 1931.
9 GZ, 'Malignant Psychoses', 15.
10 GZ to A.A. Brill, 17 December 1927, NYPSI; 'Post-Partem Schizophrenias', 370–383.
11 GZ, 'Most Common Mechanisms Met with in Psychopathology', GZB.
12 Bickel, ed., *Henry E. Sigerist: Correspondences*, 111.
13 GZ, 'The Dynamics', 763–764.
14 Email from AZ, 5 February 2018.
15 GZ to van Beuren, 3 February 1929, ASCCU.
16 GZ, 'Ausländisches Interesse', 66.
17 Danto, 202.
18 Watkins, 258; GZ, 'Ausländisches Interesse', 66, 67.
19 GZ, 'Ausländisches Interesse', 67.
20 NM, 'Rencontre', 4.
21 GZ 'Freud's Fundamental Psychiatric Orientation', 1–2; GZ, questionnaire, 30 September 1932, NYPSI.
22 Rado, 'Deutsch Psychoanalytische Gesellschaft', 1929, 366, and 1930, 133.
23 GZ, 'His Own Cook', 155–156.
24 'Group photograph, Hunger, Klebs ..., 1929', permission of Wellcome Collection. CC BY.
25 GZ to van Beuren, 3 February 1929, ASCCU.
26 Emails from and interview with AZ.
27 HMP, 70, 513.
28 GZB.
29 Freud, 'Report', 489; film: www.loc.gov/item/2018600161/
30 Van Beuren to Alan R. Anderson, 13 December 1929, ASCCU; email from Gloria Levitas, 14 October 2013.
31 GZ, 'Introduction' and programme in *Monday Night Meetings*: *1930*, 4, GZB.
32 T.H. Weisenburg to GZ, 18 February 1930 and Adolf Meyer to Weisenburg, 5 February 1930, Adolf Meyer Collection, Alan Mason Chesney Medical Archives, Johns Hopkins Medical Institutions, Baltimore, Maryland.
33 GZ to Weisenburg, 24 February 1930, Adolf Meyer Collection.
34 Meyer to Weisenburg, 26 February 1930, Adolf Meyer Collection.
35 GZ to JZ, 21 March 1930.
36 GZ to JZ, 21 March 1930; GZ to 'Très Saint-Père', 31 January 1953, APD; GZ to van Beuren, 3 July 1930, ASCCU.
37 GZ to van Beuren, 3 July 1930, ASCCU.
38 NYPS minutes, 28 January 1930, 27 January 1931, NYPSI.
39 GZ to Fielding H. Garrison, 18 February 1931, GZB.
40 GZ, 'Sidelights', 43.
41 Malcom, 47; H.D., *Tribute to Freud*, 98, 166; Quinn, 198–199.
42 GZ to GWH, 29 August 1931.
43 GWH to GZ, 31 August 1931.

Chapter 10

Private practice

1931–1933

Economic depression gripped the country by the autumn of 1931. Despite a veneer of prosperity in New York, where building projects inaugurated during the booming 1920s were defining what would become the city's iconic skyline, more than a quarter of its inhabitants were out of work. Men with sandwich boards paced the streets pleading for employment while breadlines stretched the length of city blocks. New York throughout the 1930s was the city of Edna St. Vincent Millay's poem 'Recuerdo', a metropolis in which young bohemians could spend the night on the Staten Island ferry, watching the moon set and the sun rise as 'a bucketful of gold', and impulsively give all their 'money but their subway fares' to a needy newspaper vendor, but Gregory could afford neither a bohemian life nor such frivolity.[1]

Gosselin had returned from Germany in 1930 and the two friends signed a lease from 1 September 1931 on a shared office on West 54th Street. On the same date, Gregory and Ray, now nearly eight months pregnant, moved into an apartment on East 79th Street. Two weeks later, the New York Psychoanalytic Society opened in a new building on West 86th Street, and on 24 September, during their first meeting after the summer hiatus, the Society moved forward with plans to establish an Institute, based on the Berlin model, for training future analysts. Brill, the Society's president, appointed Gregory to the board of directors of the new Institute and as chairman of the Library Committee and vice-chairman of the Committee on Research, new committees to support students and teachers. Gregory's ensuing involvement in the life of the Society and Institute would add considerably to the various demands on his time and energy.[2]

The city's cultural life was now on Gregory's doorstep. The theatre, Carnegie Hall, and the Metropolitan Opera would thrive during the depression for those who could afford tickets. Gregory would regularly dress not only for performances but for dinners at elegant restaurants and receptions at grand hotels. He would eat pastrami sandwiches for lunch with psychoanalytic colleagues at local delicatessens and meet friends after work for a whisky in stylish bars. With Ray as hostess, he would entertain at home.

Some of Gregory's first patients came to him through the New York Psychoanalytic Society. Psychiatrists who wished to become psychoanalysts needed to

DOI: 10.4324/9781003190936-10

pay for their training, and throughout his career aspiring analysts would be his patients. While his experience in Berlin had been with patients who couldn't pay much or at all, he now needed to find clients with money in their pockets. He still had friends in the theatre world and some of them still had money: Actors, writers, and producers would be among his early patients. For those who came to him needing psychiatric rather than psychoanalytic help, he suggested hospital treatment, if that was what was called for, or treated them in hours not dedicated to his psychoanalytic patients, but he soon filled his schedule. If he saw each psychoanalytic patient five times a week for a 50-minute hour each, there was a limit to the number he could accept in a working day.

In addition to obligations at the Psychoanalytic Society, Gregory had his history to finish, if and when he could find time and bring himself to the task. Henry had been right: Gregory had agreed to translate *Der Verbrecher und seiner Richter*, Alexander's book with Staub. It appeared in September with Gregory's introduction as *The Criminal, the Judge, and the Public: A Psychological Analysis*. The translation had been a distraction from the history as well as a favour for an established colleague whose English was less strong than Gregory's, but it was also the result of Gregory's efforts to please his analyst, to compensate for the negative transference during the analysis. With the translation completed, Gregory turned his attention to other projects and, freed from hospital shifts, he now made new connections and solidified old ones in ways not easy or even possible when he lived in White Plains.

Soon after Gregory opened his practice Sigerist arrived in America on a year-long lecture tour. The depression had weakened the Weimar Republic and opened the door for the National Socialists, who by 1930 had become the country's second largest political party. Not only Jews but intellectuals would struggle to sustain the lives they had made for themselves, and Sigerist, like Alexander, would join the flood leaving Europe for the United States. Most at least began their American sojourn in New York.

At the end of September Sigerist dined with Gregory at his home and rediscovered the man whose company he had so enjoyed in Leipzig. He told Temkin, who would soon follow his former boss to America, that he found Gregory 'a very nice person' whose excellent wine cellar was 'quite an asset in times of prohibition'. In addition to the fine wine and sociable company, there was probably now a servant in the household, someone who helped Ray unpack, who cooked in the kitchen and set the table, while in Gregory's shared office a secretary acted as both receptionist and accountant. The staff at work and at home would increase considerably over the next few years, but with the baby due soon and Ray physically uncomfortable and psychologically apprehensive, at least one servant helped on that convivial evening during which Gregory and Henry consolidated their friendship.[3]

Less than three weeks later, on 18 October 1931, Ray gave birth to a healthy boy whom, in popular American fashion, they named Gregory Zilboorg junior. Ray was 38; Gregory was 40. Both parents were gratified, but the weeks that followed were difficult for everyone except the baby. James and Eugenia sent their congratulations, to which Gregory was unable to respond for nearly five months. After young Greg's arrival, Ray was physically ill and more than usually emotionally fragile. At one point Gregory feared for her life, and she remained weak through December. The stress had its impact on Gregory and, in a reprise of events seven years earlier, he again had surgery on his jaw. In three operations at the end of 1931 and the beginning of 1932, all of his teeth were removed, during which time, he finally reported to James in March, he 'ate little and slept very little, but worked very hard'. He would call his surgeries and their repercussions – the blow to his vanity as well as the false teeth that took some getting used to – 'physical nonsense', and didn't attempt to explain to his brother the psychological stress underlying the physical pain, but he probably reflected psychoanalytically on the ordeal: His own teeth extracted following the birth of the baby 'extracted' from his wife; the son with his own name at once an affirmation of paternal potency and a threat not only to his mother's life and emotional stability but to his father's well-being and mortality. If Greg was the child his mother never wanted but whom Gregory had longed for – albeit in a traditional, abstract way – his physical presence would challenge their marriage. Gregory told James that, at four-and-a-half months, Greg was 'a healthy and happy little fellow', 'a strong and talkative little man', already an impressive 21 pounds. As for Ray, although still not fully recovered from the baby's arrival, she was planning to begin painting again very soon.

By March 1932, however, Gregory's practice was established and stable. He was busy with his research and once more imagined publication of his history, telling James that what he still thought of as a two-volume book would come out at the end of the summer. As usual, Gregory was attempting to cram more work into each day than even he with his high level of energy found comfortable. Working 'from early morning until late evening', he was sometimes 'a very tired man who dreams of little other than a vacation' – and when he dreamed of a vacation, Gregory dreamed of Europe, often thought of Mexico and longed to see his family, particularly his father. While a yearning for Russia had dominated his emotional life during his first years in the United States, he was aware that Russia had recently changed so profoundly that it seemed foreign to him; he felt isolated from his family and youth, nostalgic for the past, for a Russia that no longer existed. He reasoned that perhaps his emotional interest in 'the past and the irretrievable' was responsible for his interest in medical history, for the deep satisfaction and calm he only felt while working on ancient manuscripts or a fourteenth-century book.[4]

Gregory was doing his best to move the history towards publication. In October 1931 he had sent 337 typed pages to George Allen and Unwin in England, the purported first volume covering 'Primitive World, Ancient East, Greeks and Romans, Arabs, Middle Ages'. The reader had found the submission 'scholarly, well-written and most interesting' and the project 'a work on the grand scale … that needed doing' and done 'exceedingly well'. He did wonder how the author was going to treat 'contemporary psychotherapeutics' – that is, 'Freud & Co.' – but, like many editors today, his only real reservations concerned the title and production costs of such a large book. By November, however, Gregory had a commitment in principle from W.W. Norton in New York, but he was not yet ready to resume work with Henry or to involve him in any formal agreement, so he set about mining what he had written and drumming up interest, offering future copies to various correspondents and mentioning the project in lectures and publications.[5]

Gregory's overreaching and anticipating, his authoritative assertion of control of the history throughout the 1930s and of other experiences throughout his life, would offend some people who saw him as presumptuous and his apparent self-confidence as hubris, feeling he was lording his competence over them, boasting, claiming more than he could possibly deliver. Others would go so far as to suspect he was dishonest, ploughing ahead without sufficient regard for rules or realities. Gregory's high hopes and great expectations, his assumptions and – despite his brilliance – his naïveté, inevitably led him to disappointment in himself and in circumstances and to physical and emotional exhaustion.

Gregory did need a vacation, but he had his daily round of patients to see, and his history was not the only large-scale project on his mind. As chairman of the Library Committee at the New York Psychoanalytic Society his immediate task was to establish a library. Without books or appropriated funds, his committee began with personal appeals to members of the international psychoanalytic associations. Particularly generous contributions came in from Marie Bonaparte in France and Ernest Jones in England, while several Institute members, notably Brill and Jelliffe, contributed books from their own libraries and complete or partial runs of periodicals. Such gifts were gratefully received but insufficient for a large and balanced collection.[6]

Gregory's creative mind went into high gear and created two new enterprises, both of which would have independent value and help the library. The first, inaugurated in January 1932, was a bookshop, serving the needs of candidates in training and Institute course participants and open not only to society members but to the general public. One copy of each book ordered by the bookshop was donated to the library and paid for from the profit realised on the sale. This scheme reduced the cost of the library's development and kept new books coming in.[7]

The second project was the foundation with three colleagues of what would become the premier American journal in the field: *Psychoanalytic Quarterly*. Gregory's co-founders and co-editors were his friend Bert Lewin, Frankwood Earl Williams (a midwesterner interested in the Soviet Union and photography who had served for a decade as the medical director of the National Committee for Mental Hygiene), and Dorian Feigenbaum (an Austrian who had studied under Kraepelin in Munich and worked in Switzerland and Palestine before immigrating to the United States in 1924). Williams and Feigenbaum were firmly established in their careers, but Gregory and Lewin were members of a younger psychoanalytic generation. Williams had been analysed in Vienna in 1924 by Freud's colleague Otto Rank, and Feigenbaum had been analysed by Freud's maverick disciple Otto Gross, while Gregory and Lewin had received systematic training in Berlin. Gregory's friendship with Lewin dated back to their work on Ward's Island, yet he also felt a bond with Feigenbaum, a fellow immigrant, a widely travelled Jew. Gregory would have seen Williams's fascination with Soviet communism as the product of ignorance, and the two men would have had a great deal to talk about, including photography. Such alliances would be important in the highly politicised international psychoanalytic community as well as in the particular political environment of the New York Psychoanalytic Society, while the journal would be useful as subscriptions could be offered in exchange for library subscriptions to American and international periodicals.[8]

Gregory had hoped to go to Mexico over Christmas, but decided to postpone the trip. Despite Bloomingdale's general unease with psychoanalysis, some of Gregory's younger colleagues had admired him as Freud's champion, among them Bettina Warburg, who had joined the staff as an assistant physician in October 1930. The daughter of Paul Moritz Warburg and Nina Loeb, Bettina was related to two German-American banking families, both Jewish, and had startled her extremely wealthy parents by deciding to become a doctor and then specialising in psychiatry, apparently rejecting marriage and motherhood for professional life. Her rebellious brother James had followed tradition and become a banker, and marriage – often into other banking families – as well as philanthropy were a family pattern. Bettina began analysis with Gregory in New York in September. The experience would serve as a training analysis (Bettina left Bloomingdale for private psychiatric practice and teaching in autumn 1932, although she would not join the New York Psychoanalytic Society until 1938), but the duration of her analysis (nearly four years) suggests she came to Gregory out of personal need and continued as a result of trust, respect, and a sense that her work with him was helpful and satisfying.[9]

As Paul Warburg struggled with fatigue and 'eyestrain' in autumn 1931, the family suspected his physical problems had a psychological cause; in November Bettina called upon Gregory. Initially a consultant, he was soon asked to take over the case and cared for Paul as his health declined following a cerebral haemorrhage in early December. On 24 January 1932 Warburg died, but no one had expected Gregory to work miracles and the family were grateful for his support. It seems unlikely the Warburgs knew Gregory was deferring a trip to Mexico, but they probably realised he was working when most private physicians were taking time off rather than accepting new patients. For Gregory's part, he felt it would have been foolish to decline such a prestigious case. Indeed, his acceptance was logical, given the difficult financial times, the personal request from a colleague who was also a dependent patient, and his tendency to take on work whether as an intellectual challenge, a strategic favour or generous kindness.[10]

Gregory now thought of going to Mexico in the summer, but if he could not take a vacation before then, he recognised he needed to relax, to leaven the intensity of professional life. His solution was to try to develop hobbies. From childhood he had enjoyed playing chess so now thought about chess, thought it might be nice to own a beautiful chess set. On Bloomingdale's verdant grounds, he had come to appreciate trees and flowers, shady walks, and quiet evenings far from street lights and traffic; he had not learned to swim in the hospital pool, but he had learnt the rules of tennis by watching matches on its courts; he had enjoyed the sport's individual competitiveness, the displaced psychological aggression of the physical game. By the time he left White Plains he knew how to hold a racket, the right way to stand while waiting for a ball. He began to think he should take up tennis. The fascination with technology that had led him to splurge on a radio in the early twenties led him, a decade later, to purchase a camera. Gregory believed in what he called 'good goods' and in 1932 he bought a top-of-the-line Contax, produced for the first time that year by the German optical company Zeiss. He would teach himself to use different lenses and filters, learn to develop film. Some of his patients had country houses in Westchester and Connecticut or on Long Island, and he started to think that what he needed was a rural retreat away from the city's melee. If he had a country property, he imagined pastoral weekends, listening in peace to the new Saturday afternoon radio broadcasts from the Metropolitan Opera. He would buy a Cadillac, learn to drive. A country place might be good for Ray, and he would have the space for a darkroom and a library, could plant potatoes and berry bushes, buy a cow to produce milk for the baby.

Such dreaming offered a stark contrast to Gregory's professional life during a particularly taxing spring. Reviewing submissions for *Psychoanalytic Quarterly* was a constant process: When the journal's first issue appeared in April, he was already reading articles for future issues. He had his own writing to think about, too. At the Society's meeting in March, he presented 'Problems in Suicide'. At the end of May he travelled to Philadelphia to present a paper at the American Psychiatric Association – 'Present Trends in American Psychiatric Research' – jointly authored with J.C. Whitehorn and prepared for the association's Committee on Research, on which Gregory was now serving. His papers needed additional work before publication, and he was also preparing independent articles, continuing to draw on his clinical work and on his reading and thinking about medical history.

Gregory during a pensive moment, early 1930s

Gregory was also expending a tremendous amount of effort on committees at the New York Psychoanalytic Society and Institute as well as on the library and bookshop, which by May stocked over 3,000 books. Having contributed some of his own money to the shop as well as a desk and chair, he donated 'cataloguing equipment' to the library and helped two Library Committee members – Gosselin and Susanna Haigh – to develop a cataloguing system, generating psychoanalytic subheadings following the Dewey Decimal System. Realising he couldn't continue to underwrite the bookshop, before the summer recess Gregory proposed that the Institute recognise the bookshop and offer it a line of credit. Because the two entities were closely linked, he also requested that the Institute's board of directors appoint the librarian (the Library Committee chair) as bookshop manager, a role he had assumed from the start.[11]

Meanwhile, by the time the dogwood bloomed in Central Park, Gregory had indeed bought a Cadillac, learned to drive, and rented a cottage in Connecticut. Ray and the baby decamped to Westport while Gregory visited on weekends, looking about and then finding a property to buy: a colonial house with 12 acres of land, a guest house, and a caretaker's cottage, as well as barns, chicken houses, a pond and tennis court in Pound Ridge, New York, 20 miles north of White Plains.

The farm's main residence

The farm was more than an hour from Manhattan by car; the nearest train station was a 15-minute drive away in New Canaan, Connecticut. Gregory was delighted. He signed the papers at the end of June, then finally turned his attention to arranging his commitments so he could go to Mexico in August. While he cancelled psychiatric appointments, he didn't feel he could leave his all his psychoanalytic patients, and Bettina Warburg, C.J.F. Parsons (a doctor in general practice in Dobbs Ferry, New York), and Henry Rawle Geyelin (the Warburgs' family physician) would accompany him.

The fact that he was travelling with this entourage was delicate. While Gregory thought of the trip as 'a sort of a rest cure', it was imperative that he keep personal and family matters separate from his professional life, and not only for professional reasons was Gregory always guarded about his private life. Aware of his own volatility and vulnerabilities, his culpability and insecurities, he took a defensive posture towards the outside world; his first impulse in relationships was discretion rather than confession, and despite his capacity for bonhomie, his sense of humour and charisma, his sincere warmth and sociability, he protected himself from perceived threats by trying to keep his personal life private. It is possible to see his discretion as well as many of the other attributes of his personality as defence mechanisms, as the probably not entirely conscious methods by which he kept most of the people in his life at a strategic distance. There is no evidence to suggest that any of his patients ever knew his family lived in Mexico City. Even those patients and colleagues who would later become friends did not know his parents had immigrated to Mexico, though some were aware he had a brother who worked there. Travel with three patients would limit the time Gregory could spend with his family and distract him from the intensity of the reunions. Consciously and unconsciously, the limitation and distraction were likely part of Gregory's plan.[12]

Too busy now to write to his brother himself, he resorted to delegating the responsibility to Pauline Turkel, who was now his secretary. She explained to James that Gregory would not be staying with him but hoped he could recommend the 'very best' and least 'commercial' hotel in Mexico City. Specifically, 'Dr. Zilboorg would like the nicest suite they have', a bedroom with a bath and a parlour with 'a comfortable couch'. Pauline added that Gregory also wanted 'a comfortable car and a good chauffer' during his nine days in Mexico, emphasising, 'The plans of several people depend on the arrangements the Doctor will make.'[13]

These requests as well as his purchase of the camera and the farm indicate that Gregory had what could generously be called a disposable income or – more crassly – a lot of money. Ironically, he wasn't wealthy now any more than he had been when he had stayed at the elegant Park Hotel in The Hague or booked first-class passage from Rotterdam in 1919. He was doing what he had always done and would always do: He was spending what he had, and in 1932 he had quite a bit to draw on. He didn't consider the future or what Ray and little Greg or even he himself might need next year or in due course. It was useful if friends or acquaintances or interested patients helped out, voluntarily or at his request, as the latter logically would during this trip, but his thinking was always that money was only money; if more funds were needed, he would simply work harder.

While Gregory wanted recommendations, he didn't want James to make reservations. Despite the extra cost, Gregory booked his accommodation as well as first-class cabins on the outgoing and returning ships through a New York agent because he wanted to help a friend who had been a patient. Gregory invariably stretched the boundaries between his role as psychoanalyst and his role as a socially responsible person with the means to do and ask for favours, but this first trip to Mexico made him think carefully about the separation of his professional and personal life. Knowing that he couldn't count on the family to restrain themselves and behave 'appropriately', he made it clear to James that if he decided to meet the ship when it docked in Vera Cruz or the train from the port when it arrived in Mexico City in early August, he was to be discreet and come alone:

> This is very important for professional and psychological reasons: Patients will be with me, and the ethics and psychology of my work are such that my patients should not see me in my private life or have anything other than purely professional impressions of me.

Balancing conflicting responsibilities and anticipating potential difficulties, Gregory wanted to do the right thing by everyone to the degree this was possible. On the familial front, he was eager to see his brother, but he particularly he wanted to bring presents for Moses and concluded this letter by asking for their father's 'shoe size and the number or size of his suits'.[14]

Gregory on a New York City tennis court, 1932

While Gregory didn't plan to rush about sightseeing, he was also eager to visit Pueblo, the pyramids at Teotihuacan, and Cuernavaca, where he would see murals by Diego Rivera, whom he may well have met during an exhibition of his work at New York's new Museum of Modern Art. He also hoped to have time for some tennis, explaining to James that it was his favourite sport. For a man generally spending 16 hours or more in his treatment room and at his desk, it was in fact his only form of exercise.

Throughout June the etiquette and ethics of travelling with patients weighed on his mind. Reduced to dictating a letter, he asked his brother to reserve places for him and his patients on the morning train from Vera Cruz to Mexico City and to arrange that his seat be a few seats away from the other three or – better yet – at the opposite end of the car, reiterating, 'Psychoanalysts avoid as much as possible any informal social congress with their patients', yet defending the situation as 'unavoidable' since 'It is no more possible for an analyst to go away without practicing a couple of hours a day than for a violinist.' His parallel suggests that it was he who needed to continue to work with his patients rather than they who needed to continue with him. His 'rest cure' did not, in other words, mean a complete cessation of work, something impossible for a man as driven as Gregory, although it did mean that he could leave Ray and Greg in the country apparently without qualms. Indeed, the vacation Gregory needed might well have necessitated a break from his unfulfilled wife and ten-month-old son.[15]

Travel by ship took five days each way, so Gregory spent as long at sea as he finally did in Mexico. In the time not devoted to psychoanalytic sessions, sightseeing, photography, or a set on a tennis court, he saw his father and Basia for the first time since 1918 as well as his mother, whom he had not seen since 1929, and James, whom he had not seen since he left for Monterrey a decade earlier. He met two of his nieces – 12-year-old Nadia and 3-year-old Lydia – and saw Eugenia and 11-year-old Natalie, whom he had not seen since they passed through New York on their way to Mexico from Danzig in the summer of 1923. The reunions were intense and bittersweet. Reflecting on the visit on the elegant *S.S. Oriente* en route back to New York, he wrote a reflective letter thanking James and Eugenia for their warm and generous welcome. In short, he told them he felt 'wonderful', deeply happy to have gotten 'reacquainted', and lovingly disposed towards everyone.

Whether his mother and widowed sister, however, were included in 'everyone' is debatable. He had wanted nothing directly to do with them before the trip but had felt sorry for them. After seeing them in Mexico, he no longer even pitied them. It seemed to him their misery was of their own making at every turn. They lived 'in the aftermath of the bitterness and malice created on a Sabbath in Kiev 35 years ago or during a quarrel or woe of 30 years ago', existing in a hypothetical 'if only' world. He would continue to help with monthly financial contributions, but found Anna and Basia 'beyond repair' and felt very sad for his father, who was subject to their carping.

Moses was less than happy in Mexico. Having left Kiev with mixed feelings as a result of Basia's impulsive decision, he resented the pressures his family continued to attempt to impose upon him. When Fera and James arranged for passports so their parents could go to New York for a long visit, he had flatly refused, feeling he was being treated as 'a bit dead or some kind of idiot'. Having made what he saw as a mistake in going to Mexico without thinking it through, Moses rejected out of hand what seemed to him only 'another mistake'.

Understandably disheartened not so much with Mexico, where he had resourcefully begun to make a new life, but with being taken for granted and manipulated, he responded to much that went on around him by withdrawing and holding his tongue. Although Moses was better able to control his emotions and more fatalistic than his eldest son, they had much in common. It is no wonder Gregory was particularly concerned for him.

Gregory also worried about James and his family. His brother was depressed by his inability to leave Mexico and his lack of advancement at work and relatively low salary. Responsibility for his wife and daughters as well as for his parents, sister, and Nadia weighed heavily. Gregory understood Anna and Basia's narrow outlook as a consequence of their 'psychological and intellectual breakdown', but felt his brother was in danger of falling into the rut of 'repetitive compulsive patterns'. Sharing his perceptions in his kind and gentle letter, he hoped James would give serious thought to his analysis and encouraged him to write frequently in the hope that together they could find a solution.[16]

Gregory returned to New York with his spirits renewed. He had missed little Greg and by the end of August, in an affirmation of family, Ray was pregnant again. Resuming work on his history in early September, Gregory wrote the Library of Congress in search of a book in Spanish by Marcelino Menendez y Pelayo on the Renaissance humanist Juan Luis Vives. The shipboard letter would be his last to James in Russian; from now on he would write in the English that had become natural to him despite rather charming turns of phrase that reveal his Russian roots: Reimmersed in New York, he reported that 'Basia wrote to Fera a letter' and asked his brother to telephone 'to' a friend.

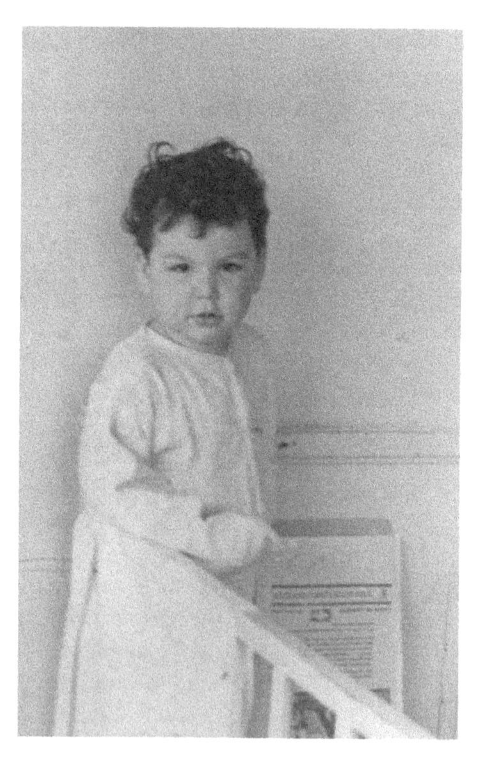

Greg in 1932, photographed by his father

Gregory's exhilaration was short-lived, and by the end of September he was once more exhausted by 'a whirlwind of work' and beginning to wish he had extended the visit to Mexico. His schedule would simply not permit long holidays, however, and he confessed to James that he didn't want to be away from little Greg: 'my attachment to the child grows with every day and it is somewhat difficult for me to part with him'.

Following his brother's example, James had taken up photography, and Gregory was eager to have photos and films of the family. With typical generosity he told his brother to let him know how much the supplies cost because he wanted to pay for them. He was, in fact, acutely lonesome for his family, and before the end of the month put together a parcel of carefully chosen presents: a large album for Natalie, for whom he had begun to save stamps, and clothing, including ties and a sweater he contended he no longer needed but thought his father could use. For his mother he enclosed a cheque for $150, twice the monthly amount he was now contributing towards his parents' household. With another visit out of the question for the foreseeable future, in October he decided Fera should go to Mexico, he told James, 'instead of me'. Sol was still earning very little and the home atmosphere was tense. Gregory felt the trip would be psychologically good for Fera, and of course he would pay for it.[17]

Throughout the autumn Gregory was busy not only with patients but with responsibilities at the New York Psychoanalytic Society and Institute. The board of directors did indeed make the bookshop an official part of the Institute, and on 1 October 1932 Gregory, now officially the bookshop manager, submitted the first annual report. He summarised the shop's activities and indicated that, drawing on $150 of its profits, a professional librarian had been engaged to catalogue the library's holdings. Brill, the executive director, was more than pleased, remarking in his October report that the bookshop, which now stocked 3,878 books, was 'a successful undertaking' without indebtedness.[18]

Gregory had assumed other professional duties as well: In addition to membership in the International Psychoanalytic Association, the American Psychoanalytic Association, and the American Psychiatric Association, he became an elected member of the New York Academy of Medicine. Awash in such public and social obligations and preparing a celebration of the first anniversary of the *Quarterly*, at which he hoped Sigerist would speak, he confessed to his friend that at times he had 'painful moments of cultural loneliness'. His current life, satisfying in many ways, was a far cry from the scholarly solitude he also craved. His farm, whose house he was redesigning with the help of an architect and local workmen, was a great solace, a physical retreat that also offered him psychological security. He hoped it would be habitable by Christmas.[19]

The Pound Ridge house would not be finished by the end of the year, but 1932 ended well: Fera thoroughly enjoyed her trip to Mexico, and one can only imagine how pleased her secretly sentimental father was to see her. It was over a decade since he had watched her leave Kiev in the farmer's cart with the gold coins for her wedding ring sewn into her hem. Basia, too, must have been overjoyed to see her sister, to reintroduce her to Nadia, who scarcely remembered her aunt. With all of this reaffirmation of family, James and Eugenia decided in November to visit New York for two weeks over the holidays. Gregory drove them into the country to see the progress on his property where he had plans for shelves in his future library and a dark room. In town they went to the theatre and attended concerts, had what Gregory would call 'some fun'. Indeed, he needed some fun in his life, but in addition to moments of levity, his family as always presented him with emotional as well as practical challenges.[20]

Now that he had money, that seemed to be what the family wanted. He was contributing a third of his income to the Levitas family and his relatives in Mexico: $75 a month went to James for their parents' household, but the rest went out in response to requests for financial help or as gifts of his own choosing – funding for Fera's trip, for example, or physical presents such as film for his brother or clothing for his father. This situation put everyone in a difficult position: Gregory was bothered by constant demands for money that he frequently felt compelled to refuse, while family members, generally through James or Fera, tried to justify their requests even as they resented Gregory's capacity to be munificent. The explanation of their needs drew Gregory uncomfortably into his family's daily lives. Although more than willing to prescribe a routine for Eugenia, who was struggling with depression, he was less willing to be 'a cash cow' whom everyone unfairly resented. Reflecting on Basia's complaints, he concluded philosophically, 'People in this universe almost never change, particularly if they do nothing about changing. Just as Lenin, Mussolini and Hitler are inevitable, so are inevitable certain people's patterns of living, doing, and feeling.' He was less equanimous in expressing his resentment to James, irritated because 'people have been spitting in the well they are drinking from', apparently deeming it fair to criticise him, assuming they were justified in using him, then gossiping about him and his financial capacities and propensities in a manner he found disagreeable and unfriendly. He asked, 'If an economic turn takes place, as it inevitably will, who will help me? Could I, or *would* I, ask for help?' Aware of his own abilities and limitations, he pointed out to his brother that he was neither a businessman, nor a speculator, nor a juggler with papers and tricks; he worked hard and felt he exploited no one and lived on no one's efforts except his own. He had little sympathy for his female relatives, although he made some exception for Fera. For years he had avoided having anything to do with relatives, having deadened his emotions towards them. He told James bluntly that he now wanted 'to re-establish them in that status of being dead' as far as his mind was concerned.

Upset by the family's demands on his finances, he was also working extremely hard: In January he had been elected secretary of the New York Psychoanalytic Society, while in February Brill had reappointed him for a third year in a row to the Educational Committee, a post confirmed by election for a three-year term in March 1933 as the Institute developed what would become its regular and more democratic procedures. Gregory's expression of understandable frustration and resentment with his extended family had its source at least in part in exhaustion. Typically, while he felt physically at the end of his rope, he also felt he had to 'push on', unable to foresee 'any rest for at least another six months'. His only consolation was his anticipation of the completion of his farmhouse, to which he soon hoped to escape at weekends.[21]

In Mexico Eugenia and James were expecting their third child, and Eugenia and Ray had likely confided in each other during the Christmas visit. Eugenia's depression had more to do with her husband's frustration at work and the worldwide economy than with her own situation, and she generally enjoyed motherhood. Ray's problems were less cosmic and had their source in her resentment of the responsibilities children inevitably brought as well as in her limited ability to create an independent life for herself while her busy husband was busy. At the age of 40 Ray had a difficult labour, and on 19 May Nancy was delivered by caesarean section. The popular name must have sounded American to both her parents, though of course it was a gesture towards Anna just as Greg echoed his father's name. Such naming was at once a rejection of the Jewish tradition of calling a child after a deceased relative and an affirmation of family in the Anglo-Saxon tradition. For Gregory his family was now complete: first a boy, then a girl – what the French call '*le choix du roi*', the choice a king would make if he had the power. For Ray, children meant a home with servants and the freedom to paint when she felt up to painting.

In June Eugenia gave birth to Olga. Three girls wasn't anyone's choice, but James and Eugenia were more worried about finances than not having a son. Once again, James turned to Gregory: Eugenia's brother Yousik was studying in New York and required support until he received his diploma; her mother was unwell in Palestine and needed expensive medicines, although the doctors saw her illness as terminal. James felt he could no longer comfortably contribute the $25 he regularly added to Gregory's monthly payment. Could Gregory contribute to these causes as well as increase the sum for their parents?

Gregory would mull the matter over throughout the summer. By August he had agreed to support Yousik, reasoning that sooner or later he would have a job, but decided it was simply impossible to undertake additional responsibility for Eugenia's family or his parents' household. He explained firmly to his brother: Their parents were not his only obligation and their demands and needs were not among those to which he was most sympathetic. If he let himself go without brakes (which, he joked, 'are frequently out of order anyhow'), he would be working like a slave without a penny of his own. He was sorry for Eugenia's mother but as a doctor accepted the inevitability of the facts: He knew of no illness which in its terminal stages would require expensive medicine; the matter finally seemed to him a subsidy to Eugenia's father, to whom he owed nothing. And then there was Fera. She had not requested money, but when she asked him for an old suit for Sol, he understood that she needed his support and resolved to do something about it. To his credit, James accepted Gregory's response with relative calm and cordial coolness, but he didn't grasp the limits his brother was trying to set nor the extent to which Gregory drove himself.[22]

Gregory took no summer holiday in 1933. He saw his family a couple of hours a day – more than he did in the winter when he was even busier – and dreamt of a break in the autumn or the winter, perhaps in Mexico or somewhere Mediterranean. In New York, however, he found no time to relax at all: Despite the time he spent imaging trips and cruises, he actually saw only a few blocks of the city on his way to and from the office – always the same blocks only hastily registered.

He often felt there was little *joie de vivre* in his life. As hard as he tried, he found it difficult to espouse a Nietzschean love for the distant and the invisible; waves of quite the opposite sometimes rose up in him.[23]

Gregory's patient roster was full. Bettina had spoken highly of him and the experience of psychoanalysis, and his timetable now included her brother James (Jimmy) Warburg as well as his wife Kay Swift, who were struggling to maintain their marriage. Bettina's cousin Edward (Eddie) Warburg also became a patient at about this time, and in June Gregory had found a daily hour for Jimmy's friend Marshall Field. Gregory had in addition at least two or three associate members of the New York Psychoanalytic Society in training analyses. In addition to psychiatric patients he saw less frequently, Gregory saw patients on a consultancy basis for one or more sessions at the request of general practitioners or psychiatric or psychoanalytic colleagues. In these cases, he might recommend further treatment by others or hospitalisation, although occasionally he would take on the referral himself.

Consonant with his socialist convictions and the principles underlying his training in Berlin, Gregory believed psychoanalysis could help anyone serious about self-examination. One did not need to be particularly neurotic to benefit from the process, although he would argue that everyone had individual neuroses, but his patients tended to come to him out of personal distress whose source was frequently circumstantial. Among the circumstances that brought patients to him was their ability to afford psychoanalysis. That they could spend both the money and time meant most of his patients were wealthy, and ironically their very wealth was in many cases part of the reason for their distress. The situation made Gregory uncomfortable: He was catering for the most part for rich people whose leisure, choices, and opportunities often made them self-indulgent and potentially frivolous. His patients frequently drank too much, but while alcoholism was a problem he had dealt with from his early days at Bekhterev's institute, working-class alcohol consumption in Russia was quite a different matter from overindulgence among New York's cocktail set. Payment was another issue: Like other psychoanalysts then and now, Gregory charged a sliding fee intended to be at once affordable and sufficiently substantial; the patient should view the sessions as valuable and important, commitments not worth missing. In the depressed 1930s, Gregory thus ended up with a good income from clients who could afford his services at a time when almost everyone except the exceedingly rich was struggling to make ends meet and not even considering psychoanalysis. His patients' wealth and the fact that their resources were at least in some measure the source of their emotional difficulties would trouble him throughout his career. Starting out in private practice at the height of the depression, he couldn't afford to refuse such patients, felt at least at first that he was lucky to have them at all.

The specific problems his patients struggled with can in most instances only be inferred. Gregory did not generally take notes, and if he did, they have not survived. Only a few of his patients wrote personally about the experience in published or unpublished accounts, and they were understandably self-protective, discreet, and sometimes defensive. Contemporary letters document some patients' issues, but Gregory himself was circumspect and reserved, rigorously maintaining professional discretion even with colleagues. While Bettina Warburg considered her analysis with Gregory as her training analysis, her relationship with her parents and her decision to practise medicine must have posed emotional problems she wanted to address. That she was unmarried and apparently did not want children may well have been another issue. Jimmy Warburg and Kay Swift initially sought help in defining and resolving their differences, but Gregory refused to be a marriage councillor. Swift had begun an affair with George Gershwin soon after meeting him in 1925. She and Jimmy divorced in late 1934, while both were still in analysis. Jimmy would marry Phyllis Baldwin in 1935, and less than a year after that marriage ended in divorce in 1947, he married Joan Melber. Swift and Gershwin never married, although their affair would continue until his death. Marriage was also an issue for Eddie Warburg, who would marry for the first and only time in 1939 at the age of 31. His closest friends at Harvard had been homosexual and bisexual men, and he had followed them into the world of visual art and ballet. Sexuality was likely an issue that troubled him in various ways for years. Following standard practice, Gregory routinely cautioned his patients not to make life decisions during analysis, although of course they did. They also often wanted him to tell them what to do: Should they marry or divorce? Stop drinking or keep drinking? Have children, move to the country, quit one job, take another? Such questions he regularly refused to answer, although his cautions and refusals were probably frequently and understandably misinterpreted as positive or negative responses.[24]

Gregory's treatment of Marshall Field offers a case in point, although Field's problems were evidently less distressing and of shorter duration than those of many other patients. Gregory saw him regularly at first, then less regularly until he stopped being a patient two years later. Like many of Gregory's other patients, he, too, entered analysis because of 'considerable tension due to marital difficulties'. After 15 years his first marriage had ended in divorce in 1930. He remained close to the children – Barbara, Marshall, and Bettine – but in the same year had married the British socialite Audrey James Coats, who had recently divorced her first husband. Independently wealthy, he had left investment banking in 1926 to create 'Caumsett', an enormous estate at Lloyd Harbor on Long Island, but by 1933 the property no longer needed his full attention, nor did the polo ponies raised and trained there. Field was feeling at loose ends both personally and professionally. His marriage to Audrey was rocky: Her behaviour was erratic and by the summer of 1933 he had fallen in love with Ruth Pruyn Phipps, whose husband was reluctant to divorce the mother of their two boys aged two and not yet one. Depressed and suffering from occasional dizziness and headaches, Field sought help. After their initial sessions, Gregory logically sent him to his former patient

Henry Geyelin for a complete physical examination that revealed 'nothing abnormal of any significance'. Gregory would later summarise the analysis:

> At no time during the period of our professional contact did I find in Mr. Field any evidence of nervous or mental disease, or severe incapacitating neurosis. The problems he was facing were created by a series of unfortunate circumstances of a personal nature.

He added that since his second divorce and subsequent marriage, Field had been well adjusted, happy, and serene. Such an analysis gratified both patient and doctor, but frustrated with many of his wealthy clients, Gregory confessed to Sigerist being 'thoroughly disgusted' by having to treat rich people who did not seem to him to care about anything but 'their pocket-books'.[25]

Events Germany in 1933, however, were more disturbing to Gregory than the ethical issues of working with so many affluent patients. In early May students in Berlin began a campaign of book burning; works by Marx and Freud went up in flames. In mid-July all political parties except the National Socialists were banned. In October, calling into question the entire diplomatic aftermath of the war, Germany withdrew from the League of Nations. The news that blared from the papers reminded Gregory of his Russian past, his own roots on the other side of the Atlantic, his revolutionary principles and political convictions. In November he wrote Sigerist, who had accepted a post as professor of the history of medicine at Johns Hopkins University in Baltimore: He was very glad his friend had left Leipzig before 'the whole nation became crazy', concluding simply and soberly that 'Europe certainly is in a terrible mess.'[26]

Indeed, Gregory needed a friend. While his patients confided their marital problems, he confided in no one. He could no longer attribute Ray's psychological frailties to the absence of progeny. She tended to regard their two children as a burden and a distraction. The classes she took at the New York Art Students' League and additional domestic help apparently did little to relieve her disappointment and frustration, and it was difficult for her to understand Gregory's sense of isolation, his fellow feeling with other Europeans, and his intellectual frustration.

Among his colleagues, Gregory was wisely wary. The atmosphere at the New York Psychoanalytic Society was at once professional and replete with internecine tensions. Sigerist was not the only intellectual to flee Germany, and the influx of European psychoanalysts that had begun in the early 1930s was increasing dramatically. Rado had arrived in New York in 1931 at the beginning of over a decade of psychoanalytic immigration. In 1932, Sachs left Berlin for Boston and Horney headed for Chicago, where Alexander was now the director of the Chicago Institute for Psychoanalysis, yet after falling out with Alexander in 1934, Horney would join the flood of psychoanalysts for whom New York was the city of choice. Heinz Hartmann, who arrived in 1941, and Rudolph Loewenstein, who came in 1942, would be among the last of this wave to immigrate. New York thus became '*Mitteleuropa* on the Hudson', and the New York Psychoanalytic

Society became riven with conflicts affecting everything from training practices to theoretical assumptions, from the power of elected officials to the policing of the profession.[27]

Gregory was, of course, no novice to internal discord. He had witnessed divisive power struggles during the revolution while subsequent political conflicts had resulted in his flight. He had been present during violent arguments in the Duma and the Reichsrat, had seen individuals rise to power and fall from grace. He had become aware at Bloomingdale of some of the specific differences that divided psychiatry, including psychoanalysis itself and anti-Semitism. At the international congress in Oxford much bitter debate had concerned lay analysis. The Europeans didn't see a medical diploma as necessary – Anna Freud, analysed by her father, had no medical credentials and was by 1929 not only Freud's ardent supporter but his representative. In contrast, psychoanalysts from the United States, where quackery had long threatened scientific practice, were convinced that only analysts with medical diplomas would make the profession respectable. Despite his energy and enthusiasms, as a Russian Jew Gregory had learned when to be strategically inconspicuous; despite his strong opinions, he had learned how, when the occasion demanded, to pass without comment. In sum, he knew that life in a group was a risky business, and although it was his tendency to take centre stage and dominate a conversation, he was wise enough to realise that, while sticking to principles, keeping one's head down was often the best policy. He could be elegantly polite as well as forthright, carefully courteous and sincerely generous as well as brash and egoistic; while striving always to do the morally right thing, he recognised on the basis of experience that, to the degree it was possible, everything might finally come down to the survival of the individual.

The fracas that ensued at the New York Psychoanalytic Society in 1933, with its roots in its shifting politics and widening membership, would upset him profoundly. Tension within the society grew increasingly personal and Gregory was a polarising figure, supported primarily by young psychoanalysts, many of them Jews, and often accepted begrudgingly by older, predominantly Gentile established members. There were some newly arrived Europeans who saw him as a sympathetic colleague educated abroad, but others resented him as an immigrant a decade ahead of them in language mastery and integration.

The Society did not normally meet over the summer. In 1933, there was a particularly long hiatus and no official meetings between 20 April and 28 November. But during the late spring and summer, Gregory became aware that some colleagues questioned his management of the library and bookshop; perhaps some members had also become uncomfortable with how he carried out his other responsibilities as a member of the Educational Committee and the board of directors or even with how he fulfilled his role as secretary of the Society, in which by 1933 he wielded considerable power. By September, Gregory felt he had no recourse but to withdraw from his activities in both the Society and Institute.

He began by writing to Lewin, then chairman of the Council, pointing out the obvious: 'The atmosphere of tension in our Society and Institute interferes with their smooth and normal running.' Stating formally that this situation was hurtful to psychoanalysis in New York and in general, he had concluded, 'for the sake of peace in the Society' and 'for the good of psychoanalysis', he should temporarily withdraw from his activities in both the Society and the Institute. Gregory's decision for the sake of the profession was no hubristic assumption of self-worth; the reputation of psychoanalysis was a major concern of the New York Psychoanalytic Society and Institute, which collectively had taken on the policing of psychoanalysis in America. It was not only a question of defending the profession against malicious insinuations in newspaper gossip columns; there were feelings among some members that psychoanalysis was threatened from within by those who diverged from Freud's ideas or who failed to do things as they had been done or ought to be done, though there were often no clear rules or regulations. The 'atmosphere of tension' likely had its roots in personality conflicts as well, but certainly the influx of analysts from abroad exacerbated matters.

Gregory insisted that he was not resigning but merely withdrawing in the hope that his absence would lead to 'a clearing up of all personal issues' and facilitate 'unimpeded peaceful work'. On the same date, on bookshop letterhead that listed him as manager, he sent a letter to Monroe Meyer, then director of the Institute, enclosing his letter to Lewin as 'self-explanatory'. Gregory was deeply sorry for the inconvenience his withdrawal would cause, but rather obsequiously informed Meyer that he was sure the director's skilful management would allow the educational programme to continue without any disturbance. Washing his hands of the entire business, Gregory finally indicated he had instructed his secretary to furnish Meyer with any further information he might want about the library and bookshop accounts.[28]

At the Society's November meeting, the first since Gregory's withdrawal, concern was formally raised about the bookshop. Apparently not having understood how its finances functioned, Brill wanted to know specifically how it could have generated a $300 profit while also showing a $200 deficit and suggested Gregory might furnish more information. Although some members evidently wanted a professional audit and were only deterred by its expense, Rado proposed that the Library Committee should first be asked for a report. Edward Liss reported that the Bookshop Committee had decided that the shop should continue as a financially viable entity that supported international psychoanalytic publications as well as the Society's library. The minutes, despite their formal discretion, reveal some of the animosities that pervaded the membership, and Gregory was not the only member to want to distance himself. Perhaps out of solidarity with Gregory but surely also in response to the pernicious atmosphere that prevented 'peaceful work', Dudley D. Shoenfeld, the psychoanalyst who had profiled the kidnapper in the 1932 abduction and murder of Charles Lindbergh's baby, at this time also submitted his resignation from all offices in the Society and Institute.

Notwithstanding his measured letters to Lewin and Meyer, Gregory was emotionally devastated by his colleagues' antagonism. There was talk in the Society's corridors of the necessity for 'fierce reprisal' for his behaviour, even of his expulsion. While Jelliffe, chairman of the Educational Committee in 1933, personally objected to what he saw as Gregory's disruptive manner, to his 'final cannibalistic oral grin' when he finished a sentence (in all fairness the result as much of Gregory's dentures as of his satisfaction at having made a point), even he found the group's attitude towards Gregory 'typically paranoid'. For over a year after his withdrawal Gregory did not attend Society meetings and kept his distance from the Institute in general, shocked by an experience in which his competence was questioned and his honour maligned. Indeed, he was so deeply distressed that for nearly six months he felt unable to work with students in training analysis. It was not in his nature to sulk, however, and as with previous setbacks and hurdles in his life, he quickly directed his intellectual and emotional energies to other pursuits.[29]

Notes

1 Millay, 2–3.
2 NYPS minutes, 24 September 1932, NYPSI.
3 HES to Owsei Temkin, 10 October 1931, Bickel, ed., *Correspondence: Sigerist-Temkin.*
4 GZ to JZ, c. 6 March 1932.
5 'Reader's Opinion', George Allen and Unwin; GZ from Clement Collard Fry, 7 December 1931, and from George M. Kline, 9 March 1932, all GZB.
6 GZ, 'Report', 1 October 1932, NYPSI.
7 GZ, 'Memorandum', 22 May 1932, NYPSI.
8 GZ, 'Report', 1 October 1932, NYPSI.
9 *Annual Reports: The Society of the New York Hospital*, 1931, 1933; Bettina Warburg's CV, NYPSI.
10 Chernow, 330; GZ to JZ, c. 6 March 1932.
11 GZ, 'Memorandum', 22 May 1932; 'Extracts of the Report of the Executive Director', 9 October 1932, both NYPSI.
12 GZ to JZ, 23 March 1932; Chernow, 346; Leffert, 427–428; Pollack, 199; Rimler, 119–120.
13 Pauline Turkel to JZ, 6 June 1932, JEZB.
14 GZ to JZ, c. 16 June 1932.
15 GZ to JZ, 1 July 1932.
16 GZ to JZ, 19 August 1932; MZ to JZ and EZ, 28 September 1927.
17 GZ to JZ, 21 September, 18 October 1932.
18 GZ, 'Report', 1 October 1932; 'Extracts of the Report of the Executive Director', 9 October 1932, both NYPSI.
19 GZ to HES, 31 October 1932.
20 GZ to JZ, 2 November 1932; cable, JZ to GZ, 2 December 1932.
21 NYPS minutes, 28 February, 30 March 1933, NYPSI; GZ to JZ, 6 February 1933.
22 GZ to JZ, 27 July, 31 August 1933; JZ to GZ, 5 September 1933.
23 GZ to JZ, 15 July, 31 August 1933.
24 Hellman, *Unfinished Woman*, 166–167, *Pentimento* and *Scoundrel Time*, passim; Ingersoll's autobiography, multiple unpublished versions, Howard Gotlieb Archival Research Center, Boston University; Hoopes, passim.
25 Henry Rawle Geyelin to GZ, 11 August 1933, with medical report on Marshall Field, 2 August 1933, GZB; GZ to Clinton Davidson, 8 July 1940, GZB; GZ to HES, 25 October 1937.

26 GZ to HES, 14 November 1933.
27 Makari, '*Mitteleuropa*', passim.
28 GZ to Bertram D. Lewin and Monroe Meyer, both 27 September 1933, NYPSI.
29 NYPS minutes, 28 November 1933, NYPSI; Jelliffe to Karl Menninger, 12 June 1933, in Burnham, *Jelliffe*, 127–128; GZ, NYPSB, 323.

Chapter 11

Alternatives

1933–1935

There were many psychological, psychiatric, and psychoanalytic issues that interested Gregory and had nothing to do with the Society and Institute. In the autumn of 1933 his patients claimed his days in the office he shared with Gosselin, but he had no intention of taking on any more translations and, having liberated himself from Society and Institute responsibilities, he again began to think seriously about the problem of suicide and the relationship between psychology and law, a complex matter and life-long interest that his translation of *The Criminal, the Judge, and the Public* had brought into focus. With his history still unfinished, he was also reflecting on the kind of professional life he wanted to lead.

By the end of the year Gregory had begun work with inmates at Sing Sing, a maximum-security correctional facility an hour's train journey north of the city. With the support of the warden Lewis E. Lawes, Gregory offered *pro bono* services to inmates. His interviews combined research and treatment, what he called 'investigative psychotherapy', and informed his understanding of crime, particularly homicide, and its relation to suicide, which he understood in part as homicidal anger turned inward, while inversely homicide seemed to him in part suicidal anger turned outward. Psychotherapy with inmates contrasted sharply with psychoanalysis in a comfortable Manhattan office, but while Gregory's work at Sing Sing was more in keeping with his commitment to social service, he certainly recognised that only income from private practice allowed him to treat prisoners for free.[1]

The Daily Mail Sunday Magazine

The Relation Between Homicide and Suicide

Neurologists, Making Study of the Mental Attitudes of Prisoners, Discover Many Facts Concerning Causes of Crime

Syndicated newspaper article, March 1935

DOI: 10.4324/9781003190936-11

After his annual 'open house' on Christmas eve, Gregory and his family likely headed for their country home to celebrate his 43rd birthday and the new year. He had regularly managed weekend escapes at the rural property where by 1934 his livestock included not only chickens but several pigs and a couple of cows. In the spring there would be piglets and calves while fresh eggs were available throughout the year for the kasha he enjoyed with his Saturday lunch. He was proud and happy about his farm, as he confessed to his friend Sigerist, whose convenient geographical and professional distance from psychoanalytic politics made him a precious confidant and colleague.[2]

Gregory's physical and emotional separation from the Society and Institute not only freed him to interview prisoners but to resume work on his history, yet it was friendship with Sigerist that permitted him to rethink the entire project. Although Gregory was not yet ready to finish the book, he now drew on it in ways he had not previously considered and revelled in a renewed enthusiasm. He visited Sigerist in Baltimore in the late autumn, and in February Sigerist came to New York. They attended a Friday evening performance of Eugene O'Neill's *Ah, Wilderness* and on Saturday a *Psychoanalytic Quarterly* dinner; after midnight, Gregory drove them to Pound Ridge. On Sunday they relaxed with the family and animals before returning to New York. Throughout the characteristically busy weekend, the two men talked and talked and talked.[3]

One of the ideas they arrived at was a symposium that fired Gregory's imagination. In a long letter to 'My dear Sigerist', Gregory revealed his rigorous thinking on the subject of the history of medical psychology as well as his energy and practicality. He proposed specific sessions beginning with a survey of 'the field up to and including' the British physiologist William Harvey to illustrate 'the sum total of what Psychiatry in the main uses today': 'the fundamental concepts of Hippocratico-Galenic humoral trends' – endocrinology – and 'Harveyan influences with regard to circulation', to show that 'associativistic psychology from Wundt on to Bleuler' took root in this early period. Another session, on 'the Pinel and Tuke tradition', would show the cultural trends and forces that gave rise to 'the humanistic "organizatory" and custodial tradition'. A second day would feature a session on 'Psychiatric Nosology' from the French physician Bossier de Sauvage to the German psychiatrist Emil Kraepelin, while a final session would be devoted to 'The development of the psychiatric concepts of disease' and 'various therapeutic trends'.

Sigerist had requested suggestions for possible speakers and moderators. Although Gregory felt that his friend knew the field and was 'a better chooser', he proposed that Sigerist present the session on the French psychiatrist Philippe Pinel and the British psychiatrist William Tuke, feeling the subject should be considered 'as a characteristic result of liberal humanism of the eighteenth and nineteenth centuries'. Sigerist might also lead the discussion on nosology, while Gregory himself would speak on the psychiatric concept of disease and proposed a sequence of topics: A consideration of 'Hippocrates-Galen' ideas, mediaeval notions up to the thinking of the Dutch scholar of medicine and psychiatry

Johannes Weyer, understanding from Weyer to the mid-nineteenth century, views from the mid-nineteenth century to Kraepelin, and finally concepts from Kraepelin to the sociological influences proceeding modern twentieth-century thinking.

While volunteering to speak on historical material, Gregory's passion was not proprietary. If Sigerist preferred to assign him another topic, he would gladly accept 'if I happen to know enough about it'. Aware, however, that his energy tended to overpower and restraint was not his first impulse, Gregory concluded by apologising for his long and detailed letter: 'My own enthusiasm for the subject carries me perhaps to greater length than is necessary.'[4]

Such enthusiasm, planning, and friendship were not enough to assuage the pain and frustration of the library and bookshop fracas, and despite visits from friends in both New York and the country and his delight in his young children, family life was insufficient to calm Gregory's unquiet spirit. On 18 February he left with Gosselin on a ten-day trip to Bermuda. The few days on shipboard both going and returning as well as the island's sunny warmth offered the rest that only complete separation from daily life could provide.

Gregory returned to New York on March 1 and, without a pause, resumed work: He had papers to write, *Quarterly* articles to edit, and patients to see. Eddie Warburg was still in analysis, as were Bettina and Jimmy Warburg and Kay Swift. Still struggling with the issue of divorce, Swift, whose relationship with Gershwin was now central to her life, encouraged him to seek analysis, and by the spring of 1934 Gershwin, too, became one of Gregory's patients. The immediate cause for his seeking help was what he termed his 'composer's stomach', a mixture of stage nerves and general anxiety about artistic productivity and success. Less easy to define and confront but as practically and emotionally pressing was his romance with Swift: If she and Jimmy divorced, could he commit himself to marrying her? At the age of 33 Gershwin was an established composer with an international reputation. *An American in Paris* had premiered in 1928 at Carnegie Hall to mixed reviews, but following an abortive attempt to work in Hollywood, Gershwin had returned to New York and Broadway musicals. By 1934, however, he was working on his most demanding composition, the jazz opera *Porgy and Bess*. His daily sessions with Gregory would last for a year and a half.[5]

Marshall Field was also still in treatment. Despite 'the exhilaration of his private merry-go-round', he had come to Gregory at a time of psychological crisis. While Field had voted for the Republican Herbert Hoover before the crash and again at the height of the Depression in 1932 when Hoover lost to Roosevelt, in 1936 Field voted – as Gregory had in 1932 and thereafter – for Roosevelt. Always generous and considerate, committed to justice and gentlemanly fair play, Field's changing perspective went deeper than merely a political *volte face*. His childhood in England and America, his father's suicide, and his mother's social conscience were surely topics raised during the analysis, as was the matter of money and its privileges. Self-examination under Gregory's guidance brought him to see *noblesse oblige* as insufficient. As with his other wealthy patients, Gregory had begun by charging a substantial fee, but when he realised that paying by cheque made him in Field's eyes simply an employee, he asked him to stop paying for a while. The turnabout enabled meaningful psychoanalytical work as Field focused, involving himself in causes he came to care deeply about. Gregory did not direct Field's attention to specific ends, but the analysis gave Field the confidence to take on public service and commit himself to things larger than himself.[6]

Field's correspondence with Gregory – beginning 'Dear Doc' and signed 'Yours ever, Marshall' and 'Marshall F.' – suggests the affectionate respect of a struggling student for an admired teacher. On holiday in the summer of 1934 he sent Gregory a cigarette case but directed it to the wrong address. Writing about the mistake, Field told him he would hold it for him till they saw each other again. The psychology of this gift – something of value a patient wanted to give his analyst, then misdirected only to have it returned so that it was still in the patient's possession, then held onto until their next meeting – would not have gone unanalysed by Gregory. The two men would maintain a friendly relationship after the conclusion of the analysis: Field would always feel positively about his treatment, grateful for the psychological clarity and professional direction he achieved, while Gregory was happy to remain in touch in with the gracious and honourable man whose principles and work he came to admire.[7]

Family matters, however, as well as professional life and the state of the world continued to command Gregory's attention in the spring of 1934. Fera informed him their mother was unwell, but James suspected Anna's complaints were due to 'extreme sensitiveness to any illness, fear of it at all times and excess of cures' recommended by the 'all-knowing' Basia, who was now studying nursing. If their sister succeeded, James declared somewhat bitterly, 'something useful may come out of her after all' and she might become able to support her child and contribute to their parents' household. As for himself, James continued to be discouraged about the limited professional opportunities. There was little Gregory could do about the global economy or matters in Mexico, although he asked his brother to keep him informed about Anna's health before adding his wry but not particularly comforting assessment of life in general: 'The world is going crazy slowly, surely, and quite effectively – so are we all individually and jointly.'[8]

James put Anna's German doctor in touch with Gregory, establishing a pattern whereby their parents' physicians would communicate with Gregory, in German or Spanish. He would then, from his medical perspective, explain the situation to James and send extra money to cover expenses, relieving his brother of the responsibility and stress such family matters generally produced. Enclosing a cheque for $100 over and beyond his monthly cheque to support his parents, Gregory told James, 'it appears quite definitely that mother suffers from a severe form of arteriosclerosis and that it is obviously a more or less terminal stage.' Invariably a realist, Gregory did not soften what he saw as the truth. In language elegant even in its foreignness and occasional mistakes, he explained that the 'sudden drop in her blood pressure is not of good omen. Her vascular system has lost its electricity'. By 'electricity' Gregory surely meant 'elasticity', but perhaps he was just trying to make physiology comprehensible to a mechanical engineer. He elaborated:

> her blood vessels became as hard as iron pipes and therefore harder pumping is required to circulate the blood. This gives higher blood pressure. On the other hand, the pump, in this case the heart, can work well and hard only if its muscles are rugged; however, this muscle itself feeds on blood transmitted into it by special blood vessels which are hardened.

Choosing non-technical vocabulary (healthy muscles are 'rugged'; the heart is at once a pump and a muscle which is fed by 'special blood vessels'), he elucidated the 'complex situation':

> more and harder work is required of an instrument which is increasingly less and more poorly fed. Hence a severe weakening of the heart, a corresponding reduction in its efficiency, and poorer propulsion of the blood into the system – called a fall in blood pressure – a veritable vicious cycle.

Such phrases as 'well and hard', 'more and harder' and 'less and more poorly' charm in their simultaneous grammatical correctness and odd unnaturalness to the ear of a native English speaker, which despite his fluency and eloquence Gregory would never be.

His explanation was typically kind, generous, and helpful, even if it probably contained more information than his brother needed or wanted. Gregory gave similarly lengthy explanations to colleagues and students, to friends and his own children, all of whom would be impressed and at least slightly overwhelmed. He didn't offer such disquisitions to flaunt his erudition or linguistic competence, and he never modified this approach to imparting information and his opinion, but he was aware – as in his enthusiastic letter to Sigerist about the symposium – that other people could and often did misunderstand his tone and purpose. He told James, 'I write you all this not because I want to impart some medical wisdom, but because I think you will see a little better what to expect if you know what is going on.' Gregory didn't like his mother and was repelled by her approach to the world, but he had compassion personally and as a doctor for all human beings and told James he nursed the hope she would not develop 'any of the dragged out types of suffering'.[9]

Having given James the benefit of his opinion as a dispassionate doctor, two days later he added his view as the experienced psychoanalyst and son that he also was. Sorry he couldn't suggest anything constructive and in the spirit of 'medical directness', he believed that 'Mother will never be able to follow any rational regime' and was incapable of contributing anything towards prolonging her own life. Putting aside his irritation with Anna's character and behaviour, he pointed out that her neurotic symptoms were of secondary importance – even 'absolutely non-neurotic individuals' whose cardiovascular trouble included cerebral involvement usually develop 'emotional upsets, depressive states, tearfulness and great anxiety'. Simply and kindly he told James what he had to tell himself: In the current situation, their mother was 'entitled to her psychological symptoms'.[10]

Professionally Gregory's work was advancing well and by the spring he was ready to present the preliminary results of his ongoing research and broad thinking. In April he delivered a paper to the New York Neurological Society on what he understood as various types of suicide. His argument had an historical as well as a theoretical context (Saint Augustine and Freud) and offered both case studies and cross-cultural data, in which his intellectual objectivity was tempered by compassion. In full and characteristic flow, he reached his perceptive conclusion:

> The problem of early diagnosis of possible suicidal outcomes in patients is of paramount importance in the treatment of suicidal trends. Such diagnosis is possible on the basis of observations of mental mechanisms and anamnestic data, which become valuable criteria before the suicidal tendency comes out fully in the trend of the patient. Suicides can be differentiated on the basis of the mental mechanisms, this proving that there are many psychologic types of suicide – a point of diagnostic and therapeutic importance.[11]

The issue of suicide would require more research than Gregory could do on his own, and he soon realised he would need staff and funding. His view of the project like his view of the world was large and wide, ethical as well as psychological, sociological, historical, and theoretical. He was meanwhile acutely aware of events in Europe, where he planned to attend the 13th International Psychoanalytic Congress in Lucerne in August. Having travelled to Mexico in the summer of 1932, he had missed the 12th congress held that year in Wiesbaden, a meeting which Freud had been too ill to attend but to which many analysts went, even Jews such as Alexander, Rado, Sachs, and Ernst Simmel, who had by then also left Berlin for America. Switzerland was a strategic choice in 1934 as even Gentile psychoanalysts had difficulties in the Third Reich. On 30 June, in what became 'The Night of the Long Knives', the Nazi party purged the Stormtroopers of committed socialists and others whose politics differed from Hitler's. A month later, on 2 August, President Hindenburg died and, combining the post of president with chancellor, Hitler proclaimed himself 'Fuhrer'. On 18 August, leaving the children in Pound Ridge with servants, Gregory and Ray sailed for Le Havre on the *Ile de France*.

The trip would be 'a vacation without rest and a holiday with a lot of work': Not only did Gregory have the congress ahead of him, but he was again travelling with two patients, Bettina and Eddie Warburg. From Le Havre via Paris Gregory and Ray went on to Switzerland, but Eddie – alone or with his cousin, who probably attended the congress – continued to Italy. While as a newly qualified psychoanalyst Gregory had not addressed the Oxford congress in 1929, here at the stylish lakeside Hotel Beau Rivage he was an established analyst fast creating an international reputation. On the penultimate day of the proceedings, he spoke brilliantly on the subject of suicide, but even before the congress concluded on 31 August, he headed more hastily than planned to Venice.

He had hoped to see Sigerist, on holiday just south of Lucerne, but Eddie was apparently in some psychic distress and needed Gregory's attention. The youngest of the Warburg cousins was one of Gregory's more dependent patients: A 'hail fellow well met' renowned for his clever, joking manner, he was intelligent and energetic but unfocused. When he first met with Gregory, he had described himself as out of balance, uncomfortable in his own shoes, not yet able to stand on his own two feet. Eddie's turns of phrase had been revealing to Gregory, who had asked him during their first session to take off his clothes, walk towards him, turn, and walk away from him. Gregory then asked him if anyone had ever told him that one of his legs was shorter than the other and sent his new patient to an orthopaedist. Eddie would wear a shoe with a graded sole for the rest of his life. His sense of deeper psychological unbalance, acute in the 1930s, was less readily addressed.[12]

Gregory and Ray must have had some relaxing and convivial moments during a fortnight with the two Warburgs in Italy. After Venice they travelled to Florence and then Siena for a few days at the Hotel Palazzo Ravizza, whose opulence was typical of the first-class accommodation Gregory invariably sought. Their itinerary likely included a short visit to Rome before their return to Paris. The foursome left Europe, travelling first-class on the *Ile de France*, on 19 September. Six days later they were back in New York and Gregory was back at work in a new office on East 75th Street.

From the autumn of 1934, Gregory would no longer share a workplace with Gosselin. Their relationship was collegial, but with a full roster of patients Gregory was ready for a space of his own. Indeed, physical space was one of the reasons for the move: With additional staff because of his work on suicide and historical research, he required more than a secretary-receptionist; he needed someone to type documents, someone who knew French and German, someone who could help with the increasing volume of correspondence and files, and someone to manage accounts. With Pauline as his personal secretary but devoting much of her time to clerical work for *Psychoanalytic Quarterly*, he engaged a part-time accountant to come in once a week and began to think of hiring a research assistant, a multitalented native speaker of English who could type and take shorthand, understand history, appreciate language, and follow his intellect wherever it and his emotional explanations might lead. That this was a tall order probably did not cross his mind.

Gregory felt lucky, however, to be back at home with an ocean between him and the events in Europe that seemed to him 'thoroughly crazy'. Visiting the farm on weekends, he relaxed and took photos of the children that he sent to James in Mexico where, according to the reports he received, family life was seldom calm and every minor crisis resulted in a request for money. The newest development concerned not his mother but Basia. Having finished her nursing course, she wanted $500 ($9,000 today) to set up a gynaecology clinic with a local doctor.

Gregory was generally disposed to be generous. In October he sent James $150 as a birthday present. Hoping to diminish his fretful brother's many worries, he additionally decided to assume full financial responsibility for Moses and Anna: Starting in November, he sent James $100 a month instead of $75, releasing his brother from contributing (and worrying about contributing) $25 a month to their parents' support. Basia's idea, however, seemed to him 'a very stupid and shady venture' and he refused point blank.

His reasoning offers insight into his understanding of medicine and its practice. He advised Basia to find paid work rather than go into business, for work meant income, while business meant responsibility and expenses, neither of which he thought she could handle. Further, he felt that a 'gynaecological business', inevitably involving abortions (spontaneous or induced), was a particularly delicate affair. Serious and even fatal infections, he argued, would be almost inevitable in a clinic with inexperienced staff; while a certain mortality rate was inevitable, if it were high (and he thought it would be high under the circumstances), the whole venture would become 'a frightful flop' even when and if and as it succeeded commercially since 'the more successful commercially' such a medical venture was, 'the shorter the road to jail'. His argument was principled:

> Anyone who has anything to do with sick people, must first be ready to work – work day and night, work hard and work seriously. The financial reward for such work always comes – perhaps never a very great reward – but it comes.

He concluded bluntly, 'anyone who looks into a throat and sees a dollar and not a pair of tonsils, will get the dollar perhaps but will let the patient bleed to death.' Basia should not have imagined he would respect her plan: Medical people 'make a living by treating people but as soon as they insist on treating people in order to make a living they are no good.'[13]

Gregory made two significant points: Commercially successful medical ventures court danger from resentful patients and the law, and 'treating people' (as opposed to 'making a living') is the purpose of medical practice. He was well aware in his explanation that he was speaking on the basis of his own experience. His financially successful practice had probably already contributed to his colleagues' resentment of him, as evidenced by recent events at the New York Psychoanalytic Society, where the proposal of a professional audit had come close to an accusation that he had done something not only irregular but illegal, something punishable within and perhaps even beyond the Society's remit. From childhood Gregory had recognised that success was often resented while merit alone was seldom sufficient for advancement or respect. Further, 'Treating people', medicine itself, was a moral calling. Not treating individuals properly – and to the extent of one's capacity through hard and serious work – was not merely an ethical but a moral failing that rendered one completely 'no good'. Gregory's concern with moral value went beyond his fear of political or legal consequences. He worked 'day and night', hard and seriously, to fulfil what he saw as a priestly vocation and to be a good person. His compulsion was an effort to avoid being 'no good', to do what he thought was necessary to his calling. Gregory's efforts to stand up against censure and to be both a good doctor and a good man would more and more consciously and explicitly shape his life. The reasons he gave for rejecting Basia's request were particular to her situation, but the thinking behind them went deep and remained on Gregory's mind.

On his mind throughout the autumn of 1934 was the issue of raising funds not only for work on suicide but for both the *Bulletin of the Institute of the History of Medicine*, Sigerist's new journal and a department of medical sociology within Johns Hopkins' Institute of the History of Medicine. In November Gregory spent the weekend in Baltimore on the first of many trips. Impressed with the physical space and the Institute's work under Sigerist's direction, Gregory went into high gear to muster financial backing among the friends, acquaintances, and colleagues he had interested in work on suicide.[14]

Before the end of the year, with Mortimer Williams Raynor's encouragement, Gregory had organised a Committee for the Study of Suicide: Gerald R. Jameison, Head of the Women's Division at Bloomingdale, was president; Marshall Field was vice-president; Henry A. Riley, Professor of Neurology and Neuroanatomy at Columbia, was treasurer; and Gregory himself was secretary and director of research. Sigerist and Edward Sapir, Professor of Anthropology at Yale, were 'consultant members'. Field had a personal as well as social interest in the issue of suicide and he, like Bettina Warburg, who was also a committee member, contributed funds. Among the other members were Elizabeth G. Brockett, Chief Psychiatric Social Worker at New York State Psychiatric Hospital, and Franklin G. Ebaugh, Professor of Psychiatry at the University of Colorado Medical School, as well as two of Gregory's colleagues at the New York Psychoanalytic Society and Institute: the Polish psychiatrist and neurologist Hermann Nunberg, who had come to New York from Vienna in 1932, and Dudley Schoenfeld. The configuration of the committee is evidence of the scope of Gregory's reach by the mid-1930s. By the time it was formally incorporated in December 1935, the committee also included Gosselin as assistant secretary and Field's lawyer Louis Weiss, who had a special interest in psychoanalysis, as the committee's official counsel.

The symposium Gregory had been so enthusiastic about never came to be, but through Sigerist's auspices the Institute of the History of Medicine invited him to give three lectures slated for February 1935. An endowed series named in honour of the Japanese bacteriologist Hideyo Noguchi, the lectures could concern any topic in medical history and would result in a published volume. The opportunity concentrated Gregory's attention: Rather than speak for an afternoon on psychiatry from Hippocrates to Freud, he decided to focus on the medical man and the witch during the Renaissance, a topic which would allow him to discuss psychopathology not only from a scientific perspective but from the point of view of both medieval law and religion.

By the time Sigerist and his wife Emmy dined with Gregory and Ray on a December visit to New York to meet prospective backers Gregory had lined up for the history of medicine journal, he and Sigerist were friends with not only common interests but common and parallel projects. With Gregory's encouragement, Sigerist bought a movie camera, so filmmaking as well as photography soon became a shared hobby. For his part, having been impressed by the staff available to Sigerist in Baltimore, before the end of the year Gregory hired his own research secretary. With a degree in French from the University of Chicago and a master's in library science from Columbia, Marjorie Milde was just the sort of person Gregory needed as an assistant: energetic, intelligent, bilingual, and orderly.

As Gregory returned to the history of medical psychology, his correspondence with Sigerist included not only professional matters and their mutual leisure interests, but topics ranging from world events to office supplies. Paradoxically at once unmaterialistic and attracted to 'good goods', Gregory enjoyed showing people the things he admired, pointing out their fine material, shape, and craftsmanship, their art and attractiveness, their elegant combination of form and function. He was thus particularly fond of cameras and watches (of which he now had a small collection) but also of fountain pens, cutlery, and cufflinks, yet he was not possessive and took as much pleasure in giving as in acquisition. Gearing up to rework his history, Gregory told Sigerist in mid-December that he had obtained three 'organizers' of the sort he had shown his friend on his recent visit. 'They are in leather', he reported, 'and cost $3.50 each'. He wondered if Sigerist wanted all three of them or if he should send him only two, as beyond the virtue of their attractiveness, they were now particularly valuable, 'the last three to be had as the manufacturer has gone out of business'. Socialist to his core, Gregory also saw nothing unacceptable in asking for items he liked, although he was quick to offer to pay if the exchange seemed to require it. The week after posting the organisers, he mentioned a 'bagatelle': Sigerist's 'very nice paper clips', which Gregory thought not only 'good looking' but 'quite convenient'. He asked if Sigerist's secretary could post him the box so he could order some himself, or it were not too much trouble, could she order them for him: 'one box of the smallest size, one of the largest (for bulky papers), and one box medium size'. He would naturally mail a cheque 'immediately upon receipt'. Gregory saw nothing presumptuous in asking, nothing awkward about giving or receiving, nothing embarrassing about money – which was, after all, only money.[15]

With various projects on the go and lectures to write, Gregory spent a calm but social Christmas break with his family. Returning to work in good spirits with a full schedule of commitments, in January 1935 he delivered two papers to the New York Academy of Medicine, the first on 'The Medical Man and the Witch Towards the Close of the Sixteenth Century' – an abbreviated version of the Baltimore lectures – and the second on 'Some Physical Aspects of Mental Disease'. His historical research as well as his entire medical training from his earliest days at the Psycho-Neurological Institute had linked the physical with the psychological, and the reciprocal relationship between body and psyche was a matter he confronted on a daily basis with his patients. He told his audience at the New York Academy that 'deliria of organic origin in no way solve the psychiatric problems with which the medical man has to deal', while 'psychogenic forces' in no way dispose of anatomy and physiology as 'unnecessary appendages to our psychic life'. Emphasising the importance of working together on patients' behalf, he observed that a therapeutic result based on the difficult art of careful diagnosis was the motivation for both psychiatrists and 'medical' doctors.[16]

Cooperation was also on the minds of the membership of the New York Psychoanalytic Society and Institute. More than a year after Gregory's strategic retreat, in an effort to resolve ongoing differences at a meeting on 18 December 1934 he did not attend, the Society had approved a motion to expunge from the minutes the entire proceedings concerning a conflict between the Educational Committee and Paul Ferdinand Schilder, an Austrian psychiatrist and student of Freud's who had come to New York in 1929. These proceedings involved a 'special Investigating Committee', but while both the Educational Committee and Schilder regretted 'the grievances' and deemed 'them extinguished in the interests of a peaceful solution', the matter was by no means settled. Because of 'personal difficulties' between Schilder and 'certain members' of the Educational Committee, 'a special supplementary committee' was appointed 'to judge the merits of Dr. Schilder's claim to be authorized as a training analyst'.

At this last meeting of the year yet more business occurred, including the nomination of officers for 1935. When Brill was re-elected as president by acclamation, he accepted with a short speech mentioning his desire for 'better cooperation among the members'. Such cooperation, however, continued to be an issue among these contentious psychiatrists. Brill's friend Philip R. Lehrman, a Russian-born Jew analysed by Freud, nominated for secretary Gregory's Bloomingdale colleague George Daniels, who had taken over the office on Gregory's withdrawal, while Shoenfeld put Gregory's name forward, provoking Brill to question Gregory's standing within the Society and raising all over again the matter of what seemed to some members an incomplete report on the bookshop. It was pointed out that Gregory had withdrawn from active participation on his own personal initiative and not as a result of any action taken by the Society, so he was indeed a full member 'in good and regular standing'. His name thus remained in nomination.

At the next meeting on 29 January 1935 Gregory was present for the first time since April 1933. In a fruitless effort to maintain a low profile, he withdrew his name; Shoenfeld is recorded as concurring. The matter of the bookshop, however, remained unsettled and in the interests of clearing it up – 'in fairness', Lawrence Kubie suggested, to Gregory – the original Library and Bookshop Committee was asked to look into the matter again. Monroe Meyer then resigned from the committee. When Gregory asked whether the Society had been informed that 'not a single penny' of its money had been given to the bookshop or to the Library and Bookshop Committee, Meyer quoted the treasurer's annual report from 1933 to confirm that the bookshop's operation was at that time entirely financially independent from the Society. Gregory then volunteered that at the end of 1933, the Society owed him $90 and still owed him $24 ($1,700 and $450 today), funds he had personally advanced to keep the bookshop operational, a point confirmed by Edward Liss.

The matter of the bookshop and Gregory's part in it was finally concluded at least formally by the report of the Special Committee on the Library and Bookshop on 30 April 1935. After careful examination of the accounts and interviews with individual Society members, it found 'nothing to justify the assumption that the entire enterprise was not carried out with complete candor, good will and honesty' and suggested 'the entire matter be dropped once and for all' from the Society's deliberations. Gregory could not, however, let the matter go without having the last word. He again called attention to the fact that, at the inauguration of the bookshop and library, funds for the acquisition of books and journals had come largely from his own pocket. He once more defended his bookkeeping methods, submitting sample cards in illustration. Mentioning a letter from Adolph Stern, who had succeeded him as librarian in November 1933, stating that Gregory was owed $84, Gregory indicated he felt Brill had been 'misinformed' about records received by Meyer and turned over unopened to Stern, who corroborated the sum and added that he sympathised with Gregory's bookkeeping methods. Brill then rallied, saying he had never questioned Gregory's integrity. Gregory's friend Lewin went further and proposed a vote of thanks to Gregory for 'his contribution and devotion in regard to the library and bookshop'. The motion was carried with acclaim, but Gregory, the consummate orator, wanted the very last word: He requested that the secretary make it a matter of record that despite the discussion at the meeting at the end of November 1933, he had never been asked for the bookshop accounts.[17]

There the matter finally rested and Gregory returned to active participation in the life of the Society and Institute. Even if the issue was now formally concluded, the tensions that had provoked it inevitably continued. Apparently the problem had never actually been the bookshop accounts, which had been regularly submitted and in which no inaccuracy of method or sums was ever discovered, but the suspicion by some society members that Gregory was not to be trusted, that he was somehow dishonest, manipulative, and secretive for his own ends, guilty of 'shady dealings'. These suspicions had their roots in anti-Semitism, in professional and political jealousies, and in personal confrontations with his challenging personality. That suspicions in the case of the management of the library and bookshop had proved groundless only piqued resentments. The tense atmosphere did not abate, and despite the exoneration and vote of thanks, Gregory had not seen the last of the New York Psychoanalytic Society's special investigative committees.[18]

1935 was nevertheless a good year. The Noguchi lectures were well received and Gregory spent four intense weeks preparing them for publication. The result was a substantial volume on the history of medical psychology in northern Europe during the Renaissance. Quoting extensively from contemporary sources – particularly the German monk Heinrich Kramer's *Malleus Malleficarum* (1487) and Johann Weyer's *De Praestigiis Daemonum* (1563) – Gregory argued with Weyer that those accused of witchcraft suffered from mental illness and needed medical attention rather than ecclesiastical exorcism or legal judgement. Fascinated by the many cases recounted in both documents, Gregory pointed out the possible psychiatric conditions from which the individuals suffered, although his purpose was to elucidate rather than to impose his own medical understanding on the past. Detailing the period's clerical and folk culture, Gregory claimed Weyer as 'the founder of medical psychiatry' whose historical significance was not only his humane attitude towards witches and recognition that many witches were in fact mentally ill but his championing, in the face of ecclesiastical and popular opposition, of 'a real clinical psychopathology'. Specifically, Gregory felt that Weyer, a student of the German physician Heinrich Cornelius Agrippa, had introduced 'the scientific, descriptive, observational method to clinical psychopathology' and 'reclaimed the whole field of psychopathology for medicine'.[19]

Gregory's estimation of Weyer, whom he saw as anticipating Pinel and his follower Jean-Étienne Dominique Esquirol, reveals his own commitment both to treating individual cases individually and to rigorous clinical observation and evaluation. The rationality, particularity, sensitivity, and kindness he praised were what he demanded of himself in his treatment of patients. Gregory's own values and attitudes indeed inform the entire book, including the issue of cultural and particular attitudes towards women. He saw the historical treatment of witches, most of them female, as evidence of obvious and detestable misogyny, while one of the elements he most admired in Weyer's life and work was that his first wife and, after her death, his second were not only personal companions but scientific and clinical collaborators.[20]

Gregory's revision of the lectures on top of his psychoanalytic work and research for the Committee on Suicide left him little leisure. Without hosting responsibilities, Ray had less to occupy her and left in mid-February on a 21-day Caribbean cruise. When Gregory briefly managed to put professional responsibilities aside, he felt rather lonely and his thoughts turned to his family in Mexico. Writing to James he accounted for his solitude by explaining with good-humoured irony that he and Ray had agreed to cooperate in their 'common endeavors': He was very tired; hence she went to have a rest for him since he didn't have time to do it himself. But by 1935 it was clear at least to Gregory that he and his wife didn't have many common endeavours.[21]

Gregory was delighted, however, to be working on a book of his own for the first time since 1920, and he began to anticipate a revision of his history as soon as he could bring himself to work again with Henry. The men couldn't have avoided meeting professionally both in New York and at the annual conventions of the American Psychiatric Association; by 1935 their relationship was cool but cordial. Although Gregory had moved on, Henry was still at Bloomingdale, constrained not only by the hospital hierarchy but by his wife's health: Eleanor had developed a 'mild depression', from which he would regularly insist she was recovering, but she would remain mentally frail throughout the rest of her life. In January Gregory hoped that, with Eleanor supposedly improving, they could soon get together to see if the history could be 'whipped into shape' for publication by the end of the summer.[22]

Indeed, Gregory considered *The Medical Man and the Witch during the Renaissance* as partly publicity for the project, and Sigerist, paraphrasing Gregory in a letter to him, stated in the foreword, 'The present lectures are not an incidental study, but the result of many years of research that will finally lead to a History of Medical Psychology that Dr. Zilboorg is preparing in coöperation with Dr. G. W. Henry.' By the time Gregory completed the revision in March, creating in the process a meticulous index, the manuscript was all he had hoped: work so well done that it wouldn't require the usual secretarial attention. Sigerist confessed, 'the editor's task was never easier than in this case', while the index itself he found 'beautiful' with its precise and elegant headings that included 'epidemics' ('in cattle' and 'in monasteries'); 'hair, removal of'; 'hystero-demonopathy'; 'instinctual life'; 'swallowers, pathological'; 'women, hostile attitude towards' as well as 'sympathetic attitude towards'; and a final entry: 'Zilboorg, Gregory'.[23]

Gregory's thesis was persuasive based on the examples he cited, although he incorrectly assumed that almost all people considered to be witches were mentally ill and, even less convincingly, that almost all people with mental illnesses were perceived as witches. He also assumed the *Malleus* represented general attitudes at the time at least in Germany and by implication throughout Europe, assumptions later historians have questioned. Recent historians have even objected to the elegance and accessibility of Gregory's language, bewailing that his history, like most history until the end of the twentieth century, was unscientifically written 'in prose accessible to nonhistorians'.[24]

Gregory's contemporaries, however, admired not only the author's learning and conclusions but the work's scope and attractiveness. Unsurprised by Gregory's choice of sources, familiar to scholars in the field, the pioneering historian of science George Sarton was nevertheless impressed with Gregory's point of view and praised the volume as 'a psychopathological study' by a distinguished psychiatrist whose 'technical remarks' he felt merited a wide readership especially within 'medical circles'. Sarton also drew attention to the book itself as 'handsome' and 'beautifully got up'.[25]

Revealing throughout Gregory's characteristic attention to detail, the book was indeed elegant both linguistically and aesthetically. Impressed with the galleys in May, with the appearance of both the text and his carefully chosen period illustrations in a work that reflected his own performance as a lecturer and historian of medicine, he decided this personal book should feature his own photograph as a frontispiece over a reproduction of his signature.[26]

Frontispiece for *The Medical Man and the Witch during the Renaissance*

In the spring of 1935 Gregory felt he had come into his own. As if to celebrate his return to psychiatric history, in March Gregory bought an additional 30 acres of farmland, expanding his country property to an extensive 42 acres. He would manage to relax there on occasional weekends during the spring and summer, devoting time to family, reading, and photography, to music on the radio and record player, to writing and reflecting on matters other than psychiatric and psychoanalytic practice. Indeed, he needed a social life apart from his daily hours at the office, apart from his work on the *Quarterly* and his many collegial relationships. If solitude was necessary to what Gregory saw as spiritual life, so was the psychological nourishment of unfettered companionship and intellectual exchange. Partly as a result of their work on the lectures and the resulting book, Gregory and Sigerist had become close friends; the only closer friend was Abe, who had established a private surgical practice in Manhattan with privileges at Lenox Hill Hospital on 77th Street. Proximity meant that despite their busy professional lives Gregory and Abe saw each other regularly; young Greg and Nancy would call the balding bachelor with the gentle voice 'Uncle Abe'. Gregory shared with him, as with Sigerist, an interest in photography, and the two former classmates met as trusted companions even though they had pursued divergent specialties and different paths in their personal lives. On the occasional evening they could manage, Gregory and Sigerist would talk over all manner of things at will, preferably over a good meal. Shortly before Sigerist left for his annual summer abroad, including this year a visit to colleagues in the Soviet Union, Gregory stopped in Baltimore en route to Washington for an American Psychiatric Association meeting. He strolled with his friend on the shore of the Chesapeake Bay, discussing the state of the world and taking photographs before dining together on seasonal softshell crabs 'in all their glory'.[27]

Life in Mexico was less happy. When in late May Basia asked Gregory to underwrite their mother's visit to a health resort, he wrote James to determine if such a trip was necessary and how much it would cost. After his farm's expansion, Gregory admitted he was feeling 'somewhat cramped' financially, 'not in a position to be too liberal'. James responded that he was stressed, financially pressed, and extremely tired from overwork, but didn't want to treat his brother as a 'milk cow'. He tried to clarify: Their father had savings but was stingy; James had even occasionally borrowed money from him and felt Moses, not Gregory, should pay for their mother's treatment. Relaxing on his farm and looking forward to receiving copies of his book, Gregory accepted this typically gloomy report with undampened spirits. He sent James news about his thriving livestock and, despite depleted funds, a cheque for $50 for Anna's trip, declaring with trenchant humour that when he failed in his own productivity, his cows and the printer compensated for his deficiencies. In July he sent his brother a copy of *The Medicine Man and the Witch.*

It took James six weeks to respond, but he might be excused for being distracted. At the end of the summer, having evidently decided against opening a clinic, Basia suddenly announced she was getting married. This time her choice seemed wise: A Russian immigrant who, like Basia, had been previously married, David Bekman Lejtman was not young – but at 41, neither was Basia – and ran a successful leather business in Mexico City; moreover, he was highly regarded in the orthodox Ashkenazy community. Moses and Anna were thrilled and involved themselves enthusiastically in the wedding planned for late September. Almost as an afterthought, James told Gregory that their parents were proud of him, too, and wished they could show him off as they showed off James as a 'great engineer'. He finally got around to telling his brother just how impressed 'the old folks' were with the book. A few weeks earlier James had stopped by on his way home from work and shown them the copy Gregory had sent. As usual, their apartment had been filled with visitors; his eyes aglow, Moses had passed the book around with trembling hands. Talking in a very low voice, he had shown each of them the frontispiece. Gregory must have been moved by this vignette: his reserved father at last so pleased with his eldest son's achievement.[28]

In New York that autumn Gregory once more plunged into his hectic professional life. Having concluded his analysis with Bettina Warburg in June and Marshall Field in September, Gregory's schedule quickly filled with new patients. Although Jimmy Warburg as well as Kay Swift may still have been claiming some of his psychoanalytic attention, he continued daily sessions with Eddie Warburg and George Gershwin at the same time that he resumed his research and committee work on suicide and attendance at professional meetings, including those at the New York Psychoanalytic Society and Institute. His editorial duties at the *Quarterly* had not stopped during the summer, but as his colleagues returned from their holidays, his reviewing responsibilities intensified. He now began to write 'Suicide among Civilized and Primitive Races' for presentation at the Boston Society of Neurology and Psychiatry in October.

Despite his obligations, he hoped to see Sigerist and hear about his summer experiences. Gregory told his friend modestly his desire was selfish since he felt he had nothing new to contribute to their historical discussions while supposing that Sigerist had 'a mass of newly acquired and important knowledge'. Adding that he was sending samples of Belgian photographic paper on which he had a discount, he wanted to know which surfaces Sigerist preferred and how much of each he might want. It is unclear if Gregory considered the paper a gift or expected Sigerist to pay, but the offer was typical: a degree of pride in having negotiated something advantageous mixed with generosity, an almost paradoxical combination of attitudes other people frequently found difficult to understand. With some of the same pride and generosity, Gregory mentioned the 'great success' of a new 'purely modern opera' he urged Sigerist to see when he was next in New York: Gershwin's *Porgy and Bess*.[29]

Gregory managed a weekend in Baltimore in early November. After Sigerist's Friday evening lecture on his Russian experiences, the men spent two intense days talking about almost everything except philosophy and religion: The history of medicine was naturally a topic, but also Russia, wars, revolutions, theatre, music, and photography. An accomplished cook, Sigerist prepared elegant meals they enjoyed with good wine and much laughter, and there were hands-on hours in Sigerist's 'laboratory', where they worked with the new papers and Gregory explained why he had put aside his Contax and was now 'a Leica man'. Sigerist would call it 'a great weekend', while Gregory promised his friend tickets to the opera he had touted as a theatrical triumph.[30]

In fact, *Porgy and Bess* was not a great success; reviews were at best condescending, at worst dismissive. Gershwin himself was more than disappointed; he was angry and depressed by the rejection of work on which he had spent two years of creative energy. Gregory probably suggested getting away from New York for a while. Gershwin had previously found inspiration in Paris and Cuba; with Europe out of the question, Mexico seemed an attractive destination, although the choice was likely Gershwin's rather than Gregory's. Three years earlier Gershwin had accompanied the Mexican painters Diego Rivera and Frida Kahlo and the Mexican composer Carlos Chavez on a chartered train from New York to Philadelphia for the premiere of *Horsepower*, a ballet by Chavez with sets and costumes by Rivera. Gershwin's friend and fellow musician Vernon Duke had contacts in Mexico and put Gershwin in touch with the international socialite Estrella Elizaga, then living in Mexico City. Gregory – whom Gershwin expected to accompany him as his psychoanalyst – welcomed the incidental opportunity to see his family, but he also recoiled, recognising the challenge of keeping his personal and professional lives separate. The task had been difficult during his first visit to Mexico; it would be more problematic with Gershwin at a time when he was particularly sensitive and distressed, while Eddie Warburg as a dependent patient would need to go along as well.

Gregory mentioned the trip to Sigerist during the weekend in Baltimore, but only on his return to New York did he notify James of his 'quite unexpected' decision. Gershwin had made plans according to what appealed to him: The three men would leave New York on 15 November by train via Saint Louis to Mexico City, where they would stay at an elegant hotel in the San Angel district. A car would be hired for visits to Taxco, Acapulco, Guadalajara, and Mazatlan on Mexico's west coast, where in early December they would board a cruise ship bound for New York via the Panama Canal and Havana. Despite the trip's impromptu nature, Gregory looked forward to discovering a country about which he knew comparatively little. He told his brother that 'Edward Warburg and George Gershwin' would be his 'two travelling companions', who would inevitably have claims on his time, and emphasised that for 'obvious reasons' of discretion he didn't want anyone except perhaps James to meet his train. Even before his arrival, Gregory was juggling his responsibilities and preferences but had already resolved to spend the first evening with his brother and 'the old folks'.[31]

The weeks in Mexico turned out to be gratifying in ways Gregory could not have anticipated. He managed to spend the first evening with his family at his brother's home, although a visit there was always difficult for Moses and Anna, who refused to eat in a non-kosher household. Having failed to understand Gregory's situation, James compounded the awkwardness by regretting that Ray and the children had not been able to come along, but the reunion must have been sweet: Basia showing off her new husband; Nadia, Natalie, and Lydia markedly taller since Gregory's last visit and eager to introduce two-year-old Olga to her uncle; Anna seated in a comfortable chair as *mater familias*; Eugenia welcoming everyone to her crowded house; Moses at last able to express his pride to his son the distinguished psychoanalyst, the author of books.[32]

The next day would set the tone for the rest of the trip. In the morning, Gregory would have analytic sessions with Eddie and Gershwin. After a good lunch, there would be sightseeing, shopping, and encounters with local people, followed by dinner with interesting guests and discussions of music, art, culture, and politics; if there were a piano, Gershwin would play. On the second evening, Elizaga arranged a party at the San Angel Inn, the converted Carmelite monastery where the group was staying. Guests included the painters Miguel Covarrubias, Roberto Montenegro, and David Siqueiros plus artists Gershwin already knew: Diego Rivera, probably with Frida Kahlo; one of Kahlo's lovers, the sculptor Isamu Noguchi (who had made a bronze bust of Gershwin in New York in 1929); and Carlos Chavez. Gregory was in his element and Gershwin found him 'particularly amusing' as he spoke with the other guests in both English and Spanish. The Mexican revolution, Marxism, fascism, and political art were all topics, but in addition to serious intellectual discussion, there was surely much laughter as well as song.[33]

During the hours Gregory had to himself, he saw his family. He also arranged to meet medical colleagues and learned of good work being done on the history of both Aztec and Mayan medical practices. With Gershwin and Eddie he visited Alberto Misrachi's modern art gallery in the capital's historic centre and discovered a specialist camera shop around the corner where he examined lenses and filters and German cameras, but he had his Leica with him throughout the trip and took photographs, including an impressive series of portraits.

Gregory's portrait of Diego Rivera, 1935

Gregory's portrait of David Siqueiros, 1935

On a foray south the three men admired Taxco's colonial architecture and browsed in the silver shops before travelling north and west to Mazatlan where, on 3 December, they boarded the *Santa Paula* for the leisurely journey home. Having started in Seattle the ship made various stops along the California and Mexican coast. The urbane New York actor Frank Morgan, who had played King Cyril in Gershwin's 1928 Broadway musical *Rosalie*, had boarded in Los Angeles. The trip back to New York turned out to be almost as stimulating as the weeks in Mexico and offered Gregory the time away he often longed for but found so difficult to organise.

At Gregory's urging and likely on his brother's funds, James joined the group when the ship docked in Havana. In republican Cuba's sophisticated capital there was music of all sorts in the streets and nightclubs, where everyone was offered highballs of rum and Coca-Cola, while the island's balmy temperatures would be a stark contrast to the snow flurries that greeted the travellers in New

Gregory on the S.S. *Santa Paula* in December 1935 with George Gershwin, Alma Muller Morgan, Frank Morgan, and an unidentified passenger

York on 17 December. Gershwin, who had not finally been creatively inspired by the trip, concluded his analysis on his return to the city. His relationship with Gregory would remain amicable and he would turn to his psychoanalyst for medical advice, but his formal treatment was over as he cast about for a new direction in his career. Gregory, however, was in high spirits: He had found Mexico 'even more fascinating' on his second visit, while the entire trip had proved a 'very delightful holiday'.[34]

Notes

1 GZ, 'Investigative Psychotherapy'.
2 GZ to HES, 18 January 1934.
3 GZ to HES, 24 January, 7 February 1934; HES to GZ, 22, 25 January 1934.
4 GZ to HES, 7 February 1934.
5 Pollack, 207–208; Leffert, 146.
6 Becker, esp. 134–138, 150–151.
7 Marshall Field to GZ, nd, GZB.
8 JZ to GZ, 9 April 1934; GZ to JZ, 21 March 1934.
9 GZ to JZ, 16 April 1934.
10 GZ to JZ, 18 April 1934.
11 GZ, 'Differential Diagnostic Types', 291.
12 GZ to HES, 28 September 1934, Bryher to H.D., 30 August 1934, in Friedman, 415.
13 GZ to JZ, 16, 18, 22 October, 2 November 1934.
14 GZ to HES, 13, 15, 21 November 1934; HES to GZ, 16 November 1934.
15 GZ to HES, 13, 18 December 1934; HES to GZ, 14 December 1934.
16 GZ, 'Some Physical Aspects', 1, 5.
17 NYPS minutes, 18 December 1934, 9 January, 30 April 1935, NYPSI.
18 Quinn, 342.
19 GZ, *The Medical Man*, 205.
20 GZ, *The Medical Man*,163–164.
21 GZ to HES, 25 February 1935; GZ to JZ, 23 February 1935.
22 GZ to GWH, 10 January 1935; GZ to JZ, 23 February 1935; GZ to HES, 29 March 1935.
23 GZ to HES, 15, 29 March 1935, and to Helen Brooks, 15 March 1935; HES to GZ, 6, 10 April 1935; GZ, *The Medicine Man*, 210, 211, 214, 215.
24 Wallace, *History*, xx; Mora, 'Early American Historians', 63, 'Renaissance Conceptions', 238.
25 Sarton, 147, 150, 152.
26 GZ to HES, 7 May 1935.
27 GZ to HES, 18, 29 April 1935.
28 GZ to JZ, 27 May, 26 June, 30 July 1935; JZ to GZ, 1 June, 12 September 1935; marriage certificate, BZ-Lejtman, 28 September 1935.
29 GZ to HES, 16 October 1935.
30 GZ to HES, 24, 30 October 1935; HES to GZ, 8 November 1935; GZ, 'His Own Cook', 156.
31 GZ to JZ, 6 November 1935.
32 JZ to GZ, 11 November 1935.
33 Pollack; 199; Rimler, 119.
34 GZ to HES, 19 December 1935; GZ to JZ, 18 February 1936.

Chapter 12

Divided attention

1935–1937

Gregory enjoyed a few free moments during the 1935 holiday season, but his desk both at home and at work was piled with papers. Just before the end of the year, the Committee for the Study of Suicide was formally incorporated and in January began its substantial programme. In addition to his privileged patients – who now included the witty writer Beatrice Kaufman and the playwright Moss Hart – Gregory's research brought him into contact with people who were neither rich nor famous as he and his colleagues worked with the families of New York City policemen who had attempted or succeeded at suicide and patients at Bellevue Psychiatric Hospital. This work also confirmed his friendship with Karl Menninger, whose thinking on suicide differed from Gregory's but whose shared interest would increase their respect for one another as they respected their differences.[1]

In part as a result of Gregory's trip to Mexico, he was also thinking a great deal about visual art. Two of his photographs of Sigerist featured in December 1935 and January 1936 at the Second International Leica Exhibition at Rockefeller Center, a show that included Carl Van Vechten's portraits of Gertrude Stein and Theodore Dreiser. In February, when Siqueiros visited New York to set up his Experimental Workshop, a year-long 'laboratory for traditional and modern techniques in art', Gregory was among the first visitors. While Siqueiros was a Stalinist – in contrast to Rivera, a Trotskyite in the schism that was in the 1930s splitting the Communist world – Gregory sympathised with the socialist principles that informed the art of both painters. Fascinated by the Workshop's technical goals, he commissioned three paintings from Siqueiros: 'Collective Suicide', 'Cosmos and Disaster', and 'The End of the World'. All three reflected Gregory's thinking about individuality, suicide, homicide, fascism, and war as well as illustrating the artist's goals during this period: 'dialectical methodology coupled with technical breakthroughs'. 'Collective Suicide', a work on a grand scale depicting Chichimec Indians killing their children and themselves rather than submit to the conquistadores, is often considered the crowning achievement of the Workshop and must have been influenced by Gregory's discussions with Siqueiros of 'Suicide among Civilized and Primitive Races', in which he had referred to native suicides in response to the Spanish invasion. Although Gregory did not specifically mention the Chichimecs

DOI: 10.4324/9781003190936-12

in the article, which wasn't published until May 1936, the fact that it was first presented as a paper in October 1935 meant that the history of suicide in Central and South America was on Gregory's mind even before he met Siqueiros.

Much too big even for the walls of Gregory's large apartment, the painting remained on display at the Workshop until the end of year when Gregory lent it to the exhibition 'Fantastic Art, Dada and Surrealism' at the Museum of Modern Art, where Eddie Warburg had been a member of the board of trustees since 1932. When the exhibition closed in January 1937, Gregory would offer 'Collective Suicide' to the museum as a gift, perhaps his intention from the start. Eddie and Gershwin, too, would purchase and donate paintings by Siqueiros to the museum in 1936 and 1937, but Gershwin notably commissioned for himself a personal work, 'George Gershwin in a Concert Hall'. This painting depicted Gershwin on stage and the mostly faceless audience in the background, but in the front row Siqueiros depicted people particularly important in Gershwin's life: members of his family, close friends, Kay Swift, Siqueiros himself … and Gregory Zilboorg.[2]

Gregory would keep 'Cosmos and Disaster' and 'The End of the World', which had more meaning for him personally. Inspired by recent events in Spain, these paintings offer apocalyptic visions of violent destruction. In 'Cosmos and Disaster', a devastated landscape suggests not only the Spanish civil war but the trenches of 1914–1918: A barren black and brown 'no man's land' in the distance gives way to broken timbers and lines in the foreground where a small, barely identifiable red figure lies alone amidst the wreckage. In 'The End of the World', huge red, yellow, and eerily green flames in the night sky throw into sharp contrast a broken building and enormous cave at whose entry, on a grey stretch of rough ground, stands a minute red figure whose white face and raised arms intensify the horror. In each painting, the solitary figure draws the viewer's attention, emphasising the effect of devastation and finality on the single person who remains visible. Gregory's concern with political and social equality depended on his valuing the individual, and it is not surprising that these smaller works whose landscapes menace lone individuals remained throughout his life in his own collection. Indeed, the inclusion of these tiny figures in commissioned works suggests a fascinating collaboration between artist and patron. In 'George Gershwin in a Concert Hall', the faces in the audience were initially anonymous, but the painter was willing to modify his work at Gershwin's request. Gregory may well have discussed with Siqueiros the addition of a single person to his two paintings, a detail that in each case increases the menace of the landscapes and poses questions important to both artist and psychoanalyst about survival and significance.

Gregory would never be a patron of the arts like Gershwin and particularly Eddie – he would never have their fortunes nor their leisure – and in 1936 his nights and days were typically 'crowded with matters that required immediate attention'. Between bouts of writing and seeing patients, he reflected on his principles and experience of family life in Mexico, wondering what he might do to make things easier for James, whose financial situation the brothers had discussed frankly when James visited New York in December. James was living with his family in a small rented house because his straitened circumstances made purchasing a place of his own impossible in the present and improbable in the future. Despite his generosity, Gregory's finances would not stretch to buying a house or land in Mexico during the depression years. Having paid $2,000 ($35,000 today) for 'Collective Suicide' and likely as much again for the other two paintings, he had little extra to give away. After a great deal of thought, he proposed a temporary solution: His brother could rent a larger place whose additional cost Gregory would pay. This unsolicited offer was characteristic, and his proposal, detailed in an important letter devoted to persuading his reluctant brother to accept his suggestion, reveals his complex and persistently socialist attitude towards money as well as his own comfortable situation.[3]

James naturally had scruples, feeling he would lose his own self-respect by becoming even more dependent on his brother, but Gregory didn't share his compunctions, labelling them 'prejudices'. Acknowledging that both men were typical products of capitalistic life, Gregory nevertheless felt that only in 'a purely small bourgeois society' were human relationships measured 'on the basis of one's pocketbook'. Although James was exploited by his employers, even a self-employed psychoanalyst was not outside 'the capitalistic regime'. He explained:

> I seem to be independent because I make and pay myself for the productive work I do. Whatever the causes of it all, I suffered the pleasant accident of making more money than thousands of others who work harder and have more responsibilities.

With sincere humility and modesty, he insisted his 'success' was only 'a capitalistic accident' and denied that his financial situation was the result of talent, pointing out that in Spain or Japan his 'so-called services' would be neither needed nor so well paid. In both cases, he would have to live hand to mouth or 'play politics' with his medical judgement to 'drum up trade' and thus become 'a petty shopkeeper with a few honest and mostly dishonest medical articles in stock'.

Gregory maintained that his offer wasn't a matter of generosity or prompted by 'a sort of sentimental splashiness of feeling and money'; he simply saw that 'accidents of a capitalistic world' kept on increasing his needs in proportion to the growth of his worldly goods, while his brother's needs increased disproportionately to his material capacity. Neither benevolence nor duty, he insisted, led him to advise renting a larger house, but 'the simple desire to square my accounts'. At this point in this significant letter, however, the thrust of Gregory's argument as well as his generosity, sense of responsibility, and even a degree of guilt got the better of him. He went so far as to reconstruct their past, contrasting his brother's hard work, sacrifice, and suffering with his own life defined not so much by agency as by 'various queer accidents'. Gregory was playing to his audience, not actually distorting the past so much as glossing over his own struggles, whose pain he still felt, while trying to encourage and support his able but often pathetic brother. He told him that 'fate constantly smiled on me'; while James was 'starving in New

York', he was sitting in the Marble or Winter Palaces where, except for the fear of being shot, he claimed he had had 'a good and thrilling time'.

Gregory could not deny the bitterness he still felt at their American reunion, however. When their paths crossed in the New World, they had shaken hands, but James, Gregory asserted, had wanted to pull away as if it were humiliating to 'get on along the road together'. Gregory might gloss over his difficult years in Russia before, during, and after the revolution, but his bitterness about his brother's rejection during his first years in New York would persist. Gregory would always feel sorry for James at the same time that he tried to make amends for his role in the revolution, his refusal to sacrifice his medical education, and his successful multifaceted career.

Invariably the perceptive psychoanalyst, Gregory advised James to consult his inner self, sure he would find there 'a couple of unnecessary remnants of the old psychology' he could 'readily and profitably throw out'. Fearing property prices would continue to rise, James worried he would miss his chance, but Gregory counselled that 'it is always cheaper to do a thing when one can do it with ease than when one feels cramped'; at present he had 'so many obligations to meet and so many expenses, such as taxes' that he would be 'considerably embarrassed, if not seriously cramped' if he undertook to purchase property in Mexico. He urged James to 'quiet' his 'quite intelligible impatience' and wait until he was ready to contribute, to relax and depend on Gregory's interest and assistance, even insisting that James would be doing him a favour in accepting his offer. He then sent his brother two cheques: one for $100 ($1,800 today) for the monthly support of their parents and another for $200 'in addition' towards the year's increased rent.[4]

Throughout 1936 Gregory directed his vast energies in ever more multiple directions. His family in Mexico and at home commanded his attention; in addition to seeing patients, research, writing, editing, and committee work claimed his time as did travel for conferences in Chicago and Philadelphia and for presentations in Boston, Baltimore, and Washington. In February he moved into a larger office in the same building. His files and library were expanding as he took on new projects and staff, but he may also have wanted additional space for himself. Like those of his medical colleagues, his office was in fact a comfortable apartment adapted to his requirements, including a 'treatment room', with a chair and couch as well as a desk, and a waiting room. The kitchen and living room with a fireplace retained their integrity as did at least one of the two bedrooms, but the rest of the space was quickly filled. In addition to Pauline, his staff included his research assistant and another secretary, who shared typing responsibilities and received patients, filed notes and correspondence, took dictation, answered routine letters, made phone calls, and arranged hotel reservations as well as performing editorial duties that ranged from checking Gregory's spelling and references in various languages to looking things up in his office library or in the New York Public Library. On Fridays an accountant came in to sort out payments by cash and cheque for services rendered and owed, while in the background, preparing lunch for everyone at mid-day and returning to empty paper-filled bins in the evening, there was Della, who carefully wrapped leftover sandwiches in waxed paper and dusted with quiet gravity.

An even larger staff at home in town and on the farm enabled the social and personal life Gregory also needed. Four servants lived with the family in New York: a cheerful American cook, a German maid, a Swiss butler, and the affectionate nursemaid Miss Hutt, who accompanied the children to Pound Ridge while the others stayed in the city to look after Gregory. In the country a local woman cared for the house while her husband and son saw to the fruit and vegetables, the dogs, chickens, pigs, and cows. Only such support permitted dinner parties in the city or overnight guests on the farm, attendance at the theatre or the Metropolitan Opera or Carnegie Hall, and the hours so important to Gregory in the dark room in the Pound Ridge barn, where he developed, enlarged, and printed photographs.

Gregory hoped for another holiday in Mexico and the publication of his history; he hoped to help his brother and to hear better news on the radio. Such hopes did not mitigate, however, the heavy professional and personal responsibilities he was shouldering or improve the international situation, and he felt seriously stressed by the spring. His friendships lightened his mood while occasional days on the farm were a welcome distraction, but he was increasingly burdened by obligations and too much of a realist to think even for a moment that he could change the course of Nazi politics or the civil war in Spain.

Hobbies like photography and chess helped, as did the new interest in cooking Sigerist had inspired, but moments of relaxation were offset by his concerns about democracy, and he was bothered by finding his name in gossip columns and in articles on his prominent patients in the popular press. Never good with money, he was unable to be as generous as he liked; not knowing where the pennies went, he worried as he did every year about paying his income tax as the March deadline approached. He could analyse the world economy and understood capitalism, but the daily ups and downs of the stock market and keeping accounts were beyond him. He read the papers and worried about world affairs; he ate his toast with marmalade for breakfast, drank his tea with lemon, and kept his worries about Ray, who often seemed physically and mentally unwell, to himself. In early March he addressed a combined meeting of the New York Neurological Society and the New York Academy of Medicine on 'Varieties of Aggression in Parenthood', a paper that extended his earlier thinking on parental antagonism towards children and reflected not only on what his patients had revealed to him since he first formally considered the problem five years earlier but what he had discovered through his own experience as a father and husband to a woman who remained deeply uncomfortable with motherhood.

Gregory's bonhomie, however, could be summoned in even the most difficult times. With witty self-deprecation, he wrote Sigerist in late March, 'I have an idea. It is strange that I have one, but it just happens. Would you and Mrs. Sigerist spend a week-end with us?' Ray and Emmy might go to the theatre on Friday evening, he thought, while he and Sigerist printed photographs. Later that night they would drive to the country, where his programme included 'some walking and photography', before returning Sunday afternoon to the city for another evening enlarging. The Sigerists could, he proposed, take the midnight train home. For these impressively energetic and busy men, such a weekend took careful coordination and would not take place until late April, when the two couples attended a formal dinner to celebrate Freud's 80th birthday before heading to Pound Ridge for the walking and photography. Gregory must have thoroughly enjoyed the experience; Sigerist, who found the farm 'marvelous', pronounced the weekend one of the 'most delightful' he had ever had.[5]

The farm captured Gregory's heart and imagination, and he told Marshall Field he was even looking for a second bull. No longer dependent on his analyst, Field was now not only a colleague on the suicide committee but a respected friend. Declining his offer of a mature animal in exchange for a cow bred at 'Caumsett' and now thriving in Pound Ridge, Gregory explained he had in mind 'a real youngster a couple of months old who could run along growing up on my place, reach manhood under my psychoanalytical guidance, and then be duly provided with the bullish wherewithall'. He continued in the same humorous vein:

> I have one mature male now who is doing his duty credibly, but in another year and a half the gentleman will have so many ladies as his descendants, that to protect my good name against being besmirched by King Oedipus, I would like to raise his successor from another strain.

Enjoying his psychoanalytic trope, he concluded,

> As to exchanging your cow, I have a severe resistance to it and I refuse to analyze it. She is my prize animal. Her name according to your papers is Northern Sunshine and Sunshine she truly is. How could I part with her for a mere male?

Friendship, like the farm, lifted Gregory's spirits, and he was pleased that Field had found his way. When Ruth Phipps went to Reno in late April for the divorce that allowed her to marry Field, Gregory sent her flowers, risking more gossip but honouring his former patient for whom he wished the happy marriage that had eluded Field in his first two unions.[6]

Moments of levity and occasional weekends with friends finally did little, however, to lighten Gregory's burdens. Preoccupied with the great number of things that filled each day but remained unaccomplished and generally fatigued, he had 'a sense of slipping', felt unable to modify his schedule or eliminate the things to be done. He was, in short, 'laboring under a severe sense of dissatisfaction with things as they have been, are, or are going to be.' The publisher Alfred A. Knopf had evinced interest in Gregory's history, and the two men had met in March over a drink at the Plaza Lounge Bar, where Gregory explained his agreement in principle with Norton and shared with a fellow Jew the reasons the book had stalled. He had sent Henry a copy of *The Medical Man and the Witch*, but the history had still not moved along and, working on Sigerist's recommendation from the second edition of 1567, Gregory began translating *Von den Krankheiten so die Vernunfft Berauben* ('The Diseases that Deprive Man of His Reason') by Paracelsus. One reason Gregory's name so often appeared in Walter Winchell's embarrassing columns was that academic work was not the only writing coming from his pen. Ever the journalist as well as the scholar, he wanted to reach a wider audience and by the summer had begun a lengthy piece, 'Aggression: Savage and Domesticated', for the *Atlantic Monthly*. James tried to encourage his troubled brother: Gregory's failure to achieve all he attempted was only natural since he invariably attempted about five times as much as James thought humanly possible.[7]

Gregory took no summer holiday in 1936, but the farm continued to provide consolation. There, when he pried himself from his desk, he enjoyed being both gentleman farmer and *pater familias*. Nancy, who had turned three in May, and young Greg, almost five and barely kept in line by Miss Hutt, were a source of delight, while the flora and fauna, including two young heifers and a new five-month-old bull, bloomed and multiplied. Gregory ebulliently reported to James that the family was eating 'fresh eggs, fresh eggplant, young ducks, and squabs' while 'the poor eunuchs, officially called capons' were growing like the apples, although as yet neither was ripe. Peter and Ramsey, the country dogs, were successfully hunting woodchucks as 'big as racoons' and running into the lake with Greg while hummingbirds more peacefully fed on the gladiolas.

The pastoral world Gregory enjoyed describing contrasted starkly with his pressured daily life. He had considered an early autumn trip to Mexico, but too many 'circumstances' made this impossible, and he was already anticipating a long vacation in November and December. Along the lines of the Mexican holiday in 1935, he had begun to plan a six-week tour of South America. It would similarly involve travelling with dependent patients, who would share the costs, but in an effort to lift her spirits, this time Ray would go, too. The vacation was something to look forward to during what in late 1936 increasingly seemed to Gregory dark times.

On the global front, the news was deeply unsettling. The Nuremburg laws forbidding relationships between Aryans and Jews had come into force in September 1935, new rules many American regarded as a merely local matter, but in March 1936 Hitler had ordered the reoccupation of the Rhineland, calling into question the terms of the Versailles Treaty and provoking international concern. The Olympic Games in Berlin in August did nothing to allay Gregory's unease. Strikes and riots in Spain throughout the spring had given way to civil war, with Stalin supporting the Republicans and Hitler, Franco's Nationalists. Before the end of the summer International Brigades from throughout the world joined on the Republican side, while in America Roosevelt prepared to run against Alf Landon for a second term in a contest that was widely expected to result in the incumbent's landslide victory. In Mexico labour unrest had provoked a summer strike against the Mexican Power and Light company and its American, Canadian, and

British owners, depriving the capital of electricity for 90 consecutive days. Gregory could be brutally sarcastic. There was, he told James in August, 'No news, of course, except the Mexican Power strike and the Spanish revolution. Otherwise everything is quiet, dull, stupid, bland, and provincial in this greatest of all great presidential campaigns.' He concluded, 'My views on the essential condition of the universe have not undergone any serious change nor has my disgust.'[8]

Before Gershwin left New York for Hollywood in August, he and Gregory surely had a farewell drink together. Their relationship was now informal and jocular, but Gregory sincerely hoped Gershwin would find in California the inspiration he sought and urged him to keep in touch. Shortly after his arrival in Los Angeles the composer duly wrote that he hadn't started work yet, but was getting his bearings. Addressing him as 'My dear Goish' in affectionate imitation of a Brooklyn accent, Gregory responded in early September. He was suitably friendly and general, noting the sultry weather oppressing New York's congested streets and writing of himself only that he was working 'as usual'. He reassured Gershwin that it was quite all right that he wasn't yet composing for that meant 'all is in the future'. Expressing his confidence in Gershwin's potential, he told him to 'write again and write soon and write a lot', implying not only that further correspondence would be welcome but that Gershwin's creative energy should and would 'again' and 'soon' and bountifully go into writing music.[9]

In the crowded and steamy city Gregory was typically working hard on the five times as much as his brother thought possible, to which James now added yet another item: Could Gregory with his influential contacts help him find a new job? He was truly unhappy in his current position, felt neither secure nor rewarded, frantic to move on at the same time that he dithered, hesitating to spend his limited funds to meet possible employers in the States and wondering what might be available in public or private 'power supply management' in New York or Philadelphia – indeed anywhere but Mexico.

Gregory responded as was his wont by offering money for the trip, but he was not encouraging. He carefully explained that while government jobs might be interesting, they didn't pay well and were uncertain because they were 'mixed up with politics and factional rivalry'. Private enterprise jobs were even more difficult to get since commercial companies were closed corporations – one had to be 'an "insider"', play the same games, be they 'golf or cocktails', and 'vote Republican' – a situation made worse in that anti-Semitism in the United States, in his experience, had reached 'barbaric proportions'. To illustrate, he reported that his barber had recently told him he preferred the Eighth Avenue to the Lexington subway because the cars were cleaner and '"not so many Jews ride in it"'. Perhaps, Gregory suggested, there might be something for James in Argentina.[10]

Gregory's life was so hectic in the autumn that he had no time even to see Sigerist before he set off for South America. The intensity of his work was part of the problem, but so was his home life. He insisted in his correspondence that he found his children a constant joy, yet while little Nancy was generally biddable, young Greg was wearing not only on his parents but on his governess, who had trouble controlling the headstrong child whose difficulty following rules and paying attention tried everyone's patience. Before Gregory and Ray's departure, the decision was taken to replace Miss Hutt with Katherine Darroche, a no-nonsense Irish woman supposedly particularly capable with boys.[11]

Nancy, aged three, photographed by Gregory

Gregory's photography continued to offer him unalloyed solace, however, and anticipating the trip, he enrolled in masterclasses on spotting, retouching, and chalking. Scratches and poor distribution of light would no longer bother him, and he submitted portraits to various salons. From late October to mid-November his photograph 'Blind' was shown at the First Annual Photographic Salon of the Philadelphia Art Alliance and two additional photographs had already been accepted for winter shows.[12]

Gregory may have found the 1936 presidential race lacklustre, but he voted for Roosevelt with some enthusiasm on the first Tuesday in November. Indeed, he probably did some active campaigning, for he was invited by the Democratic National Committee to listen to the returns on the radio in the Biltmore Hotel's Music Room. A week later he was in Richmond, Virginia, where he gave two talks, the first to a group of doctors at the home of the pioneering psychiatrist James King Hall, co-founder and president of Richmond's progressive Westbrook Sanatorium. With particular interests in the history of psychiatry, the relationship between physical and mental illness, and the psychiatric treatment of criminals, King and Gregory would discover they had much in common. The afternoon talk, however, was political rather than professional – on democracy, fascism, and communism. The account in the *Richmond Times-Dispatch* gives a vivid portrait of the mature man who had spoken on similar topics as Skobelev's representative during the revolution and an itinerant Chautauqua lecturer 15 years earlier. Now a 'noted New York psychiatrist', he was described as a 'swarthy Russian-American with big black moustaches on a keen and thoughtful face', a 'realist' who informed the group that in his opinion there would be another war. He spoke with grim frankness: 'Politics, you say, is a little dirty. Everything is a little dirty. Our bodily functions are not all so pretty and nice. Neither are the human sides of relationships which deal with power.' Yet he believed in democracy, whose 'greatest contribution to civilization' was 'the awareness of the individual that he is his own master'. Democracy faced particular challenges, however, and the most crucial, he pointed out insightfully, were those resulting from economic disparity: 'An Eastern banker and a West Virginia miner necessarily have different conceptions of citizenship. To harmonize these', he declared, 'is the job of democracy.'[13]

In the evening, at the Richmond Academy of Medicine, Gregory spoke on a professional topic about which he had also thought a great deal: 'The Problem of "Organic" versus "Mental" in Medicine and Psychiatry'. Here he echoed what he knew from his own professional training and practical experience and what he had told the New York Academy of Medicine a year earlier: Anatomy and physiology could not be separated from psychiatry, for emotional illness was integrally related to physical illness; the good psychiatrist would necessarily work with other physicians in both diagnosing and treating any patient.

Four days later, with their numerous suitcases and flowers from well-wishers filling their staterooms, Gregory set sail at noon on the *S.S. Southern Prince* with Ray and three patients, Eddie and Jimmy Warburg and Jimmy's second wife Phyllis. The cost for travel alone, exclusive of hotels, was $6,437.83 (over $100,000 today); on every ship they had the best cabins and on every train their compartments were 'luxe'. This extravagant trip was paid for proportionally, but the wealthy Warburgs may indeed have footed most bills in exchange for daily psychoanalytic sessions. However payments were arranged, Gregory could not have left his practice for six weeks without his patients' financial support, and in 1936 these patients felt they could not travel freely for an extended period without his psychoanalytic care.

The five travellers spent their first 12 days at sea, celebrating Thanksgiving off the coast of Brazil with a sumptuous dinner that included beluga caviar, lobster Newburg, and the obligatory pumpkin pie. On 27 November they landed in Rio and two days later boarded an overnight train to Sao Paolo, then another train south to the port of Santos where, on 2 December, they boarded the *S.S. Augustus* for Uruguay. Two days later they departed from Montevideo by night steamer for Argentina and on 9 December they left Buenos Aires by plane for Santiago. Having crossed the continent by flying over the Andes, they made their way by train to Vina del Mar, but saw most of the western coast of South America from the sea. Departing on 12 December from Valparaiso, the *S.S. Santa Lucia* stopped at the Chilean ports of Chanaral and Antofagasta before calling at Mollendo, Callao, and Talara in Peru, Guayaquil in Ecuador, and Buenaventura in Columbia. On 22 December the group recapitulated Gregory and Eddie's experience of the previous year by passing through the Panama Canal and spent the next few days cruising the Caribbean, where they celebrated not only Christmas but Gregory's 46th birthday, before disembarking in Havana. On 27 December they boarded the *S.S. Florida* for Miami, where they finally set off for home on the 'Orange Blossom Special', the most luxurious train on the Eastern Seaboard. They arrived at New York's Penn Station on the afternoon of 29 December 1936.

After six weeks away, Gregory and Ray must have looked forward to seeing the children, to sleeping in their own beds and simply catching their breath after their spectacular whirlwind tour of South America. In their absence, James and Eugenia had spent a few weeks New York, where they had seen Greg and Nancy at the apartment. They even spent a weekend on the farm with the children and Miss Darroche but also Pauline Turkel. The visit gave James and Eugenia a vivid glimpse of Gregory's life: the busy office, the vivacious youngsters, the country estate whose expanse and bounty, even in winter, were impressive. By 29 December, however, James and Eugenia were back in Mexico, and Gregory and Ray spent the final days of 1936 readjusting to family life and the climate in the northern hemisphere.[14]

For the duration of the holiday Ray's depression had lifted, but Gregory began to suspect that a physical illness might be at least partly responsible for her emotional instability and consultations were arranged. Gregory did not share his suspicions with his wife and Ray apparently remained unaware of his worries, periodically sad and unsatisfied, especially when on her own, but content in her role as her husband's wife in social situations, pleased when he spent time with her, when he told her about his day, when they were in bed together at night, when they didn't argue about the children.[15]

The new year did not start well. While Gregory was ready to resume work with renewed energy, even before he returned to the office he received the distressing news that Feigenbaum, the *Quarterly's* editor-in-chief, had died suddenly from influenza on 2 January. Gregory was personally upset, but his friend's death also meant that immediate responsibility for the journal fell heavily on him and Gosselin. Marjorie Milde was expecting a baby and had left the office before Christmas, and the new secretary, Ruth Mattison, was much less experienced and younger, had graduated from Vassar College only the previous June, and while qualified, didn't yet know the ropes. Gregory had evidently found Miss Mattison through the Vassar careers office, thus sparking interest in his speaking at the college. By January a date had been arranged for the spring.

Gregory had not seen Sigerist since before he left for Europe and was eager to catch up. Reflecting on his own holiday, he wrote Sigerist with characteristic good humour and wit that he was 'back from South America where dictatorships prosper and bubonic plague or dysentery is still in the full bloom of vigorous youth'. He had been impressed with the dramatic Andes, but dismayed to find that 'the

Inca culture has been duly destroyed as all other Indian cultures'. In another indication that the trip had been a mixed experience, an escape from the daily round but less stimulating than he might have liked, he told Sigerist his camera had been kept busy but not his mind.[16]

Gregory also made time to tell James that he was back, head over heels in work, and distressed so many people had influenza. He wanted to know if his brother could find him an electric timer that could be set remotely – a typically blunt request for something material and specific. Having gotten to know James, Pauline also wrote, informing him that Gregory had been rushing every minute since returning from his 'wonderful trip' and wouldn't be pursuing his brother's recommendation of a new secretary because he had already hired someone. Gregory had plunged back into the professional life he had left in mid-November but with the added burden of needing to make up for his six weeks away.[17]

Two topics were particularly on his mind as he wrote papers and prepared articles for publication: suicide and the understanding of self and others. The context for both topics was simultaneously historical (with references to Aristarchus of Samos, Galileo, Herbert Spencer, Oliver Wendell Holmes, Freud, and Einstein) and contemporary (communism, revolution, and war were the immediate backdrop). In 'Considerations on Suicide, with Particular Reference to That of the Young', a long presentation for the Orthopsychiatric Association in New York on 18 February 1937, he discussed both the history of suicide among young people across cultures and the moral attitudes associated with interpreting their behaviour, presenting suicide as neither courageous nor cowardly nor even generally the result of mental illness, although 'common sense' might not deem suicide reasonable. The understanding of who we are, what we do, and why we do it – and of what shapes, limits, and even blocks that understanding historically, socially, theologically, and psychologically – was a topic he focused on throughout the spring in 'The Heritage of Ignorance', an article for the *Atlantic Monthly*. Gregory's writing was in full flower: elegant, wide-ranging, provocative, meticulously researched, and pointedly pertinent to his contemporaries. His consideration was not only intellectual and professional; these were matters with personal resonance as he reflected on his own life and psyche and on the self-knowledge he hoped to enable in his patients.

For his talk at Vassar, he prepared something less wide-ranging and addressed again the relationship of the mental and the organic under the title of 'The Psychological and Biological Aspects of the Freudian System'. This familiar topic ironically had immediate relevance when he received a worried phone call from Gershwin in mid-February. During a rehearsal in San Francisco, Gershwin had briefly blacked out; during the performance itself, his fingers had at least once struggled to find the right piano keys. Gregory advised him to consult a doctor for a thorough medical examination. Not having seen Gershwin professionally for over a year – nor even socially since he left New York over six months earlier – Gregory was in no position to diagnose much less treat psychological or physical problems from over 3,000 miles away. If no organic cause were discovered,

Gershwin should follow up with further psychoanalysis and Gregory gave him the name of his Berlin colleague Ernst Simmel, now settled in Los Angeles.

The spring was particularly busy. Gregory lectured in Baltimore in mid-March and managed most of a Sunday there with Sigerist. In mid-April he was in Poughkeepsie, New York, to give his Vassar talk, while at the end of the month he addressed the Association for the History of Medicine in Atlantic City. Meanwhile, the news from Europe went from bad to worse, and on 26 April, Franco's German and Italian allies bombed the city of Guernica in a strategic operation that killed hundreds of civilians. International outrage meant Spain was in the headlines for over a week, and Gregory impulsively decided on a brief visit to Mexico. He had no commitments to lecture until the annual meeting of the American Psychiatric Association in Pittsburgh in the middle of May and felt a sudden urge to get away, to see his brother and father, perhaps even to be in a Spanish-speaking country where no bombs were falling.

This third trip to Mexico, the first without patients, was fatiguing rather than restorative. Gregory barely had a chance to see his parents, though he spoke at some length with James and even spent an hour in Misrachi's gallery, where he bought a watercolour for 900 pesos ($4,000 today). Such a hasty visit offered little respite from his frantic schedule, and he returned to New York regretting particularly not having spent more time with his father. Perhaps he also regretted not spending more time with his own children, but he was present to give Nancy a Bedlington terrier for her fourth birthday. Bobo, as Nancy promptly denominated her, was probably chosen because the breed was reputedly good with children and relatively easy to care for. The servants would walk her, but Gregory had a soft spot for animals and liked the idea of a dog in the apartment, a guileless creature who would please his daughter and demand little from him apart from affection.[18]

While Gregory felt burdened and frustrated, his fretful brother was feeling used and useless, overtaxed at home and at work, imposed upon without being able to impose himself on his world. In contrast, whatever complaints Gregory made to friends and family, his tremendous energy, determination, imagination, and wit managed to carry him through each day, while his passion for social justice and commitment to his profession never wavered and his essential *joie de vivre* took pleasure in cameras and cows, reading and writing, jokes and generosity, conversation and contemplation. Never the most considerate of men and often egotistic even when kind, he was a good psychiatrist, a good psychoanalyst, and a good analyser of people and situations; even when he didn't seem to be listening or didn't like what he heard, he registered what others were saying, was deeply sensitive when it concerned himself, could strike out quickly in retaliation of actual or anticipated criticism, but his counsel was always well-considered and generally wise. He now took it upon himself to advise his brother.

Gregory's approach reveals how he must have responded to many of his patients. He tried diplomatically to help James see that much of his current difficulty was of his own making. He posed questions ('I wonder whether you realise …?') and couched his views carefully ('The impression I have is …', 'I don't feel in sympathy with …'), then moved on to logical analysis using everyday rather than psychoanalytic terminology before concluding with firmly suggested remedies and reassurance. As he well knew, he told James that when a man is overloaded with responsibilities, they are not always inevitable or necessary. Specifically, he felt James didn't need 'to tutorize' his children: It was foolish and inefficient, creating unnecessary psychological dependence while failing to awaken that curiosity which he saw as the only motivation for education and culture. He didn't think it right that his brother's office telephone buzzed the whole day with calls from home, so that even when he left home, he didn't actually leave it.

James had mentioned a 'nervous breakdown', but Gregory attempted to allay his fears: 'such a condition exists only in the mind of the layman' and was simply a common abstraction 'covering a multitude of sins'. By seeing everything in his life – not only his girls' academic achievement but even a cocktail party or housework – as a 'duty', James fooled himself into believing that everything depended on him, so it wasn't surprising he sometimes felt, whether or not he admitted it, in need of 'a good cry or a good drink'. Such a way of thinking was simply messing him up 'inside and outside'. Gregory urged James to take a few moments for himself, 'to walk out, sit under a tree, light a cigarette and get lost in wondering what would happen … if Hitler were the Duke of Windsor and if the Duke of Windsor were Stalin'. Such musing wouldn't change the world of course, but the reverie would relax him and make him feel better. As for the rent, one of his brother's many worries, Gregory reassured him this was merely a practical matter and never in question: He would immediately, as previously, send a cheque for $200.[19]

As his brother's worries indicated and as Gregory was reminded every time he picked up a newspaper, one thing could so easily lead to another on life's grand and smaller stages. To avoid a constitutional crisis, Edward VIII had abdicated the previous December for the woman he loved and, as the Duke of Windsor, married the twice-divorced American Wallis Simpson in France in June. In early July, at Lugou Bridge southwest of Beijing, tensions between China and Japan escalated into a battle whose impact on world peace would not have gone unnoticed by Gregory, who could remember the Russo-Japanese war that had triggered the 1905 revolution. Then, on the front page of the *New York Times* on 12 July 1937, a headline announced, 'George Gershwin, Composer, Is Dead'. The lengthy obituary was subtitled 'Master of Jazz Music Dies in Hollywood at 38 After Operation for Brain Tumor'. Gregory's first response was undoubtedly shock as well as sadness.[20]

Gershwin had followed Gregory's advice to seek medical attention, but the physicians who had examined him in February and March had found nothing physically wrong. When his symptoms didn't improve, on 9 June he had finally consulted Simmel, who referred him to an internist, who recommended a neurologist. Tests at Cedars of Lebanon Hospital in Los Angeles a fortnight later were inconclusive, and the doctors decided his symptoms must be psychosomatic. After leaving the hospital on 26 June, his health had deteriorated dramatically. On 9 July he had fallen into a coma and been rushed to hospital, where a lumbar puncture indicated a brain tumour. Despite immediate surgery, he never regained consciousness.[21]

As a responsible psychoanalyst Simmel had in all likelihood telephoned Gregory before meeting with Gershwin; as a professional courtesy, he had probably also, by telephone or letter, reported his opinion after the consultation. It is conceivable that some of Gershwin's symptoms during the time of his analysis might have been partly attributable to the tumour, and certainly Gregory – who had lectured on the connections between the mental and the organic in psychiatry throughout the period of Gershwin's treatment – would have reflected on what might have been done differently or in addition to their psychoanalytic sessions, but sad as he was at the death of a man whom by 1937 he counted as a friend as well as a former patient, Gregory was not one to dwell on 'what ifs' in history or in medicine. Members of Gershwin's family and biographers would later blame Gregory, but that was inevitable, as he had pointed out to his brother when declining to support Basia's clinic.

Gershwin's songs now dominated the airwaves. New York stations broadcast everything from the sunny 'I Got Rhythm' to the bittersweet 'But Not for Me'; even classical WQXR was playing 'An American in Paris' and 'Rhapsody in Blue'. On Thursday 15 July Gershwin's body arrived in New York for a funeral at Temple Emanu-El, a 12-minute walk down Fifth Avenue from his former psychoanalyst's office. It seems likely that Gregory was one of the nearly 3,000 people who jammed the enormous synagogue to pay homage. Listening to the heavily throated incantation of Hebrew prayers familiar from childhood, he could not have failed to reflect on the arc of life – Gershwin's, anyone's, his own – but he had living patients to see and work inevitably waiting for him at his desk.

Notes

1 GZ to Karl Menninger, 6 April 1937, Faulkner and Pruitt, 239–240.
2 Schlemowitz, 59, 70, and email, 8 August 2018; Debroise *et al.*, 178; GZ, 'Suicide', 1352–1353; David Alfaro Siqueiros, 'Artist's Questionnaire' (1970) and loan files, 'Fantastic Art', Museum of Modern Art, New York, where 'Collective Suicide' is on permanent display; 'Portrait of George Gershwin in a Concert Hall', Blanton Museum of Art, Austin, Texas; 'Cosmos and Disaster', Tate Museum; 'The End of the World', Harvard Art Museums, Cambridge, Massachusetts.
3 GZ to JZ, 4 February 1936; loan files, 'Fantastic Art', Museum of Modern Art.
4 GZ to JZ, 4, 18 February 1936.
5 GZ to HES, 25 March, 8 April 1936; HES to GZ, 30 April 1936.
6 Marshall Field to GZ, 7 April 1936; GZ to Field, 8 April 1936, both GZB.
7 GZ to JZ, 12 May 1936; JZ to GZ 28 May 1936; Alfred A. Knopf to GZ, 25 March 1936, and GZ to Knopf, 27 March 1936, both GZB; HES to GZ, 15 May 1936.
8 GZ to JZ, 5 August 1936.
9 GZ to George Gershwin, 9 September 1936, George and Ira Gershwin Collection, Library of Congress, Washington, D.C.
10 JZ to GZ, 5, 15 September 1936; GZ to JZ, 9, 30 September 1936.
11 Email from AZ, 18 August 1918.
12 GZ to HES, 14 October 1936.

13 'Psychiatrist Sees Collapse of Democracy in Next War', *Richmond Times-Dispatch*, 11 November 1936, np.
14 GZ to JZ, 2 November 1936; JZ to GZ, 31 December 1936.
15 GZ to JZ, 27 October 1938.
16 GZ to HES, 5 January 1937.
17 GZ to JZ, 5 January 1937; Pauline Turkel to JZ, 4, 5 January 1937, JEZB.
18 GZ to JZ, 5 May 1937; email from AZ, 17 August 2018.
19 GZ to JZ, 23 June 1937.
20 *New York Times*, 12 July 1937, 1, 17.
21 Pollack, 211–213.

Chapter 13

'World affairs'

1937–1939

In the late 1930s Gregory realised that his life lacked coherence. He was pulled hither and yon by various projects, by lectures not only in New York but in Boston and Baltimore, Washington and Chicago, by his family not only at home but in Mexico. Music and theatre and visual art tugged him out of the apartment into the social whirl of the bustling city, while his farm pulled him into the countryside, where he longed to spend more time with his cows and in his darkroom. Solitude was hard to come by in his busy office, while writing required not only solitude but quiet as well as peace, and peace was a rare commodity in a world hurtling towards war.

The remedies in his daily life were more and more clearly inadequate. Silence at Friends' meetings did not stimulate his active mind or calm his uneasy spirit. His short temper was not improved by his patients, many of whom continued to drink too much and wanted him to solve practical problems in their economically comfortable lives, and he grew increasingly impatient with his brother, who was a less and less satisfactory confidante. Reading the news only further depressed his flagging spirits, while getting away didn't change the world at large nor the one he returned to where correspondence piled up on his desk in his absence. Gregory began to consider re-entering analysis – the psychoanalyst's first response to an analyst in psychic distress was to prescribe more analysis; he now started to think of prescribing it for himself.

In September 1937, three months after Gregory had suggested that his brother imagine Hitler as the Duke of Windsor, James declared with wry humour that he was amused at the comparison with Gregory's own life: What was Gregory doing if not attempting to do the work of a dozen men? Wasn't he trying to be a doctor, scholar, writer, farmer, and photographer as well? The wear-and-tear was terrific and not at all surprising. James did not, however, propose a remedy. Natalie, now settled at Oakwood, a Quaker boarding school in Poughkeepsie probably chosen at Gregory's suggestion, had spent a few days with Gregory and Ray en route, and James was grateful, but his letter quickly descended into a typical litany of family doings and woes. Basia was ill again. Although James did not quite see how it would be possible, Moses was anxious make a trip to the United States, to visit relatives in New York and elsewhere, to see Gregory, to look at a different and

DOI: 10.4324/9781003190936-13

larger world. 'The old man' was getting on in years, 'becoming softer and ever wiser', but he was 'pretty much alone in his surroundings of wailing women'. James could only find the situation sad.[1]

Gregory had no solution for either Basia or Moses and didn't feel he could visit Mexico. He had taken no holiday over the summer but now decided to stay home throughout the coming winter to attend to his writing: The history still awaited him, and he had essays to finish as well as a book he was considering on suicide. He confessed to Sigerist in October that his mood had 'not been of the best'; the 'utterly depressing turn of events in "world affairs"' made him 'relive a number of apprehensions'. The Nationalists were advancing in northern Spain while in Germany it had become illegal to employ Jews. It is impossible to underestimate the impact of such news on Gregory's psychic life. He informed Sigerist that although his photography was progressing, 'the course of the Loyalist's cause puts a damper on it.' He was disgusted at having to treat so many people whose priorities in life seemed to be financial, but the source of his melancholy was not only world events and materialistic patients. Without revealing specifics of which he himself was possibly unaware, he simply told Sigerist, 'My fortunes, in some respects, have turned on me, and this adds a hue of unhappiness to the already existing depressive mood. Perhaps it is only Weltschmerz, but it is rather painful.'[2]

During autumn 1937 and well into the following year Gregory's attitude towards his work and the topics he chose to speak and write about were shaped by his depression, by his deeply emotional response to 'world affairs' and the daily life that failed to offer the consolation he needed. At the end of November, he chose to address the New York Psychoanalytic Society on 'The Sense of Immortality', but what he talked about was fear. Drawing on his own experience, he mentioned having been unafraid in two automobile accidents at the moment the cars collided, had felt no fear when he witnessed battles in the streets during the revolution or in the trenches. Rather, he contended, one feels in such situations calm and serenity – until one sees someone fall; then anxiety mounts. Considering an invitation to present a paper at the 1938 congress of the International Society for the History of Medicine to be held in Yugoslavia, he hoped Sigerist would also attend; if he weren't going to be there, Gregory told his friend, he would feel lost.[3]

Aware of his vulnerabilities, Gregory also chose to speak on topics that avoided both direct autobiographical reference and current international instability. In December he addressed the Boston Psychoanalytic Society on 'Some Observations on the Transformation of Instincts'. Despite his liberal social conscience and abhorrence of misogyny, he was a man of his era working within a Freudian framework. Here he returned to the relatively safe territory of the clinical case study. Among the patients he described was a sexually frustrated woman able to have 'clitoral' but not 'vaginal' orgasms. Her floods of tears after intercourse and in analytic sessions suggested to him her desire to urinate like a man. He considered her 'frigid' even though she climaxed during 'her own manual masturbation or by the friction of her husband's penis against her clitoris' and argued that her tears apparently 'took the place of a neurotic, symbolic, substitutive, masculine orgasm'. Such tears seemed finally the behaviour of 'a child who has not had enough sucking' and thus an 'infantile' rather than a 'masculine' protest. Building on and modifying Freudian theory, in this paper Gregory paralleled the penis with the breast and food with faeces as well as oral with anal eroticism while adding to narcissism and the castration complex the trauma of weaning. Such a theoretical focus on what he understood as female experience allowed him to sidestep world affairs and his own life very neatly – unless, of course, in focusing on a woman's sexual frustrations he was consciously or unconsciously attempting to address his wife's continuing unhappiness and her sense – as well as his – of her inadequacy.[4]

The Christmas period wasn't particularly festive. Sixteen-year-old Natalie joined the family over the fortnight and Gregory was keenly aware of the additional responsibility: A niece he didn't know well was completely different from his own young progeny consigned to a governess. Ray might or might not take her shopping or to a Broadway matinée, but he had little idea what to do with a teenager, no idea how to be a good uncle. Apparently using his work as a buffer between himself and his family, he spent 27 December with Sigerist in Baltimore en route to a meeting in Washington.[5]

Natalie's return to Oakwood in January must have relieved him slightly, but Gregory recognised that he needed to address his emotional fragility and re-entered psychoanalysis. It was, however, neither in his character nor financially possible for him to have anything less than a full schedule. Some of his patients had moved on – Moss Hart, who at Gregory's recommendation had continued analysis with Simmel when he moved to Hollywood in 1936, on his return to New York in 1937 had entered analysis with Lawrence Kubie, likely also at Gregory's suggestion. Gregory may have felt that Kubie was a better analyst for Hart at this point or simply not have had a free hour. Gregory was certainly unable to accept everyone who wanted to work with him, but early in 1938 he agreed to treat the independently wealthy journalist Ralph Ingersoll.[6]

In his autobiography, Ingersoll is overwhelmingly affirmative about his experience of psychoanalysis. Despite success in the world of New York newspapers, he sought help because in his relationships with women he was 'a mess'. Recently divorced, his current relationship with the writer Laura Z. Hobson was fraught. She was in an apparently successful analysis with Kubie, and when Ingersoll decided to seek analysis, Kubie recommended a number of colleagues. Ingersoll selected Gregory because his address was close to his own. Ingersoll's charming simplicity often lacked understanding or even responsibility, but allowed him to cut to the chase: If he committed himself to seeing a psychoanalyst five times a week, it would be easier if he didn't have far to go. His vivid account of his analysis offers a privileged glimpse into Gregory's approach to treatment.

Initially the two men discussed why Ingersoll was seeking psychoanalysis and what he expected to gain from it. Ingersoll was a heavy drinker and, like many of Gregory's patients, suffered from frequent headaches and chronic indigestion in response to stress. Ingersoll felt encouraged and affirmed from the start. Like many people he noticed Gregory's European moustache and long black hair, but it was Gregory's extraordinarily expressive dark eyes that dominated the encounter, and he found them 'at once warm and intense'. At the end of their second session, Gregory finally told the undisciplined journalist that he was 'very ill', but a good candidate for analysis because he reacted positively to life and was extremely curious, energetic, and driven.

Ingersoll was not put off by being told that he was even sicker than he thought. He saw Gregory as 'a truly exceptionally able professional' and came to have 'complete confidence' in his judgement and trusted he would exercise it in Ingersoll's best interest 'as a human being'. The analysis, which cost Ingersoll $20 per hour, was quite traditional: He would enter the treatment room, lie down on the couch, and free associate. The sessions were often anguished; sometimes Gregory would speak, although occasionally he would say nothing at all. Ingersoll – who saw Gregory as 'a very level-headed advisor', a 'wise and loving man' trying to 'save' him – would find the experience deeply moving and helpful. Gregory didn't always sit out of sight behind the couch but sometimes across from Ingersoll at his desk in order to speak with him as a psychiatrist. Feeling that Ingersoll couldn't raise money for a newspaper of his own, Gregory at one point advised him to abandon the idea and stick with his present job rather than commit a kind of professional suicide with complex emotional elements. While at first their relationship was formal, by the time the analysis concluded five years later, Ingersoll would feel they were not only doctor and patient but friends. Reflecting on his psychoanalysis in the late 1960s, Ingersoll would declare that from no other experience in his life had he benefitted so much.[7]

Gregory wrote articles, delivered papers, and treated patients effectively in 1938, but his undulant depression continued. It was less a neurotic sadness than a normal reaction to the state of the world, overwork, and an unfulfilling marriage, and in retrospect he understood his psychological state as the result of a spiritual crisis. He had been concerned about his spiritual life even as a young man in Russia, where the Russian word he often used in his early letters that can be translated as 'spirit' or 'spiritual' means more than the English conveys. In the context of late nineteenth- and early twentieth-century Russian culture, one's spiritual sense had to do with identity; it encouraged individual awareness, artistic refinement, and conscience. A spiritually healthy man led a carefully examined moral and cultural life; he held himself responsible for the quality of social and intellectual life around him. This powerful and affective concept of spirit was a strong element in Gregory's sense of moral and social duty and the basis for his revolutionary activity. It also contributed both to his valorising the individual and to his commitment to medicine and specifically psychiatry and psychoanalysis.[8]

Gregory was examining his moral and cultural life carefully in 1938 at the same time that he was keenly aware he had little control over general social and intellectual life around him. In an attempt to come to terms with his emotional state, he read widely not only newspapers and contemporary psychoanalytic material but history, fiction, philosophy, and the Bible. In a related attempt to address human social and intellectual life more generally, he wrote essays, reviewed books, and presented papers to various audiences. For his own anxiety and depression, however, psychoanalysis would not by itself be sufficient; inasmuch as his difficulties were spiritual, they would require a spiritual solution.

Reviewing Mortimer Adler's *What Man Has Made of Man* for *Psychoanalytic Quarterly* early in the year, he criticised the author as much for his spiritual flaccidity as for his lack of historical understanding, sociological naïveté, and limited comprehension of psychoanalysis. Like Adler, Gregory admired Thomas Aquinas, but he didn't consider him out of context nor admire him to the exclusion of other philosophers. Gregory argued that Adler was a typical critic of psychoanalysis: He erroneously believed in 'free will and autonomous reason', asserting that together they worked for the good of humankind and the world, made humans the crown of creation, and brought people 'ever closer' to their God. Gregory pointed out the foolishness of this position: Since the 'good' is necessarily 'postulative in nature', such trust in will and reason led as easily to communism and fascism as to benevolent religion. In his view, 'Man is human not because he is not a "brute animal" (he is one) but by virtue of his ability to be one self-consciously.' Adler also erred when he equated health and happiness, and writing personally Gregory paraphrased Freud: Psychoanalysis may relieve people of their symptoms, but it leaves them with the unhappiness which is the human lot. The unhappiness Gregory felt wouldn't be relieved by psychoanalytic self-consciousness.[9]

In 'Loneliness', which appeared in the *Atlantic Monthly* in January 1938, Gregory attempted to explain an unhappy phenomenon. Here his context was literature rather than philosophy and history, but his point of view remained psychoanalytic. Citing Tolstoy and Sinclair Lewis's *Babbitt*, *Robinson Crusoe*, Dostoyevsky, and Strindberg, he anchored loneliness in the 'deeply seated psychological triad' of narcissism, megalomania, and hostility. Like a headache, which might be serious – perhaps indicative of early pneumonia or a brain tumour – loneliness could be a mild headache or 'a psychological typhoid fever'. Wiser than Adler with his misplaced confidence in reason, he observed that emotional knowledge precedes rational knowledge and reason often serves emotions rather than the other way around; loneliness wasn't often logical but a result of 'too severe an arrest of emotional development'. Gregory sidestepped treatment – offering a cure for loneliness was beyond the scope of his article, a matter of psychoanalytic work with an individual patient. He didn't say that a cure for some sorts of loneliness, for a *Weltschmerz* whose source probably had little to do with arrested development, might be a matter for a priest, yet he was beginning to wonder in his own case if this might not be so.[10]

All in early 1938 was not doom and gloom, however, and photography could lift Gregory's spirits as could moments with Sigerist, who joined him in the country for an entire weekend in late January. Gregory had taught Sigerist a great deal about photography; Sigerist in turn had taught Gregory about cooking. By now they were partners in each other's kitchens: In Baltimore, Sigerist was the chef and Gregory the kitchen maid; on Sigerist's visits to New York, the roles were reversed. Following his friend's example, Gregory recorded his favourite recipes in a notebook, among them 'Scallops à la Henry' and Sigerist's 'Chicken à la Portugaise,' while he had contributed pirog, borscht, and 'Boeuf à la Stroganoff' to Sigerist's repertoire. *Weltschmerz* put to one side, they cooked together throughout the late 1930s with joy and laughter, conversing about 'any theme from cabbages to kings' while frequently tasting and exclaiming 'This is fun!' and sometimes even 'This is superb!'[11]

Nevertheless, playful moments were rare. During hectic days that offered Gregory little time to reflect, his energy went increasingly into his writing. In Chicago in February he addressed the annual meeting of the American Orthopsychiatric Association on the 'Overestimation of Psychopathology'. Surprised when they saw analysed individuals 'really angry or truly sad', some people concluded that they had been incompletely analysed because they were not better 'adjusted'; others decided these feelings indicated psychoanalysis was worthless. However, such people endowed psychoanalysis with miraculous powers: 'It is the return of the repressed demand for the Kingdom of Heaven to be inaugurated forthwith and here on earth.' Gregory rejected out of hand the idea that the socially well-adjusted person is in tune with society and by extension 'a glorified, serene Babbitt' – such a concept of mental health contained the very 'dis-individualized submissiveness' he argued we should be fighting against. Our narcissism, he suggested, causes us to overestimate the tools we have invented; we become angry and resentful when they aren't perfect solutions to our problems and blame them rather than ourselves. This paper is concerned with history, with Freud, Jung, and Adler as well as Machiavelli, Hobbes, Mussolini, and Hitler, but it is also transparently about Gregory himself as he struggled to understand and take responsibility for his real anger and true sadness.[12]

By March Gregory began to wonder if he were physically ill. He had definitely not felt well since Christmas. Having recently consulted a physician about a subnormal temperature, he had 'certain ideas about the nature of the condition' but avoided specifics when telling James there wasn't apparently a remedy: It would either pass or get worse. 'Naturally', he pointed out, 'this does not add much to the gayety of nations'. As to the nations themselves, 'they contribute even less to the gayety of things.' Whatever may have been physically wrong, when Hitler invaded Austria on 12 March 1938, the psychological impact was immediate.[13]

Gregory's response went beyond concern for Austria's Jews or even specific worry for Freud and his family in Vienna; it went beyond distress at the Nazi menace of Europe and the grim understanding that war was now probably inevitable. Gregory reacted to the Anschluss as if he had witnessed one person falling: It was a personally shattering event inducing what today would be termed post-traumatic stress. For more than a fortnight he felt so vulnerable he was unable even to write to Sigerist, a fellow European with whom he usually shared his views of current events. At the end of March, he explained his silence: Since 'the Hitler Austrian démarche', he had been 'in the same mood as on the day of the Pogroms in 1905 in Russia'. Images from his personal experience were revived with such acuteness that he felt as if he were 'always in the presence of a final débâcle'. He briefly digressed to the practical matter of fundraising for Sigerist's new American Association for the History of Medicine, for which he had just secured a pledge for $1,000 ($18,000 today) from Eddie Warburg, but he needed to work through his anxieties, felt disengaged from ordinary life and emotionally overwhelmed. 'Somehow', he told his friend, 'I feel that I need to have a talk with you; the disturbing developments of the past three weeks are a bit too much in an atmosphere of bourgeois contentment, which is characteristic of the populace.'[14]

Indeed, his sense of isolated impotence in the face of what as a revolutionary socialist he saw as a deluded bourgeoisie disturbed him almost as much as the threat of war. He would need to marshal his composure to respond calmly to his brother's current worries. What concerned James that spring was neither Gregory's physical heath nor the state of the world but paying the rent and the Mexican economy. In mid-March President Lazaro Cardenas had nationalised Mexico's oil industry by expropriating all foreign oil assets, a move that satisfied Mexican workers but provoked international trade difficulties. James conceded that Gregory had been in worse situations and thus would perhaps regard the falling peso with greater poise than James could muster, but he was feeling desperate. Resentful of his dependence on his brother, he even wrote Pauline, who had recently spent a holiday in Mexico. Complaining that he had already had to move house three times for financial reasons, he asked if she thought Gregory had changed his mind about splitting the rent with him.

Gregory, who was feeling at least physically better, finally responded to James in early April. With great patience he admitted that events Mexico were interesting and important – his way of beginning a disquisition when he wanted to dismiss someone's argument – but indicated he didn't share his brother's pessimism. As a psychiatrist, Gregory pointed out that anxieties always run ahead of actual events, but politically he thought Mexico would benefit from anti-capitalist policies and didn't restrain himself from giving James a harsh dose of his socialist thinking: In their treatment of 'backward' countries, 'civilized' nations acted as if they had 'an irrevocable diploma for economic wisdom and superiority'. The sooner this diploma was taken away from them, the better for everybody. Those who, like James and Gregory, were privileged through no particular merit of their own might become poorer as well as less secure and 'cocky' as a result, but Gregory felt they deserved the comedown and would be better for it in the long run. Predictably, such philosophical thinking would fail to comfort his anxious brother.[15]

Natalie joined the family in New York over her Easter holiday. Having turned 17 in January, she was eager to spend time with friends in the big city. It was just as well that she was an independent and responsible young person, for neither Ray nor Gregory was willing or able to spend time with her. A contretemps inevitably occurred when she stayed out one night until three in the morning. The honest and only slightly defensive account she gave to her father offers a glimpse of a household in which everyone apparently led separate lives. The children played in their nursery when not at school. Ray was out all day and Gregory never said more than ten consecutive words to her. Her aunt and uncle were 'nice' but didn't seem to care what she did, so Natalie had used 'Grisha's place' more or less as 'a parking station'. When she told her aunt that she was going to a party and wouldn't be back till late, Ray had evinced no interest in the details, had simply given her a key to the apartment. Feeling the heavy responsibility as the minutes after midnight ticked by, Gregory had taken the matter more seriously. Probably aware of having shirked their duty not only to their niece but to her parents, he and Ray had stayed awake until they heard Natalie return.

The fallout occurred the following morning. Ray told Natalie that she had done the wrong thing, as if staying out late were a social faux pas that might be acceptable in Mexico but simply, Ray had said, 'wasn't done' in New York. Gregory, however, who in anger often lost control of linguistic register, had gotten on his high horse and written Natalie a note in arch language incommensurate with the offence: He objected to her indulging in 'this manner of living' and called her behaviour 'disorderly and unpardonable'. He finally set down rules: She was to be home and in bed by ten each night, keep her room tidy, and turn out her light when absent. Trying for the correct level of both authority and diction, he explained that the issue was responsibility and 'grown-upness'; staying out till three in the morning did not make a person grown up but 'taking care of your own things does'. He signed the note pompously 'Gregory Zilboorg'.

Natalie was mortified, but nothing more was said or written and nothing changed in her aunt and uncle's treatment of her. As he was wont to do, Gregory had lost his temper and expressed himself as judge and rule-maker, but having done so, as far as he was concerned, the case was closed. He probably didn't reflect on the psychology behind his initial failure to set limits or on the effect of his harsh scolding on a sensitive youngster. He had made his own way against the old order in Europe, had developed independently the socialist principles and high moral standards according to which he tried to lead his life. None of his experiences had prepared him for being a good parent.[16]

Gregory didn't mention Natalie when he next wrote her fretful father, with whom he was now growing annoyed. Concerned by his brother's gloom and sense of panic, by what he considered neurotic anxiety, he wanted to be supportive, yet hoped James would not take it 'amiss' if he shared what was on his mind. He reminded his brother that they had specifically discussed the instability of employment in a volatile country when evaluating the risks involved in purchasing a property. He then recapitulated his socialist views, gearing up to a typically eloquent exposition: 'foreigners from North of the Rio Grande' had entered Mexico 'in a spirit of superior colonizers'; knowing how to handle drills and screwdrivers and turbines, they felt 'more deserving'. Their standard of living was higher than that of their native colleagues, even higher than that of colleagues back home. James belonged to 'a privileged class in an unprivileged country', paying out in pesos to live 'on a dollar standard'. Living in an ex-pat community with its own schools, clubs, and American imports, James had remained an exploitative invader. He had been taught from childhood to be a revolutionary and

Gregory now urged him to stop complaining and 'take it on the chin'. If James believed in his principles, he should live and work in Mexico on its terms; if not, he should pack up and return to whatever job he could find in the United States. Shouting 'Hélas Revolution! Hélas débâcle!' was ridiculous. Irritated that James apparently hadn't noticed that the world was disintegrating until the peso began to fall, Gregory accused him of having stifled his spirit of enterprise and adventure with petty bourgeois anxiety and pseudo-liberal bigotry. What he wanted from his brother was friendship and intellectual exchange, not complaints.

Despite Gregory's sincere expression of concern and effort at diplomacy, James was peeved by the lecture and had little patience for theory while struggling with hard economic facts. Affirming the warm relationship Gregory had managed to establish between the two men, he nevertheless insisted defensively that Gregory had misinterpreted what were simply 'gloomy reflections'.[17]

As the trees came into leaf in Central Park, Gregory recovered from his lingering physical illness but remained particularly emotionally sensitive. When Nancy's Bobo produced puppies, he was delighted; when the highly strung Bedlington killed them, he was devastated and could not tolerate keeping the dog. Burdened by work he had to catch up with, he reluctantly cancelled his attendance at the meeting of the American Association for the History of Medicine in early May, but there were commitments he felt unable to refuse, topics on which he felt compelled to speak out. International events having brought back past traumatic experiences, he was reacting very personally to much that occurred not only on the world stage but in his daily life. This state of mind contributed to his overreaction to Natalie's behaviour and his exasperation with his brother's pessimism; it also influenced the subjects he chose for presentations, the essays he chose to write, and the groups he agreed to address.[18]

On 11 May Gregory spoke at New York's Biltmore Hotel during an awards dinner for the National Institute of Immigrant Welfare. The honours this year went to the Serbian-American electrical scientist Nikola Tesla; the Austrian-American lawyer Felix Frankfurter, a professor at Harvard Law School who would become a justice on the U.S. Supreme Court; and the Italian-American Metropolitan Opera tenor Giovanni Martinelli. Gregory chose as his topic 'The Vicissitude of the Intellectual Immigrant of Today'. Although he didn't speak in the first person about individual difficulties, this is transparently the most personal of all his work. He spoke of the psychic trauma of integration to people of achievement from his own position of achievement, addressing them as an accomplished psychoanalyst who had become American in many ostensible ways, but whose experience of leaving home for a new life had shaped him permanently, made him acutely and defensively aware of difference, isolation, and otherness.

After movingly describing the psychological impact of the new country, the crushing of unreasonable hopes and the enduring sense of loss, he talked about standards and vulnerability. His accent alone would have revealed to his sympathetic audience how much he was still at some level foreign, an outsider who needed to hold himself to particularly high ethical criteria because he could never forget any more than his listeners could the instability of his identity. If it was important for Americans in general to be virtuous, it was even more important for the intellectual immigrant, just as every member of any marginalised and disenfranchised group needs to work harder for acceptance than those entitled by birth. Thus Gregory pointed out,

> it must be borne in mind that the psychiatrist like any other physician can ill afford to make mistakes. A misconstruction in the psychological evaluation of a man's behavior, like a mistake in physical diagnosis, may and most frequently does prove injurious to the patient as well as to the physician. Hence the medical man is thoroughly aware of the need for intellectual honesty and psychological accuracy.

Gregory's speech was a tour-de-force whose brilliant use of language offered his listeners impressive evidence of his own apparent assimilation. Nevertheless, a 'double allegiance', however harmoniously synthesised, was an essential element of immigrant psychology, the longing for 'home' that could only be assuaged, although never eliminated, by integration into the new country, 'the new family'. Without such psychic integration, Gregory contended, the immigrant would struggle with antagonism and suspicion, lack of mutual understanding and psychological reciprocity, and a spiritual separation – exactly the difficulties with which Gregory continued to contend during these pre-war years.[19]

Two years earlier, trying to convince his brother to accept the contribution towards his rent, he had insisted fate had always smiled on him. With the reality of his early experiences on his mind, Gregory now tried to get their relationship back on an even keel by being direct. He reminded James that he knew what it was to feel insecure: Not so very long ago he had been 'starving in the streets of Petrograd' and having his teeth fall out, facing death 'on the barricades in Petrograd, in the trenches of the Dvinsk front', starving in Vienna and feeling insecure in New York. Yet during all those 'long stretches of great discomfort' he had 'never failed to welcome true revolutionary changes in this world'. If James had expressed his 'gloomy reflections' in purely personal terms, he explained, he would have had had only 'friendly understanding feelings about it', but he had been disturbed by his brother's 'social rationalization'. Gregory's limited sympathy did little to smooth his brother's ruffled feathers.[20]

At the end of May, James turned again to Pauline. Gregory's kindness and generosity had seemed so strange and sudden to him, he had been unable to respond properly. Although always uncomfortable with 'material attentions', James had sensed real affection. After a good deal of persuasion, he had caved in, something he now bitterly regretted. Nonplussed, Pauline tried to explain one brother to the other. She told him that Gregory was probably as fond of James as he was of anyone. He liked to give when moved, although if he suspected that money or deeds were expected of him, he was irked. Impressively adaptable in any situation, he was surprised at others' inflexibility. James was somewhat appeased by her words and the cheques that continued to arrive, but her impression that Gregory was incapable of being fonder of anyone than he was of James certainly must have given him pause, must have made him wonder about Gregory's capacity for love.[21]

In early June Gregory attended professional meetings in Los Angeles and San Francisco, leaving Ray and Pauline to attend Natalie's graduation from Oakwood and James to cope with the instability of Mexican life. In addition to his disappointment in the falling peso, Basia's marriage hadn't proved the success everyone had counted on. With Nadia due home after her first year at the University of Texas, where she had without irony anglicised her name to 'Hope', Basia had moved back in with her parents, who with mixed feelings accepted the reconstitution of a home life that once again included their oldest daughter and granddaughter.

During the mildly restorative fortnight in California Gregory saw colleagues, some of whom had become friends, among them the psychiatrist Portia Bell Hume, whose husband Sam Hume had served with Gregory on the Chautauqua Drama Board in the early 1920s. Once again, however, Gregory took no real holiday over the summer. With the family in Pound Ridge, he had the weeks to himself and tried to get away to the farm at the weekends. He left the oversight of a move to a larger apartment at 885 Park Avenue to the servants and, in an effort to avoid the inevitable chaos, probably spent nights as well as days at his office.

As Germany escalated its claims on the Sudetenland, Gregory's article 'Propaganda from Within' appeared in the July issue of *The Annals of the American Academy of Political and Social Science*. His good sense, wisdom, wide reading, psychiatric principles, and trenchant humour informed his explanation of propaganda for an audience made up neither of general readers nor his medical peers but politicians and social scientists. In discussing 'how salesmanship works', he cited Rousseau in repeating his classic contention that people always feel first and think afterwards even if they seldom own up to it, aware of what they think but not always of what they feel. Propaganda appeals not only to this human 'passivity' but to human aggression. Offering the example of a boxing match, Gregory analysed the psychological dynamics of fighters who warm up, become 'on edge', strike the first blow followed by retaliative blows in a combination of fear and hatred. Spectators follow the same emotional pattern as they watch the game 'fought on a very earnest primitive level of mutilation and murder'. Peace, Gregory argued, depends on such 'safety valves', on 'civilised' expressions of hatred in political campaigns, in violent sports and vicarious participation in crimes as well as in 'that form of public revenge which is known as criminal justice'. In regimented and uniform states, however, where individual citizens are subjugated and have few 'normal' outlets, their aggression is directed either against the states in revolution or outward in war. In Germany, Italy, and Russia, war propaganda was thus effective because of their citizens' suppressed aggression. It was important for him that his perceptive analysis reach this journal's audience; he was writing to try to make a difference.

Gregory returned to more traditional psychiatric ground, however, when at the end of August he contributed 'Some Aspects of Suicide' to a panel presentation at Saint Elizabeth's Hospital in Washington. Having presented his talk, he refused with characteristic cleverness and eloquent humour to go as far as Karl Menninger, the director of the private Menninger Clinic in Topeka, Kansas, who had spoken of all illnesses as full or partial suicides. Indeed, Gregory found it rather remarkable that this conception should appear in the mind of a midwesterner, while

> I who am a Russian – and the traditional Russian is bent on destruction – should come out with the cheerful and altogether American idea that to attribute all forms of illness to suicidal drives is too Russian for me even though I were in Kansas.

His audience must have laughed, but in poking fun at his friend Menninger, Gregory significantly declared himself 'a Russian', albeit one with American ideas. However playful, he was well aware that his identity remained anchored in the vicissitude of 'doubleness'.[22]

As Chamberlain headed for Munich in September in an effort to appease Hitler and avoid the inevitable, Nancy and Greg, now five and a half and almost seven, headed back to Dalton, their progressive private school. In Mexico Basia's divorce became official while Gregory's widely ranging mind took on yet another topic, attempted to define if not resolve another conflict. He addressed the New York Neurological Society on 'Misconceptions of Legal Insanity', examining with engaging precision important differences between medicine and law. In a dense historical discussion, he explained that 'legal insanity' is a product of the judiciary and not of medicine, which doesn't concern itself with the 'ethico-legal' aspects of a phenomenon. Law and psychiatry were thus often diametrically opposed: 'Justice must be done' was understood by the psychiatrist as 'ill or well', the criminal must be punished, while the psychiatrist's 'Treat, do not beat the ill' was interpreted by the jurist as 'guilty or not', the criminal must be treated. Gregory went further than merely describing the 'misconceptions' and insisted the psychiatrist had a moral obligation to confront the fundamental 'duality' as 'scientifically untenable and sociologically unreasonable'. The incongruity might appear to be the fault of the law, but it was up to the psychiatrist to reject the 'antiquated speculations' offered by embattled lawyers by bringing to the witness stand the objective clinical standards of the profession.[23]

Chamberlain's declaration of having achieved 'Peace for our time' rang hollow for Gregory as Czech refugees from the Sudetenland fled eastward. Doubtful that war could be negotiated away, throughout the autumn he continued to think about the nature of suicide, the workings of propaganda, the challenges of the law, and the significance of the individual. In early October he addressed the Southern Psychiatric Association in Atlanta on 'Ambulatory Schizophrenias', a term he had coined at Bloomingdale to refer to schizoid patients who despite incipient psychosis were capable of coping with life outside a hospital. Much as his attention was drawn to the news and topics of immediate moment, he was invariably also drawn to the larger moral issues behind those topics and to what seemed to him true and lasting and transcendental. It is not surprising that sometime in the autumn he purchased Honoré Daumier's small bronze bust of Jean-Claude Fulchiron, the French politician and man of letters. The figure with its arched brows and regal nose regards the world from under hooded eyes with composed scepticism.

The autumn was a disturbing time for Gregory. He confessed to James at the end of October that he was 'under a state of tension' which had little to do with the 'frightfully difficult' world situation; he had 'no financial difficulties', but 'worries that are both deeper and more complex than mere finances'. Without going into detail, he admitted that for over two years he had been seriously concerned about Ray, even recently suspecting that she might be suffering from a fatal illness. He had been unable or unwilling to share with her either the degree of his concern or the medical details of her physical and emotional health, and although he had recently received an indefinite yet 'rather encouraging' report, he continued to worry. Indeed, his concern for Ray compounded his own distress at a time when he particularly needed the emotional support she was unable to offer. Writing to Sigerist two weeks later, he apologised for not having responded to his last letter, similarly explaining that he had been going through 'a period of trouble – personal and otherwise'. Specifically, 'Among other things', Ray appeared to have had 'a cardiac attack' and hadn't yet fully recovered. Gregory needed Sigerist as a friend outside the family circle, a confidante, a European intellectual with whom he could exchange ideas, someone with whom he could relax and play at his hobbies and talk at length. He simply told him, 'I want to have a visit with you very soon.'[24]

On 9 November a Nazi pogrom began throughout Germany: Tens of thousands of Jews were rounded up and sent to camps, hundreds of synagogues were burnt and shop windows smashed during the night soon known as *Kristallnacht*. The news provoked international outrage, but given American anti-Semitism, Jewish organisations in the United States were reluctant to protest and, despite brief discussions in Congress, there would be no change in U.S. policy towards Germany or lifting of immigration quotas.

American passivity towards such a grand scale pogrom galvanised Gregory. Alexander had invited him to give five fortnightly lectures on the history of psychoanalysis at the Chicago Institute for Psychoanalysis early in the new year, and their preparation demanded significant literary energy, but as Christmas approached he shifted his attention to a dramatic monologue he entitled *I Won't Apologize: Two Letters*. He arranged for 500 copies to be published privately in December, followed in January 1939 by a second printing of five thousand copies.

The fictional letters explore political, moral, personal, and spiritual issues. In the first, dated 25 October 1938, a few weeks after the Anschluss, Dave, an assimilated Jew, responds to John, a nominal Christian, about American 'Jew-baiting'.

Hardened by historical antagonism, Dave has avoided discussing anti-Semitism with his friend, but he is now angry because John has asserted that Jews 'must do something about it'. Insisting that 'the Jewish problem is as much a Gentile problem as a Jewish one', Dave claims that in face of diaspora, Jews have assimilated the best of different cultures. Thus Dave – like Gregory, a Jew with Quaker sensibilities – tells John, 'When you hate us, when you kick us, when you destroy us, you are killing in yourselves the most valuable thing there is in man ... your tolerance, your ability to live with your fellow-men.' Accusing John of a 'complacency of security', Dave insists that 'history guarantees you no security whatsoever. Your safety lies, not in your good background, not in your racial origin, or social adherence, but only in your ability to be tolerant, and peace-loving, and liberty-loving.' Dave insists, 'I won't apologize for our vitality any more than I will apologize for being a hated Jew', declaring that Jews 'ought to stand in full view of those who hate us, fearful for the world but fearless for ourselves'. Dave concludes,

> the inroads Hitler makes into the minds of many people are not roads to a new racial glory of the Nordic, but obscure channels through which the termites of intolerance crawl. They will eat up all your houses. They will reduce to dust your museums and your churches.

Gregory's persona as 'a disenfranchised Jew' here polarises the conversation. Unity of Jew and Gentile may be his overriding point, but his plea for tolerance in no way elides the differences between Dave and John, and the Christian in this first letter remains the other.

The second letter, dated 11 November 1938, the Armistice Day just after *Kristallnacht*, moves towards healing divisions. Dave is sceptical about the value of John's charitable work on behalf of the Jews persecuted by the Nazis. In one of Gregory's typical figures of speech, Dave explains, 'Ministering to the victims of an epidemic – imperative as it is – does not stop the epidemic.' He declares that Jesus understood 'what man is and ought to be to his fellow-man' as well as 'the psychological difficulties man has to face', aware of 'the tragedy that might befall the man who, accepting Christ, rejects the Jew, in whose tradition and walk of life Christ chose to appear'. Locating the roots of modern democracy in Christianity, Dave presents the tension between 'extreme self-denial and acquisitive self-assertion' as 'the story of the Christian, the Gentile, for the past nineteen centuries'. Thus tyrants are unchristian because they reject tolerance and the 'love of one's fellow-man'.

Specifically, Dave tells John,

> the man of today may become cruel and relentless in order to assert his will to vicarious mastery, which is actual slavery – a bondage to his pseudo-godlike leader – but he may achieve this abnormal state only if he first succeeds in overthrowing the god within himself.

People hate to be reminded of tolerance and love, Dave writes, but the danger is almost greater for the Gentile (the hater) than the Jew (the hated), because the Gentile destroys himself. With the world on the brink of a sort of suicide, Dave argues not without irony that Jews are survivors because they have been such poor world politicians and imperialists, but Gentiles need to realise that civilised life is not a Wagnerian opera: 'It isn't necessary to scheme, persecute and kill one another to get the Rheingold; it's not necessary to commit suicide to enter Valhalla.' The persecution of Jews is finally 'a symptom of a very serious disease of our civilization'. Drawing on Paul, a Jew who persecuted Christians before himself becoming one, Dave suggests in his conclusion that reconciliation of Jew and Christian is indeed possible.[25]

I Won't Apologize did not make Gregory a consistently kind or forgiving person any more than it made him less Jewish or more Christian, but it assuaged his depression and calmed his nervous response to the coming war, made him feel he had done something significant and bolstered his capacity to cope in matters of serious psychological, personal, and professional moment. *I Won't Apologize* would not make Gregory less of a bully in the one-on-one confrontations in which he held at least the verbal cards, but it enabled him to take a stand; absenting himself when push came to shove – as he had finally done in the matter of his contretemps with Henry and the fracas over the bookshop and library – would no longer be personally acceptable.

Gregory sent copies, bound in a beige cover overlaid with lavender stars of David and Christian crosses, to friends and colleagues at home and abroad. He was proud of what he felt he had achieved in the pamphlet, while its wide distribution and two printings are further evidence of his shift in attitude towards his own visibility. For years he had been willing to stand in the limelight but only on relatively small professional stages. As a young immigrant he had been self-protective, anxious about maintaining a low profile, concerned about keeping out of official notice. He was still displeased to see his name bandied about in the popular press, but on matters important to him, he was now ready to seek a public platform.

The response was positive, and many readers went beyond kind or perfunctory acknowledgement. Apparently failing to understand that 'apologise' in the title had nothing to do with regret and everything to do with defence, Sigerist, who found the pamphlet 'very illuminating', agreed with all Gregory had written but felt there was no reason the author should apologise. Harvey Cushing, Sterling Professor of Neurology at Yale University School of Medicine, also told Gregory that he certainly needn't apologise for the letters, which he had read 'with the greatest sympathy and interest'. Among the editors to whom Gregory sent copies were Morris Fishbein, editor of the *Journal of the American Medical Association*, and Clarence B. Farrar, director of the Toronto Psychiatric Hospital and editor of the *American Journal of Psychiatry*, who called the letters 'an eloquent appeal'. Other prominent figures were also impressed. Haven Emerson, the inventor of the iron lung, praised Gregory's 'attitude and understanding', while Jelliffe, by 1938 a venerated 'old man' in his seventies, sent his warm congratulations. Gregory's distribution, however, went beyond those he knew in his own profession. He sent copies to President Roosevelt as well as to the international journalist Frederic William Wile, who sent the letters to prominent Washington lawmakers including Supreme Court Justice Louis Brandeis and Attorney General Homer Cummings, who found the pamphlet 'deeply interesting'.

Jewish readers particularly understood the anger that had prompted the pamphlet and the courage involved in writing it. Anna Freud, who had fled to England with her father after the Anschluss, told Gregory that she had enjoyed the letters more than most things she had recently been reading and mentioned her own experience of the 'growth in antisemitic feeling' in people who had been 'free from it before'. Ernst Kris, who had also fled Vienna for London, was so deeply touched that he circulated his copy among his friends and hoped Gregory would 'give more publicity' to what he considered 'a most important contribution to the sociological and political problems of our time'. Gregory would continue to distribute *I Won't Apologize* into the autumn of 1940, when he gave a copy to the New York bookseller Max Breslow, who found the pamphlet's substance still very timely and its attractive appearance 'in perfect harmony with thoughts beautifully expressed'.[26]

Gregory's commitments barely allowed him to catch his breath. No sooner had he celebrated his Christmas birthday with the family than he was off to Richmond, Virginia, to address the American Association for the Advancement of Science on the limits of psychoanalysis, a lecture in which he returned to his mainstay: Only the individual could be the object of direct, 'true' scientific investigation and treatment; one could not 'depart from this fundamental principle without becoming confused'. Back in New York for New Year's, he was in Chicago in early January for the first of his five lectures. Between the first and second lecture, he went to Los Angeles for ten days of winter sunshine and yet more lecturing, but fell ill and spent most of the sojourn in bed. Two days before his return to Chicago, he cut his right hand sufficiently badly to injure a tendon. He would for weeks have difficulty writing, but no minor physical impediment would prevent his travelling or addressing various audiences. Back in Manhattan at the end of the month, he spoke at the Julliard School of Music on 'Music and Medicine, as Seen by a Psychiatrist'. At the beginning of February, he addressed a group in Hartford, Connecticut, before returning to Chicago for a public lecture sponsored by the Chicago Institute on 'Recent Progress in Psychoanalysis in Relation to History'.[27]

Throughout the first half of 1939 Gregory divided his time between New York and the Midwest. The former meant his home and office, but the Midwest was a regular element in his life until June 1939 probably in part because, when he re-entered analysis, he hesitated to work with a New York colleague. He definitely did not want to reanimate the complicated and fraught transference with Alexander, but the Midwest offered him the choice of a number of European as well as American analysts. He may well have sought out Karl Menninger, with whom he had much in common intellectually but who was different from both

Alexander and Gregory in background and temperament. Born, bred, and established in Kansas, Menninger was midwestern in sensibility: direct but reserved, kind but savvy, an enlightened and liberal American aware of Europe but in no way European, a writer whose *Man Against Himself*, published the previous year, examined self-harm and suicide as evidence of Freud's 'death instinct'. Menninger's training analysis with Alexander in 1932 had left much unresolved, while differences provoked by *Man Against Himself* renewed the conflicts between the two and provoked an intractable disaffection. Menninger would visit New York frequently throughout 1939 for a second analysis with Ruth Mack Brunswick, but by 1939 Menninger was a friend and Gregory may well have sought out a different analyst in Topeka or Chicago or Detroit – or even settled after all on a New York colleague.[28]

The lectures enabled by Alexander would certainly have dovetailed nicely, however, with analytic treatment in the Midwest, and Gregory found excuses to extend his visits. In March he addressed a joint meeting of the Detroit Pediatric Society and the Wayne County Medical Society. In April he addressed the Michigan Society for Mental Hygiene in Grand Rapids. In Chicago in May he spoke at the annual meeting of the American Psychoanalytic Association, where his presence was less incidental than in Detroit or Grand Rapids and the roster of officers and other speakers included friends, acquaintances, and mentors. Brill was honorary president; Alexander, president; Kubie, secretary; and his Boston colleague Moses Ralph Kaufman was treasurer. Among the speakers were European Jews who had immigrated to the United States (including Helene Deutsch, Kurt Eissler, Otto Fenichel, Robert Fliess, Sandor Rado, Frieda Fromm-Reichmann, Annie Reich, Ernst Simmel, and Fritz Wittels) as well as native-born Americans (including Karl Menninger, Smiley Blanton, and Bert Lewin). In such company, all conveniently in Chicago, Gregory must have spoken passionately on the subject that continued to weigh on his mind, 'The Psychology of Racial Intolerance'.

Gregory was in obvious overdrive. On his return from California, Ray had become ill and spent time in hospital, then Greg had come down with mumps, but Gregory, while his hand healed, had resorted to dictating and carried on. At the end of February he had served as moderator at a round table discussion on 'Capital Crimes and the Conflict of Adolescence' at the annual meeting of the American Orthopsychiatric Association in New York. The group included Alexander as well as Menninger and Winfred Overholser, the superintendent of Saint Elizabeth's Hospital. The topical session received coverage in the *New York Times* and the *New York Herald Tribune*, both of whom quoted Gregory at length; indeed, only the *Times* mentioned any of the other participants. *Time* also covered the meeting: Two columns described the 'more than 1,000 enthusiastic orthopsychiatrists' who buzzed in the Commodore Hotel's ballroom, yet only Gregory's photograph appeared in the magazine, while under 'Highlights of the Meeting', the reporter focused on the round table, mentioning comments by a psychiatrist at Macy's department store but devoting a detailed paragraph to Gregory's remarks. Gregory's dramatic energy and passionate conviction had made him a star.[29]

During this spectacular spring almost no topic escaped his interest. In March he addressed the New York Psychoanalytic Society on the Oedipus complex in Marcel Proust. Photography continued to be important to him, and at the end of the month he submitted four photographic portraits to a competitive exhibition at Kent State University in Ohio: 'Dr. S. B.' (perhaps his colleague Smiley Blanton), 'Blind', 'Maestro Artur Rodzinski' (the Polish musical director of the Cleveland Orchestra), and 'A Cruel Face', a photograph taken in Brazil. A first and second prize were chosen from the 268 submissions as well as five honourable mentions, among them 'A Cruel Face'. In April, under the pseudonym 'Medicus', Gregory analysed Hitler's psychology in an article for *The New Republic*, and finally managed a weekend break on the farm with Sigerist and his wife. As usual, Ray and Emmy found something to do on their own while the children, under Miss Darroche's watchful eye, romped on the lawn with the dogs and the two hard-working men spent hours talking and cooking and pottering in the dark room. In the spring sunshine on nearby Byron Lake, they even got in some fishing, a new if not enduring hobby that offered them time and peace, two rare commodities as spring edged towards summer.[30]

Gregory's analysis evidently helped him to understand his feelings, but it did not make him happy. Intense intellectual activity masked an abiding melancholy and marginalised family life in which he didn't expect these days to find much solace. With his attention focused on world affairs, he resented the intrusion of personal matters, yet felt impotent to do anything about the events he was following so closely, well aware, as he wrote James, that 'history is a captious patient and never recognized any specialty in the field of medicine'. He was living in a state of foreboding, not so much wondering when the sky was going to clear but when the storm would break. He found it strange to be wishing for war all the while knowing that 'a more generalized blood-shed' would 'solve as little as the many blood-sheds that go on and bring us less than we have even now of spiritual security and hope'. He had, after all, witnessed world affairs for almost half a century and at no time had history given 'human blood a chance even to dry up before fresh blood was spilled'. He was not discouraged by all this or even disgusted but 'just angry', so angry that whenever he felt kindly towards things and people in general, he caught himself resenting that very kindness. He concluded, 'one must be cruel, fearless, and very dogmatic, or absolutely dumb to be more or less happy'.[31]

Notes

1 JZ to GZ, 5 September 1937.
2 GZ to HES, 25 October 1937.
3 GZ, 'The Sense of Immortality', 180–181; GZ to HES, 7 December 1937.

4 GZ, 'Some Observations', 2, 16, 20.
5 GZ to HES, 7, 14 December 1937; telegram, GZ to HES, 24 December 1937.
6 GZ, NYPSB, 543; Bach, 115, 143; Hoopes, 169.
7 Hoopes, 7, 51, 170–173; Ingersoll 'High Time', 15 December 1969, 2, 4, 6–7, 10, 14, 'The Story of PM', August 1970, 9, Howard Gotlieb Archival Research Center, Boston University.
8 'Духовно' ('spirit') and 'духовный' ('spiritual') are explained in Chamberlain, 44; emails from Judith Hehir, 26, 27 March 2018.
9 GZ, 'What Man Has Made', 388, 393, 394, 397.
10 GZ, 'Loneliness', 50, 54; GZ to 'Très Saint-Père', 31 January 1953, APD.
11 GZ, 'His Own Cook', 156–157.
12 GZ, 'Overestimation', 93, 94.
13 GZ to JZ, 4 March 1938; GZ to HES, 31 March 1938.
14 GZ to HES, 31 March 1938; HES to GZ, 12 May 1938; 'Acknowledgement', *Bulletin of the History of Medicine*, vol. 6, June 1938, 676.
15 JZ to Pauline Turkel, 6 March 1938 (JEZB); JZ to GZ, 31 March 1938; GZ to JZ, 4 April 1938.
16 GZ to Natalie Zilboorg, 12 April 1938; Natalie Zilboorg to JZ, 3 May 1938, both JEZB.
17 GZ to JZ, 15 April 1938; JZ to GZ, 24 April 1938.
18 Email from AZ, 18 August 2018; GZ to HES, 25 April 1938.
19 GZ, 'The Vicissitude', 393–397, passim.
20 GZ to JZ, 19 May 1938.
21 JZ to Pauline Turkel, 31 May 1938; Turkel to JZ, 15 June 1938, both JEZB.
22 GZ, 'Some Aspects of Suicide', 139.
23 GZ, 'Misconceptions', 540, 543, 553.
24 GZ to JZ, 27 October 1938; GZ to HES, 15 November 1938.
25 GZ, *I Won't Apologize*, passim.
26 GZ from HES, 7 January 1939; GZ from Harvey Cushing, 10 January 1939; Morris Fishbein, 31 March 1939; Clarence B. Farrar, 25 December 1938; Haven Emerson, 14 January 1939; Smith Ely Jelliffe, 3 January 1939; Marguerite LeHand, 23 December 1938; Frederic William Wile, 4 March 1939; Anna Freud, 12 April 1939; Ernst Kris, 4 March 1939; Max M. Breslow, 26 September 1940; Homer Cummings to Frederic William Wile, 27 March 1939.
27 Jane Stafford, 'Psychiatry Suffering from Overpopularity', *Science Service*, 9 January 1939, np; GZ to HES, 1 February 1939; GZ to JZ, 24 February 1939.
28 Faulkner and Pruitt, 102.
29 'Orthopsychiatrists', *Time*, 6 March 1939, np.
30 GZ, 'The Discovery', 'A Psychiatrist'; GZ to HES 2 March 1939; HES to GZ, 14 April 1939.
31 GZ to JZ, 24 February 1939.

Chapter 14

Other affairs

1939–1940

By the time Gregory finished his analysis in May, he was at least accepting of the tensions and contradictions he had reported to James. Although he wasn't happy, he was no longer so depressed, and despite his anger at the state of the world, he continued to ride a crest of productivity. Likely in part as a result of this analysis, he now also felt able to deal with his feelings about the anti-Semitism that had prevented his collaboration with George Henry; at the end of the month, he was finally ready to resume work on his history of medical psychology.[1]

Henry had left Bloomingdale for private practice in Manhattan, where he was also a consulting psychiatrist at New York Hospital's Payne Whitney Psychiatric Clinic. Eager to sign a contract with Norton, Gregory wrote a formal letter inviting him to his office to discuss the legal details. Henry had done nothing with his section of the history, and they had a good deal to work out during several meetings in June. Henry must have harboured some resentment and felt abandoned as well as outdone by his accomplished colleague. For his part, Gregory needed to put aside the issue of anti-Semitism and push ahead with a co-author with little of his motivation or intellectual rigour. They finally agreed that Henry would condense his two chapters on organic psychoses and hospitals, which Gregory would then edit to bring in line with the other 12 chapters. On the point of authorship, Henry conceded that the title page would read 'A History of Medical Psychology' followed by 'Gregory Zilboorg, M.D. in collaboration with George W. Henry, M.D.' Whether out of impatience to get on with the project or frustration at having yoked himself to an uncongenial collaborator or guilt that he had not pushed himself ahead sooner or simply as a generous sop to the less capable man, Gregory agreed that Henry would receive one-third of the royalties.[2]

With the history once more at the top of Gregory's agenda, he decided to close his office for two months as of July and take 'the first real vacation' in several years. In the relative calm of the summer, he also turned his attention again to his family in Mexico. Oblivious to the turmoil in Europe, the farm was flourishing in the warm sunshine and Gregory wanted his father to visit, to see the cows, drink the fresh milk, walk with him into the garden with the dogs, to watch Greg and Nancy splash in the pond. Fera had kept him informed about their parents even when her brothers failed to communicate. Nothing much had changed, but

DOI: 10.4324/9781003190936-14

everyone's life was naturally moving on. Nadia had fallen in love with a New Yorker, a fellow student at the University of Texas. Moses and Anna were aging, and Moses especially seemed tired. Feeling despondent, James now wondered if Gregory could buy a house in Mexico that he could then rent. While assuring his brother of his good will, Gregory refused outright: He felt that the economic and biological 'burdens of life' were becoming heavier and he was simply 'unable to undertake any more burdens'. When Fera informed him that their mother had suffered another 'heart attack' and urgently needed specialist treatment at a rural clinic, Gregory immediately sent a cheque for $100, then felt foolish when Fera reported a few days later that Anna was working 'like a truck horse' to arrange a party. Pointing out that a cardiac condition 'is more aggravated by parties than alleviated by a trip to the country', he informed James bluntly that he was uncomfortable at the thought that he was being exploited.

Now that Gregory had suggested their father visit, James acknowledged that Moses had been yearning for such a trip for years, but insisted that 'he would not and should not go now.' Basia was taking care of the household because Anna had been in bed and needed constant attention, wasn't even able to walk about the apartment unaided. In his opinion, their father's trip 'would just be preposterous'. While detaching himself from family melodrama, Gregory felt sincerely sorry for his mother, 'true angina pectoris' being both painful and fatal, but worried particularly about the impact on his father. He advised James not to give him too much hope in order to prepare him 'for all eventualities' and reluctantly agreed that, under the circumstances, Moses shouldn't visit, but added with rather touching hopefulness that perhaps he could come 'later' when it would 'do him much more good'.[3]

As his mother's undulating health improved and declined, Gregory found plenty to think about in his country library. Questions he raised in 'The Fundamental Conflict with Psycho-analysis', which appeared at the end of the summer in the *International Journal of Psycho-analysis*, weighed on his mind. It was not only as a Jew with a European background that he felt beleaguered. He found psychoanalysis itself 'in the paradoxical state of unpopular popularity or popular unpopularity – depending on the place or the group where it is being discussed'. In his view, a sort of 'war on psychoanalysis' was going on. 'Sex' used to be the reason for the hostility, but it seemed to him that people were generally becoming more open and relaxed about sex, so the reason for their opposition must be something else or something more. He argued that it was not the acknowledgement of the unconscious that made people antagonistic to psychoanalysis but defections within psychoanalysis (such as Mortimer Adler, Alfred Adler, and Carl Jung) and hostility from without to what was perceived as a threat to the idea of free will and 'the companion conviction of immortality'. Anxious detractors (Karen Horney but also Otto Rank, Sandor Rado, and Wilhelm Reich) made a significant mistake by equating psyche and soul; Freud, he stressed, 'never dealt with the soul'. Gregory saw the source of the misunderstanding in 'man's most profound narcissistic tradition to make a megalomanic introjection of the father (free will) and a similarly megalomanic projection of his unwillingness to die (immortality, soul)'. His conclusion was subtle and succinct: 'A confusion of the psyche as a scientific concept and the soul as a theological one mobilizes within us a complex mass of narcissistic cathexes which constitutes the fundamental source of the well-nigh invincible opposition to psycho-analysis.' This perceptive analysis of the problem in which the psyche and the soul occupied separate spheres nevertheless posed for Gregory further questions at once personal and professional about the matter of the soul and spiritual life, but whatever answers he was beginning to imagine for himself lay outside the realm of what he wrote for publication in 1939.[4]

With these matters on his mind, however, it is not surprising that he agreed to review Freud's *Moses and Monotheism* for the *Atlantic Monthly*. Admitting for his audience of sophisticated general readers that the book's contents, 'its inner logic and method of exposition', would remain 'more or less obscure to those who are not sympathetically familiar with psychoanalysis', he summarised Freud's account of Moses's life while pointing out that it was impossible to prove or disprove something at once 'legendary and so deeply bound with religious emotions'. Gregory reviewed Havelock Ellis's autobiography for the *Atlantic* in the autumn. Reflecting on what it meant to expose oneself personally in print and citing the confessional tendency among authors from Saint Augustine to Rousseau and Tolstoy, Gregory noted Ellis's curious lack of insight, calling him 'a sexologist rather than a psychologist of sex'. Both reviews were confident and critical as Gregory publicly defined himself in contrast to these two well-known figures in the field.[5]

Amid his reading and reviewing, Gregory was beginning to recast his history, but the history happening daily in Europe also claimed his attention. As he packed his papers for a return to the city at the end of August, the war he had long anticipated was suddenly becoming a reality. During the last weekend of the summer Nazi bombs began to fall on Warsaw and on the towns and villages between the capital and the Russian border to the east where the train line ran straight on to Kiev. As the family prepared to drive back to Manhattan on the first Sunday in September, Britain and France declared war on Germany. Gregory returned to his office on Monday; on Tuesday the United States declared its neutrality. Before the end of the month Freud died of cancer in London, but he now seemed a war casualty as the Nazis and the Soviets, whose August pact had provoked international outrage, divided Poland between them. How quickly all the dominoes would fall wasn't clear to anyone, but it must have been difficult for Gregory to concentrate on his patients' inner lives as the news blared and hundreds of German panzers rolled across Eastern Europe.

He did his best during the first autumn of the war to fulfil as well as limit his responsibilities. He proposed to James that Moses defer visiting until spring, giving as an excuse that the weather would then be better, but he didn't feel, as his brother had suggested, that he could write directly to his parents since they would be unable to read his letters. Pointing out that 'The world situation has not simplified matters', he urged James to tell them he had informed both children that their grandmother was seriously ill and everyone was grieved and wished her well. The message cheered them, but the details James continued to report weren't encouraging. Anna seemed to be improving but had frequent crying fits after attacks of pain; she complained about the medical costs, felt she would never be able to leave her bed. The medical expenses were indeed a burden, and James hoped that Gregory could 'raise her allowance a little'. Moses, meanwhile, continued to worry, was 'terribly clumsy and of no help at all'.[6]

Fera's reports were marginally more reassuring, and at least the Levitas family finally seemed to be finding its feet. Fera was holding down the domestic fort in the Bronx where Nora and Misha were doing well in local schools. Sol had joined the staff of the liberal anti-communist *New Leader* as business manager in 1936, but there were rumours that the editor was considering retirement and Sol was in line to take over. Beyond giving Sol more creative scope, such a promotion, for which everyone hoped, would relieve Gregory of his regular contributions to the family's finances. Pauline was right: Gregory much preferred to be in a position to offer munificent gifts rather than provide obligatory subsidies – even if the obligation was merely a matter of his conscience.

Henry had been less productive over the summer. Like everyone else he had probably been distracted by the headlines, but he was also preoccupied with personal and professional matters. Like Gregory he had two children, but his wife was less stable than Ray. By the summer of 1939, probably in part out of concern for Eleanor, Henry had accepted a post as medical director of Brooklea Farm, a private sanitarium near Bloomingdale in Port Chester, New York. The family was comfortably accommodated on the large estate where Eleanor led a sheltered life with psychological support from the staff, but she still needed attention from her husband, who commuted between Brooklea and his commitments in the city.

In 1938, as an executive member of the Committee for the Study of Sex Variants at Payne Whitney, Henry had begun to work with the homophile activist Alfred A. Gross, a defrocked Episcopal priest who had come to him for therapy in 1937. Their research, which in 1941 would result in *Sex Variants: A Study of Homosexual Patterns*, a book of over a thousand pages, was a dodgy collaboration. Neither a physician nor a psychologist, Gross profited from his relationship with Henry, who gave his work respectability and authority as well as the 'cover' he needed as a closeted homosexual. Henry, in turn, depended on Gross, an enterprising man with advanced degrees in divinity and philosophy, who provided contacts and conducted interviews with minimal involvement from Henry. Indeed, Gross probably wrote up most of their research. *Sex Variants* would contain virtually no references to psychological literature on homosexuality, no references to the sexologists Magnus Hirschfeld or Havelock Ellis, and only passing general mention of Freud. Depending on a simplistic gender-inversion model of homosexuality, the book's clinical interpretations were 'guided more by folk wisdom than coherent theory'. Clarence Arthur Tripp, a psychologist who would work with Henry as a researcher and photographer during the war and later with the sexologist Alfred Kinsey, would – like Gregory – find Henry unreliable and 'intellectually shallow'.[7]

Although Gregory was probably not surprised, he must have been irritated that it took Henry until mid-October to post signed copies of the publishing contract to Louis Weiss, now Gregory's personal lawyer. Aware that he was slow, Henry nevertheless proclaimed that he was 'ready at any time to rewrite' his section, although he unfortunately no longer had a copy and would need to borrow Gregory's.[8]

Gregory had little time to focus on the history during the unsettled and unsettling first months of the war. Soviet troops attacked Finland in November, although not until December was the Soviet Union expelled from the League of Nations. Sigerist, caught in South Africa by the advent of war, was unable to return to the United States until the end of the year. Yet as blackout restrictions came into force in England, the lights in New York continued to glitter. The period in Britain would retrospectively be called 'the phoney war'; in the United States, as Gregory waited with mixed feelings for more 'blood-sheds', the months before the Japanese attack on Pearl Harbour would be filled with ironic contrasts. On Broadway R.C. Sherriff's moving First World War drama *Journey's End* had a brief revival in September, while Lillian Hellman's *Little Foxes*, a grim examination of greed produced and directed by Herman Shumlin, ran for almost a year. America's theatre audiences, however, preferred lighter fare. George S. Kaufman and Moss Hart's comedy *The Man Who Came to Dinner* began a long run in October, while Clarence Day's affectionate *Life with Father*, which opened in November, would become a Broadway staple throughout the war. As cinema newsreels documented 'the winter war' in Finland, Ingersoll continued his struggle on behalf of his liberal evening paper that would carry no advertising. Pleasing his psychoanalyst with a scheme for intellectual and political independence might have contributed to Ingersoll's motivation, but the idea of his own paper fired his imagination. Hellman, meanwhile, whose torrid affair with Ingersoll had ended nearly four years earlier, began analysis with Gregory, whose roster by 1940 included Shumlin, Hellman's ex-husband Arthur Kober, and in all likelihood Beatrice Kaufman's playwright husband George.[9]

Despite spending portions of his working day with privileged patients, Gregory's politics and sense of social responsibility meant that he did what he could for those victimised by the war. Hitler's persecution of European Jews had galvanised international aid organisations. Eddie Warburg – who had recently married a wealthy divorcée, Mary Prue Currier, who would soon begin working in the Office for Inter-American Affairs to counter German and Italian propaganda in Latin America – was chairman of the American Jewish Joint Distribution Committee; Jimmy Warburg was actively working to persuade the government to abandon its policy of neutrality. As Ingersoll rushed about putting together a newspaper staff of 'non-professional intellectuals', 'intellectual non-professionals', and 'professional intellectuals', Gregory made donations, gave talks, attended dinners, and did everything he could to help refugee psychoanalysts struggling to get practicing privileges. He did little, however, to make family life run more smoothly, probably because he felt there was little he could do. By the end of the year even six-year-old Nancy was aware of the tensions. In clear and careful handwriting she addressed several notes formally to 'Dear Father', hoping he was feeling well or having a nice time, but in one particularly poignant message she hoped that 'Gregory is not a nuisance to you'. Young Greg was often a nuisance to his preoccupied father.[10]

James was also irritating. When Jimmy and Phyllis Warburg went to Mexico on holiday in March, Gregory arranged a meeting with James, who failed to maintain the discrete reserve his brother expected. On their return, Jimmy reported that Moses was too old and ill to make the often-debated visit to the United States. Gregory was scarcely able to conceal his anger and told James in early April that he took this information 'as a message', for he couldn't imagine his brother's saying this 'and other things' to the Warburgs 'merely as a topic of conversation'; 'she as a former patient' of his and 'he as a patient' weren't people with whom James should discuss his 'personal affairs and characteristics'.

As for their father's trip, while Moses was mentally fine, he was aging physically; travel would be impossible unless someone could go with him – perhaps, James suggested, a friend of Fera's returning from Mexico later in April might accompany him. The prospect of a visit from his frail and traditional father, with whom he had to communicate in Yiddish, was suddenly overwhelming. Citing horrible weather and family illnesses, Gregory told James it would be better to wait at least until after the annual meeting of the American Psychiatric Association in May.[11]

Gregory's letter provoked a six-month hiatus in their correspondence. He would continue to receive reports from Fera, but James was apparently as irritated by Gregory's scolding as Gregory had been by his brother's indiscretion. Yet Gregory didn't need to rely entirely on Fera for news of Mexico, where Trotsky had been granted asylum in 1937. Befriended by Rivera and Kahlo, Trotsky lived in the artists' large compound for over three years. At the end of May 1940, a violent attack on the premises, led by Siqueiros, made international headlines. Having broken with Rivera in April, however, Trotsky was no longer in residence and would live until August 1940 when he was murdered by a single assailant with a pickaxe, an event again reported in the New York papers. With Russians in Mexico and the Soviets supporting the Axis powers in Europe and the Far East, Gregory was reminded daily of the revolution he helped to make and the country from which he was exiled that still had a claim on his heart.

Yet the spring of 1940 was not without its lighter moments, and Gregory was capable even in wartime of amusing ripostes, elegant asides, riveting conversation, generosity, and bonhomie. He addressed the Baltimore Medical Society in mid-March and spent a convivial weekend with Sigerist, sent him with his thank-you note a brace of pheasants raised on the farm and asked for a recipe. When the recipe arrived, he was typically gracious, thanking his friend on behalf of 'myself, the culinary department of my household and all the prospective eaters at my table'. Back in Baltimore at the beginning of April Gregory addressed Sigerist's seminar on the history of psychiatry. At the end of the month he spoke on 'The Sense of Reality' to the New York Psychoanalytic Society, a typically wide-ranging talk scintillating with references to psychiatrists, philosophers, Chekov, and Dostoyevsky. In early May Gregory and Sigerist spent another weekend together, taking photographs and talking, this time in Pound Ridge. Among other topics they discussed what they might write for the 'medical department' of Ingersoll's paper, now called *PM* and slated to begin publication in June. Sigerist inevitably returned to Baltimore laden with farm produce.[12]

As usual Gregory was juggling commitments and responsibilities, but Ingersoll's passion was contagious and by the time *PM* hit the newsstands, it had Gregory's psychological support as a viable project. When Sigerist evinced new interest in the translation of Paracelsus Gregory had begun four years earlier, he became enthusiastic about contributing to a volume that would illustrate different aspects of his personality and work. There were, however, projects and even patients Gregory felt obligated to refuse. Although he had treated anti-Semites before Hitler's rise to power, he now interrupted treatment of a Nazi sympathiser, unable to control his revulsion. Then there were tasks he had to do simply to keep his office running. Ruth Mattison, who was getting married in the summer, had inconveniently handed in her notice. She contacted Vassar for a recommended replacement while Gregory hoped for someone more experienced than his research secretary had been when he had hired her two years earlier.[13]

As the German army rolled through Holland and Belgium in late May, Gregory interviewed Margaret Stone. Having graduated from Vassar in 1938, she had been working for two years but looked awfully young. In the waiting room she had been absorbed in a paperback: the popular psychologist Henry C. Link's *Return to Religion*, a positive-thinking book that encouraged its readers to be sociable and nice as well as to make money and go to church. Gregory quipped that he didn't think Link would bring her back. The interview rapidly became as much an argument about psychology and religion as an examination of her qualifications. In the days following the debacle of Dunkirk, the Nazis marched through France and she was pretty certain such an odd and combative interview meant she wouldn't be hired, but Gregory was too distracted to interview another candidate; whatever her shorthand skills, he decided Miss Stone was intelligent enough.[14]

In *PM*'s first issue on 18 June, under the pseudonym 'Jeremiah Strapp', Gregory wrote not on medicine but on 'The Passing of France'. He felt sick at the fall of Paris not because the occupied city was 'the nightclub of the universe' but because Paris for him was the capital of European culture that had nurtured Voltaire, Rabelais, Montaigne, Pasteur, and Ignatius Loyola. He felt pain and gloom because Paris was not so much conquered by Hitler, he contended, as surrendered 'by small men, traders and petty gamblers on the stock exchange'. Closely following political developments, a month later Gregory reiterated the point in a second article, arguing that France and all it represented had been 'murdered' by Édouard Daladier, Pierre Laval, and Pierre-Etienne Flandin. When he told Sam Hume that he hoped to finish his history if the war did not distract him, the conditional phrase was not a conventional pleasantry. For Gregory, the war was a huge daily distraction; he responded to events in Europe as if they were happening on his doorstep.[15]

Miss Stone began work on July 1 at a salary of $40 a month. Miss Mattison showed her the 20 volumes of the 1911 *Encyclopaedia Britannica* in the office library, took her that sunny morning to the New York Public Library and explained how to use its resources, told her that every time Dr. Zilboorg used a name, she was to look it up because while he spoke excellent English, his spelling was 'terrible'. Excited by the job's responsibility and novelty, Miss Stone set to work in the afternoon. Gregory gave her three handwritten pages of the history to type, and she set them on the windowsill where a sudden breeze blew them over the back alley four floors below, then up over the roof of the next building. When in mortified panic she confessed what had happened, Gregory was merely concerned that she was so very upset and said he would write them again that evening. Tremendously relieved, she was completely astonished. Never in her 22 years had she met anyone like Gregory.

My mother had had a happy childhood in a family and environment not at all like my father's. She had grown up as the much-loved only girl, a middle child with an older brother four years her senior (Louis Talcott Stone, Jr., known as 'Lou'), the apple of his mother's eye, and a younger brother (George Norton Stone, known always as 'George'), born when Peg was three, a sickly infant whose scarlet fever had provoked convulsions that likely resulted in life-long epilepsy, mostly controlled by phenobarbital and kept secret, probably even from his siblings. Unlike Lou, Margaret Norton Stone, known always as 'Peg', was born in a hospital in the spring of 1918 as American troops boarded ships to rescue Europe from the First World War. She entered the world on Freud's birthday, although on 6 May 1918 Freud turned a distinguished 52, while Gregory was a revolutionary Russian journalist of 27 with his American future still before him.

Peg's parents were intelligent, capable people and above all nice – kind, traditional, and very loving of their able children. Louis Talcott Stone was a mill owner's son of English stock from western New York State. He grew up in comfortable surroundings, went to Kent School in Connecticut and then to Yale University, though he was always rather embarrassed to have taken only the three-year business degree his parents felt was suitable. He worked in New York City in the cotton trade with his friend and partner George Norton. Back and forth they went to negotiate for the harvest in the south, and when Norton fell in love with Margaret Taylor (always called 'Margo'), the eldest daughter in an old Memphis family, he urged Louis to meet her sister Louise and follow suit, which he promptly did. It was a happy marriage. Louis and Louise bought a pretty house in suburban Bronxville, an easy commute from the city and a semi-rural paradise for their children. Lou had been named after his father, while Peg was named for her aunt Margo, in consolation after the death of the Nortons' only child, who had died at birth a year earlier. Norton himself died in the post-war flu epidemic. Margo's ginger hair turned white overnight and she moved in with the Stones, with whom she would live for the rest of her life in the largest bedroom, the only one with its own bathroom. Peg's brother George was named after Margo's husband, another gesture in an effort to console a widowed sister and aunt.

Peg grew up playing with neighbours in the front garden, watching the goldfish in the ornamental pond, waiting for her father's return each evening heralded by his whistling as he came up the street from the train station. There was always a black servant, a girl from the south who invariably claimed to be 16. When the girls became young women and left to raise families, a cousin would be brought up from Tennessee to take their place.

Dressed in ruffles and lace, Peg was an adorable child with large blue eyes, light brown curls, and pale skin that soon freckled.

Peg, aged two

She learned to read early and mastered numbers with ease, a problem for her parents who asked themselves, when she turned four, 'Whatever are they going to do with her when she enters the first grade?' Lou was already tall for his age (he would grow to an impressive six feet, eight inches; George would be six foot, five), and Peg herself was a good height for a girl, but she would be the smallest child in her class, a whole year younger than her prospective classmates, when Louise enrolled her in the Bronxville school a year ahead of time. The teacher was happy to have such a bright and competent pupil, but by Christmas of 1923, it was clear Peg was academically misplaced. In January she was moved to the second grade, but by spring it was decided that even this wasn't the solution. In autumn 1924 Peg skipped another year and joined the fourth grade with children three years older and more socially mature. It is no wonder that despite her ability she was somewhat shy, concerned to do the right thing and be a good girl always.

Peg was content, however, with her books and friends. A sporty child, she adored her brothers and played with them with aptitude and skill. She paddled a canoe and swam on family holidays in summer and skated on Bronxville's ponds in winter. She learned to shoot a BB gun and got wading boots one Christmas so she could fish in local streams with Lou and George. Her parents read to her at bedtime, attended services at the Episcopal church every Sunday, and told her nothing at all about sex.

October 1929 hit the cotton trade hard, and Louis's investments melted away in the crash. Norton had been wiser and luckier, having invested most of his savings in IBM during the war, and Margo would weather the depression in benevolent gentility, although the family would inevitably resent her munificence and their dependence. Margo paid for Lou and George to attend Kent and Yale and for Peg to attend college, albeit as a scholarship student, yet she provided more than money. She tutored both boys in the Latin and helped her sister make tuna fish and parsley sandwiches that throughout the 1930s Louise took down to the tearoom of the New York Exchange for Women's Work. Both women learned to type, likely Margo's idea, and got secretarial work in a community welfare office.

As a youngster during the depression Peg learned to economise and had little trouble obeying her elders and following directions; she was not an especially imaginative or creative child and didn't question doing what she was told. She liked to have fun and was content within the boundaries of her world where parents knew best and people didn't talk about what they didn't talk about. When she first got her period, she had no idea what was happening. Held back at 15 on the advice of her school principal, who judged her simply socially unready for college, she spent her last year of high school reading history and literature with slight supervision and taking extra classes in mathematics and French with a teacher who had never been to France. She invited her older brother as her partner to her senior prom.

When Peg went off to Vassar in September 1934, she was the youngest freshman in her year and still thought that a woman could get pregnant by kissing. Her goal was to learn the name of every girl in her class before graduation, and she started on the project immediately. Blissfully happy, she would count her four college years as amongst the best in her life and cherish the friends she made there. Boyfriends were another matter. At dinner dances students from Yale or Williams College were bussed to Vassar and she had admirers; there were stolen kisses after champagne and awkward embraces after evenings drinking beer in Poughkeepsie pubs, but physical or emotional intimacy didn't particularly interest her. When she was taken out for an expensive dinner in New York, the young man who drove her home expected more than a brief kiss good night. Peg rejected him out of hand and ended the relationship, such as it was, then and there. Before she shut the car door, he told her he thought he had made a very poor investment. She knew enough to find that an insulting confirmation of her judgement.

Peg did well in all of her college classes and majored in English but never grasped the thrust of literary history. She thoroughly enjoyed her course in the history of Western art and her two semesters on the Romantic poets, was amused that despite the name they didn't write really about love, yet what the Romantic movement meant for her finally came down to wonderful paintings and poems about nature.

It was decided that Peg should go to Europe in the summer of 1936 as a companion to her cousin whose horizons were going to be widened by six weeks in Italy and France with her mother, Peg's paternal Aunt Bette. Peg's horizons were broadened by transatlantic crossings on elegant ships and stays in comfortable hotels; she went to the Louvre, strolled through ruins in Rome, and ate too many figs. Never to be outdone, the following summer Margo took both girls abroad again. They went to Ireland and England, rented a car, and drove through the Lake District as far north as Edinburgh, took an overnight train to London, saw Big Ben and the Elgin Marbles. That Europe was on the precipice of another war did not make much of an impression on

Peg at Vassar

Peg's mind. Her father and mother did not discuss politics and the only time she ever heard them argue was over the comparative merits of Margaret Mitchell's *Gone with the Wind* and James Fenimore Cooper's *Drums along the Mohawk*. Louis subscribed to the *New York Times*, Louise to the *New York Herald Tribune*. He voted the Republican ticket while she voted Democrat. When Roosevelt ran for a second term in 1936, her mother wouldn't reveal if Louis had voted for the much-admired Democratic president who was putting the country back on its feet. She simply told her daughter she thought the Bronxville school had just fallen down. Peg had a good sense of humour, but her mother was even funnier; Lou and especially George were killingly funny, could turn a phrase and make one weep with laughter.

After graduation, Peg spent her godmother's gift of $100 on a month's secretarial training in New York City. Mary-Alice Hunter, her best friend at Vassar, joined her, doing what female graduates did in 1938. Still shy but good at editing, Peg quickly mastered the rudiments of shorthand and perfected the touch typing that she had learned in high school and used to earn pin money at college. Occasionally she spent the night in Manhattan with Mary-Alice, who found work with Lever Brothers and had a tiny apartment of her own, but Peg continued to live at home and commuted to the city for her first real job – as a receptionist for a travel agency. On payday Peg sometimes splurged on a five-cent Coca-Cola and would sip it slowly through a straw, watching the world go by from a stool near the drugstore window. When Hitler invaded Czechoslovakia in October 1938, the travel business went bust.

Louis had his first stroke while Peg was still at Vassar. By 1938, he was no longer able to work; Louise and Margo were supporting the family with what they could earn as secretaries and counted on Peg's contribution of $5 each week from what she knew even in hard times was a miserable salary. She didn't dare tell her family when she lost her job. She went down to a city employment agency each day on her usual train and soon accepted a place as the third secretary to the head of the legal department of the National Broadcasting Company.

While Peg was quick to say that she didn't hate the NBC, she confessed to friends that she hated the job. She didn't like commercial life. She wasn't in fact very good at shorthand, though she did get better at it; she diligently took the contents of the wastepaper basket home with her at night to practise. The main secretary was having an affair with the boss, and she didn't like either of them, thought the woman was 'cheating'. She stayed on conscientiously, feeling she was being treated like an old dog but determined to appear dependable and acquire a job history. When in spring 1940 her application for a raise from $30 to $32 a week was refused, she applied for a secretarial post at a school in Baltimore, but when she got the offer, she turned it down. Baltimore hadn't seemed very nice when she went for the interview and suddenly felt too far from home. Peg told the head of the school her father wasn't well, but she felt she was taking 'a sissy way out'. As soon as she returned to Bronxville, however, she took another tack and contacted Vassar's vocational bureau.

Working for Gregory would turn out to be far more interesting than anything Peg could have imagined. Before the end of July she couldn't eat and had lost ten pounds, was shocked by the seriousness of her feelings for someone so much older than she, her employer, a married man with two dependent children, a Jew. For Gregory, Peg was sweetness and light, kindness and consideration, his better self, his *Amérique à lui*. At his request and her inclination, she was soon working late, often staying in the city into the evening. He played records for her in the office living room and dined with her in local restaurants before she caught the late train back to Bronxville. He began to leave her little notes when he passed her desk, asked where she bought her clothes, how much a new suit cost at Lord and Taylor. When she reluctantly admitted she had seen one she liked for $45, he told her not at all reluctantly he thought she should have it. Starting that summer, Peg would edit everything Gregory wrote, recasting awkward phrasing, suggesting colloquial expressions, restructuring sentences, inserting punctuation, striking out redundancies. Never again would Gregory dangle modifiers or get away with writing that someone did something 'unawarely'. Before the first German bombs fell on London at the end of August, they were lovers.[16]

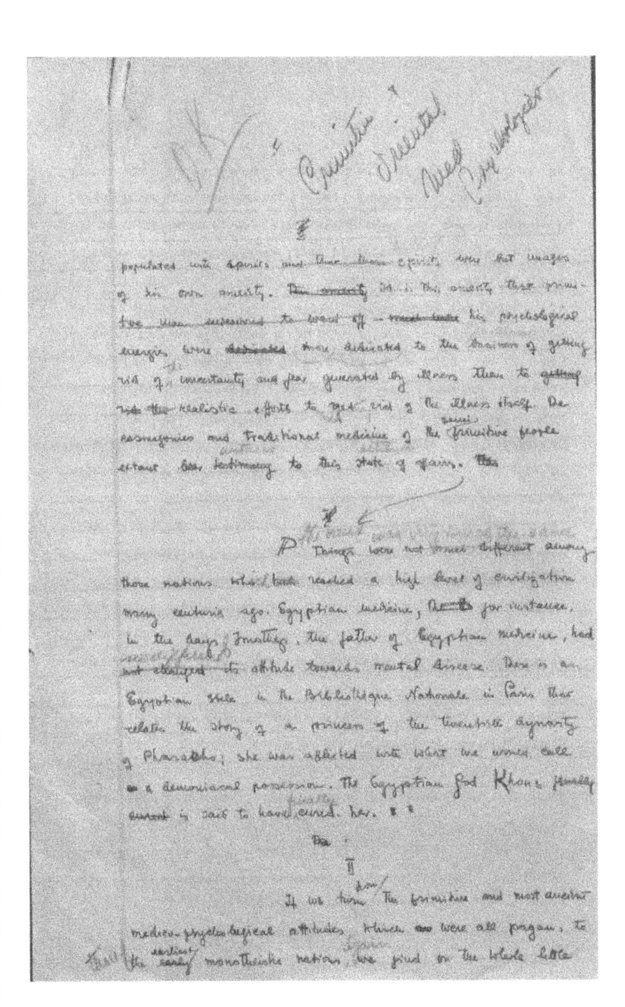
populated with spirits and [illegible] spirits were but images of his own anxiety. It is this anxiety that primitive man [illegible] his psychological energies were more dedicated to the business of getting rid of the uncertainty and fear generated by illness than to realistic efforts to get rid of the illness itself. The cosmogonies and traditional medicine of the primitive people extant bear testimony to this state of affairs.

Things were not much different among those nations which had reached a high level of civilization many centuries ago. Egyptian medicine, for instance, in the days of Imhotep, the father of Egyptian medicine, had [illegible] its attitude towards mental disease. There is an Egyptian stele in the Bibliothèque Nationale in Paris that relates the story of a princess of the twentieth dynasty of Pharaohs; she was afflicted with what we would call a demoniacal possession. The Egyptian god Khons [illegible] is said to have cured her.

II

If we turn from the primitive and most ancient medico-physiological attitudes, which were all pagan, to the earliest monotheistic nation, we find on the whole little

A draft of page 28 of Gregory's *History of Medical Psychology* with Peg's corrections in pencil

Autumn 1940 was a period of suspension. Campaigning for a third term, Roosevelt promised not to intervene in 'foreign' wars while in October the country's first peacetime draft required the registration of all men between the ages of 21 and 36. Lou and George both had to enrol, although at 49 Gregory was exempt. Despite wide isolationist sentiment, the United States was becoming the 'arsenal of democracy', supplying the Allies in a policy soon known as 'Lend-Lease'. What Gregory was going to do about his affair with Peg was up in the air.

In October James asked why he hadn't heard from Gregory since April. While James in fact owed Gregory a letter, Gregory hadn't written for various reasons. Rather than explaining about work on his history, about world affairs or affairs of the heart, he told his brother he found it difficult to be inspired or disturbed by 'the chronic bickerings that go on in the small circle of so-called family'. He claimed he was interested in what his brother was doing and in what was happening around him, but he had no interest 'in stamping on the same spot and considering it walking'. Gregory was harking back to their unbalanced correspondence years before in Russia when he had longed for a fraternal relationship with the brother James had never been and was never going to be. He signed this letter frankly and without irony 'as always', but the truth of the matter was that he no longer expected or needed the intimacy he had repeatedly sought from James.

For his part, James was hurt and angry. Accusing his brother of having 'toyed' with him, he declared that Gregory's 'visions of being exploited' and his 'tendencies to lecture' had managed to stifle any natural impulse to write about matters 'more transcendental'. Gregory would continue to send monthly cheques to their parents as well as the regular rental subsidy to James, but he wouldn't respond to his brother's fury. Fera would keep Gregory informed about the 'chronic bickerings' and the state of everyone's health in Mexico, but there would be no direct communication between the two men for over a year.[17]

Brooding was not in Gregory's nature, however; he saved reflection for more immediate intellectual and emotional matters, and he inevitably had so much on his plate, so many interests, responsibilities, obligations, and enthusiasms, that his relationship with James seems simply to have fallen by the wayside. He was working hard on the history, played chess occasionally with Greg and Nancy during country weekends, spent creative time in the barn not only in his darkroom but in a workshop now equipped with circular saws and power drills, clamps, and substantial planks of oak and birch. As 'Jeremiah Strapp' he wrote for *PM*. Ever the caustic observer, in 'Contributions to the Dictionary', he defined 'Communist' as 'Any man of whom you are suspicious'; 'Fascist' as 'Any man you do not like'; 'Nazi' as 'Any man you hate'; and 'Alien' as 'A foreigner who does not play polo'.[18]

Throughout the autumn Ingersoll kept him abreast of ongoing dramas as *PM* battled its way into the rough-and-tumble world of New York's newspapers. Gregory heard about internal power struggles that were quickly followed by distribution problems involving 'sabotage' by the circulation managers of other evening newspapers 'in the best tradition of American racketeering'. The excitement of vicarious journalism must have been stimulating for the former revolutionary, but professional responsibilities claimed his more sober attention. The Committee for the Study of Suicide was working on its final report and preparing to disband, while his translation of Paracelsus had stalled during a summer that, he told Sigerist, had been 'strenuous but not very fruitful'. The two men had not seen each other since an evening with Ingersoll in late June spent discussing the 'medical department' for which Sigerist had submitted 24 articles during a productive summer vacation in the American West. Although Gregory was now 'very, very eager' to see his friend, they were so busy that an opportunity to meet wouldn't be possible until after the new year.[19]

Had Gregory seen Sigerist during the autumn, he might well have confided his affair with Peg, but as things were, he told one. By November, however, Peg had unburdened her heart to her brothers during a family weekend in Bronxville. George's letter to Peg on his return to Yale reveals some of the challenges she faced. He acknowledged that Peg was confronting 'something so unmanageable, so tough and important' that 'Sunday school standards and opinions' were 'laughably small time'. Their parents would be hard to persuade, but her own 'mulishness', her 'amused defiance and superiority' in the face of the challenges would, he felt, carry her through.

Peg and Gregory had evidently already discussed marriage, but that possibility was predicated on a divorce from Ray. It was one thing for Marshall Field and Jimmy Warburg to divorce and remarry – even to divorce a second time and marry a third time – but as far as Peg's parents were concerned, ordinary people simply didn't do such things. Conventional people who were neither millionaires nor movie stars made their beds and slept in them; if they slept in other people's beds, they were 'trash', and it was better that nobody knew and nothing was said. Obviously, Gregory couldn't get divorced without anyone knowing; he and Peg couldn't marry without anything being said. The discrepancy in age would also challenge Louis and Louise and most of the people they knew and Peg knew, as would the facts that Gregory was a Jew, a Russian, a socialist, and a psychoanalyst. Naïve and supportive, George had some idea of what his sister expected from the relationship and hoped she would be 'happy and fascinated even beyond those expectations'. As if the hurdles were already overcome and the result a fait accompli, he was convinced in November 1940 that she was about to enter an 'outstanding' marriage, but Gregory had been married for over 20 years and had two dependent children; he wouldn't find it easy to leave Ray. Peg was less naïve than George, and Gregory was more experienced than either of them, but even he couldn't have imagined the difficulties that lay ahead.[20]

Notes

1 GZ, NYPSB, 543.
2 GZ to GWH, 31 May, 7, 20 June 1939; GWH to GZ, 1, 8, 21 June 1939, GZB.
3 GZ to JZ, 8 June, 28 July, 8 August 1939; JZ to GZ, 20, 29 June, 2 August 1939.
4 GZ, 'The Mental Health Aspect', 279; 'The Fundamental Conflict', 8, 9, 12, 13.

5 GZ, Review, '*Moses and Monotheism*', np; Review, '*My Life*', np.
6 GZ to JZ, 11 September 1939; JZ to GZ, 3 October, 15 November 1939.
7 Minton, 102, 104, 119, 301n.
8 GWH to GZ, 13 October 1939.
9 Hellman, *An Unfinished Woman*, 143; GZ's secretary to Lillian Hellman, 14 October 1941, and Beatrice Kaufman to GZ, GZB; Gallagher, 90.
10 Hoopes, 219.
11 GZ to JZ, 8 February, 1 April 1940; JZ to GZ, 5, 25 March 1940.
12 GZ to HES, 18, 25 March 1940; HES to GZ, 30 March, 9 April 1940; GZ, 'The Sense of Reality', 183.
13 HES to GZ, 9 April 1940; GZ to HES, 10 April 1940; GZ, 'Social Convictions', 416–417; Ruth Mattison to MSZ, 16 May 1940.
14 MSZ, Dar interview.
15 GZ, 'The Passing of France', 3, and 'Where Are the People?', 18; GZ to Samuel Hume, 11 June 1940, Samuel J. and Portia Bell Hume Papers, Bancroft Library, University of California, Berkeley.
16 MSZ, Dar interview; MSZ to Zita L. Thornbury, 24 November 1939; GZ, Review, '*My Life*', np.
17 GZ to JZ, 2 October 1940; JZ to GZ, 8 October 1940.
18 GZ, 'Contributions', np.
19 GZ to HES, 3, 10 October, 16 December 1940.
20 George Stone to MSZ, 10 November 1940.

Works cited

NB. A full bibliography of Gregory Zilboorg's work is available at https://sites.google.com/view/gregory-zilboorg/bibliography.

Abraham, Richard. *Alexander Kerensky: The First Love of the Revolution.* New York: Columbia UP, 1987.

Aleichem, Sholom. *The Bloody Hoax*, transl. Aliza Shevrin. Bloomington: Indiana UP, 1991.

Alexander, Franz, and Hugo Staub, *The Criminal, the Judge, and the Public: A Psychological Analysis*, transl. and introduction, Gregory Zilboorg. New York: Macmillan, 1931.

Andreyev, Leonid. *He, the One Who Gets Slapped*, transl. and introduction, Gregory Zilboorg. New York: Dial Press, 1921 and (as *He Who Gets Slapped: A Play in Four Acts)* New York: Brentano, 1922.

Annual Reports: The Society of the New York Hospital. New York: Society of the New York Hospital, 1923–1942.

Bach, Steven. *Dazzler: The Life and Times of Moss Hart.* New York: Knopf, 2001.

Becker, Stephen. *Marshall Field III: A Biography.* New York: Simon & Schuster, 1964.

Bickel, Marcel H., ed. *Correspondence: Henry E. Sigerist-Chauncey D. Leake, 1930–1955.* Bern: online publication, Institute of the History of Medicine, University of Bern, 2012.

———. *Correspondence: Henry E. Sigerist-Gregory Zilboorg, 1931–1956.* Bern: online publication, Institute of the History of Medicine, University of Bern, 2012.

———. *Correspondence: Henry E. Sigerist-Owsei Temkin: 1931–1956.* Bern: online publication, Institute of the History of Medicine, University of Bern, 2012.

———. *Henry E. Sigerist: Correspondences with Welch, Cushing, Garrison, and Ackerknecht.* Bern: Peter Lang, 2010.

Burnham, John C. *Jelliffe: American Psychoanalyst and Physician & His Correspondence with Sigmund Freud and C.G. Jung*, ed. William McGuire. Chicago: The University of Chicago Press, 1983.

Chamberlain, Lesley. *The Philosophy Steamer: Lenin and the Exile of the Intelligentsia.* London: Atlantic, 2006.

Chernow, Ron. *The Warburgs: The Twentieth-Century Odyssey of a Remarkable Jewish Family.* New York: Random House, 1993.

Clum, Woodworth. *Making Socialists Out of College Students: A Story of Professors and Other Collegians Who Hobnob with Radicals.* Los Angeles: Better America Federation of California, 1920.

Coolidge, Calvin. 'Enemies of the Republic: Are the "Reds" Stalking Our College Women?' *Delineator*, June 1921, 4–5, 66–67.
Danto, Elizabeth Ann. *Freud's Free Clinics: Psychoanalysis and Social Justice, 1918–1938*. New York: Columbia UP, 2005.
Debroise, Olivier, Mari Carmen Ramirez, and James D. Oles. *David Alfaro Siqueiros: Portrait of a Decade, 1930–1940* (exhibition catalogue). Mexico City: Instituto Nacional de Bellas Artes y Literatura, 1997.
'Dr. Gregory Zilboorg: The Emancipation of Liberty the Theme of Address', *Chautauquan Daily*, vol. 47, no. 34, 1 August 1922, 1–2.
Faulkner, Howard J., and Virginia D. Pruitt, eds. *The Selected Correspondence of Karl A. Menninger*. New Haven: Yale UP, 1988.
Figes, Orlando. *A People's Tragedy: The Russian Revolution, 1891–1924*. London: Pimlico, 1997.
Freud, Anna. 'Report of the Eleventh International Psycho-Analytical Congress', *Bulletin of the International Psycho-Analytic Association*, vol. 10, 1929, 489–510.
Friedman, Susan Stanford, ed. *Analyzing Freud: Letters of H.D., Bryher, and Their Circle*. New York: New Directions, 2002.
Gallagher, Dorothy. *Lillian Hellman: An Imperious Life*. New Haven: Yale UP, 2014.
Hamm, Michael F. *Kiev: A Portrait, 1800–1917*. Princeton: Princeton UP, 1993.
H.D. *Tribute to Freud*. New York: New Directions, 1974.
Hellman, Lillian. *An Unfinished Woman: A Memoir*. Boston: Little, Brown, 1969.
———. *Pentimento*. Boston: Little, Brown, 1973.
———. *Scoundrel Time*. Boston: Little, Brown, 1976.
Henry, George W. *Sex Variants: A Study of Homosexual Patterns*. New York: Paul B. Hoeber, 1941.
Hoopes, Roy. *Ralph Ingersoll: A Biography*. New York: Atheneum, 1985.
Ingersoll, Ralph. *Point of Departure*. New York: Harcourt, Brace, 1961.
Korolenko, Vladimir Galaktionovich. *In a Strange Land: The Story of Every Immigrant*, transl. Gregory Zilboorg. New York: Bernard G. Richards, 1925.
Leffert, Mark. 'The Psychoanalysis and Death of George Gershwin: An American Tragedy', *Journal of the American Academy of Psychoanalysis and Dynamic Psychiatry*, vol. 39, no. 3, 2011, 421–452.
Mailloux, Noël. 'Rencontre avec … Noël Mailloux', interview with Josette Garon, Jacques Mauger, François Péraldi, Gabrielle Clerk, and André Lussier, Montréal, 5 February 1987, *Revue Québécoise de Psychologie*, vol. 20, no. 1, 1999, 1–14.
Makari, George. '*Mitteleuropa* on the Hudson: On the Struggle for American Psychoanalysis after the *Anschluss*', *After Freud Left*, ed. John Burnham. Chicago: The University of Chicago Press, 2012, 111–124.
Meir, Golda. *My Life*, New York: Dell, 1976.
Meir, Natan M. *Kiev, Jewish Metropolis: A History, 1859–1914*. Bloomington: Indiana UP, 2010.
Menninger, Karl. *Man Against Himself*. New York: Harcourt, Brace, 1938.
Millay, Edna St. Vincent. 'Recuerdo', *A Few Figs from Thistles*. New York: Harper, 1922.
Minton, Henry L. *Departing from Deviance: A History of Homosexual Rights and Emancipatory Science in America*. Chicago: The University of Chicago Press, 2002.
Mora, George. 'Early American Historians of Psychiatry: 1910–1960', *Discovering the History of Psychiatry*, ed. Mark S. Micale and Roy Porter. New York: Oxford UP, 1994, 53–80.

———. 'Renaissance Conceptions and Treatments of Madness', *History of Psychiatry and Medical Psychology*, ed. Edwin R. Wallace and John Gach. New York: Springer, 2008, 227–254.

Nathans, Benjamin. *Beyond the Pale: The Jewish Encounter with Late Imperial Russia*. Berkeley: University of California Press, 2004.

Paskauskas, R. Andrew, ed. *The Complete Correspondence of Sigmund Freud and Ernest Jones: 1909–1939*. Cambridge: Harvard UP, 1995.

Pollack, Howard. *George Gershwin: His Life and Work*. Berkeley: University of California Press, 2006.

Quinn, Susan. *A Mind of Her Own: The Life of Karen Horney*. Reading, MA: Addison Wesley, 1987.

Rado, Sandor. 'Deutsch Psychoanalytische Gesellschaft', *International Zeitschrift für Psychoanalyse*, XV Band, Heft 2/3, 1929, 365–368.

———. 'Deutsch Psychoanalytische Gesellschaft', *International Zeitschrift für Psychoanalyse*, XVI Band, Heft 1, 1930, 132–134.

Rappaport, Helen. *Caught in the Revolution: Petrograd 1917*. London: Hutchinson, 2016.

Reed, John. *Ten Days That Shook the World*. New York: Boni and Liveright, 1919.

Rimler, Walter. *George Gershwin: An Intimate Portrait*. Urbana: University of Illinois Press, 2009.

Rischin, Ruth. 'Andreev', *Encyclopedia of Literary Translation into English*, ed. Olive Classe, London and Chicago: Fitzroy Dearborn, 2000, vol. 1, 50–54.

Ross, Edward Alsworth. *The Russian Bolshevik Revolution*. New York: The Century Company, 1921.

Russell, Charles Edward. *Bolshevism and the United States*. Indianapolis: Bobbs-Merrill, 1919.

Sarton, George. 'Review' (of *The Medical Man and the Witch During the Renaissance*), *Isis*, vol. 25, no. 1, May 1936, 147–152.

Schlemowitz, Emily. *David Alfaro Siqueiros's Pivotal Endeavor: Realizing the 'Manifiesto de New York' in the Siqueiros Experimental Workshop of 1936* (MA Thesis, Hunter College, 2016). CUNY Academic Works. https://academicworks.cuny.edu/hc_sas_etds/68.

Slater, Wendy. *The Many Deaths of Tsar Nicholas II: Relics, Remains and the Romanovs*. Abingdon: Routledge, 2007.

Sorokin, Pitirim A. *A Long Journey: The Autobiography of Pitirim A. Sorokin*. New Haven: College and UP, 1963.

Stoddard, Lothrop. *The Revolt against Civilization: The Menace of the Under Man*. New York: Scribner, 1922.

Terry, Jennifer. *An American Obsession: Science, Medicine, and Homosexuality in Modern Society*. Chicago: The University of Chicago Press, 1999.

Wallace, Edwin R., and John Gach, eds. *History of Psychiatry and Medical Psychology*. New York: Springer, 2008.

Watkins, C. Edward, Jr. 'The Beginnings of Psychoanalytic Supervision: The Crucial Role of Max Eitingon', *American Journal of Psychoanalysis*, vol. 73, 2013, 254–270.

Weber, Katharine. *The Memory of All That: George Gershwin, Kay Swift, and My Family's Legacy of Infidelities*. New York: Crown, 2011.

Zamiatin, Eugene. *We*, transl. Gregory Zilboorg. New York: Dutton, 1924.

———. *We*, transl. Gregory Zilboorg (second edition). New York: Dutton, 1959.

Zilboorg, Gregory. *A History of Medical Psychology* (with two final chapters, 'Organic Mental Diseases' and 'Mental Hospitals', by George W. Henry). New York: W.W. Norton, 1941.

———. 'A Psychiatrist Looks at Hitler' (as 'Medicus'), *The New Republic*, vol. LXXXXVIII, no. 1273, 26 April 1939, 326–327.
———. 'A Psychosis Caused by a Latent Focus of Infection (Ischio-Rectal Abscess)', *New York State Journal of Medicine*, 1 July 1927, 1–8.
———. 'About Actors: The Municipal Theatre of St. Louis', *Drama*, vol. 14, no. 11, October 1923, 16–18.
———. 'Affective Regeneration in the Schizophrenias', *Archives of Neurology and Psychiatry*, vol. 24, August 1930, 335–347.
———. 'Against Kerensky: A Piece of Bad Journalism That Serves No Purpose', a review of Andrew Kalpashnikoff, *A Prisoner of Trotzsky's*, *The Evening Post*, 7 August 1920, np.
———. 'Aggression: Savage and Domesticated', *Atlantic Monthly*, September 1936, 298–307.
———. 'Ambulatory Schizophrenias', *Psychiatry: Journal of the Biology and Pathology of Interpersonal Relations*, vol. 4, no. 2, May 1941, 149–155.
———. 'Ausländisches Interesse an Institut: Aus Amerika', *Zehn Jahre Berliner Psychoanalytisches Institut: Poliklinik und Lehranstalt*, ed. Deutschen Psychoanalytischen Gesellschaft, Foreword by Sigmund Freud. Vienna: Internationaler Psychoanalytischer Verlag, 1930, 66–69.
———. 'Behind the Screen', *Pearson's Magazine*, June 1920, 916–921.
———. (transl.) *The Criminal, the Judge, and the Public: A Psychological Analysis*, Franz Alexander and Hugo Staub. New York: Macmillan, 1931.
———. 'Chautauqua and the Drama: Impressions of a Traveling Stranger, Theatre Soliloquies VI', *Drama*, vol. 12, nos 1 & 2, October–November 1921, 16–18, 40.
———. 'Concerning a Kolchak Picture', *The Globe*, 15 September 1919, np.
———. 'Considerations on Suicide, with Particular Reference to That of the Young', *American Journal of Orthopsychiatry*, vol. 7, no. 1, January 1937, 15–31.
———. 'Contributions to the Dictionary' (as 'Jeremiah Strap'), *PM*, vol. I, no. 26, 23 July 1940, 13.
———. 'Depressive Reactions Related to Parenthood', *American Journal of Psychiatry*, vol. X, no. 6, May 1931, 927–962.
———. 'Die Unmittelbare Verwirklichung des Socialismus, von einem Russischen Socialisten', *Der Friede*, 12 November 1918, np.
———. 'Differential Diagnostic Types of Suicide', *Archives of Neurology and Psychiatry*, vol. 35, February 1936, 270–291.
———. 'Foreword', *In a Strange Land: The Story of Every Immigrant*, Vladimir Galaktionovich Korolenko, transl. Gregory Zilboorg. New York: Bernard G. Richards, 1925, v–ix.
———. 'Foreword', *We*, Eugene Zamiatin, transl. Gregory Zilboorg (second edition). New York: Dutton, 1959, xiii–xviii.
———. 'Freud's Fundamental Psychiatric Orientation', *International Journal of Psycho-Analysis*, vol. XXXV, Part II, 1954, 1–5.
———. 'His Own Cook', *Journal of the History of Medicine and Allied Sciences*, vol. VIII, no. 2, 1958, 155–159.
———. 'Intellectual Ice Cream and Native Drama: Theatre Soliloquies, Impressions of a Traveling Stranger, III', *Drama*, vol. 11, no. 9, June 1921, 319, 335–337.
———. 'Investigative Psychotherapy in Certain Types of Criminals', *New York State Journal of Medicine*, vol. 43, no. 10, 15 May 1943, 928–930.
———. *I Won't Apologize: Two Letters*. New York: Privately printed, December 1938 and January 1939.

———. 'Leonid Andrieyev – The Self-Defeat of a Revolté', *Soviet Russia*, 15 May 1920, 488–490.
———. 'Loneliness', *Atlantic Monthly*, January 1938, 45–54.
———. 'Malignant Psychoses Related to Childbirth', *American Journal of Obstetrics and Gynecology*, vol. XV, no. 2, February 1928, 3–16.
———. 'Masculine and Feminine: Some Biological and Cultural Aspects', *Psychiatry: Journal of the Biology and Pathology of Interpersonal Relations*, vol. 7, no. 3, August 1944, 257–296.
———. 'Maxim Gorky: The War and the Revolution', *Evening Post*, 12 June 1920, np.
———. 'Medical History as a Force in Medical Functioning', *Victor Robinson Memorial Volume: Essays on Historical Medicine*, ed. Solomon R. Kagan. New York: Froben, 1948, 3–8.
———. *Mind, Medicine, and Man*. New York: Harcourt, Brace, 1943.
———. 'Misconceptions of Legal Insanity', *American Journal of Orthopsychiatry*, vol. IX, no. 3, 1939, 540–553.
———. 'Mr. Zilboorg's Position', *Evening Post*, 28 August 1919, np.
———. 'Overestimation of Psychopathology', *American Journal of Orthopsychiatry*, vol. 9, no.1, 1939, 86–94.
———. 'Post-Partem Schizophrenias', *Journal of Nervous and Mental Disease*, vol. 68, no. 4, October 1928, 370–383.
———. 'Propaganda from Within', *Annals of the Academy of Political and Social Science*, July 1938, 1–8.
———. 'Psychological Sidelights on Andreas Vesalius', *Bulletin of the History of Medicine*, vol. XIV, no. 5, December 1943, 562–575.
———. 'Reflections on a Century of Political Experience and Thought', *Political Science Quarterly*, vol. XXXVI, no. 3, September 1921, 391–408.
———. Review, *Moses and Monotheism* by Sigmund Freud, *Atlantic Monthly*, vol. 164, no. 3, September 1939, np.
———. Review, *My Life: Autobiography of Havelock Ellis* by Havelock Ellis, *Atlantic Monthly*, vol. 164, no. 5, November 1939, np.
———. Review, *The Life and Work of Sigmund Freud: The Last Phase, 1919–1939* (vol. III) by Ernest Jones, *Psychoanalytic Quarterly*, vol. XXVII, 1958, 253–262.
———. 'Russian Psychiatry: Its Historical and Ideological Background', *Bulletin of the New York Academy of Medicine*, vol. 19, no. 10, October 1943, 713–728.
———. 'Sidelights on Parent-Child Antagonism', *American Journal of Orthopsychiatry*, vol. II, no. 1, January 1932, 35–43.
———. 'Social Convictions and Clinical Psychiatry', *Bulletin of the New York Academy of Medicine*, vol. 29, no. 5, May 1953, 411–419.
———. 'Some Aspects of Psychiatry in the U.S.S.R.', *American Review of Soviet Medicine*, vol. I, no. 6, August 1944, 562–575.
———. 'Some Aspects of Suicide', *Suicide and Life-Threatening Behavior*, vol. 5, no. 3, Fall 1975, 131–139.
———. 'Some Observations on the Transformation of Instincts', *Psychoanalytic Quarterly*, vol. VII, no. 1, 1938, 1–24.
———. 'Some Physical Aspects of Mental Disease', *New York State Journal of Medicine*, vol. 35, no. 14, July 1935, 1–8.
———. 'Suicide Among Civilized and Primitive Races', *American Journal of Psychiatry*, vol. 92, no. 6, May 1936, 1347–1369.

———. 'The Changing Concept of Man in Present-Day Psychiatry', *American Journal of Psychiatry*, vol. III, no. 6, December 1954, 445–448; reprinted in *Freud and the 20th Century*, ed. Benjamin Nelson. New York: Meridian, 1957, 22–31.
———. 'The Death of Nicholas II' (in Russian), *The People's Cause* (?), c. mid-July 1918, np.
———. 'The Deeper Layers of Schizophrenic Psychoses', *American Journal of Psychiatry*, vol. XI, no. 3, November 1931, 493–511.
———. (transl.) 'The Diseases That Deprive Man of His Reason' by Paracelsus, with an introductory essay, *Four Treatises of Theophrastus von Hohenheim Called Paracelsus*, ed. Henry E. Sigerist. Baltimore: Johns Hopkins, 1941, 135–212.
———. 'The Discovery of the Oedipus Complex: Episodes from Marcel Proust', *Psychoanalytic Quarterly*, vol. VIII, no. 3, July 1939, 279–302.
———. 'The Dynamics of Schizophrenic Reactions Related to Pregnancy and Childbirth', *American Journal of Psychiatry*, vol. VIII, no. 4, January 1929, 733–766.
———. 'The Fundamental Conflict with Psycho-Analysis', *International Journal of Psycho-Analysis*, vol. XX, Parts 3 & 4, 1939, 1–13.
———. 'The Heritage of Ignorance', *Atlantic Monthly*, June 1937, 728–736.
———. 'The Invisible Lenin', *Pearson's Magazine*, September 1920, 80–81.
———. *The Medical Man and the Witch during the Renaissance*. Baltimore: Johns Hopkins, 1935.
———. 'The Medical Man and the Witch towards the Close of the Sixteenth Century', *Bulletin of the New York Academy of Medicine*, vol. 11, no. 10, October 1935 (second series), 579–607.
———. 'The Mental Health Aspect of the Communication of Ideas', *American Association for the Advancement of Science*, no. 9, 1939, 279–283.
———. 'The Passing of France' (as 'Jeremiah Strap'), *PM*, vol. I, no. 1, 18 June 1940, 3.
———. *The Passing of the Old Order in Europe*. New York: Thomas Seltzer, 1920.
———. 'The Psycho-Social Paradoxes of Returning from the War', *Mental Health Bulletin* (of the Illinois Society for Mental Health), vol. XXIII, no. 2, March–April 1945, 1, 4–8.
———. 'The Russian Invasion', *Drama*, vol. 13, no. 4, January 1923, 127–130.
———. 'The Sense of Immortality', *Psychoanalytic Quarterly*, vol. VII, no. 2, 1938, 171–199.
———. 'The Sense of Reality', *Psychoanalytic Quarterly*, vol. X, 1941, 183–210.
———. 'The Star and the Ensemble on the Russian Stage', *Drama*, vol. 11, no. 3, December 1920, 95–96.
———. 'The Struggle of the Patient Against the Doctor', *Journal of the Michigan State Medical Society*, vol. 52, April 1953, 424–428.
———. 'The Theatre of the Past in Soviet Russia', *Drama*, vol. 12, no. 6, March 1922, 195–196.
———. 'The Vicissitude of the Intellectual Immigrant of Today', *Journal of Social Psychology*, vol. 12, 1940, 393–397.
———. 'Thirty-Five Years Later', *We*, Eugene Zamiatin, transl. Gregory Zilboorg (second edition). New York: Dutton, 1959, xix–xx.
———. 'What Man Has Made of Man', a review of Mortimer J. Adler, *What Man Has Made of Man: A Study of the Consequences of Platonism and Positivism in Psychology*, *Psychoanalytic Quarterly*, vol. VII, no. 3, 1938, 380–398.
———. 'Where Are the People?' (as 'Jeremiah Strap'), *PM*, vol. I, no. 24, 18 July 1940, 18.
Zilboorg, Margaret Stone. 'Introduction', Gregory Zilboorg, *Psychoanalysis and Religion*. New York: Farrar, Straus and Cudahy, 1962, vii–xi.

Abbreviations and notes

APD	Noël Mailloux Papers, Les Archives Provinciales Dominicaines, Montréal, Québec, Canada
ASCCU	Archives and Special Collections, A.C. Long Health Sciences Library, Columbia University
AZ	Anna (formerly Nancy) Zilboorg
BIO	GZ, biographical statement, 4 January 1925, ASCCU
BZ	Basia Zilboorg Berdychevsky
EZ	Eugenia Zilboorg
FZ	Fera Zilboorg Levitas
GWH	George W. Henry
GZ	Gregory Zilboorg
GZB	Gregory Zilboorg Papers, Yale Collection of American Literature, Beinecke Rare Book and Manuscript Library
HES	Henry E. Sigerist
HMP	*A History of Medical Psychology*
JEZB	James and Eugenia Zilboorg Papers, Yale Collection of American Literature, Beinecke Rare Book and Manuscript Library
JZ	James Zilboorg
MMM	*Mind, Medicine, and Man*
MSZ	Margaret Stone Zilboorg
MZ	Moses Zilboorg
NM	Noël Mailloux
NYPS	New York Psychoanalytic Society
NYPSB	Minutes, special meetings of NYPS Board of Directors
NYPSI	Archives and Special Collections of the NYPS and Institute
POOE	The Passing of the Old Order in Europe

Russia used the Julian calendar until 14 February 1918, when the Soviet government adopted the Gregorian calendar. I use Julian ('Old Style') dates for historical events and documents written in Russia before its adoption of the Gregorian calendar. For international events before 1918, however, I use Gregorian (New Style, 'NS'). 'OS' dates are 13 days earlier than 'NS' dates.

Saint Petersburg, Russia's imperial capital, became Petrograd in 1914, Leningrad in 1924, then Saint Petersburg again in 1991. After the revolution, Lenin moved the capital to Moscow; I refer to Saint Petersburg/Petrograd as the capital in early chapters.

In Britain 'psychoanalysis' often appears as 'psycho-analysis' until the mid-twentieth century; I have preserved the orthography without the use of *sic*.

Gregory Zilboorg's writing in English generally followed American conventions for spelling and punctuation. I have followed the conventions of the originals when quoting while following in English translations of his letters the same British conventions I myself follow.

I have generally chosen to refer to my father as 'Gregory'. Similarly, I refer to my paternal grandparents as 'Moses' and 'Anna'. Other family members and friends, whom I knew or who were spoken of throughout my childhood, I also refer to by their first names: Edward Mortimer Morris Warburg appears as 'Eddie' and Abram Abeloff as 'Abe', while Henry Sigerist sometimes appears as 'Henry'.

Index

Chapter titles are accompanied by dates and are generally descriptive; many events and institutions (such as the Russian revolution, the First and Second World Wars, Bloomingdale Hospital, the Berlin Psychoanalytic Institute, and Columbia University) can be easily found and do not appear here. For similar reasons, the entry for Gregory Zilboorg is brief and does not attempt to recapitulate the trajectory of his life. Since the biography draws throughout on Henry Sigerist's correspondence, the entry for Sigerist is also brief. Most Zilboorg family members, mentioned throughout the text, are listed here only to indicate specific images. The entry under Sigmund Freud's name directs readers to references to Freud as a person and not to the many references to Freudian psychoanalysis.